Reflection

What a Difference a Day Makes,
What About
100 Years?

Reflection

What a Difference a Day Makes,
What About
100 Years?

KAREN SLOAN-BROWN

A Reflection:
What a Difference a Day Makes, What about 100 Years?
Copyright © 2013 by Karen Sloan-Brown

All rights reserved.
No part of this work may be reproduced or transmitted in any form or by any means, electronic or mechanical, including photocopying and recording, or by any information storage or retrieval system, except as may be expressly permitted by the 1976 Copyright Act or in writing from the publisher. Requests for permission should be addressed to Heritage Publishing, 102 Ivy Hill Lane, Goodlettsville TN, 37072

Library of Congress Cataloging-in-Publication Data on file
ISBN: 978-0-578-13644-8

All quotations are used by permission. All rights reserved.

All material of Martin Luther King, Jr. are reprinted by arrangement with The Heirs to the Estate of Martin Luther King, Jr., c/o Writers House as agent for the proprietor New York, NY. Copyright: 1963 Dr. martin Luther King, Jr. Renewed 1991 Coretta Scott King.

Table of Contents

Introduction 7
Current State of Affairs 8
A Bit of Background 10
1909 12
    Demographics 13
    Mood of Black Community 14
    Political Climate 15
    Leadership 16
    The Black Church 18
    Education 20
    Employment 21
    Extraordinary African-Americans 23
    The Black Press 24
    The Issue of Crime 25
    Health 27
    Housing 29
    Family Structure 30
    Black Entertainment 32
    Black Athletics 34
    Memorable Moments 34
    Reflections on a Decade 37
1919 38
    Demographics 39
    Mood of Black Community 40
    The Great Migration 41
    The Red Summer of 1919 43
    Lynching 45
    Political Climate 46
    The Black Church 47
    Leadership 48
    The Black Press 51
    Education 52
    George Washington Carver 54
    Employment 55
    The Issue of Black Crime 56
    Health 57
    Housing 58
    Family Structure 60
    Black Entertainment 61
    Sports and Black Athletes 63
    Memorable Moments 64
    Reflections on a Decade 65
1929 66
    Demographics 67
    Mood of Black Community 68
    Political Climate 69
    Black Leadership 71
    The Harlem Renaissance 73
    The Black Church 75
    The Black Press 76
    Black Literature and Art 77
    Education 80
    Bessie Coleman 82
    Black Businesses and Professionals 84
    Employment 85
    Social Clubs and Fraternal Orders 86
    Crime 87
    Health 88
    Housing 90
    Family Structure 91
    Entertainment and Artists 93
    Sports and Black Athletes 96
    Stock Market Crash 98
    Memorable Moments 99
    Reflections on a Decade 99
1939 101
    The Great Depression 101
    Demographics 103
    Mood of Black Community 104
    Political Climate 105
    Leadership 107
    The Black Church 108
    The Black Press 110
    Black Businesses and Depression 112
    Black Professionals 113
    Mary McLeod Bethune 114
    Ernest Everett Just 116
    Employment 117
    Education 119
    Crime 121
    Scottsboro Boys 122
    Health 125
    Housing 127
    Family Structure 128
    Art and Entertainment 130
    Black Athletics 135
    Memorable Moments 137
    Reflections on a Decade 139
1949 141
    Demographics 142
    Mood of Black Community 144
    The Second Great Migration 145
    Political Climate 146
    Leadership 148
    Civil Rights Movement 150
    Race Riots 152
    Black Churches 153
    The Black Press 154
    Employment 156
    Black Businesses 157
    Black Professionals 158
    Charles Drew 159
    Education 161
    Black on Black Crime 163
    Health 164
    Housing 166
    Family Structure 168
    Black Athletes and Sports 170
    Cultural Expression 173
    Entertainment 175
    Memorable Moments 178
    Reflections on a Decade 179
1959 182
    Demographics 183
    Mood of Black Community 184
    Legal Victories against Segregation ... 185
    Political Climate 186
    Black Leadership 188
    The Civil Rights Movement 191
    The Black Church 193
    The Black Press 195
    Black Businesses and Professionals .. 197
    Percy Lavon Julian 198
    Employment 200
    Education 201
    Issue of Crime 203

Health Issues	204
Housing	205
Family Structure	208
Black Athletes and Sports	209
Black Literature	213
African-American Art	214
Black Entertainment	215
Memorable Moments	217
Reflections on a Decade	218
Reflections on Fifty Years	
1969	**221**
Demographics	222
Mood of Black Community	223
Civil Rights Movement	224
Political Climate	230
African-Americans and Vietnam War	232
Black Riots Reign	234
Black Leadership	236
The Black Panther Party	238
Nation of Islam and Malcolm X	239
The Black Church	241
The Black Press	242
Martin Luther King, Jr.	244
Berry Gordy, Jr.	247
Black Businesses and Professionals	249
Employment	250
Education	252
The Issue of Crime	254
Health Issues	255
Housing	257
Family Structure	259
Black Athletes and Sports	260
Literature	265
African-American Art	266
Entertainment	267
Memorable Moments	270
Reflections on a Decade	272
1979	**274**
Demographics	275
Mood of Black Community	276
Political Climate	278
Black Leadership	279
The Black Church	281
The Black Press and Media	283
Black Businesses and Professionals	284
John Harold Johnson	286
Employment	289
Education	291
The Issue of Crime	293
Health Issues	294
Housing	296
Black Family Structure	298
Black Athletes and Sports	300
Black Culture	304
Literature	305
Entertainment	306
Memorable Moments	309
Reflections on a Decade	310
1989	**312**
Demographics	313
Mood of Black Community	314
Political Climate	315
Black Leadership	317
The Black Church	319
Black Press and Media	321
Black Businesses and Professionals	323
Black Employment	325
Education	326
The Issue of Crime	328
Health Issues	330
Housing	332
Family Structure	334
Sports and Black Athletes	336
Black Literature	341
Artists of the Decade	342
Black Entertainment	344
Memorable Moments	349
Reflections on a Decade	350
1999	**352**
Demographics	353
Mood of Black Community	354
Political Climate	355
Black Leadership	358
C. Delores Tucker	360
The Black Church	362
Black Press and Media	364
Black Businesses and Professionals	366
Black Employment	367
Education	369
The Issue of Crime	371
Health Issues	373
Housing	375
Family Structure	377
Sports and Black Athletes	378
Black Literature	383
Artists of the Decade	384
Black Entertainment	386
Memorable Moments	391
Reflections on a Decade	392
2009	**394**
Demographics	395
Mood of Black Community	396
Political Climate	397
Hurricane Katrina	399
Black Leadership	400
Barack Obama	402
The Black Church	404
Black Press and Media	406
Black Businesses and Professionals	408
Black Employment	401
Education	411
The Issue of Crime	414
Health Issues	416
Housing	418
Family Structure	420
Sports and Black Athletes	422
Black Literature	426
Artists of the Decade	427
Black Entertainment	429
Memorable Moments	434
Reflections on a Decade	435
Reflection on 100 Years	436
Bibliography	**440**

Introduction

The year 2009 was monumental in terms of the fulfillment of dreams that most black people, including myself had considered impossible within their lifetimes; the inauguration of a Black president in the United States of America. Was this the signal that the quest for the ever elusive equal opportunity and judgment not by the color of their skin but by the content of their character had successfully been achieved, or was this just a blip on the radar? This state of affairs calls for a progress report or at the very least a reflection on the advancement of African Americans.

Examining the state of African-Americans, or referred to in my era, black people, might take a rocket scientist. Determining the progress or the lack thereof is difficult due to the many contradictions that are always present in any worthwhile analysis. The dilemma is deciding on what criteria to use for judgment. What time frame will serve as the reference, and when have the greatest changes been evident? There is a propensity to look at changes in the United States over a century, the period of 100 years. So keeping with the trend I'll focus on the last 100 years, beginning with the year 1909, the year the NAACP was formed, and when my alma mater Tennessee State A & I was founded.

Reflection over one hundred years will remind us of the trials and the triumphs of a people, along with the missteps that hinder our ability to progress. As a people we have made tremendous strides, but are we continuing to move forward, or are we losing ground? What are the changes that have taken place in our leadership, business and personal finances, our thinking and aspirations, our culture, values, and attitudes, and how have they affected the quality of life and personal growth for African Americans today? What are the factors or influences that have brought us to this present point of circumstances?

Change is often described as evolution. This evolution is a slow process of change in a population that is spread over many generations that introduces many variations as we adapt to our environment. What are the results of the evolution of Black people over the last one hundred years? What have been the catalysts for the changes or evolution? How have we evolved economically, socially, educationally, politically, and artistically? Has this process of change been a 180 degree transformation, or have we come full circle, or is it more likely that we have detoured on some tangent from an obtuse angle? These are the questions I hope to answer by retracing our history over the past 100 years.

Martin Luther King spoke of reaching the Promised Land, and dreamed that we would "Overcome" as a people, that we would all be assured of our unalienable rights. Has the majority benefited as a whole in a normal distribution or have the results been positively skewed for only a select few. There is always a range in the strides toward a particular

A Reflection

destination; some have taken a more straightforward route, others in less traveled routes, and then the incessant wanderings of those who have lost their way. Langston Hughes' poem asks what happened: "Has the dream been deferred, or has it dried up like a raisin in the sun?"

Recalling my own life; I have seen many changes over the decades, the developments in civil rights, education, and numerous opportunities in various fields. I have seen many doors open and many attitudes changed, but over the last twenty years I have seem some backtracking, some reverses economically, educationally, and socially. I have given much thought to where exactly did this freedom train jump the track. Where did so much hope give in to hopelessness? Was there a specific chain of events? Have our reactions and behavior been influenced by outside forces or are the changes simply manifestations of different behavior. Was there a systematic campaign perpetrated to orchestrate our destruction or is our self-destruction just a greater magnification of what's taken place in America as a country.

John Hope Franklin, the premier United States historian and author of *From Slavery to Freedom,* said it best, *"If the house is to be set in order, one cannot begin with the present; we must begin with the past."*

Current State of Affairs

There have always been exceptional African Americans in this country with extraordinary intelligence and talents who have pushed themselves forward to achieve phenomenal success. In spite of the prejudice and discrimination that have been permanent fixtures in our society, many have found the inspiration, motivation, and energy to fulfill their potential and accomplish great things. Blacks are represented in greater numbers among the forefront in all arenas and professions. Participation in politics on the local, state, and national level has increased; blacks have served as mayors, governors, senators, and in the House of Representatives. They have served as district attorneys, judges, Attorney General, and all the way up to the Supreme Court. Economically we have built and run businesses, earned prominence in medicine and research, education, entertainment and the arts, and amateur and professional athletics. We have served as ambassadors to other countries, rose in rank in the military, and won Nobel prizes, and numerous other accolades.

The doors of opportunity are open to us by rights, but there are factors that affect our ability to walk through them. Even though the "good ole boy" network is alive and well,

Introduction

our main adversary against moving forward may come from within. With all the progress that we have made as a people we still have inherent problems. For all of the positive forces and individuals propelling us toward our destiny there are many negative forces contributing to our downfall. These diametrically opposed forces leave us captured in a state of inertia lacking any forward momentum. Economically we have the highest unemployment rate among whites, Asians, and Hispanics, with the highest proportion of those living in poverty. Education having been our strongest weapon in the fight for equality is showing signs of a weakening arsenal. The high school graduation rate has been declining for over four decades particularly among the black male, with less than 50 percent graduating.

The typical nuclear family in America is fading, but for African Americans it's already a rarity, single parent homes are the norm. A staggering number of more than 70 percent of black children are born into single parent families. This breakdown in the family structure is inarguably one of the main factors contributing to the continuing cycle of poverty. The lack of education and training in the black community leave many ill-equipped to enter the competitive job market. Chronic unemployment is a precursor for illegal activity that disproportionately affects poor black neighborhoods.

"Black on black" crime specifically among the youth has reached crisis proportions; evidence shows blacks have the highest incarceration rate, with 11 percent of males between the ages of 20 and 34 behind bars. No improvements on disparities in household income and healthcare have been manifested despite programs developed to address education and disease prevention awareness. Has poverty or decreased employment opportunities led to these statistics? There seems to be a breakdown in morals or in our value system. Has the lack of morals lead us to the present circumstances or is it the lack of opportunity?

The African American church has always served a dual role in the black community, more than a place of worship; it serves as a source of leadership. The contemporary church may be neglectful in its role as guide or moral authority. What has taken us from the point of 1909 to 2009? What has happened from the time my Grandmother Althea Frierson was born February 19, 1909 in Tennessee to this time in 2009 where two of my daughters, Kimberly 18, and Casey 10, live with less than optimistic statistics concerning family, health, and their pursuit of happiness? Can we identify our shortfalls and make the necessary changes for better opportunities for more than a few?

A Reflection

A Bit of Background

The end of the Civil War yielded immense changes in the South amid the devastation prompting the North to proceed with the mind-boggling task of rebuilding the country. This period of repairing the destruction left in the Southern states was referred to as Reconstruction. These reparations not only included the entire infrastructure for the South, but also granted full rights as citizens to the newly freed slaves. These political rights were set forth in the Thirteenth Amendment banning slavery; the Fourteenth Amendment granting them their civil rights along with equal protection under the law, and the Fifteenth Amendment giving them the right to vote.

During this period African Americans were active participants in the political process with 2000 blacks holding public offices, ranging from state legislature to the U.S. Senate. Their participation as delegates and voters was instrumental in ratifying the 14th and 15th Amendments. They also helped pass broad legislative reform programs where former slaves were permitted to acquire the land of former owners, work where they wanted, and use public accommodations.

Congress also established the Freeman's Bureau, a key agency developed to assist the newly liberated slaves after the Civil War. Initially it functioned as a unique social welfare program, offering legal advice, food and housing oversight, education, health care, and employment contracts with private landowners. It was most widely recognized for its accomplishments in the field of education. Public support for higher education for black students was demonstrated in the enactment of the Second Morrill Act that required states with racially segregated public higher education systems to provide a land-grant institution for black students whenever a land-grant institution was established and restricted for white students. This led to new public black institutions, and several formerly private black schools came under public control. Teachers of both races and missionary organizations worked with churches and schools to educate the great numbers of African Americans wanting to learn to read and write.

Over one hundred of the African-American members of these reconstructed state legislatures were ministers and seventy were teachers, evidence of the importance and influence of religious organizations and education in the political life of the black citizens in the South. Freed African Americans began to establish separate congregations making black churches the primary link between the black and white communities. Many whites and opponents in the white legislators viewed this time where blacks were politically active and exercised power at all levels of government as a period of "Negro domination."

1909

The end of reconstruction started with violent and political revolts against racial equality particularly in the Southern states, perpetrated by those determined to reverse gains made by black people, intent to "keep Negroes in their place." Elite white legislators began campaigns to systematically take back the rights of African Americans by passing Jim Crow laws and legalizing racial segregation in public and private facilities. Between 1890 and 1908, every state in the Deep South had written new state constitutions and passed new laws to complicate voter registration, including the Grandfather Clause, poll taxes, and literacy tests. African Americans had effectively been disenfranchised, removed from voter registration rolls across the South, left without any political representation, and without any legal recourse. By the end of the century few Blacks held office and they rarely voted.

Mandated segregation separated Blacks in schools and hospitals, restricted seating in restaurants, and on trains and other public transportation systems. "White Only" signs went up in parks, libraries, theaters, and hotels. White supremacist organizations like the Ku Klux Klan sprung up across the country terrorizing African Americans with lynching, intimidation, and attacks on their property.

A Reflection

1909

Black sharecroppers pick cotton in Georgia in 1898. Library of Congress, Washington, D.C.

Viewing the year 1909 from the perspective of one who lives in the new millennium inspires a newfound appreciation for Blacks living in that era. Most homes were one-room cabins heated by wood-burning or coal stoves, which were also used for cooking. There was no running water or indoor plumbing; fortunate families drew their water from a nearby well. Electricity had not yet reached rural areas; rooms were lit with kerosene lamps. There was no refrigeration, ice blocks were purchased from the "iceman." The mode of transportation was the horse and buggy or either on foot, only the very wealthy had cars. Most roads were unpaved paths of dirt through fields in rural communities. Urban cities had the benefit of streetcars, while state-to-state travel was by trains that carried 95 percent of all travelers, the balance walked to their destinations.

1909

The drive and resourcefulness of black people in 1909 was awe-inspiring. Today it's difficult to comprehend the harsh conditions African-Americans had to contend with in an average day; survival was arduous at this point in history with trouble on every hand. The scripture verse from Thessalonians 3:10 comes to mind, "If a man will not work, he shall not eat." This Bible verse speaks the reality facing African-Americans, not from a lack of will to work, but from limited opportunities for blacks who were deprived on so many levels. Scratching out a living from the earth was not for the weak under the best of conditions, but in the midst of bigotry and injustice it was death-defying.

Demographics

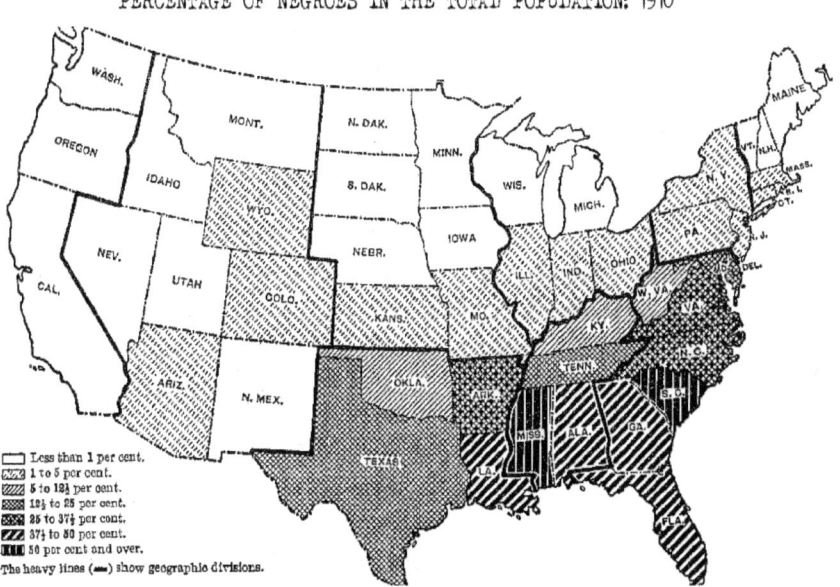

In 1909 the life expectancy for Black Americans was 33 years, with the death rate of blacks being higher than whites in every state, particularly in the South. African Americans made up 10.7 percent of the population, nearly 10 million, with more than 90 percent living in the South. Mississippi and South Carolina had the highest percentage of blacks, with black people constituting more than half of their populations. Georgia, Louisiana, Alabama, and Florida were close behind with populations that were over 40 percent black. Three out of four blacks lived on farms with their livelihood centered on the Southern cotton industry.

A Reflection

In 1909, the largest black urban population in the United States was in the District of Columbia, numbered at 94,446, while the second largest was in New York City, with a count of 91,709. Philadelphia, with a total of 84,459, ranked fifth among cities in the number of blacks, close behind New Orleans and Baltimore. The economics and employment of Blacks during these years was aggravated by the increasing numbers of poor immigrants from Europe who took unskilled and service jobs previously left for blacks.

The lack of non-agricultural jobs contributed to large gains in the number of Negro farmers in the country with 14.5 percent of farms being operated by blacks, a larger proportion than their number in the overall population. Close to 99 percent of the farms operated by black farmers were located in the South, with them owning more than 16 million acres of farm land, the majority of which was located in Mississippi, Georgia, Alabama, and South Carolina. According to the Census, the total value of farm property operated by blacks was $1,141,792,529, an increase of more that 128 percent from the previous decade. Negro farmers who did not own land grew cotton as tenant farmers, sharecroppers, or as temporary laborers.

Mood of the Black Community

The state of affairs for African Americans in the South had become intolerable; patience was being replaced with resentment. Blacks had witnessed the reversal of many civil liberties they had waited so long to obtain. Some of the liberties had been removed by unjust laws; others were suppressed through fear and intimidation, and racial tensions had reached a fever pitch. African-Americans tried to maintain some semblance of normalcy amidst the hostility of racist whites who with little provocation would metamorphose into a savage and bloodthirsty mob. The black community was being terrorized through lynching and rioting by organized white supremacy groups and out of control vigilante crowds, not only in the South, but in the North as well. An article in the Chicago Defender on Jan 1, 1910, spoke of the horror of 325 Negro men and women lynched for fun, and the rape of 28,000 colored girls between the ages of 12 and 18 years without any government justice or intervention.

In the summer of 1909, one of the four regular black regiments of the Tenth United States Calvary Regiment, better known as the "Buffalo Soldiers" returned to the states. A large crowd of blacks gathered in New York and cheered and welcomed back 750 soldiers as they marched down Wall Street and up Broadway. Black veterans were a symbol of strength and courage for the black community, a contrast from feelings of

1909

helplessness and victimization under Jim Crow. The Black community gained a sense of pride and hope in the belief that fighting for their country would secure them the rights and dignity they had been denied.

Education and employment opportunities were meager in the South, and unsanitary living conditions and working environments were beyond miserable. Black people had become tired of being treated as second-class citizens with total disregard. The circumstances in the South had reached the breaking point, weary of the indignities and degradation of segregation, blacks began to fight back in every way they could.

Political Climate

The political climate is a reflection of the current policies of the governing bodies. This climate may be directed at individuals or groups in society and may be dissimilar on a variety of levels. The political climate is dynamic, changing over time, at times being receptive and hospitable, while at others times hostile and unyielding. Social change occurs under wide-ranging conditions of the political climate, making it a powerful entity that controls policy and decision-making. The climate may also be manipulated by the media, swayed by public opinion, or influenced by organized movements for change.

The political climate in 1909 was cool to African Americans. Teddy Roosevelt was the President and was unwilling to confront the race issue; his position on the plight of blacks was not a sympathetic one, believing that blacks were inferior to whites. Teddy Roosevelt supported Booker T. Washington and the National Negro Business League, admonishing blacks that the league *"teaches you not to whine and cry about privileges you do not have."* In 1906, Roosevelt decided to dishonorably discharged 160 black soldiers accused of a shooting spree without a trial in Brownsville, Texas, this decision destroyed their lives and the lives of their families. The soldiers were denied back pay and their pensions were terminated.

Life for Black Americans in this year was a constant struggle against external forces that robbed them of their civil rights, mainly the legalization of segregation. State legislatures throughout the South enacted Black Codes or "Jim Crow" laws that disenfranchised African Americans, raising barriers that blocked most of them from voting and undermined their constitutional rights. Segregation was the law and enforced fully throughout the Southern states, forming two separate and unequal societies. Blacks were no longer served in restaurants, having to tolerate the indignity of going in back doors. Railroads and bus stations touted "if you're black, get back." There were separate

A Reflection

waiting rooms, separate ticket booths, separate schooling of children, separate bathroom facilities, separate military troops, separate nurses in hospitals, separate prison quarters, and it was definitely unlawful to cohabitate or marry outside your race.

"Jim Crow" was cruel and roguish, creating conflicts that led to race riots and 82 recorded lynchings of blacks in 1909. The "black man's place" was being debated among black people as well as whites. Should second class citizenship be accepted or should we strive for equal opportunities. Should we move cautiously, taking baby steps, or should we forge ahead boldly. Two political leaders, Booker T. Washington and W.E.B. Du Bois, with two opposing philosophies for the advancement of civil rights for African Americans were the dominant voices around this decade.

Leadership

Booker T. Washington was born into slavery on April 5, 1856, his father, an unknown white plantation owner, and his mother, Jane, a slave cook. After the Emancipation and the end of the Civil War, he worked a variety of jobs before enrolling at the Hampton Normal and Agricultural Institute, in Hampton, Virginia at the age of sixteen. Students with little or no means could pay their way by working at the school. Washington was trained as a teacher at Hampton and also attended and graduated from Wayland Seminary where he completed his instructor preparation. In 1881, Hampton President, Samuel C. Armstrong, recommended Washington to become the first leader of the new all-black Tuskegee Normal and Industrial Institute, a position he held for the rest of his life.

Booker T. Washington, the major Black leader of his time, was the last of the generation of leaders born into slavery. He became the representative and spokesman for Blacks living in the South. His philosophy was "accommodationism" and his approach was non-confrontational, calling for cooperation with whites as the optimal method to attack racism, not questioning white supremacy, accepting the sacrifice of political power, civil rights, and higher education that existed with segregation. His emphasis was on earning citizenship privileges through a combination of academic training and practical training, building intelligence and character, making the change from within. He thought that through hard work the Negro could build wealth and capital and through this ownership gain respect, educate his children, and increase his standing in the American society. Washington felt Negroes should not be misled or inspired to ambitions they were incapable of realizing. Washington focused on the dignity of labor and encouraged blacks to work hard, stay in the South, and buy property to improve their lives. Booker

1909

T. Washington's principle based on accommodation of segregation made him a liaison between races, with a large network of supporters of black ministers, businessmen, and educators.

W.E.B. Du Bois was an only child born to parents who had never been slaves and whose families had been landowners. His father, Alfred, deserted his mother, Mary, before William was two years old. Wanting to help his mother as he grew older he felt he could better their situation through education. Du Bois earned a degree from Fisk University, and went further to become the first African American to earn a Ph.D. from Harvard University. He thought that Blacks should pursue higher education, challenge and question, not trust the leadership of whites, but look to the guidance of the "Talented Tenth" of the race who would direct them to higher cultural possibilities.

Du Bois advocated an organized and aggressive defense of Negro civil rights. In 1906, he and William Monroe Trotter had organized a group of business owners, teachers, and clergy to form a movement to legally combat racism; to deal with issues of economics, education, crime, religion, and heath. The group, named after the city where they formed, the Niagara Movement, took offense to the lower expectations for blacks held by Booker T. Washington and opposed his principle of "Accommodation" by explicitly demanding equal rights and opportunities. Du Bois called for an end to segregation and discrimination.

Anti-black riots and hostility towards blacks was out of control in the North and the South prior to 1909. During this decade opposition to "Jim Crow" began to grow among Blacks, particularly the young and educated, they were becoming less intimidated by the lynching and forcefully defended their homes and property. After the Springfield, Illinois race riot in 1908, in which eight blacks were killed, the Niagara members, made up of black and white activists, felt they needed a more powerful organization to combat racism and to help migrating blacks find homes and jobs. In February of 1909, W.E.B. Dubois, Ida B. Wells, along with an interracial group of supporters, founded the National Association for the Advancement of Colored People, the NAACP, to restore the legal rights of Black Americans.

The five major demands put forth during the conference were to ensure voting rights, to ban "white only" policies in public accommodations, to promote free labor relations, to urge school programs that would not educate youths as "servants and underlings," and to require equal justice under the law.

Du Bois later wrote an essay discussing the controversy between Booker T. Washington and himself:

A Reflection

"Since the controversy between me and Washington has become historic, it deserves more careful statement than it has had hitherto, both as to the matters and the motives involved. There was first of all the ideological controversy. I believed in the higher education of a Talented Tenth who through their knowledge of modern culture could guide the American Negro into a higher civilization. I knew that without this the Negro would have to accept white leadership, and that such leadership could not always be trusted to guide this group into self-realization and to its highest cultural possibilities. Mr. Washington, on the other hand, believed that the Negro as an efficient worker could gain wealth and that eventually through his ownership of capital he would be able to achieve a recognized place in American culture and could then educate his children as he might wish and develop their possibilities. For this reason he proposed to put the emphasis at present upon training in the skilled trades and encouragement in industry and common labor. These two theories of Negro progress were not absolutely contradictory. Neither I nor Booker Washington understood the nature of capitalistic exploitation of labor, and the necessity of a direct attack on the principle of exploitation as the beginning of labor uplift. I recognized the importance of the Negro gaining a foothold in trades and his encouragement in industry and common labor. Mr. Washington was not absolutely opposed to college training and sent his own children to college."

The Black Church

In 1909, there were 35,000 black churches across the country with a seating capacity totaling 10,481,738, enough for nearly every black person in the country to sit in a pew simultaneously. The value of the church properties totaled more than 56 million dollars. There were more Blacks in the ministry than any other profession at this time among nineteen denominations, with more than half being Baptist and the next largest denomination being African Methodist Episcopal. The number of churches had grown by 48 percent over the last decade, with 91 percent of the churches located in the South.

The church has always been a place where Christians can congregate in worship, fellowship, and encourage one another. For black people it was additionally a place to escape the oppression and abuse of racism and prejudice, a respite behind church walls. Members gained a sense of identity from being a part of the church group. The church was also a community court; it solved disputes and acted as a support group. Members in rural areas came to church to get the latest news, men came to meet women for marriage, farmers came to learn of business developments, and craftsmen came to learn the demands of the community.

Another vital function of the Black church was the promotion of education. During this period women were not permitted to be ordained or hold any leadership positions. Middle-class women organized missionary societies that raised funds for African missions; they also provided reading education and job training. The black church created and/or maintained the first black schools and encouraged community members to nurture and fund these schools and other public services.

Families were participants in all aspects of the church; children attended Sunday school, there were youth groups, and men and women groups that served as social outlets. Black churches sponsored all-black church baseball leagues in the 1900's and church teams played in competitions against each other at picnics and other outings.

The role of the Black Church in the Black community cannot be overstated; it has served as the first institution in the Black society, functioning not only for spiritual and social growth, but also as a meeting place for a host of organizations. The formation of black secular organizations made it possible for Blacks to be politically and socially engaged. Most of the social organizations connected to the church were based on Christian principles and positively impacted the black church community, these included sororities, fraternities, lodges, Masons, and civic clubs. These organizations aided the poor, infirmed and elderly, as well as provided child-care and rescue homes for young black women.

Customarily the black ministers were the most educated and articulate members in the community and were held in high esteem. Black preachers were multi-faceted leaders; aside from heading the church they served as political leaders, encouraged education and economic growth, and were the main link between the black and white communities. Churches became organizations with social power with concerns linked to political goals of advancing the race. The church also served as a safe haven for political activities. The NAACP was formed as a vehicle in which different denominations of black churches could work in concert on political issues. The Black church was instrumental in raising necessary funds for legal fights challenging segregation.

A Reflection

Education

Literacy is defined as the ability to write, regardless of the ability to read. According to census statistics the literacy rate for African Americans in 1909 was 70 percent. The portion of the black population that was unable to write was centered in the southern portion of the country; the cities having the largest percentage of illiteracy were Birmingham, Alabama, Nashville, Tennessee, and Atlanta, Georgia. Illiteracy was much higher in older age groups and increased with age, with the greater number being over 65 years, the individuals who had previously been slaves.

Public education in America was still in its infancy, and operated on the premise of "separate but equal," having been supported by the Supreme Court's Plessey v. Ferguson decision. Local politics dictated the educational provisions at this time and Negro schools were being radically discriminated against in the distribution of state funds. Black schools were so underfunded that most of them were overcrowded and under the supervision of one teacher who taught all subjects, ages, and grades. Teachers in rural areas were most likely poorly trained and lacked an adequate and comprehensive education.

The South was slower in providing public education particularly in rural areas. School terms varied, ranging 10 to 51 percent shorter than school terms for whites. The percentage of school attendance was much lower in the southern sections of the country, about 50 percent of black children 10-14 attended school, and the numbers decreased to about one third by the time the children were 16 and 17 years old. School attendance tended to be erratic in the southern states particularly in rural areas, mainly because black farm children typically helped their parents work the land. Census data shows that a higher proportion of black females attended school than black males in all age levels from 6 to 20 years old, while white females and males attended school in equal proportion. The proportion of blacks attending school was higher in urban areas versus rural communities, a factor attributed to urban areas in the North having school facilities that were higher quality than those in the South.

Blacks continued to see education as the primary route of advancement and critical for the race, many talented blacks went into teaching, which had high respect as a profession. In 1909, black teachers represented 45 percent of all professional blacks with 3 out of 4 being women. Nannie Burroughs, unable to teach within public schools in Washington, D.C. because of her darker skin tone, joined the Women's Convention, a fundraising organization, to achieve her goal of establishing a school for girls. In 1909, her dreams were realized when she opened the National Training School for Women and Girls in Washington, D.C. Through her efforts the first all-female school operated by black women outside of the South grew and achieved national distinction.

Education was the cornerstone of the "New Negro's" identity as it was the means of attaining other middle-class traits such as wealth and culture. The importance of providing sons and daughters with educational opportunities, which took precedence over current material prosperity, reflected the "New Negro's" orientation toward the future. Virtually all white institutions refused to admit black applicants with few exceptions. Between 1826 and 1910, only 693 blacks had graduated from predominantly white colleges in the United States, (JBHE, 2010). In this year only 5000 black students were enrolled in college. The Freedman's Bureau was instrumental in the initiative to develop higher education institutions for African-Americans, joined by black churches and white philanthropists.

The first schools were privately funded, established without state government support. These included Howard University, Atlanta University, and Fisk University. The Morrill Land-Grant Act of 1890 declared that states must integrate their schools or allocate money for segregated black colleges. By 1909, more than 80 of the 104 Historically Black Colleges and Universities were established. These HBCU's were fundamental for the education and development of black professionals.

Employment

In this decade the majority of the black population lived and worked in sixteen states that made up the southern census region. The black community, unrecovered from the hardships of slavery remained impoverished. Their employment or means of earning a living was centered on agriculture or the farming of cotton. According to Census data, more than 87 percent of black males 10 years and older were gainfully employed and nearly 55 percent of black females were also working. Work as a farm laborer was plentiful, unemployment was not the issue; getting paid a fair wage for your efforts was the drawback. Employers and labor unions generally confined African Americans to the worst paid and least desirable jobs. Black women and children needed to work to supplement the low pay received by black men.

Fifty-six percent of the black male workers were farmers or farm laborers, and 52 percent of black female workers were also employed as farm laborers. Black farm

A Reflection

owners had no access to the usual sources of credit and were exploited by merchants who inflated the costs of necessities and reduced the market price for their crops. Landowners took advantage of sharecroppers, charging high rents, supplying them with seed and fertilizer at exorbitant costs, usually increasing their debts over the years. Sharecropping was just another form of slavery.

For black workers not employed in agriculture, men had a wider range of occupations to pursue than women, another 11 percent were laborers in construction on the railroad, others worked the mines or in construction. Black women were still relegated to domestic service, 18 percent were classified as laundresses, 10 percent were cooks, and some worked as seamstresses.

Professional black male workers were spread across a variety of occupations in much smaller numbers, usually less than 1 percent. Most of the professional men were barbers, clergymen, teachers, lawyers, musicians, and physicians. The majority of black women professional workers were teachers, hairdressers, and lawyers.

In 1909, 45 percent of black professionals were teachers, with 76 percent of those being women. Teaching and the ministry were among the few occupations available to college educated blacks, with teaching being open to women on an equal basis. Black women were able to exert leadership primarily through teaching roles.

Professional African-Americans were largely excluded from professional associations operated by their white counterparts. Successful blacks were still contested daily, ostracized and rejected by whites. The proportion of doctors and lawyers in the black population plummeted due to segregation limiting their practices, and did not recover for three generations. The Journal of the National Medical Association was first published in this year to assist and unify black health professionals in medicine, dentistry, and pharmacy. The National Association of Colored Graduate Nurses was a union established to support the growing number of black women entering the nursing field, to build upon their training and improve the quality of graduates. These organizations sought to provide a voice for these African American professionals in the often-hostile and racist world of medicine.

Black businesses and professionals thrived under segregation because black consumers were limited to where they could do business. Those who were able to run a successful business were more often located in communities with higher percentages of blacks in the population. Small business ventures that catered to the needs of the African American community included grocery stores, barbershops, restaurants, and funeral homes. Black owned banks had opened in Richmond Virginia in 1899, and by 1909, there were thirty-two new branches.

Extraordinary African Americans

Superstars are defined as persons widely-known, prominent or successful in some field. Quite a few African-Americans were able to achieve phenomenal success in their chosen areas, but they were exceptions, not the rule. The status of a professional or business owner did not make you immune to the cruelties of Jim Crow. Successful blacks were still ostracized and rejected by whites. Robert Reed Church Sr. was one of those exceptions; born in Holly Springs, Mississippi in 1830, he was the South's first millionaire, a tremendous accomplishment by anyone, but a major feat by an individual who had been born a slave. Church built his fortune through real estate; he also owned a hotel, a restaurant, and a saloon. A political leader and community activist he used real estate holdings to purchase the first city bond issued in Memphis, TN to help the city regain its city charter from bankruptcy. In 1909, Church also founded the Solvent Savings Bank and Trust Co, the first black bank in Memphis. In the same year, Church, also a philanthropist, saved the Beale Street Baptist Church from foreclosure.

Annie Turbo Pope Malone was the first to build an empire on the manufacturing of beauty products for African-American women. Having a talent for hair-dressing, Malone studied chemistry and through her research developed several preparations for the hair and scalp, the first named, "Wonderful Hair Grower." Some historians also credit Malone with developing the pressing iron and comb around this time. Having no access to traditional distribution systems, she hired and trained assistants and began providing free demonstrations and selling her products door-to-door. They traveled to churches, community centers, and to women's clubs.

Everywhere she went, Malone recruited women to serve as local sales agents, and they in turn followed suit increasing the number of sales agents. Malone also used contemporary business practices such as press conferences and advertising in black newspapers. By the end of the decade, her distribution had extended nationally. Mrs. Malone had created a unique distribution system that helped thousands of black women gain self respect and economic independence. One of her sales agents was Madame C.J. Walker.

Madame C.J. Walker, a former laundress, learned much from Annie Malone. Walker left to develop her own hair and cosmetics line using similar distribution practices. After

A Reflection

a short time Walker moved to Denver, Colorado, and opened an office there. An eastern division opened the following year with an office in Pittsburgh, Pennsylvania. By the end of 1909, Walker soon to become one of the first black millionaires, transferred her successful hair products business called the Madame C.J. Walker Manufacturing Co. to Indianapolis, IN. She was widely regarded as the most successful black entrepreneur of the early 20th century in the United States.

The Black Press

The famous quote, "the pen is mightier that the sword," was put to the test by African-American newspapers during this time in America. The black press was set to take up the fight against the injustices of segregation and push for equal rights and opportunities for black citizens. Black newspapers sprung up across the Midwest and into the North. Over 275 newspapers were in print in 1909 with a combined circulation of more than 500 thousand, and the church also served as a major site of print production.

Black people were basically unseen in the white newspapers unless a crime had been committed. The black press acknowledged their people and gave them a voice that created a sense of unity. The Negro press was crucial in keeping readers informed of important issues for the community. Through this vehicle blacks were able to have their say, express hopes and protests, announced births, deaths, and marriages, as well as civic and social concerns. The black press, through advertisements, promoted black businesses and free enterprise among entrepreneurs in the black community.

Prominent newspapers of the day were *The Chicago Defender*, the *Pittsburgh Courier*, the *New York Amsterdam News*, the *Afro-American*, the *California Eagle*, the *Norfolk Journal and Guide*, and the *Crisis*. These papers served as catalysts for political and social change amid this time of continuing prejudice and discrimination among African Americans. These times produced a new generation of black press principals like Robert S. Abbott of Chicago and Henry Allen Boyd of Nashville. In 1909, these impassioned and purposeful men joined forces and organized the National Negro Press Association (NNPA) in Louisville, Kentucky. Members were African American editors and journalists coming together to strengthen the influence of the African American press.

Robert S. Abbott, the founder of the *Chicago Defender*, started his newspaper with seed money totaling a mere 25 cents. He worked out of the kitchen in his small apartment, producing a press run of 300 copies. Abbott's journalistic venture progressed to produce the country's most influential black weekly newspaper, with the greatest portion of his readership being outside of Chicago.

The *New York Amsterdam News*, established with an initial investment of $10, published its first issue on December 4, 1909. It was founded by James H. Anderson, named after the street where he lived, and operated out of his home before relocating to Harlem. It is among the oldest published African-American newspapers in the United States.

Black newspapers were not in place to be objective; they all had an agenda, mainly for the education and uplift of their readers. Booker T. Washington had immense influence over the Negro Press during his leadership through associations with editors and publishers. Washington used this influence to quiet criticism of his policies and approach to blacks achieving equal status and their inalienable rights. Press outside of his influence took a much more independent stance. The *Crisis*, the magazine distributed by the NAACP, and edited by W.E.B. Du Bois, held a much more militant tone. Du Bois stated the objective of the paper was to "set forth those facts and arguments which show the danger of race prejudice, particularly as manifested today toward colored people." The policy of THE CRISIS will be simple and well defined:

> "It will first and foremost be a newspaper: it will record important happenings and movements in the world which bear on the great problem of inter—racial relations, and especially those which affect the Negro—American.
>
> Secondly, it will be a review of opinion and literature, recording briefly books, articles, and important expressions of opinion in the white and colored press on the race problem.
>
> Thirdly, it will publish a few short articles.
>
> Finally, its editorial page will stand for the rights of men, irrespective of color or race, for the highest ideals of American democracy, and for reasonable but earnest and persistent attempt to gain these rights and realize these ideals. The magazine will be the organ of no clique or party and will avoid personal rancor of all sorts. In the absence of proof to the contrary it will assume honesty of purpose on the part of all men, North and South, white and black."

The Issue of Crime

Crime among the black population was a problem in 1909 with the incidence of black crime being at high levels, and is still a very serious issue today. According to the 1910

A Reflection

Census on Prisoners and Juvenile Delinquents, there was proportionately more crime committed among the Black population than whites and any other race. At this time in history blacks were 10.7 percent of the population but constituted nearly 31 percent of prisoners incarcerated. For the year 1909, blacks were 21 percent of those arrested and jailed. In as far as juveniles were concerned, white offenders in the North were sent to reformatories, whereas in the South where the majority of offenders were black, there were no reformatories.

Some have used these statistics to promote negative images and racial stereotypes of African- Americans as lacking morals, more likely to commit crimes, more likely to be violent, more likely to cheat and steal, less intelligent, and lacking work ethic, thus enabling them to justify their inhumane treatment of blacks and the denial of equal rights and opportunity. A survey taken by Tom Smith of Chicago's National Opinion Research Center in 1990 showed that even today large percentages believe these racial stereotypes to be true.

The justice system was a contradiction to its own description, for it was not fair or impartial. Black men and women both suffered violence at the hands of white men in an atmosphere nonchalant to the wrongs committed against them. The injustice was further evident in the average length of sentences, jail time for black men were three times that for whites, and black females were six times more likely to be imprisoned than white females. Closer analysis of the crime statistics in 1909 would take into account that African-Americans were more likely to be arrested and sent to jail than their white counterparts, and also due to their economic condition they were unable to afford counsel, or if fined, unable to pay. These circumstances would inflate the numbers of blacks incarcerated relative to whites.

Scientific research requires that you first define the issue under discussion before you can approach any resolution. What provokes the criminal act? Disrespect in every aspect of life to the point it where it becomes a hindrance in one's ability to earn a living or provide for family breeds dejection. Loss of self-respect clouds reasoning, making individuals feel they are deserving of the ill-treatment they received. They feel powerless and rebel against society; stealing to survive, while venting pent-up anger through violence. Willie Webb (1990) defined violence and the meaning gives great insight into the root causes for the persistence of these anti-social behaviors:

> To be without hope is violence. To be without love is violence. The deprivation of justice is violence. Ignorance is violence. Unemployment

is violence. To be hungry and without shelter is violence. Poverty is violence. To be helpless and misrepresented is violence. To be without liberty and freedom is violence. To be forced to live without human dignity is violence.

W. E.B. Du Bois conducted an in-depth analysis into the variables that contributed to the rising crime levels of blacks. He recognized the difference between the pressures on southern blacks and those on northern blacks because the strains of city life in the North were much different from those of the southern rural sharecroppers. In his study he found that the incidence of crime can be attributed to structural forces in urban areas. These forces are a legacy of slavery; they include poverty, an inferior education, a lack of skills, unemployment, compounded by segregation and racism.

In his research Bu Bois divided black populations into four classes:
1. The well-to-do.
2. Hardworking laborers who were doing fairly well.
3. The "Worthy poor" who were working but merely carving out an existence.
4. The "submerged tenth," merely existing.

Du Bois found direct correlations between low levels of education and employment and high levels of criminal activity. Crime and violence are related to the social class. Those individuals with lower socioeconomic status were more likely to be perpetrators and victims of lawlessness. During the early years of the century, poverty and the inability to find work caused desperation and pushed some blacks to commit crimes for survival. The African-American community had been marginalized and dehumanized by Jim Crow, who reserved opportunities for upward mobility for "white only." Du Bois deduced that black crime declined as the African-American population progressed and moved toward a more equal status with whites.

Health

Disparities between the races were prevalent in every facet of life in the early years of the twentieth century, but particularly devastating in mortality rates. Whites lived an average of 17 years longer than blacks at this time. Urban cities had higher mortality rates than rural areas, the larger the city, the greater the mortality. New York being among

A Reflection

the largest cities had exacerbated issues of overcrowding, spreading of infection, and the lack of sewage disposal. The black mortality rates in Buffalo stood at twice that of whites: 30 to 16.3 in 1910. Infant mortality rates are another health marker that revealed special problems for blacks in New York. As early as 1910, death rates in New York City for blacks in the one-year old and younger age group stood at a shocking 333 per 1,000 live births in contrast to 144 for whites.

Central to the generally higher death rates for the black population in northern states like New York was the disproportionate illness blacks experienced from communicable diseases. During this decade, among infectious diseases, only tuberculosis was more deadly than pneumonia and influenza. These chronic respiratory illnesses were formidable accounting for 28 percent of African American deaths in 1909. The greatest disparity in mortality among blacks and whites was due to tuberculosis and pneumonia. The greatest proportion of black mortality was caused by tuberculosis; being the number one killer among New York City's black and white populations.

The single most important chronic illness predicting black mortality in 1909 was a cardiovascular conditional called arteriosclerosis, which was the hardening of the medium and large arteries. A study done on race, infection, and arteriosclerosis in the past by Costa, Helmchen, and Wilson (2007) found that chronic mild stress may induce or accelerate the development of atherosclerosis, suggesting that low socioeconomic status and limited legal protections may have directly worsened blacks' health outcomes. Black rates of arteriosclerosis were double that of whites and 47 percent of blacks had congestive heart failure compared to nine percent of whites. The greater risk factors for blacks were due to incidences of infection; black people either had greater exposure to infection because of living conditions or were more susceptible to infectious disease because of poorer nutritional status.

The health of African-Americans or also referred to as the "Negro Problem" was the subject of much study and analysis that drew a variety of conclusions. In 1910, the American Medical Association's prestigious journal published an extensive article by a southern medical professor entitled "Syphilis and the American Negro: A Medico-Sociologic Study." In this rant, the author cautioned that because the benevolent system of slavery had been eliminated, the health of the nation's blacks had been "crushed." One extreme researcher, Frederick Hoffman, a statistician for insurance companies had predicted the 'Negro' was destined for extinction, faulting their tendencies, immoral living habits, and their susceptibility to disease. His theory was refuted by research done by W.E.B. Du Bois, which was published in a 1906 paper titled "The Health and

Physique of the Negro." Du Bois concluded that "If the population were divided as to social and economic condition the matter of race would be almost entirely eliminated." His data showed that the death rate and sickness among blacks were relative to environmental conditions not racial traits and tendencies.

Mortality is determined largely by the socioeconomic status; persons with adequate income have more access to medical care, better nutrition, higher quality of water and air, and sufficient shelter and clothing. Du Bois postulated, "With the improved sanitary condition, improved education and better economic opportunities, the mortality of the race may and probably will steadily decrease until it becomes normal."

Probably the most significant factors contributing to the higher mortality level is the inadequate medical services and the un-attendance of a physician. In 1909, there were only about 3500 black physicians in America; not nearly enough to administer to the segregated black population. Access to hospital facilities was limited at best; white doctors simply denied them admitting privileges, forcing black doctors to leave patients who required hospitalization or surgery at the entrance door. Black patients were hesitant to use the services of black physicians who were unable to provide necessary hospital medical care. These doctors were hugely disadvantaged by the low or uncollectable fees from the generally poorer black clientele, limited access to capital, and the hostile working relationships with white physicians.

Housing

Fundamental to the laws of Jim Crow was the enforcement of residential segregation. Blacks and whites were not to live in common neighborhoods or in close proximity to one another. Segregation in housing was maintained in both the North and the South. When a black family moved into a white area, white residents fled the neighborhood, and it soon became a black neighborhood. Most black neighborhoods were created on the least desirable land containing substandard structures. In urban cities black families were forced to live in tenement houses described as uninhabitable slums. One-room crowded apartments of the city and the one-room houses in the country had similar drawbacks; poor ventilation and inadequate plumbing, both conditions contributed to and aggravated the health issues of the black community.

The health and mortality rate of Blacks in urban areas was greatly affected by their living conditions. Many were forced to live "on the other side of the tracks" along river banks and streams on the outskirts of the city. More were forced to live in alleys and

A Reflection

on unpaved streets in slum areas in buildings that were damp and in disrepair. Black neighborhoods were overcrowded in areas where the garbage collection was irregular. Landlords kept rental costs high. Most could not afford to move to better neighborhoods, while others were threatened when they attempted to move in white residential areas. Campaigns to discourage Black home buyers sparked race riots. The National Urban League was formed and they worked diligently with the NAACP to improve labor and housing conditions in the cities.

Home ownership and better living conditions were positive factors in the decrease of the death rate for blacks over the past decade. Even though only 23.7 percent of African Americans owned their homes in 1909 this was nearly a 31 percent increase from 1900. Over 45 percent of the owned homes were on farms in rural communities. The 76.3 percent of blacks who rented properties found their options undesirable, most often having to live in rough and degrading conditions. Real Estate agents had listings separated into "white property" and "colored property" with the colored properties being of low quality, and unsanitary.

During this year Los Angeles had the highest percentage of black home ownership in the country, more than 36 percent of black residents owned their homes. Racial discrimination was less of a problem for blacks there, mainly due to their small population in the city; racial tensions were largely between the whites and the Mexicans.

Philip A. Payton Jr., a successful real estate entrepreneur in New York, was known as the Godfather of Harlem for his investment deals that provided housing for African-Americans in Harlem. He was instrumental in starting the trend where prominent black churches became dominant property owners renting to members of their congregation. By 1907, black churches began moving to Harlem, sometimes buying up apartment houses when they came. A few years later John E. Nail served as the agent for St. Philip's Protestant Episcopal Church, considered the wealthiest black church in the state and maybe in America. The church purchased prime properties totaling $1,070,000 in Harlem, which included a row of 13 apartment houses on 135th Street, between Lenox and Seventh Avenues, for $620,000. The church then proceeded to evict all of the white tenants and rented the apartments to blacks.

Family Structure

There are immense contradictions on the status of the black family in 1909. Some research data stated that the black family had been disintegrated by emancipation. The view that slavery

1909

could have possibly been beneficial to the stability of any family is preposterous. Countless tainted perspectives viewed black people as having low morals, promiscuous, and prone to irresponsible behavior. Their relationships were thought to be informal extensions of plantation life. Before W.E.B. Du Bois conducted his research, most of the opinions were from individuals looking at a race of people as if they were another species.

A stable family environment is defined as one in which adults marry and live together in their own homes, and children are born and raised by both parents. Opposing observations see the turn of the century black family as having no structure and discipline, while at the same time centering their lives on the black church. African-Americans have historically been religious; God-fearing Christians, with faith and worship being a high priority. Based on the definition of family stability and the Census results for this year, the black family was stable and intact. Data showed that most black adults were married and lived with their spouses. Eighty-seven percent of black children lived in households with their mother; the majority being legitimate and living with both parents.

Blacks had the highest rate of marriage of all races. The U.S. Census recorded that 73.1 percent of African American females aged 15 years and older were married, for ages 25 to 34 over 85 percent were married, and for ages 35 to 44 over 92 percent were married. In comparison to whites during this time, African Americans married at an earlier age and had a higher proportion of women widowed, 14.8 percent in all age groups. In urban areas the proportion of married, widowed, or divorced was lower than in rural communities particularly for younger age groups. The migration to cities or urban areas was most common among single men and women. The greater number of single women may be attributed to their increased ability to support themselves in the city.

There is consensus surrounding the major negative factor affecting the stability of the black family: the inability of the black male to obtain substantial employment sufficient to support a wife and children. Looking at employment statistics from 1909, I was struck by the number of black women who worked outside the home in comparison with other races. The reality being that their income was needed to supplement the meager wages paid to their husbands and fathers. A closer look revealed there were also many poor immigrants in the same level of poverty as black families, yet these women did not work anywhere near the proportion of black women. Was this another consequence of slavery, the assumption that black women should be servants to other women, or were white women just accustomed to black women working for them? Were we less valued as women?

A Reflection

Hard work was no stranger in the black household, but there was always some time for relaxation and escaping the pressures of everyday life. Leisure time was spent playing sports and having picnics. Churches organized and sponsored competitive baseball and basketball games. In the South, Saturday was the day blacks were allowed to come downtown, so they dressed in their "Sunday best" to stroll through town. For those a little more risqué there were juke joints and good time houses.

Black Entertainment

Vaudeville was the most popular form of entertainment in the country. It featured comedians, musician, singers, dancers, ventriloquists, acrobats, and animal trainers. Bill "Bo jangles" Robinson was the most well-known Black American in Vaudeville. He began his career as a child around eight years old earning 50 cents a night; at his peak in vaudeville he earned $6,500 a week teaming with George W. Cooper. Unfortunately most black performers on the stage circuit were controlled and exploited by white managers and producers with low wages and degrading performance stereotypes.

In 1909, there were over 3000 black professional entertainers, most of them employed in all-Negro musicals. Musical theatre was the popular genre of the day, all-black theatrical troupes toured across the country and beyond. Women were often the featured performers. Matilda Sissieretta Jones, having sung for four consecutive presidents, the last being Teddy Roosevelt, was still unwelcome to present her talents in racist American classical concert halls. After years of successfully touring abroad with the Fisk Jubilee Singers, she formed a musical and acrobatic act called the Black Patti Troubadours that included a chorus of 40 accomplished singers, comedians, dancers, and even jugglers. Several members of her troupe, like Bert Williams went on to achieve great successes. These productions provided Jones with income over $20,000 per year. The performances showcased her operatic repertoire in musicals such as "*A Royal Coon*" and "*A Trip to Africa*" in 1909, as well as collaborations with vaudeville composers, Bob Cole and Billy Johnson.

Bob Cole, the major talent in the writing of the black owned musicals, left the Black Patti Troubadours, eventually meeting two brothers, J. Rosamond Johnson and James Weldon Johnson; their collaboration would be the source of his most successful songs. The Johnson brothers would later write the Black National anthem, "*Lift Every Voice and Sing*" and James Weldon Johnson, who would soon write "*The Auto-biography of an Ex-Colored Man*." In 1909, the trio collaborated on *The Red Moon,* a Broadway operetta with sophisticated lyrics. As a team they had moved from 'coon songs' and stereotypical themes toward romantic and realistic human feelings expressed by black performers, a feat unheard of outside of New York. The cast included Abbie Mitchell, Aida Overton Walker, and Sam Lucas. James Weldon Johnson left the team to pursue other interest and Cole and J. Rosamond went back to vaudeville.

The world famous performing duo of Bert Williams and George Walker also parted ways this year after 16 successful years of song-and-dance and comedy skits, from traveling minstrel shows to starring in the first black musical on a Broadway stage, *In Dahomey,* in 1902. Williams and Walker transitioned over time from the racial minstrel formulas and went against the stereotypical standard for black musical comedy by incorporating romance into their shows. Williams was an important and outstanding entertainer, able to move past racial barriers in his career during a period of racial inequality, furthering the growth of the African-American entertainer.

Ragtime was the popular music genre of this time. The syncopated rhythms of this musical style were composed for the piano, having been influenced by vaudeville and minstrel show songs. Missouri was recognized as the heartland of Ragtime and Scott Joplin was the proclaimed "King of Ragtime." He was the composer of 44 original rags, one ragtime ballet, along with two ragtime operas. One of Joplin's first compositions, "The Maple Leaf Rag," was his greatest and most influential piece, selling nearly 500,000 thousand copies by 1909. Ferdinand Joseph LaMothe, better known as Jelly Roll Morton, started as a ragtime pianist, and was considered to be the first jazz arranger, he wrote "Jelly Roll Blues" and "New Orleans Blues," during this time period.

W.C. Handy was commonly known as the "Father of the Blues." He was born November 16, 1873 in Florence, Alabama, the son of former slaves. His father was strict, a second generation minister in the African Methodist Episcopal church. W.C. was to follow in the family footsteps but his love for music led in a different direction. Handy traveled and performed from one city to another, even taught school briefly. He worked from Chicago to St. Louis, and then to Evansville, Indiana. He even worked minstrel shows with a group called "Mahara's Minstrels."

In 1909, Handy and his band moved to Memphis, Tennessee, and made their mark on Beale Street. He wrote his first song this year, "Mr. Crump," a campaign song for a Memphis mayoral candidate, the base of the tune would later evolve into his hit "Memphis Blues." It was also the first published commercial blues song. Handy having sold his rights to the song, didn't receive the financial benefits of its success. Handy's combination of ragtime and Latin rhythms with black folk music

A Reflection

morphed into a harmonic structure that became known as the blues. The blues were essential in the future development of jazz.

Black Athletics

Marshall W. "Major" Taylor was the first athlete to compete on an integrated professional team, the first to create world records, and the first to acquire a commercial sponsor. Bicycling was the most popular sport in America between 1890 and 1910, and Major Taylor was the "Fastest Bicycler in the World." Taylor was the trailblazer for all black athletes to follow, at his peak he earned more than $35,000 a year. He completed his final European tour in 1909 before retiring.

Boxing was the most equal opportunity sport open to Blacks in this year, and Jack Johnson was the king of the ring. Born on March 31, 1878 in Galveston, Texas, Johnson won the world heavyweight title on December 26, 1908 becoming the first Black Heavy Weight Champion of the world. Racial animosity among whites was so intense that Jack London campaigned for a "Great White Hope" to take the title away from Johnson. As the title holder, Johnson had to face a series of fighters billed by boxing promoters as "great white hopes," often in exhibition matches. Johnson successfully defended his World Heavyweight champion title four times in 1909, beating Frank Moran, Tony Ross, Al Kaufman, and the middleweight champion Stanley Ketchel.

Black athletes could only compete on "all-Negro" teams at black colleges or in all-black leagues after the turn of the century. Football was the only integrated professional team sport during this decade. Charles "Doc" Baker was the second African-American to play professional football as a halfback for the Akron Indians from 1906 to 1908.

Memorable Moments

In 1909, Matthew Alexander Henson, an African American arctic explorer, accompanied Robert E. Peary on seven expeditions to reach the North Pole before they were successful. Henson was the first to reach it, becoming the first mortal to walk on the top of the world.

In this decade, the "Colored Basketball World's Championship" is established; it begins as an unofficial term coined by a New York Age sportswriter to designate the best African American "five" in the country. The Twelfth Street Colored YMCA of Washington, DC forms a basketball team, known as the "12 Streeters"; almost every player is a current or former student of nearby Howard University. The 12

1909

Streeters win the 1909-1910 Colored Basketball's World Championship with an undefeated record.

In 1908, Henry Ossawa Tanner had his first one-man exhibition in the United States showing his religious paintings at the American Art Galleries in New York. His most famous piece was The Banjo Lesson (1893).

A Reflection

1893 painting by Henry Ossawa Tanner, via http://www.artchive.com/artchive/T/tanner.html

Reflections on a Decade

This decade was characterized as a period of frustration. The incessant degradation of black men and women being called boy or gal, and auntie or nigger, while having to address whites as Miss or Mister, served as a constant reminder of the white dominated society. The unquestioned insanity of vicious mobs that meted out vigilante injustice for the crime of a black man looking at a white woman was accepted and undeterred by those who held power and control. The value of a black's man life had been so cheapened that lynching and crimes committed against them went virtually unpunished.

Black people unsatisfied with the demeaning treatment sought education and decent wages to establish a foothold or a position of security from which they could climb out of the subordinate position imposed upon them by Jim Crow, but protests against segregation and injustice were answered with evictions, loss of employment, and even the loss of your life. The misery of the moment was overwhelming, laws continued to torment the black community over this decade and we have yet to overcome the handicap.

No matter what your station in life, whether you were a share cropper or a physician your desires were the same, to live with dignity, to be independent and self-sufficient, to raise a family and provide for their needs. Along with common aspirations there were common stumbling blocks, the lack of employment opportunities, low wages, inadequate education, and dilapidated living conditions. During the early 20th century, race improvement and positive self-image were seen as a way to increase social mobility. There were the fortunate few who were able to earn quality educations and do amazing things in academia, in medicine, and as entrepreneurs.

At the close of this decade there wasn't much visible transformation in the circumstances of black people. Politically disenfranchised but strongly supported by competent leadership in and out of the church, and enlightened by a steadfast black press, African-Americans forged ahead in the journey of a better life. Education was the catalyst for change, and however inferior the public education system in the South at the time, it would have to serve. Economically, blacks wrestled with low wages, no access to capital, and the legalized discrimination of Jim Crow. Opportunities for advancement were few, but the family structure was strong, people remained hopeful in the future, doing what they had always done; keep the faith and keep fighting.

A Reflection

1919

African-American soldiers home from World War I (public domain)

A steady gaze at the decade leading into 1919 reveals a multitude of shifts in the lives of African-Americans, most of them driven by World War I. Initially the Armed Forces had denied the acceptance of Black inductees but later relented, although the soldiers were relegated to subservient duties. Blacks had rushed to serve militarily, mistakenly thinking they could ingratiate themselves into acceptance as equal citizens by offering to sacrifice their lives for their country, believing they would be rewarded with justice and equality. After the war, Black veterans returned to the same racist America they had laid their lives on the line to defend.

World War I had other life-changing affects on black people across the country. American participation in the war inadvertently opened doors that otherwise would have remained closed under a normal state of affairs. During the war the U.S. government halted the immigrations from Europe, and with millions of white men enlisting, an extensive labor shortage was created, opportunities that tens-of-thousands of African-Americans were more than eager to fill.

Circumstances in the South were at a critical point economically for most and the revival of the Ku Klux Klan, bragging of one million members, only added fuel to a raging fire. Something had to give, and by the summer of 1919, it was the sanity and civility of a nation possessed by hate. It's difficult to fathom the conditions that would motivate a million people to pull up stakes and leave all they had ever known. Seeing the disadvantages, the negative factors piling up, it's hard to grasp how any advances could be made against those headwinds. Looking closely at 1919 you have to admire the determination, the tenacity, and feel the desperation of the huge numbers of black people who packed up everything they had, and those who left empty-handed, to venture toward far away cities and states to pursue greater opportunity. To endure the hardships and prejudice and still remain hopeful enough to move illustrates the character of a people who keep it pushing.

Demographics

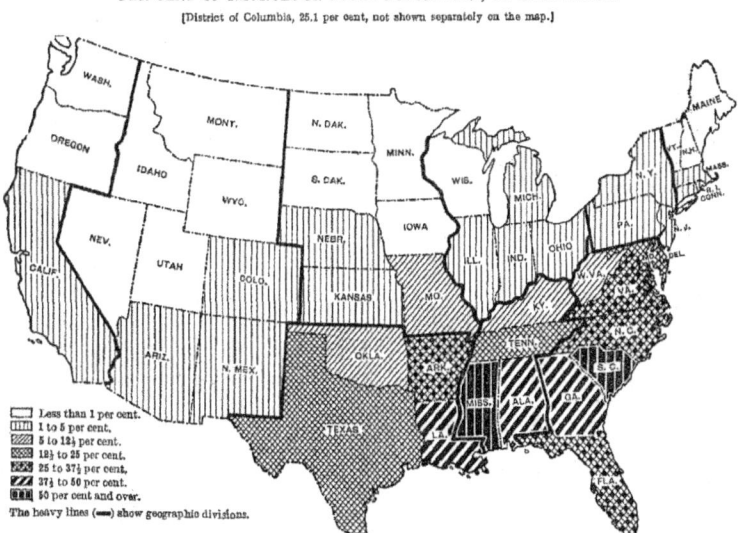

The world is still in the throes of the Influenza Pandemic that began in the fall of 1918. More than a third of the global population was infected, and an estimated 50 to 100 million died from the disease. The life expectancy for Black Americans in 1919 increased from the last decade and was now 45 years. Blacks were now 9.9 percent of the population with numbers around 10,463,000. There were 98.2 men for every 100 women. Eighty-five percent of blacks still lived in the South. Agriculture was still the

A Reflection

chief employer, and 14.7 percent of farmers in the country were African American. The increase in the proportion of black farmers is concentrated in the southern states, the result of the continued break-up of plantations operated by wage hands into small farms operated by black tenants.

Trains are still the primary mode of transportation. Urban cities like New York, Philadelphia, and Boston had trolley lines and subway systems for travel. The Ford Model T was in mass production, but only small numbers had automobiles and roads weren't always available or maintained.

Mood of the Black Community

Race restrictions were insidious throughout society; blacks weren't served in fine restaurants, were required to sit in balconies in theatres, not permitted to swim at local pools, refused lodging in hotels, and not hired in managerial and administrative positions. African-Americans were caught in the midst of a vicious onslaught of racial violence motivated by fear, prejudice, competition for employment, conflicts in housings, and by a general disregard for the rights of black people.

Yet, it was a time of awakening for Black people in America; unwilling to continue to settle for crumbs from the table, things had to change. Black pride was growing, feelings of fear and despair brought on by Jim Crow were transformed into determination, and attacks on black communities by whites were met with resistance. Blacks were moving from all-black towns in the South searching for safe havens away from Jim Crow and widening discrimination.

Discussions in churches and social gatherings always began and ended with whether they should leave their land and travel north. Black people were finding power in the press and in politics. They were becoming more militant in their responses to both physical and economical attacks. A black woman responded in a letter printed in the *Crisis* newspaper conveying the sentiments of black people: *"The Washington riot gave me a thrill that comes once in a life time ... at last our men had stood up like men. ... I stood up alone in my room ... and exclaimed aloud, 'Oh I thank God, thank God.' The pent up horror, grief and humiliation of a life time -- half a century -- was being stripped from me."*

1919

The Great Migration

Summed up simply and eloquently by Langston Hughes, the Great Migration was a...

One Way Ticket

I pick up my life
And take it with me
And I put it down in
Chicago, Detroit,
Buffalo, Scranton,
Any place that is
North and East?
And not Dixie.
I pick up my life
And take it on the train
To Los Angeles, Bakersfield,
Seattle, Oakland, Salt Lake,
Any place that is
North and West?
But not South.
I am fed up
With Jim Crow laws,
People who are cruel
And afraid,
Who lynch and run,
Who are scared of me
And me of them.
I pick up my life
And take it away
On a one-way ticket?
Gone up North,
Gone out West,
Gone!

A Reflection

Image from "Segregated waiting room at railroad depot : Jacksonville, Florida," The Florida Memory Project.

The Great Migration was just beginning to peak in 1919; over 500,000 Blacks had pulled up stakes in the South, triggered by a mixture of motivations. The boll weevil had decimated the cotton crop in the Gulf States, forcing farmers, sharecroppers, and laborers to look for alternative work. The lack of farm work in the South coincided with a shortage of laborers in the North. World War I had interrupted international immigration; new laws after the war limited the number of European immigrants, eliminating a steady source of cheap labor. Northern employers needed the black worker.

Recruiters had come to the South enticing Blacks with promises of higher wages. Advertisements for black laborers ran in black newspapers. White employers in the South did everything they could to stop the exodus; they even raided railway stations and removed blacks from the trains and placed them in jail on false charges, but the "Great Migration" had commenced. Blacks traveled in mass, leaving the terror of the South behind them, carrying high hopes of living better, and dreams of an equal education for their children. Those that didn't migrate wanted to create all-black towns. Black populations in the North grew by 43 percent, 55 percent in the West, and 2 percent in the South.

Four hundred thousand black Americans served in World War I. Black soldiers were returning home from World War I to find their sacrifice to the country had gained them nothing back at home; Black veterans were being subjected to the same racism from the country they had fought so heroically to defend. The injustice inspired black society with a spirit of militancy, part of an editorial in the *Crisis* in late 1919 stated, *"When the lynchers gather, we too must be armed. When the mob moves, we propose to meet it with bricks and clubs and guns."* Blood, sweat, and tears, had been shed in sacrifice for their country, and Blacks wanted what was due them, justice, equality, and security.

The Red Summer of 1919

If we must die, let it not be like hogs
Hunted and penned in an inglorious spot,
Like men we'll face the murderous, cowardly pack,
Pressed to the wall, dying, but fighting back!

-Claude McKay

"If We Must Die," in Harlem Shadows: The Poems of Claude McKay
(New York: Harcourt, Brace and Co., 1922)

The dramatic growth of the black populations in the North caused racial tensions; the black population in Chicago had grown 148 percent in three years, from 44,103 to 109,594. Northern labor unions were hostile to black workers barring their membership and creating more tensions, and the "new Negro" was less inclined to turn the other cheek. Blacks fighting back progressed into race riots in Washington and Chicago. The catalysts for the riots depended on whether you ask blacks or whites.

White military men were on a rampage, inflicting unchecked violence against black military persons and civilians after the war. On May 10th in Charleston, South Carolina, four U.S. sailors and one civilian led the first serious race riot that began the "Red Summer." More racial skirmishes broke out, each spurred on by the fervor of the last, the next in Gregg and Longview counties in Texas. In Houston, Texas a race war between soldiers of the 24th Infantry and a bloodthirsty white mob broke out, eleven whites and two blacks were killed, a total of 18 soldiers were hanged for their alleged involvement. The attempts made by the white persons responsible for the slaughter and destruction to justify their actions were futile, there was simply no excuse.

An article published in the October issue of the *Crisis*, written by Walter White, the assistant executive secretary of the NAACP, stated what he believed to be the eight general causes for the riots, and the same conditions, to varying degrees, could be

A Reflection

found in almost every large city with an appreciable Negro population. These causes, taken after a careful study in order of their prominence, are:

1. Race Prejudice.
2. Economic Competition.
3. Political Corruption and Exploitation of Negro Voters.
4. Police Inefficiency.
5. Newspaper Lies about Negro Crime
6. Unpunished Crimes Against Negroes.
7. Housing.
8. Reaction of Whites and Negroes from War.

During the summer and early fall of 1919, vicious and bloody riots broke out in every direction of the country. James Weldon Johnson fittingly referred to it as "The Red Summer of Hate." In total, there were 26 race riots between the months of April and October. The most violent and deadly riot occurred in Chicago on July 27, set off after police refused to arrest the white man responsible for the stoning and drowning of a black youth for swimming in an area of Lake Michigan beach reserved for whites. A total of 38 people, black and white, were killed and 500 were injured, and in the aftermath 1000 black families were left homeless.

Other severe race wars were in Washington, D.C. from July 19-23, where six blacks were killed and 100 wounded, and Elaine, Arkansas from October 1- 3, where five whites and between 100 and 200 blacks were killed. The massacre in Elaine began with an attack by white land owners on a meeting of the Progressive Farmers of Household Union where they were organizing Negro farm laborers seeking fair pricing. In Oklahoma the motive was a false accusation of assault by a white girl against a nineteen year old colored boy. The difference between these riots and previous attacks was that blacks retaliated. The militancy of the black war veterans was contagious. No longer were they going to be passive victims, they were armed with weapons to defend themselves.

Lynching

In 1919, the NAACP published, *Thirty Years of Lynching in the United States, 1889-1918*, which revealed the causes of lynching and the circumstances under which the crimes occurred. Lynching can only be described as an evil sickness; uncivilized madness driven by irrational notions of entitlement. The impulse behind lynching didn't require much incentive, the favorite excuse was the rape or offense of a white woman, guilt or innocence was irrelevant.

Eighty-three black Americans are known to have been lynched in 1919. Six Black men were tortured and strung up to be used as targets in Lake City, Fl. In Livermore, KY, admission was charged in the Opera House for whites to view a lynching and be allowed to shoot the victim, whose body was riddled with hundreds of bullets. Recounting the

Black lynching and burning of Will Brown by a white mob in Omaha, Nebraska, September 29, 1919

Image Ownership: Public Domain

horrid details of the countless lynchings of men, and even women, and most vile, the lynching of a woman in her eighth month of pregnancy and the murder of the child are so mind-boggling they would only serve to distract the reader from the focus of the writing.

Lynching was seen as the major problem in America at this time, being the most sinister of all crimes committed. Thousands of black men were lynched without justice for the victims. The despicable acts perpetrated against black men and women had to be stopped. In July of 1919, 15,000 black men and women marched in silence down the Fifth Avenue in Manhattan, NY in demonstration against lynching and the unspeakable violence black people experienced at the hands of white mobs.

James Weldon Johnson, field secretary of the NAACP, organized protests in response to the racial violence. Numerous telegrams were sent to President Wilson asking him to interject;

> "...the shame put upon the country by the mobs, including United States soldiers, sailors, and marines, which have assaulted innocent and unoffending Negroes in the national capital. Men in uniform have attacked Negroes on the streets and pulled them from streetcars to beat them. Crowds are reported ...to have directed attacks against any passing negro....The effect of such riots in the national capital upon race antagonism will be to increase bitterness and danger of outbreaks elsewhere. The National Association for the Advancement of Colored People calls upon you as President and Commander in Chief of the Armed Forces of the nation to make statements condemning mob violence and to enforce such military law as thesituation demands.
> The National Association for the Advancement of Colored People

A Reflection

respectfully enquires how long the Federal Government under your administration intends to tolerate anarchy in the United States."
-*NAACP telegram to President Woodrow Wilson*
August 29, 1919.

Pleas to political leaders for relief fell on deaf ears, leaving African-Americans with no other recourse but to defend themselves. The black community was urged to organize and take up the necessary arms for self-defense. Several instances showed that Blacks had been successful in warding off lynch mobs when they were met with resistance.

Political Climate

The political climate in 1909 was frigid at best, President Woodrow Wilson, a southerner and white supremacist was in the middle of his second term. Although blacks had supported Wilson in his election bid, he used his office to reverse the advancements made by African Americans during Reconstruction by bringing Jim Crow to the White House. Under his leadership Black federal supervisors and most black diplomats were fired and replaced by whites, refusing to be "ruled by an ignorant and inferior race." This set a national tone for open discrimination across the country, Black federal officials in the South were dismissed and the local Washington police force and fire department stopped hiring blacks.

Wilson segregated the Navy, and permitted officials to segregate the toilets, cafeterias, and their work areas, stating *"Segregation is not humiliating but a benefit"* and *"distinctly to the advantage of the colored people themselves."* In defense of the Ku Klux Klan he excused the violence; *"self-preservation [forced whites] to rid themselves, by fair means or foul, of the intolerable burden of governments sustained by the votes of ignorant Negroes."*

Black voters in the North found their independence in using their influence, gaining seats in the state legislatures of Massachusetts, New York, New Jersey, Pennsylvania, West Virginia, Ohio, Indiana, Illinois, and Missouri. More militant Blacks explored other political affiliations like the Socialist and newly formed Communist parties, others promoted Pan-Africanist nationals. Journalist Cyril Biggs started a monthly magazine called the *Crusader* that moved a step further and inspired the creation of the African Blood Brotherhood which called for complete separation. Briggs proposed, *"Government of the (Negro) people, for the (Negro) people and by the (Negro) people."* The African Blood Brother Hood was initially formed as a self-defense organization in 1919 for Blacks threatened by lynchings and race wars.

Blacks in the South *"voted with their feet,"* continuing the exodus towards cities in the North and Midwest to cities like Washington, Baltimore, Philadelphia, New York, New Orleans, and Chicago. With the growth of the black population in these cities there was also increasing racial prejudice and discrimination. Black populations had grown by such large numbers in some cities that they gained significant political clout in local elections and black urban leaders gained clout in their ability to deliver votes. This new presence was met with resistance among some candidates and a color-line was emphasized in campaigns to solicit the immigrant vote.

The Black Church

The Great Migration precipitated tremendous growth in African Methodist Episcopal and Baptist churches in the North and Western parts of the country. Olivet Baptist Church located in Chicago, the nation's largest black church had more than 10,000 members. The political strength of the black community grew with the Black church, and religion inspired hope for the future. The ties between politics and the church were closely intertwined in the black community. Black churches were independent of white society, and the only place the NAACP could meet. In 1919 the NAACP membership in the South had outgrown the membership in the North, with numbers exceeding 425,888.

Black pastors of 1919 wore many hats, in addition to their duties as spiritual leaders; they operated as peace-keepers during the riots, as well as politicians for their congregational concerns. The Reverend Doctor Junius C. Austin was indeed a political preacher who was broadly recognized as one of the great orators of his time. He received the call into the ministry at an early age and went further to complete his education with a Doctor of Divinity degree in 1910 and also a theology degree at Temple University in Philadelphia. Eventually he landed in Pittsburgh where he enlarged the Ebenezer Baptist's congregation to an imposing membership of 5,000. His leadership extended outside the church where he encouraged the migration of blacks to the North and established a financial institution, the Steele City National Bank, and a real estate office, the Home Finder's League, for support systems when they arrived in Pittsburgh.

In 1926, Austin was chosen to replace the pastor at Pilgrim Baptist Church on Chicago's South Side where he continued to pastor for more than 40 years, and by the end of the decade it had grown to be one of the ten largest church congregations in the United States. Austin was called the "dancing preacher" for the grace and power of his physical expression as well as his verbal presentation, preaching two or three sermons every Sunday. He was

A Reflection

credited for the birth of gospel music, having appointed Thomas A. Dorsey, writer and composer of *"Precious Lord, Take my Hand,"* as his Minister of Music.

Austin became active in civil rights, being elected as president of the Pittsburgh chapter of the NAACP, assisted the Urban League, supported the Sleeping Car Porters, and was also involved in the Universal Negro Improvement Association (UNIA) and its revolutionary and captivating leader Marcus Garvey. Political leaders realized the extent of Austin's appeal and influence, making his support a precious commodity sought by both political parties. Austin was instrumental in promoting the election of the first African-American U.S. Representative since the Reconstruction era, Republican, Oscar DePriest. In the words of Gates and West, Rev. Junius C. Austin was *"one of the first black ministers to demonstrate both the economic and political potential of the church."*

As African-Americans grew economically and educationally, class consciousness began to cause divisions among black people. Native urban blacks did not consistently welcome southern blacks to the cities, and this classism was also evident in the black churches. Rural blacks were uncomfortable with the dress and decorum of some middle-class churches. Storefront churches sprung up in cities like Chicago, Harlem, and Philadelphia to address the different mores of black people. Smaller congregations developed a sense of community and nurtured new arrivals as they adjusted to big city life. A more unorthodox group led by Father Divine and his disciples relocated to Sayville, New York in 1919; his Peace Mission Movement became the first black homeowners in Long Island.

Leadership

The more militant atmosphere added new dimensions to black leadership during these turbulent years of change. The rise in black consciousness produced a receptive audience for newcomers like Marcus Garvey and his organization, the Universal Negro Improvement Association, A. Philip Randolph with his union organizing, along with the steady influence of W.E.B. Du Bois and the NAACP.

Du Bois had been supportive of black participation in World War I, while Randolph was strongly opposed to it. The idea of *"making the world safe for democracy"* was *"a tremendous offense to the intelligence of the Blacks because at that time the Blacks were being lynched and denied the right to vote, in the South especially, and were the victims of segregation and discrimination all over the nation."* Different philosophies abounded, but all were unified in their efforts to uplift the race of black people to a position of equality.

1919

***

Marcus Garvey was born in St. Ann's Bay, Jamaica to Marcus Mosiah Garvey, Sr., a mason, and Sarah Jane Richards, a domestic worker and farmer. Garvey worked a variety of jobs while he attended school before working in the press, and was a master printer by trade. As he matured he became more aware of the injustices inflicted on his race. He witnessed it in his home of Jamaica, during extensive travels throughout Central and South America, and in sections of the West Indies, and London, England. Traveling in Europe he read of the conditions for blacks in America. A passion to fight the racial conflicts grew and intensified. Garvey committed himself to end the abuse of Blacks by all other races and nations in the world.

Believing that uniting blacks was the only way to improve their condition, Marcus Garvey founded the Universal Negro Improvement Association (UNIA) in August 1914 as a means of uniting all of Africa and its people who had been scattered across continents into *"one grand racial hierarchy."* He envisioned a nation of black men building a strong country and leaving their impression on all of civilization. Garvey arrived in the U.S. on March 23, 1916 for a lecture tour to raise funds for a school in Jamaica to be patterned after the Tuskegee Institute to preach his prophecy of Black Nationalism through his 'Back to Africa' movement. While in America Garvey continued to tour and speak about his separatist philosophy of social, political, and economic freedom for blacks.

Marcus Garvey eventually settled in Harlem, New York, and in May 1917, Garvey and thirteen others formed the first UNIA division outside Jamaica and by June 1919, he had established 30 branches in different cities with over 2,000,000 members. Larger numbers continued to join the UNIA motivated by pride of race and a commitment to work for the uplift of blacks around the world.

Garvey formed the Negro Factories Corporation and then launched the Black Star Shipping Line of ships, obtaining the first ship in September, the Yarmouth. His program was one of black self-determination and independence and set the theme for all black development today. He urged that black people should have a homeland of their own where they would have the greatest opportunity to develop politically; establishing their own government, industrially; through the growth of their own businesses, and socially; uniting all the black people of the world.

As Garvey's prominence grew, so did the number of his enemies. A growing group of black elites, of which W.E.B. Du Bois was one, disagreed with Garvey's philosophy

A Reflection

and his positions against integration in American. Du Bois felt Garvey was *"the most dangerous enemy of the Negro race in America and in the world."* Unfortunately, misguided business policies coupled with bad choices of associates contributed to the failing of the Black Star Shipping Corporation. This circumstance supplied ample ammunition for Garvey's enemies to instigate an onslaught to destroy his reputation and cripple his movement.

Charges of mismanagement and mail fraud were brought by the Federal government; Marcus Garvey was convicted, jailed for two years and then deported back to Jamaica. The legacy of Marcus Garvey left a lasting impression on America by showing the power of the black community, effectively giving them an influential voice within society. It showed that blacks would no longer accept white oppression and had the power to organize and fight back against corruption. The back to Africa movement served as a prelude to the Civil Rights movement, it demonstrated that blacks had the ability to unite together and play a significant role in political affairs.

***

Asa Philip Randolph was one of the most visible and influential African-American Civil Rights leaders of our time. Randolph was born in Crescent City, Florida, on April 15, 1889, the second son of James and Elizabeth Randolph. His father was a tailor and ordained minister of the African Methodist Episcopal Church, and his mother was a skilled seamstress. Lessons learned at an early age formed his approach to pursuing social equality, from his father, that color was less important that than a person's character and conduct, from his mother, the importance of education and of defending one's self physically if the need arises. The Randolph parents had great expectations for their two sons, which clashed with his ambition to be a professional stage actor. To pursue his stage career he moved to New York and spent several years acting, and even helped to organize the Shakespearean Society in Harlem. His major roles included Hamlet, Romeo, and Othello.

Randolph, an avid reader, was moved by W.E.B. Du Bois' *The Souls of Black Folk*, it changed his focus and he began his arduous struggle for social equality. Randolph joined the Socialist party and became a regular on the soapbox corner of 135th and Lenox Avenue. He lectured on socialism and craft unionism, rejecting moderate reform. By 1919, Randolph and his childhood friend, Chandler Owen, had established a monthly socialist journal called *The Messenger*. Their writings were considered radical and agitating, prompting Randolph to be labeled "the most dangerous Negro in America." In July 1919, *The Messenger*, was refused passage through the U.S. mail. In that year, A. Philip Randolph became the president of the National Brotherhood of Workers of America, the union for African-American shipyard and dock workers on the coastal plains of Virginia.

The Black Press

The major black leaders at the end of the decade were connected to some form of written media or press for mass circulation of their ideas, principles, or philosophies. W.E.B. Du Bois edited and wrote for the *Crisis* magazine; its subscription rate had grown from 1000 in 1909 to over 10,000 in May of 1919. His "Returning Soldier" editorial climaxed the era, but the May issue was held up six days at the Post Office citing the "seditious" editorial as the cause.

Marcus Garvey was heard through *The Negro World*, which was published in English, Spanish, and French. This newspaper for the UNIA spoke to black communities all over the globe. A. Philip Randolph edited and wrote for the *Messenger*, and it was known as "one of the most brilliantly edited magazines in the history of American Negro journalism."

The first national black press agency was founded in 1919 by Claude A. Barrett; the Associated Negro Press. This organization would provide news releases for close to 95 percent of all black newspapers. The number of black newspapers and magazines published grew by 50 over the last decade bringing the total up to 500. Circulation among some of the newspapers tripled over the past five years. The *Chicago Defender*, a weekly publication, was the first black newspaper to have a circulation over 150,000, while the *Crisis*; a monthly publication had more than 100,000 circulations.

Blacks were invisible in other newspapers unless accused in a crime. During this turbulent year across the country the black press kept the African-American community informed and united, giving them a voice amongst all the rhetoric. Black newspapers were an inspiration to blacks and informative to whites. The themes represented in the press were the contributions of blacks in the war effort, demands for civil rights, rising black consciousness, and the right and necessity of the black community to defend themselves. The concept of the "New Negro" was created to solidify the new image of black people.

Described as "Soldiers without Swords," the power of the black press was threatening to the status quo. Some newspapers encouraged black people towards migration; the

A Reflection

Chicago Defender was very successful in motivating blacks to come to Chicago by listing organizations and names of churches they could contact for help. Other newspapers influenced by Booker T. Washington's viewpoint advised against the exodus. The black press also encouraged blacks to participate in World War I and fight for democracy throughout the world, with the belief it would bring them more at home. When changes in justice and discrimination failed to materialize for African-Americans, the press expounded on the hypocrisy of America's ideals.

Four federal agencies along with state and local began monitoring black periodicals, charging black papers with inciting racial conflict and accusing them of stirring up an otherwise contented black population. Some even blamed the black press for the year's race riots. The more militant journals which included the *Messenger*, *the Negro World*, the *Challenger*, and the *Crusader* were harassed and investigated. The more conservative periodicals; the *New York Age*, the *Chicago Defender*, the *New York Amsterdam*, and the *Chicago Whip* rejected radical ideologies and focused on racial issues and inequities.

Radical papers had small circulations and usually had short life-spans. One of the more financially successful newspapers was the *Defender*; founded by Robert S. Abbott on May 5, 1905, referred to during this time as the most powerful black man in America. The *Defender* was the nation's most influential black weekly newspaper by the beginning of World War I with a national audience and extensively read in the South. The *Defender* was smuggled into the South, distributed by black Pullman porters and entertainers across the Mason/Dixon line.

The *Chicago Defender* launched an aggressive campaign encouraging "The Great Migration" movement in the South. White distributors refused to circulate the paper and groups like the Ku Klux Klan tried to confiscate it or threatened its readers. The newspaper was passed from person to person, read aloud by people in barbershops and beauty shops, and in churches. Estimates put its readership at over 500,000 people weekly at its height, with each paper sold being read by four to five African Americans.

Education

The black consciousness and culture grew as Negroes advanced in education and economic status. Compulsory education had become law, requiring all students to complete elementary school with the age of school attendance varying with the state. For 21 states, the age began at 7 years, and 8 years for the other 27 states and the District of Columbia. Education was still a priority for Blacks who saw it as a means of bettering

1919

their lives and achieving equal rights. Illiteracy rates continue to drop among black persons, down to 11 percent for persons between 10 and 14 years of age. The higher amounts of illiteracy were still concentrated in the South.

School attendance had increased by 50 percent over the last decade. For ages 7 to 13, 75 percent of black males and 78 percent of black females were enrolled in school. School attendance dropped as students got older, for persons 16 or 17, only 34 percent of black males and 43 percent of black females were still attending school.

Black schools were still receiving a fraction of the financial support that white schools received, and the demand for teachers far outdistanced the supply of teachers. High school education for whites was limited and for black students it was basically nonexistent. Southern school boards refused to build high schools for blacks with the reasoning they were incapable of advanced learning. Campaigns of self-help began as black people pooled their limited resources, donated their time and labor to build and fund schools for their children. These efforts were assisted by northern philanthropists who desired to support black education and increase access to public education. Julius Rosenwald the president of Sears and Roebuck during 1919 provided revenue that built schools and libraries, supplemented salaries, and funded summer schools.

In 1919, there were 107 African-American teacher training schools in the South. Teachers were uniting and organizing associations to gain better salaries, improved school houses and equipment, and quality training for educators.

Philanthropists, officials, and educators were debating the optimal programs of study to best prepare black students, specifically disagreements on industrial education to the exclusion of a classical curriculum, which was also a subject of contention between Booker T. Washington and W.E.B. Du Bois. Industrial education taught carpentry, auto repair, bricklaying, metal working, sewing, cooking, and laundry work. Supporters of industrial education considered it to be more practical, while detractors believed it limited African-Americans to low-wage jobs in the industrial workplace.

The number of students pursuing post-secondary education or college had grown over the last decade. At the end of 1919, 4040 black students were enrolled in college-level schools. However, black professional schools were suffering with revenue shortages and expenses due to a lack of students. Of the ten black medical schools operating a decade earlier, only three still continued to function, Howard University in Washington, D.C., Meharry Medical College in Nashville, Tennessee, and the College of Medicine and Surgery in Memphis, Tennessee.

A Reflection

Extraordinary Africa-American

George Washington Carver distinguished himself as an educator, agricultural researcher, inventor, poet, and artist. In 1919, at Tuskegee, Carver discovered over a hundred new and varied uses for the peanut, making it a major part of Southern agriculture and revolutionizing the Southern economy. Carver was best known for developing crop-rotation methods for conserving nutrients in soil by alternating nitrate producing legumes-such as peanuts and peas-with cotton, which depletes soil of its nutrients. This was presented at a critical time when the boll weevil had almost ruined cotton growers. As a result of his research, the South became a major new supplier of agricultural products. In 1919, the United Peanut Association of America was founded and Carver was invited to speak at their first annual meeting. Carver's promotion of peanuts before Congress made him the most famous African American of his era.

The date of George Washington Carver's birth is not known, but it is estimated to have been before the emancipation of slaves around 1864. As an infant George Carver and his family were kidnapped and resold in Kentucky, only George and his older brother James were recovered. After slavery was abolished, Carver was raised by his owner, Moses Carver, as his son. Moses taught him the basics in reading and writing, but unable to attend school in Diamond Grove he was encouraged to leave home to pursue his education. He traveled through Missouri living with foster families while he continued his studies. Eventually he moved to Kansas where he graduated from high school. Carver spent five years trying to get into college until he was accepted at Highland College, in Highland, Kansas. Upon his arrival to the college, seeing a black man, the school rejected him. He continued his travels and homesteaded a claim in Ness County, Kansas. He stayed there a few years, where he plowed 17 acres without the help of a mule or horse. He grew corn, vegetables, plants and flowers, and fruit and forest trees.

Still desiring to complete his education, he borrowed $300 from a local bank and went to Simpson College in Indianola, Iowa. Carver began studying art and piano, but his talent for growing plants and flowers convinced his art teacher that he should study Botany, and she persuaded him to study at Iowa State Agricultural College. In 1891, he became their first black student, earned his master's degree, and he later became their first black faculty member. Carver's research there in plant pathology and mycology gained national recognition. In 1896, Booker T. Washington invited George Washington Carver to head the Agriculture Department at Tuskegee; he accepted and remained there for 47 years.

George Washington Carver's discoveries included 325 different products derived from peanuts; some examples are shampoo, face powder, vinegar, soap, coffee, butter, milk, and printer ink. He later found that other crops like the sweet potato, soybeans, and pecans also enriched depleted soils, so he investigated additional uses for these products. Carver found 118 products from the sweet potato including synthetic rubber, 75 from pecans, and 500 dyes from a variety of southern plants.

Employment

During World War I, four million people entered the military, leaving large numbers of civil jobs needing workers. Farm laborers were drawn from the fields to work in factories to produce munitions and indispensable goods. The South was feeling the effects of the loss of cheap labor in the Great Migration, but was still obstinate and unwilling to change its wicked ways and improve the conditions for black workers. Labor shortages during the war brought about compulsory work laws. Federal and state laws were passed in the North and the South. Domestic and farm labor was in such great demand that labor ordinances to remedy the situation were simply manipulations to force blacks to work where they wanted them at an unfair wage. An excerpt from an essay published in The New Republic early in 1919 stated,

> "In Macon, Georgia, a colored woman was arrested for not working. She told the court at her trial that she was married, that her husband earned enough to enable her to stay at home and take care of the home and her children, and these duties kept her too busy to do any other work. Despite this statement she was fined $25.75 and told by the court that if she remained in Macon she "would either work in service or on public works" as being married did not exempt her from the provisions of the law. In Birmingham, due to the shortage of domestic labor, an article appeared on June 19th in local papers stating all women must work. White women protested and in two days another headline clarified: "NEGRO WOMEN HERE ORDERED TO WORK."

Workers were required to carry an employment card signed by their employer, showing they were in obedience to the law. Those who did not comply were arrested for vagrancy and fined, some were sent to the "State Farm" to work for free. On the first day the ordinance went into effect 20 black women were arrested. The *New York Weekly* described the condition of the vast host of colored people, just as bad as, if not worse, than it was

A Reflection

during the days of slavery. "Though today we are enjoying nominal freedom, we are literally slaves." Blacks worked 14 to 16 hours a day for $10 dollars per month, living a treadmill life, where they didn't move forward, simply working as hard as possible to stay in the same position.

In the field of agriculture, blacks were continuing to leave the land; tenancy or sharecropping amounted to slave labor. Those who chose to stay were somehow improving their status. In this year, 29 percent were laborers, 58 percent were tenant farmers, and 13 percent were land owners.

More than 50 percent of black women were employed, working as domestics, seamstresses, taking in laundry, and for small numbers the teaching profession was also an option. Black men had a wider range of options, they found work in mechanical industries, coal mining, meat-packing, and the largest increase came in building and construction work. Most were still relegated to menial jobs in factories and on the railroad. Because of the lack of steady employment and higher wages, jobs such as the Pullman Porter or hotel doorman, relatively undistinguished positions, became prestigious positions in black communities.

As black workers migrated to the North in search of better jobs their rate of employment grew. According to the census, in this year 71 percent of blacks over the age of 9 years had gainful employment, while only 51 percent of whites worked. The American Federation of Labor voted to end racial discrimination, and African Americans made substantial gains in industrial employment, particularly in the steel, automobile, shipbuilding, and meatpacking industries. Between 1910 and 1920, the number of blacks employed in industry nearly doubled from 500,000 to 901,000. In Cleveland 65 percent of black males worked in manufacturing and mechanic industries, but 73 percent of industrial workers were in unskilled labor categories.

The Issue of Black Crime

Criminal activity among African-Americans continued to be a serious and growing problem. For the black community there was more trouble on every hand, if not being victimized by racist belligerent white men terrorizing them day and night, they had to contend with the intra-racial lawlessness of their own people. The black migration was blamed for the increase in violence seen in urban cities, not only by white society, but also by elite blacks who saw the new migrants as uncivilized. White immigrants were also exposed to disproportional levels of crime committed amongst themselves in slums where they resided. The difference between the groups was white immigrants were able to prosper and rise above the fray, while blacks were mired in deprivation by prejudice and discrimination.

Black people were about 10 percent of the population, but totaled 31 percent of those incarcerated in state and federal prisons, with the average age of those imprisoned being 28 years. According to Uniform Crime Reports, homicide arrest rates for blacks were four times that for whites. Blacks were arrested at higher numbers for all offenses except for nonsupport and neglect of family. Penalties or time served was longer in Northern states. Taking into account the imbalances in the justice system during the period, the recorded numbers don't relay the inequalities of law enforcement. Blacks were more likely to be arrested, convicted, and given consistently longer sentences for comparable crimes than whites.

Contrary to the racist myth that black men had uncontrollable desires to rape white women, black men rarely committed rape; this crime was more frequently committed by white men during this time. Blacks were largely charged with assault and homicides usually perpetrated on other black people. Juvenile delinquency increased as more often both parents worked outside of the home. Census data reports that black youth made up 17 percent of juveniles aged 15-19 housed in Juvenile Correctional Facilities.

The occurrence of elevated crime rates among the population was attributed to a subculture of violence within the African-American psyche by whites seeking to justify ill-treatment towards blacks. Statistics and studies have shown that crime levels decrease as the economic level increases. Poverty was the main culprit, most responsible for anger, rebelliousness, and resentment among black people overcrowded in slums compounded with the inability to provide for their basic needs. Poverty was perpetuated by inequality in educational attainment and discrimination in employment opportunities.

Health

The year 1919 began in the middle of the influenza pandemic that had spread throughout the world for most of 1918. Before this year would close, more than 40 million people would have lost their lives to the flu. African-Americans were less susceptible to this influenza and the reasons why were feverishly debated. Some observed that the disparity may be a consequence of segregation, where blacks had limited exposure to the disease, but the cause of the difference was unclear. Other theories suggested that although blacks were less vulnerable in contracting the disease, if they did become infected, they died more frequently because of their social condition and their susceptibility to pneumonia.

A Reflection

The additional health issues for African Americans for this decade were very similar to those in 1909. The black community faced heart disease, accidental death, and pneumonia, but tuberculosis was particularly associated with black people. The living conditions for most black people in urban areas kept them more susceptible to tuberculosis and typhoid fever, diseases that appear more often among the poor. Tuberculosis is caused by bacteria and Typhoid fever is caused by ingesting contaminated water or food. Inadequate sanitation is associated with both of these infectious diseases. Infant mortality and venereal diseases were also disproportionately in the community.

For the previous 20 years, African- American physicians had proposed more than a few strategies to decrease the incidence of tuberculosis and other infectious diseases in black communities. They pressed for the enforcement of sanitation laws to clean up the tenement housing where many urban families were forced to live. Some progress was made, and black and white deaths from tuberculosis declined over the last ten years, although deaths among blacks were still three times higher than those of whites.

The African-American community had fewer trained physicians and nurses than the white community; this meant that many African Americans were unable to access sufficient health care when necessary. In 1919, there were approximately 119 African-American hospitals in operation. Racial discrimination restricted African-American physicians and healthcare professionals from utilizing white medical facilities, and few hospitals admitted black patients. Many working class migrants received care from midwives and lay healers. Forced to wait in separate waiting rooms, and charged fees above their means, most relied on home remedies or patent medicines, going to doctors only for serious health issues.

Housing

The cities with the most dramatic increases in the African-American population during this period were Chicago, New York, Detroit, and Cleveland. Scarce housing and the mass influx of migrants in urban cities created a struggle between races and social classes. Housing was a major source of contention between blacks and whites during the years surrounding 1919. For those living in larger cities, blacks were segregated in overcrowded tenements in all-black neighborhoods in undesirable parts of town that were filthy and lacked sanitation. Black neighborhoods filled to their capacity in urban cities induced blacks to find homes outside of the overcrowded ghettos. As more and more blacks moved into white areas, organized efforts to retain "white neighborhoods" went into effect to keep blacks on "their part of town."

The "Black Belt" in Chicago was a district of dilapidated accommodations that extended 30 blocks along State Street on the South Side. This area was divided into zones according to economic status. The poorest blacks lived in the oldest section, the northernmost vicinity of the black belt, while the elite resided in the southernmost section. Some blacks were living in "white neighborhoods," but with the growing numbers of new migrants some whites were sent into a panic, causing them to form "Property Owners' Associations" to preserve white communities. Drastic measures would be taken to keep blacks from buying homes where they weren't wanted, having them fired from their jobs, purchasing their mortgages, and even destroying their homes. Over the 18 months up to August, 1919, there were twenty bombings of houses occupied by blacks outside of the "Black Belt."

Between 1909 and 1919, the population of African-Americans in New York City had grown by 66 percent, with the vast majority moving to Harlem. John Nail, the wealthiest black realtor in New York was instrumental in purchasing homes for well-to-do blacks in the city but soon realized that the bulk of the new blacks in Harlem could only afford apartments. During the next few years Nail and Associates would own and manage close to 50 apartment complexes and generate an annual income of $1 million. By the early 1920's, conservative estimates placed the total value of black owned property in Harlem at $60,000,000, while others considered it might be as great as $200,000,000.

In 1919, New York City's Tenement House Department determined there were no longer any vacancies in new-law tenement buildings. Harlem was grossly overcrowded with more than 250,000 people crammed into an area 50 blocks long and eight blocks wide. Many had to sleep in shifts. Both white and black landlords took advantage of the opportunity to raise rents. Most families survived by having rent parties or taking in lodgers to lessen the rent burden. A study done by the New York Urban League concluded that, "Negroes paid from 40 to 60 percent higher rents than white people did for the same class of apartments."

Employed at low-paying jobs, new migrants were not able to buy homes. Census figures for home ownership were unchanged from 1909, with 76.2 percent renting, and 23.8 percent owning their homes, although other sources report home ownership for blacks fell after the "Great Migration" from the rural South to the urban North.

A Reflection

Family Structure

The state of the African-American family is an area of controversy in 1919. The majorities of migrants to the North were young and single, and consequently were blamed for the increases in crime, sexual promiscuity, residential deterioration, and family instability. Franklin E. Frazier, a prominent African-American social scientist who studied the evolution of black families from slavery, through emancipation, during Reconstruction, and into the period of the Great Migration, characterized the black family as disorganized and dysfunctional because of a series of disruptive social experiences. It was his claim that the black family had disintegrated into single-parent households as a result of the Great Migration after World War I.

Frazier's general beliefs about the black family were that it was matriarchal; black males were subordinate to the black female because of his weak social and economical position in society. It was also his opinion that marital instability and sexual permissiveness were "prevalent" in black family life. The word prevalent is defined as widespread, customary, or rampant.

Studies based on Census data disagree with the analysis of Frazier and others who blame migrants from the South for bringing their "sharecropping culture" to the North. The assumptions of Northerners about the social condition of black newcomers were not supported by governmental statistics. Blacks continued to have the highest rate of marriage of all races. The U.S. census recorded that 75 percent of all African American females aged 15 years and older were married or widowed. Rural areas had a slightly higher percentage of marriage, for ages 25 to 34 over 87 percent were married, and for ages 35 to 44 over 93 percent were married. In urban areas for ages 25 to 34, 81.5 percent of black females were married, and for ages 35 to 44, 88.7 percent of black females were married or widowed.

While they did have lower levels of education attainment and higher levels of illiteracy in 1919, they also were more likely to be gainfully employed, with their families intact. The children from the South were raised to be independent and learned the value of hard work early in life.

W.E.B. Du Bois postulated that there were four classes in which black populations could be divided; (1) the well-to-do, (2) hardworking laborers who were doing fairly well, (3) the "Worthy poor" who were working but merely carving out an existence, and (4) the "submerged tenth," merely existing. The foundation for these classifications is economic status. Research has shown family stability is correlated with economic stability. The instability that was observed among a portion of black urban families was due to poverty, a need for parental supervision, the absence of family tradition, and the lack of social mobility. Theories that profess black people have no source for kinship and family relationships are irresponsible.

Black Entertainment

The power of entertainment through movies and music has no boundary. It influences our thinking and can alter our perception of reality. It can stir emotions of anger, sadness, joy, and even change behavior. Media is a means of communicating ideas and information. During this time it was being used as a means to subjugate the black community as they fought against stereotypes and prejudice. African-American authors and filmmakers were stirred and began to counteract the negative descriptions and put forth realistic images of African-American life.

Oscar Micheaux emerged as one of the radical voices against the white supremacist propaganda spread throughout the media, attempting to neutralize it through literature and black cinema. Micheaux know as the "Father of Afro-American Cinema" was also the first black to write and publish a best-selling novel, selling more than 55,000 copies. He was quoted as saying *"I'm tired of reading about the Negro in an inferior position in society. I want to see them in dignified roles...Also, I want to see the white man and the white woman as the villians...I want to see the Negro pictured in books just like he lives...* "*But*," he added, "*if you write that way, the white book publishers won't publish your scripts...so I formed my own book publishing firm and write my own books, and Negroes like them, too, because three of them are best sellers."*

Oscar Micheaux was born in Metropolis, Illinois in 1884, the grandson of former slaves, and the fifth of 11 children. He tried his hands as a coal miner and a Pullman porter before moving to Gregory, South Dakota where he homesteaded 500 acres in the 1910s. Micheaux was first a writer, publishing 10 novels for black audiences. His first book was an autobiographical novel depicting his experiences as a homesteader in the West. He transitioned into his next calling; traveling and selling his books across the country. Micheaux saw the beginning of the film industry as a way to not only take the success of his books to the next level but to counter old stereotypes and present a realistic version of the African-American community. He founded the Micheaux Film Corp, wrote, directed, and produced the first full-length all-Negro movie, The "*Homesteader*," the first shown in "white" theatres.

A Reflection

Oscar Micheaux's films were bold and controversial broaching sensitive subjects that disturbed both black and whites audiences; mixed race relationships, white men who prey on black women, black people "passing," and corrupt preachers. He also presented a positive image in his films, advocating education and economic independence. Micheaux's second movie, *"Within Our Gates"* was written as a rebuttal to D.W. Griffith's movie *"Birth of a Nation"* that portrayed the Ku Klux Klan as heroes. Through *"Within our Gates,"* Micheaux dramatically depicted the racial themes prevalent in American society, Jim Crow, lynching, and the Ku Klux Klan. The role of the villain was reversed in a central scene, showing a white man attempting to rape a black woman.

A social activist, he used the big screen to illustrate the horror and inhumanity of lynching, and to display the heroism of African-American soldiers who fought in the war. Micheaux was very progressive, and understood the complexity of African-American life, willing to show a wide range of characters, heroes, criminals, some who drank and gambled, as well as blacks who were as rich, educated and cultured as whites. He was recognized as the producer and director on 44 of the 82 all-Negro pictures made between 1919 and 1948.

***

The greater awareness and race consciousness of African-Americans as they migrated north and west produced an audience starved for literature, films, and music that gave an honest depiction of the black experience. The stage was not yet available to black playwrights, scripts were printed in periodicals. The NAACP, encouraged by Du Bois, created a drama committee that would develop plays by black writers. In 1919, the *Crisis* printed a play called *"Aftermath"* written by Mary P. Burrill, which captured the essence of the day. It told the story of a black soldier who returned to South Carolina after the war and discovered his father had been lynched by a white mob. *"This ain't no time fu' preachers or prayers,"* he shouts. *"You mean to tell me I mus' let them w'ite devuls send me miles erway to suffer an' be shot up fu' the freedom of people I ain't nevah seen, while they're burning and killin' my folks here at home! To Hell with 'em!"*

Musical theatre and vaudeville went into decline during the last decade when dramatic theatre and films grew in popularity. A number of bright stars of the musical stage like George Walker had died, Bob Cole, and the Johnson brothers moved on to other projects. Bert Williams joined the Ziegfeld Follies. Williams focused most of his energy in recording for Columbia; his records were among the highest-selling songs of the age, taking up a full page in Columbia's catalog. In 1919, Bert Williams was the highest paid black recording artist in the world.

In 1919, the music of the blues moved into the spotlight. Black show business was moving away from mintrelsy, songwriters and composers were producing all-black revues featuring the blues. Talent promoter and composer, Perry Bradford, claimed his revue "*Made in Harlem*," presenting Mamie Smith, was the first stage production that brought the blues to northern audiences in Harlem. Billed as "The Queen of the Blues," Mamie Smith would be the first blues singer recorded, the song was "Crazy Blues," and it sold a million copies. The commercial success of Smith's record drove other record companies to find female blues singers to record, beginning the era of classic female blues. The recording industry door was opened for the greats, Bessie Smith and Ethel Waters. W.C. Handy, "The Father of the Blues," had already signed a deal in 1919 with Victor Company for the third recording of his "Yellow Dog Blues," and the Joe Smith rendition became the best-selling recording of Handy's music at that time.

Sports and African-American Athletes

African-Americans excelled in athletics at white universities, competing in football, baseball, basketball, and track and field. In June of 1919, Paul Robeson graduated from Rutgers University after earning the distinction of the "Greatest Athlete in Rutgers History." He starred in four sports, track and field, football, basketball, and baseball. He was most superior in football, being named to the "All American Football Team." The only black student during his four years, he received a record of 11 varsity letters. No less impressive was his intellectual prowess, he excelled academically, a member of the esteemed Phi Beta Kappa Honor Society.

The two most popular sports in the country at this time were boxing and baseball. Segregation and Jim Crow kept blacks from participating in professional sports, with boxing being the only exception. Many matches were interracial before Jack Johnson dominated and humiliated white opponents in the heavyweight division. In 1919, Harry Wills (May 15, 1889 – December 21, 1958) was the best fighter in the heavyweight division. Known as the "The Black Panther," Wills was ranked as the number one challenger for the title, but racism and the "color line" after the reign of Jack Johnson gave Jack Dempsey an excuse not to enter the ring. Never given the opportunity to fight for the title, his final record was 75 wins (with 47 knockouts), 9 losses and 2 draws.

The doors of organized professional leagues were closed to blacks in these years.

A Reflection

Before segregation, black baseball players played in white leagues. After Jim Crow laws, blacks played "independent ball" in Negro Leagues. Andrew "Rube" Foster, thought to be the best African-American pitcher of the 1900s, founded and managed the Chicago American Giants, one of the most winning teams in the Negro leagues. In 1919, Foster helped Tenny Blount put together a black baseball club in Michigan, the Detroit Stars. These and other black baseball clubs were thriving in the Midwest; the Dayton Marcos, the Indianapolis ABC's, the Kansas City Monarchs, the Cuban Stars, and the St. Louis Giants. In the following year, after being denied into the Major league, Foster and the owners of these seven clubs met to form a professional baseball circuit for African-American teams, which became the Negro National League.

The National Football League and the American Professional Football Association were also organized in 1919. Two African-American players signed professional football contracts, Fritz Pollard with the NFL Akron Pros, and Robert "Rube" Marshall for the APFA Rock Island Independents. One of the original stars on the team, Pollard's first season with the Akron Pros went undefeated, winning the first championship of the league. Outstanding in football, Fritz Pollard was the first African-American to play in the Rose Bowl when he played for Brown University and the first black coach in the NFL in 1922.

Memorable Moments

Harriet Tubman, born Araminta Ross in 1820, died on March 10, 1913.

In February of 1919, The 369th Infantry "Hellfighters" Regiment of World War II triumphantly marched through New York City in a parade led by bandleader Lt. James Reese Europe and Bill "Bojangles" Robinson.

Madame C. J. Walker died on Sunday, May 25, 1919 from complications of hypertension. At her death she was the wealthiest African-American woman in America, and the first self-made female American millionaire.

In 1919, the NAACP adopted the song "Lift Every Voice and Sing" as The Negro National Anthem, first written as a poem by James Weldon Johnson, and later put to music by his brother, John Rosamond Johnson.

On May 9, 1919, popular bandleader James Reese Europe is murdered; he becomes the first African American honored with a public funeral in New York City.

Prohibition banned the manufacture, transportation, and sale of alcoholic beverages across the nation.

1919

Reflections on a Decade

The decade leading up to 1919 was wrought with turmoil and change. Black people had the Blues, but they vowed to do whatever was needed to shake them. Changes in the attitude were evident in the leadership that emerged during this period, Marcus Garvey and A. Phillip Randolph, no longer passive, but radical and defiant. There was ample evidence that black people were moving forward with fresh determination fed with the hope for a better life in the Northern and West cities, but the effects of the Jim Crow laws would be more devastating and long-lasting than those fighting to repeal them could have ever imagined.

World War I opened up employment opportunities and widened the range of job options for black men and women, although still relegated to mostly unskilled and low-wage positions. The black church working with the Urban League, still served as major support for those in transition. The black press was strong and effective, informing and influencing the black community on all pertinent issues. Politically, blacks were regaining some semblance of relevance as they exercised their right to vote in northern cities. Black businesses were thriving in urban areas serving the needs of the black community. Progress in education persists; more children were attending school and completing higher grades.

The years of the Great Migration were constructive in the evolution of black people, but the struggle for survival continued. Negative repercussions compromised health and stirred criminal activity, creating new aggravations for migrants. The common struggle bound and united black people together in their misery. African-Americans wanted quality education, just wages, places of recreation, good homes, maintained streets, sanitation, fire and police protection, and the right to vote. Those who had the finances or the education to live better couldn't escape the boundaries of segregation. Many were forced to live in the same squalor of those without the means to do better.

When asked what Negroes thought of the race riots, a Negro teacher answered, *"The accumulated sentiment against injustice to colored people is such that they will not be abused any longer."* There was a combination of catalysts that powered this sentiment and the forward movement for African-Americans; World War I, Jim Crow, job opportunities outside of the South, and the terrorizing of the black communities. There was no doubt that black people were coming of age, there was no turning back, but segregation stood as a road block on the journey to a better life.

A Reflection

1929

Pictured here are Langston Hughes [far left] with [left to right:] Charles S. Johnson, E. Franklin Frazier, Rudolph Fisher and Hubert T. Delaney, on a Harlem rooftop on the occasion of a party in Hughes' honor, 1924.

The decade preceding, and the year 1929 demands a long-lasting look. Mixed emotions are stirred because of the brilliance of the era and the devastation that it brought beginning with the Stock Market Crash of 1929. It appeared that all that had been lost in the "Middle Passage" and through hundreds of years in slavery was found in this era of the Harlem Renaissance. The spirit of African-Americans had been revitalized and unleashed. Culture grew from the souls of a people, fed by their history, developed from the pain of the past, the struggle of the here and now, and the vested hopes and dreams of the future. It burst open in music, literature, theater, dance, and the visual arts. Black people had come into their own, discovered a sense of self, and expressed it in every way possible.

These were the 'Roaring Twenties," all boundaries would be pushed to the limit, economically, socially, and culturally. America's wealth had nearly doubled over the last ten years and people were making more money than they ever had in the history of the

1929

nation. However for African-Americans there were two views on opposite ends of the spectrum of how they fared in this period of abundance, one depicting this time as prosperous and joyous, with blacks living the high life, the other depicting a time of want and wretchedness in urban slums. Maybe the true vision is somewhere between the two extremes.

The migration of black people continued to the thriving industrial cities of the South, North and West, with one million more pulling up stakes in search of employment opportunities, civil rights, and safety and security. For blacks remaining in the South, this was a decade of racism, terrorism, and poverty. The number of Ku Klux Klan members had grown to 5 million, spreading to north-eastern cities, in their ghastly efforts to keep "niggers" in their place.

Demographics

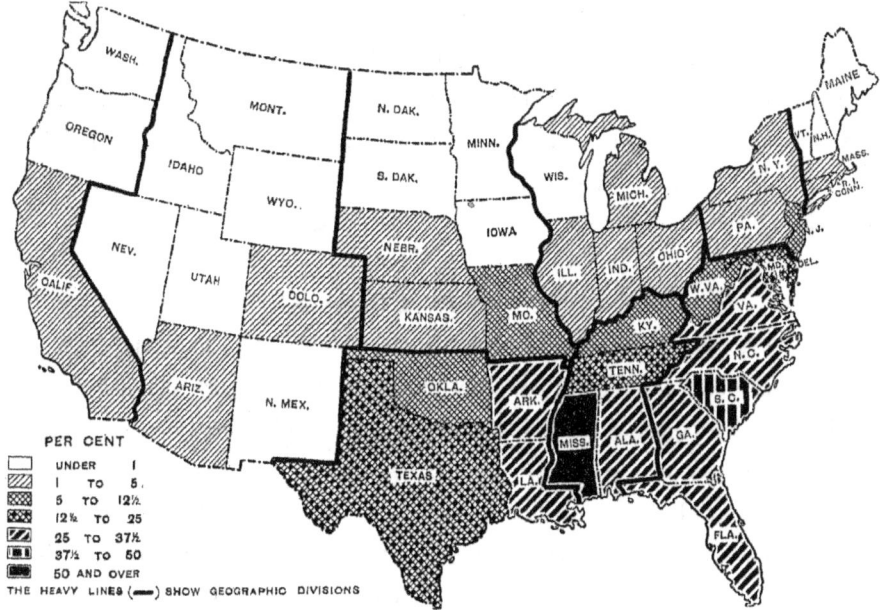

http://www.census.gov/prod/www/abs/decennial/1930.htm

The life expectancy has not changed much in the last decade, but for Black Americans it was 48 years, much less than that of white American's 61 years. Black people declined

A Reflection

in the percentage of the total population and now make up 9.7 percent with numbers around 11,891,000. There are 97 black men for every 100 women; the gender imbalance is more prevalent in the South.

In Mississippi, blacks are the majority of the population, but still have no representation. South Carolina follows with the second largest black population with similar disadvantages. Eighty percent of those living in the South were still sharecroppers. Twenty percent of blacks now live in the North, with 47.4 percent living in urban areas. Popular urban cities for migration in the South were Houston, Baltimore, and Memphis. The African-American populations in New York, Chicago, and Cleveland had more than doubled in the last decade and were close to doubling in Philadelphia. By 1929, the black communities in Los Angeles, California and Detroit, Michigan had grown by 150 percent.

Pennsylvania had the largest northern population of blacks in this year, but New York had the greatest gain in numbers; Harlem alone had over 200,000 black residents. West Indians were also migrating to the U.S. in 1929, 54,000 lived in New York, yet they didn't consider themselves African-Americans, but as black immigrants.

Blacks migrated to the Northeast and Midwest for employment in large urban manufacturing cities. The Detroit black population grew with the growth of the auto industry. Although the exodus north was not the magic bullet for blacks in America, the availability of decent employment afforded them some degree of class mobility as they transitioned from southern rural farmers into urban industrial workers.

Mood of the Black Community

The decade ending in 1909 could be seen as the childlike stage for African-Americans, they were functioning with a bevy of disadvantages. They were expressing their dissatisfaction with their second-class status but weren't able to improve their situations. Black people were caught in a reactive mode, responding to their environment but lacking the power to make changes. Moving to 1919, the struggle was in the adolescent stage, similar to the numbers in the year, moving through their teens, maturing, becoming more defiant, needing their independence, searching for their identity. When they reached the "Twenties," feelings of confidence, pride in themselves, and a self-awareness of their strength and beauty took over. Experience and greater knowledge required that they make their own decisions; they would no longer be treated as children, they demanded the respect given to adults.

1929

Black people wanted their share of the American dream, to work and earn a decent living, to raise a family and educate their children. In the decade leading up to 1929, they were determined to take charge of their destinies, to make their own moves, and not wait to be pushed around. They dared to dream bigger dreams and worked to make them happen, anything to get to the next level. Black people were more self-assured and filled with satisfaction from the successes and accomplishments of their "talented tenth," in business, education, and the arts.

It was the Jazz Age, and you had to dance. "Let the Good Times Roll." It was your station in life that dictated your level of exuberance. Black people wanted more and finally were earning the money to buy it. In 1929, the total sales for retail stores owned by African-Americans were $98.6 million. Black men and women wanted to feel good, look good, and live good. A new identity was emerging; the "New Negro" was all the rage. The music expressed our style, the flash, pizzazz, the sassiness, a new attitude, our depth, it was Jazz.

Political Climate

The politics of the 1920s was a mixed bag. Earlier in the decade, Presidents Harding and Coolidge, both Republicans, were sympathetic to plight of African-Americans, but by 1929 President Herbert Hoover could not have cared less. Harding had advocated civil rights for black people and pushed for the formation of an international commission to improve race relations between blacks and whites, but strong opposition by Southern Democrats kept these initiatives from being realized. He did place a few blacks in federal positions, one being Walter L. Cohen of New Orleans, comptroller of customs. Harding also supported the passage of a national anti-lynching law to protect black citizens. His presidency was short-lived; he died after serving the second year of his term.

In 1923, Vice President Calvin Coolidge took office with a republican philosophy similar to Harding, speaking out in favor of civil rights, and continuing to push for racial reconciliation and a commission to increase tolerance between the races. Coolidge responded to a letter that claimed the United States was a "white man's country":

> ....I was amazed to receive such a letter. During the war 500,000 colored men and boys were called up under the draft, not one of whom sought to evade it. [As president, I am] one who feels a responsibility for living up to the traditions and maintaining the principles of the Republican Party. Our Constitution guarantees equal rights to all our

A Reflection

citizens, without discrimination on account of race or color. I have taken my oath to support that Constitution....

In response to increased lynching in Southern towns and violence against blacks in Northern cities, Coolidge repeatedly called for anti-lynching legislation to be enacted, but most Congressional attempts to pass this law were filibustered by Southern Democrats. Coolidge also named African-Americans to judgeships and other major posts. Speaking at Howard University, he praised *"the progress of the colored people on this continent"* as *"one of the marvels of modem history." "Racial hostility, ancient tradition, and social prejudice are not to be eliminated immediately or easily,"* he said, *"But they will be lessened..."*

As a result of the "Great Migration," black voters held the balance of power between the parties in many states. Years after Lincoln had freed the slaves; blacks remained loyal to the Republican Party even though there had been no significant civil rights benefit evident to sustain the loyalty. The break with the GOP was precipitated by the Great Flood of 1927 in Mississippi. More than 1.5 million people were displaced from their homes. Secretary of Commerce Herbert Hoover, indifferent to the hardships experienced by blacks, a racist who believed whites were superior to blacks, was in charge of the flood relief operations. Hoover ignored the mistreatment of blacks as tens of thousands were rounded up by gunpoint in refugee camps for forced labor.

During his presidential campaign, Herbert Hoover promised further reforms for blacks if the travesties in the refugee camps were not publicized in the media, but these promises were not kept. Hoover used what is now referred to as the Southern Strategy; he forced all republican blacks to relinquish their offices to produce a lily white GOP to win the support of racist whites in the South. Hoover's legacy was the critical error of the Republican Party to renounce its commitment to civil rights and equality in order to appeal to the racist white voters in the South. While in office President Hoover upheld all Jim Crow practices. His racist actions opened the door for Franklin D. Roosevelt to solicit black voters for the New Deal.

The Great Migration produced dramatic growth of the black population in the North, particularly in Chicago. This concentrated population of blacks in the South Side of Chicago had more political muscle than any other in the country. This power facilitated the election of the first African-American, Oscar Stanton DePriest, to be elected in Congress in the 20th century, and the first from a northern state. This victory represented a breakthrough in African-American political representation on the national level, creating a foundation for future black members of the House and Senate, and ending the 28 year absence of black representatives.

Oscar Stanton DePriest was born in March 9, 1871, to former slaves in Florence, Alabama. In 1878 his family moved to Kansas to escape deplorable economic and social conditions after the end of Reconstruction. DePriest moved to Chicago in 1889 after finishing his education. He worked as a house painter and decorator, allegedly passing for white on occasion to get work. He later achieved success in his own business and real estate management firm.

DePriest's transition into politics resulted from his ability to deal and deliver the black vote in the Second and Third Wards, gaining him his first elected position in 1904, and a seat in Chicago's Cook County Board of Commissioners. He continued to climb the political ladder becoming the top black politician under Mayor William H. Thompson, who selected him as the nominee in the lakeshore congressional district that included the South Side of Chicago. Winning by a slight margin he began serving his term in 1929, fighting for civil rights of African-Americans not only in Chicago, but throughout the nation.

Black Leadership

The three prominent black leaders during this period of the Harlem Renaissance were the same men from the previous decade, W.E.B. Du Bois, Marcus Garvey, and Asa Philip Randolph. The contention between these three leaders became more intense during the twenties. The rivalry between W.E.B. Du Bois and Marcus Garvey was as much personal as it was ideological. Through their respective publications they took many opportunities to rail against each other.

> "As we study the personality of Du Bois, we find that he only appreciates one type of men, and that is the cultured, refined type which lingers around universities and attends pink tea affairs. The men of dynamic force of the Negro race, the men with ability to sway and move the masses, Dr. Du Bois cannot appraise their face value, and that is why the author of "The Souls of Black Folk," while the idol of the drawing room aristocrats, could not thus far become the popular leader of the masses of his own race."
>
> --Garvey, The Negro World, Jan. 1, 1921

"Marcus Garvey is, without a doubt, the most dangerous enemy of the Negro race in America and in the world. He is either a lunatic or a

A Reflection

traitor…..The American Negroes have endured this wretch all too long with fine restraint and every effort at cooperation and understanding. But the end has come. Every man who apologizes for or defends Marcus Garvey from this day forth writes himself down as unworthy of countenance of decent Americans. As for Garvey himself, this open ally of the Ku Klux Klan should be locked up or sent home."
--Du Bois, The Crisis, May 1924

W.E.B. Du Bois advocated the integration of blacks into white society, believing the talented tenth would lead the masses and guide them to achieve their equal rights. A. Philip Randolph also believed in the integration of black people into American society, but he thought the leadership should come from the people, the working class as the main force to struggle for their human rights. Marcus Garvey was a separatist, feeling that blacks should not seek to ingratiate themselves into white society, but be independent and self-sufficient.

Randolph opposed the back to Africa movement of Garvey, seeing the problem of black people not as a black problem, but as a social illness in the country caused by unequal distributions of wealth and power. His philosophy was a more pragmatic approach to the uplift of black people, believing that a decent and well-paying job is the first step towards justice and political freedom. The back-to-Africa movement did demonstrate the need for blacks to unite, and showed that they had the ability to organize under black leadership. Randolph also saw some redeeming qualities in Garveyism as written in the Messenger, September 21, 1921:

"It has stimulated the Pride of Negroes in Negro history and traditions, thereby helping to breakdown the slave psychology which throttles and strangles Negro initiative, self-assertiveness, ambition, courage, independence, etc. It has further stiffened the Negros's backbone to resist the encroachments and insults of white people. Again it has emphasized the international character of the Negro problem. As a propaganda organization, at one time of its history it was highly useful in awakening Negro consciousness to the demands of the times."

By 1929, Marcus Garvey's movement had collapsed, he had been convicted of mail fraud, had his sentence commuted after two years, and had been deported back to Jamaica. W.E.B. Du Bois and the NAACP were forged together in the fight against racism, pursuing one legal battle after another in their efforts toward equality. Randolph's experience as a labor organizer served him well when he formed The Brotherhood of Sleeping Car Porters one of the most successful Black unions. In 1929 they received an American Federation of Labor (AFL) federal charter for their union.

The Harlem Renaissance

Palmer Hayden, Jeunesse (1927)

The Harlem Renaissance, first referred to as the New Negro Movement wasn't triggered by any specific event or particular individual. It was the amalgamation of circumstances, the Great Migration, the Marcus Garvey movement, higher education achievement, and economic growth in black society, as well as a host of writers, musicians, and artists moving to the forefront. All of these factors brought confidence, pride, and self-awareness.

The swelling of race-consciousness during this time expanded and erupted, and a volcano of creativity opened and freed African-Americans confined by generalizations and stereotypes. Writers had opportunities to be published and the artistic freedom to choose whatever subject matter they preferred. Was this an explosion of intellectuals and artists, or was it the audience that suddenly erupted?

The writers, musicians, and artists did not initiate the New Negro or the Harlem Renaissance, the environment developed as the black people evolved from the Southern

A Reflection

farmer to urban sophisticate. The "Negro" had been transformed, not only in defiance to the present social order, but in their standards of what they wanted in literature, music, and art. The connection to African heritage was strengthened, enabling blacks to see themselves before slavery, and feel their cultural and physical beauty. Younger blacks wanted to expand their horizons, no longer seeking to imitate white customs and mores, but embracing African and African-American traditions. They wanted to see positive expressions of who they perceived themselves to be, not what white America thought they should be.

In 1927, Huber Harrison, founder of the *Voice*, the first newspaper of the "New Negro Movement," took exception to the characterization of the "renaissance." He argued that the "Negro Literary Renaissance" disregarded *"the stream of literary and artistic products which had flowed uninterruptedly from Negro writers from 1850 to the present."* The talent was always there. Writers and musicians had long yearned to express the different aspects of the black experience, but needed financial support and opportunities to perform.

Harlem, New York provided all that was needed, the population, the performers, and the venues. There were numerous publications in which to be heard, stages that welcomed black actors, and exclusive clubs that featured black musicians. Black intellectuals and artists were both attracted to Harlem, energizing and inspiring each other, making it the capital of Black America, the epicenter of publishing, drama, music, and art.

Alain LeRoy Locke, a writer and editor, a preeminent professor of philosophy at Howard University, and a patron of the arts, was credited with the promotion of African American artists, writers, and musicians. He encouraged them to focus onto African and African American subjects as inspiration, and to depict their own history as subject material. Locke's philosophy of the New Negro was based on self-confidence and self-awareness, and the potential of black equality. He was a steadfast motivator and supporter of the movement, continually injecting energy and enthusiasm, and enlightening critics to the talents imbedded in African-American culture.

Locke was viewed as the "Father of the Harlem Renaissance," and is recognized for his editing and contributions to *Opportunity: Journal of Negro Life and Survey Graphic*, specifically the issue devoted to the Harlem Renaissance. He expanded the issue later that year into an anthology of the foremost African-American literature of the era called *The New Negro; An Interpretation in 1925,* which represented the changing state of race relations in the United States.

Support of struggling artists is always crucial in fostering success. Charles S. Johnson, head of the Urban League during this time, established its journal *Opportunity: A Journal of Negro Life*, and as editor sponsored the unknown Langston Hughes and Arnaud Bontemps. Johnson, considered the "Godfather of the Harlem Renaissance," was one of the leading patrons of young writers, instrumental in the success of many promising black authors by publishing their work in the *Opportunity*.

A'lelia Walker heir to her mother, Madame C.J. Walker's hair-care and beauty empire, was also a generous patron of the arts in Harlem. She hosted and inspired many writers, artists, actors, and musicians at her lavish homes in New York. Her extravagant parties became literary events, bringing together such writers as Langston Hughes and Zora Neale Hurston. There was also the patronage of wealthy whites who wanted to promote African-American artists and their accomplishments, these included Carl Van Vechten, Charlotte Osgood Mason, and Arthur and Amy Spingarns.

The Black Church

According to the 1926 Census of religious affiliations, total membership rolls of all African-American memberships in congregations was 5 million. There were 24 denominations and 37,790 buildings, with 90 percent located in the South. Of the denominations, Baptist was still the largest with 3 million members, comprising 60 percent of total church memberships. Some of the higher education institutions sponsored by Baptist churches were Benedict College, Shaw University, Virginia Union University, Morehouse College, and Spelman College. The second largest denomination representing 30 percent of black church members was Methodist, which was divided into four groups: African Methodist Episcopal, African Methodist Episcopal Zion, Methodist Episcopal, and Colored Methodist Episcopal. Wilberforce University was sponsored by Methodist churches. The remaining 10 percent were spread across a variety of denominations.

In 1929, nearly 80 percent of urban pastors were not college educated, and more than 86 percent didn't have a divinity degree. Women outnumbered the men in membership and attendance at a ratio of ten to six. The black church was still serving as a social center and meeting place, filling the gaps in the educational and welfare needs of the congregation and community. The lives of black people, particularly in the South, revolved around activities in the church, renewing their strength in family and community.

Southern black churches in the 1920s were being stressed, not only by the depletion of members migrating to the North, but also by the agricultural depression that hit their remaining members hampering their financial support of the church. Rural congregations held tight to older customs and traditional forms of worship that carried over from slavery.

A Reflection

Many young people drifted away from the Southern church because of the lack of programs directed to the youth. Carter G. Woodson admonished the rural churches for not addressing the relevant needs of their congregations and community:

> "While the urban church is often trying to make this a better world in which to live, the rural church is engaged in immediate preparation for the 'beautiful land of by and by.' The rural church building may be used for social uplift purposes, but this is not the church thus in action."

Urban churches in the North were overwhelmed by the rapid increase in members from the South and the difficulties they experienced in their transition. In efforts to accommodate the growing congregations many church leaders expanded their buildings, those that were financially able and those who could secure loans, built brand new churches, some bought older church building from whites. Smaller sects opted for storefronts on inner city streets.

In 1929, it was estimated that 5000 blacks attended Catholic churches in Harlem; most were immigrants from Caribbean islands. These churches operated schools unlike protestant churches, with members enrolling their children as students. White control over the Catholic churches was maintained even after many congregations were majority black. There were other significant religious movements in the 1920s, Marcus Garvey founded the African Orthodox Church in 1921, and the Father Divine Peace Mission grew in popularity.

Urban churches were becoming more powerful as memberships grew, and the larger congregations had more resources. Churches developed social programs to fulfill the needs of their congregation, assisted members in finding housing and employment, and supplied adult education and daycare. They sponsored trips and concerts, and larger churches organized athletic clubs and sports teams that competed with one another.

The Black Press

In 1929, the *Pittsburgh Courier*, created by Robert L. Vann, was sold from coast to coast, having the largest circulation among African-American newspapers during this period. The second and third largest and most influential black newspapers were the *Chicago Defender*, and the *Baltimore Afro-American*. Each of these papers published national editions and local editions for their respective cities. The *Courier* also published a New York City edition, catering to the large population of blacks in Harlem, and acknowledging it as the cultural center for black America. The *New York Amsterdam News* and the *Philadelphia Tribune* were also among the top national black newspapers.

1929

The black press had always stood at the helm in the war against Jim Crow and with the changing attitudes of the "New Negro" they also became more aggressive in the battles against racial injustice. They used the newspaper as a forum to insist on improvements for black people in housing and educational opportunities. During the 1920's, the black press began to strongly assert its leadership position, using its power in national campaigns that united African-Americans in mass.

The *Chicago Whip* organized the "Don't Buy Where You Can't Work" campaign which went national after being joined by *The Courier*, *Los Angeles Sentinel*, and the *New York Amsterdam News*. These papers worked in concert to pressure white-owned businesses, specifically those located in the black community, to hire blacks. The *Chicago Defender* continuously campaigned for anti-lynching legislation, and also for the integration of sports. The *Norfolk* was busy with its campaign against the racially restrictive covenants that were being used to enforce segregation in residential housing tracts and farms in rural Virginia. The *Courier* also campaigned for the increase of black doctors and the opening of a black hospital to provide for the health needs of the African-American community in Pittsburgh. Vann as editor of the *Courier* used the newspaper as a forum to insist on improvements for black people in housing and educational opportunities.

Most black newspapers and periodicals were run by major leadership figures who wanted to change the perception of the "Negro" to erase old stereotypes and have black people seen through a different lens. They wanted to elevate the image through the exhibition of talent and intellect of the young progressive writers of the day. This platform was a mutually beneficial enterprise; publishers used the writing of these literary artists to accentuate the ideologies of their publications, while the exposure connected new authors with an audience for their works. Some these authors were equally gifted as journalists, switching between the two genres to relay not only facts but history and culture for the uplift of black people.

Black Literature and Art

The mass of literature that was produced during this period, now called the Harlem Renaissance, was especially significant in that it unleashed a flood of creativity that led to the broad dissemination of African-American culture throughout the world. Prominent authors of this decade were James Weldon Johnson, Alain Locke, Jean Toomer, Countee Cullen, Zora Neal Hurston, Claude McKay, Jessie Fauset, and Langston Hughes. Subject matter was not confined to black culture and experiences, but to the human experience of

A Reflection

love, religions, and nature, although racism was a common thread that appeared in most of the literature.

Claude McKay, a poet and novelist who migrated from the West Indies, was inspired by the current issues of the day. In his works he was defiant, as in "If We Must Die," but he was also romantic and passionate in other poems like the "Harlem Dancer." James Weldon Johnson wrote of familiar aspects of black life to illuminate the beauty of the ordinary as shown in "God's Trombones: Seven Negro Sermons in Verse."

Countee Cullen and Langston Hughes were among the most popular during the 1920s. Cullen didn't want to be restricted to black racial themes even though we naturally write about that which we are most knowledgeable about. Both he and Hughes focused on the "Negro" and their African heritage. Langston Hughes was unapologetic for his depictions of poverty and social injustice.

Several writers of the time dealt with the issue of skin color and "passing within the race." Depictions in the literary works of Wallace Thurman's "The Blacker the Berry" and Nella Larsen's "Passing" addressed the multifaceted topic in 1929. The setting for Larsen's novel was New York during the Harlem Renaissance and focused around "Negro" society. Individuals who were accomplished and educated socialized among themselves and other prominent whites. Some who were physically able passed for white sometimes as a matter of convenience. The novel "Passing" suggests that the price that one has to pay to be accepted into white society, such as denying one's racial and cultural identity is much too high.

Jessie Fauset's second novel, Plum Bun, also published in this year, explored the 'catch 22' predicament of 'passing,' and sold 100,000 copies within 90 days of its publication, elevating it to the status of a best-seller. Passing was not only a denial of your own identity; it's also an admission that you are not good enough. Trying to exist in another life that denies your own sense of self and your past every day, in addition to the fear of being discovered, destroys the individual over time.

There was no shortage of controversial topics on which to write during this time. Subjects relating to lynching, the war, gambling, violence, poverty, sexuality, and the abuse of black women were often featured in the popular literature. Intellectuals like W.E.B. Du Bois objected to writings by some authors that dealt with the harsh realities of black life, those he felt aired dirty laundry and saw them as counterproductive in the "uplift" of black people. Claude McKay's "Home to Harlem" represented the shocking details of Harlem's nightlife and blatant sexuality. Above and beyond from being a Harman Gold Award winner for literature, it was also a best seller. Du Bois was intensely critical of the novel, accusing white publishers of using these types of books to feed the appetite of white readers hungry for depictions of untamed black street life.

W.E.B. Du Bois and Alain Locke also pushed young black artists to embody their African heritage and African-American culture in their paintings and sculptures. Aaron Douglas became a leading visual artist during the Harlem Renaissance, being called the "Dean of African-American painters." Alain Locke called him a "pioneering Africanist," using his illustrations in his famous anthology, *The New Negro*, published in 1925. Douglas' work was often published in the *Crisis* and *Opportunity* periodicals. Douglas' most famous illustrations were for *God's Trombones,* James Weldon Johnson's book of poetic sermons.

Talented painters producing works during the twenties were Palmer Hayden, Archibald Motley, Malvin Garvey Johnson, William Henry Johnson, Laura Wheeler Waring, and sculptor Augusta Savage.

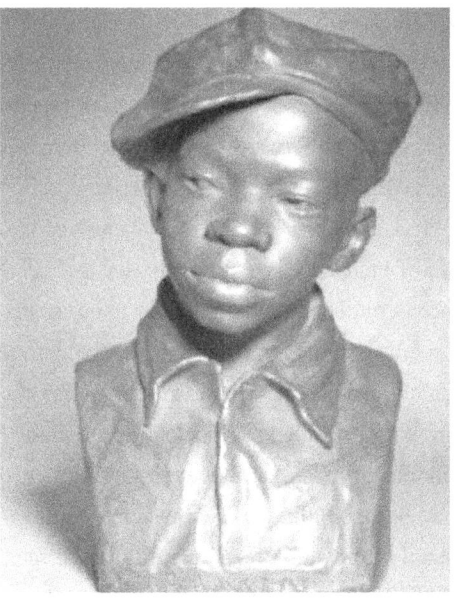

Augusta Savage, Gamin (1929), Smithsonian American Art Museum

A Reflection

Education

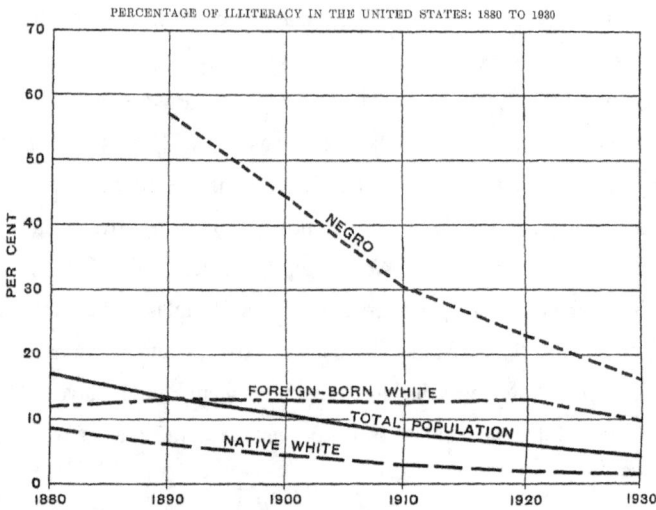

Looking back at 1929, African-Americans had made great progress in learning to read and write during the last fifty years, with illiteracy rates falling towards 15 percent. As seen in the past decade, most of the illiteracy was concentrated in southern states among the older portion of the population. In terms of moving forward beyond basic literacy black people still had far to go. According to the 1930 Census data, school attendance was increasing, with more than 94 percent of urban black children 7 to 13 years old enrolled in school. Numbers among rural-farm and rural-nonfarm attendance had also increased to 83 percent and 87 percent respectively, but attendance in rural communities tended to be erratic.

Census data also recorded a decline of school attendance with the increase of age, and the numbers were much lower in the South Atlantic region than in the Northeast. Compulsory education was not enforced for black children in the South. For persons 14 to 15 years of age, attendance dropped to 72 percent and further to 40 percent for persons 16-17 years of age in the South. Although the meager economic conditions of most black families were probably motivation for older children to seek employment, the major factor in the decline of blacks attending school after the eighth grade was attributed to the absence of black public high schools.

Most of the black schools tended to be rundown, overcrowded and underfunded, and attendance was increasing. Urban cities in the South, like Atlanta, had begun to build public schools for blacks. By 1929, the number of public funded black high schools in southern states had grown to over 900.

1929

While miniscule gains were being made in the South in the building of schools and improving education for black students, those in the North were taking huge loses. The repercussions of the Great Migration were being felt in every aspect of life for black people, particularly in education. Before World War I, northern cities like New York, Philadelphia, and Chicago had "colored" schools and mixed schools, but racial tensions and prejudices fueled by the drastic growth in black populations along with residential exclusions ignited the movement towards school segregation. By 1929, school segregation had spread into a nationwide reality.

The lack of blacks sitting on school boards and city councils left blacks powerless in the fight against the misappropriation of resources, manipulation of residential zones, and transfer policies that further entrenched segregation. The separate education or "dual education" system served to advance and develop white students, while oppressing black students; planting seeds of inferiority. School officials attempted to justify their malfeasance through the rationalization that blacks were mentally deficient, that blacks had limited learning capacity, advising that their education be adapted to their capacity for manual labor. As a result black high schools didn't have the electives and extra-curricular activities, or vocation classes offered in white schools.

Black high school students were taught an industrial arts curriculum to prepare them for low-skilled and low-paying jobs while depriving them of a quality education, ensuring they would have no chance of elevating their social and economic status. Black people were divided in their feelings about segregated schools in the North. Some protested with lawsuits and petitions, while others, including some black church ministers favored separate schools. Weighing the advantages and disadvantages, separate schools would assure that inadequate and unfair funding would continue, but it also meant employment for black teachers. Students in black schools didn't have to suffer in hostile environments or be subjected to insults and demeaning treatment, and black history and culture could be taught freely.

Higher education for blacks had similar challenges. In 1929, there were approximately 14 thousand black colleges students, 75 percent attended private institutions with a religious affiliation. Du Bois noted that 23 white colleges and universities that admitted black students provided no access to other campus facilities or transportation, and refused to let them live in dormitories. After the death of Booker T. Washington, African-Americans wanted to increase the benefits of higher education, black students protested the substandard education received at black colleges from racist white faculty members. Student uprisings

A Reflection

in the 1920's brought changes to the curriculum offered at black institutions; industrial training programs that emphasized manual labor training, including carpentry, agriculture, and brick masonry were omitted in this decade. Hence, black students were better educated and had higher aspirations.

Extraordinary African American

"If I can create the minimum of my plans and desires there shall be no regrets."
— *Bessie Coleman*

Bessie Coleman was the most famous African-American civil aviator in our history. Known as "Brave Bessie" or "Queen Bess," she was the first African American woman to earn a pilot's license, despite the racial and gender obstacles that stood between her and the realization of her dreams. Elizabeth "Bessie" Coleman was born on January 26, 1892, the tenth of thirteen children to George and Susan Coleman, sharecroppers in Atlanta Texas. Coleman, an outstanding student who excelled in math, completed the eighth grade in a one-room school house, and after turning eighteen took her savings and enrolled in the Oklahoma Colored Agricultural and Normal University in Langston, Oklahoma. Her money only lasted one semester leaving her no choice but to return home. In 1915, reaching the age of 23, she knew there was no future for her in Texas, so she traveled to Chicago to live with two of her brothers.

Working as a manicurist in a barbershop she heard the stories of pilots who had returned from World War I and began to think about being a pilot. The nonstop teasing from her brother about the superiority of French women, and how they already flew planes, pushed her to begin applying to flight schools around the country. Coleman was denied admission to every U.S. aviation school, not only for being black, but also for being a woman. She met with Robert S. Abbott, the founder and editor of the *Chicago Defender*, who advised her to move to France and study aviation and obtain her license there. Bessie began saving her money and studying to speak French. Upon receiving financial support from Jesse Binga and the *Defender* newspaper, Abbott put her in contact with the Caudron Brothers' School of Aviation in Le Ctotoy, France, and on November 20, 1920 she left for Paris. Seven months later, on June 15, 1921, she received her pilot's license from Federation Aeronautique Internationale, the first black woman to receive the international aviator certificate.

Bessie Coleman returned to the states in September 1921, beautiful, self-confident, with a flamboyant sense of style, establishing herself as a media sensation. She toured the country giving demonstrations, was interviewed by countless newspapers, and invited to numerous speaking engagements where she encouraged black men and women to learn to fly. It quickly became apparent to Coleman that to earn a living as a pilot she would have to become a stunt flier performing for paying audiences. In February 1922, she returned to Europe for additional training to further increase her skills in barnstorming. Bessie returned to Chicago, and before a huge and excited crowd, delivered a spectacular exhibition of daredevil maneuvers of figure eights, loops, and other daring stunts. Coleman's first appearance in an airshow was on September 3, 1922, at Glenn Curtiss Field in Garden City, New York, honoring the all-black 369th American Expeditionary Force veterans of World War I. The event was sponsored by Abbott who billed her as "the world's greatest woman flier."

In February 1923, Coleman experienced her first serious accident in Los Angeles when her plane stalled and crashed, she suffered a broken leg, along with cut and bruises, needing more than a year to recover. She returned fulltime in 1923, thrilling the crowds with her spectacular stunts. Bessie hated to perform for segregated audiences, insisting that black people be allowed to use the same entrance as whites. On April 30, 1926, at the age of thirty-four, Bessie Coleman tragically lost her life before realizing her dream of establishing an aviation school for African-Americans.

Preparing for an exhibition in Jacksonville, Florida, her mechanic and publicity agent, William Wills, was flying the plane with Coleman in the passenger seat. Coleman did not have her seatbelt on because she was planning a parachute jump for the next day and was scouting for landing spots. While Bessie was looking over the cockpit, the plane accelerated into a nosedive and went into a tailspin. Coleman was thrown from the plane at 1500 feet and was killed instantly when she hit the ground. William Wills unable to gain control of the aircraft died when the plane crashed and burst into flames.

Bessie Coleman was a pioneer who destroyed the stereotypes about the capability of blacks and women. She served as an inspiration for men and women who were disregarded because of their race or gender. On Memorial Day, Tuskegee fighter pilots fly over Bessie's grave and drop flowers to honor her. Lieutenant William J. Powell wrote in Black Wings, dedicated to Coleman, *"Because of Bessie Coleman, we have overcome that which was worse than racial barriers. We have overcome the barriers within ourselves and dared to dream."*

A Reflection

Black Businesses and Professionals

The number of black professionals had surged 69 percent over the last decade, doubling the increase for the 1909-1919 time period. Black chemists, engineers, and dentists were produced at a higher rate during this decade than their white counterparts. There were increases in the number of college professors, lawyers, librarians, social worker, artists, and clergy. In 1929, there were 70,000 black businesses. According to the Census, blacks operated 30,000 retail stores, employed 43,000 workers, and grossed more than 71 million in sales. There were successful restaurants, grocery stores, fuel stations, car sales, and barber shops.

During this time blacks could only get a mortgage or business loan from black owned institutions. The largest black owned business was The North Carolina Mutual Life Insurance Company. The company had 1500 employees and operated in 11 states and Washington, D.C.

One of the most successful and affluent black communities in America was Greenwood, home to 10,000 African-Americans, and located in Tulsa Oklahoma. This area was the beneficiary of an oil boom in the 1910s, and was known as the "Negro Wall Street." Greenwood was home to a number of prominent black businessmen; quite a few of them multimillionaires. There was a thriving commercial district that housed the offices of black lawyers, doctors, realtors, the buildings of groceries, barbershops, and clothing stores. Because black shop-owners provided all the needed services to cater to the black community, all monies and investment stayed within the community and it blossomed. In that 35-block span, there were 1500 black-owned businesses and houses.

Whites in Tulsa were threatened by the success of this black community, and on May 31, 1921, Greenwood was torched and destroyed by the most violent and destructive race riot in American history. Mobs of malicious white people armed with guns, spurred by the alleged assault of a white woman, killed, burned, and pillaged the businesses and homes of the black men, women, and children of Greenwood. Several witnesses described airplanes dropping firebombs on buildings and homes.

The Greenwood district was devastated; property damage was more than $1.5 million. Over 600 businesses were destroyed, including 21 churches, a hospital, a bank, libraries, schools, 21 restaurants, 30 grocery stores, and more than 1000 homes. Official death tolls stated 26 blacks and 13 whites died. The Red Cross estimated 300 died, and other sources gave much higher figures of 3000 African-Americans killed. Fourteen hundred black Tulsa residents sued to reclaim $4 million in property damages. The strength and resilience of the Greenwood community rebuilt the district within five years of the riot. The area was also known for its phenomenal jazz and blues musicians in the "twenties."

Employment

Despite the large numbers of African-Americans who migrated to the North and West, more than 80 percent still lived in the South, and of these, nearly half remained in rural communities raising crops to earn a living. Blacks still ran 14 percent of all farms, with most raising cotton, 25 percent raising sweet potatoes, and 16 percent corn. The decline of agriculture gained steam in the 1920s', and black farm owners were experiencing significant losses of owned land. In this last decade, an area of 4292 square miles, 2,749,619 acres had changed hands, with large amounts of land being abandoned. The amount of land lost was twice the size of the state of Delaware. From 1920 to 1930 the number of black farm owners dropped by 37,596, a 17.2 percent decrease, and the number of those sharecropping dropped by 42,850. Unfortunately, 79 percent of those still working the land were tenants cheated out of the fair prices for their crops and barely earned enough to survive.

From 1909 to 1929, manufacturing and mechanical industries saw the number of black workers increase by 368,750. According to the 1930 census, 30.8 percent of black laborers were in manufacturing and mechanical industries, 34.3 percent worked as domestics, personal service, or janitors. Transportation or railroad track labor and mining also employed large numbers of black workers. Although black employees were at the bottom of the working class, they were still better-off than they had been in the South. Eighty percent of employed black women over 10 years of age were servants, hairdressers, laundry workers, waitresses, or boarding house operators. The cities also offered agencies that protected black women from the sexual abuse, false accusations of theft, and the economic exploitation they suffered in the South.

A black working class developed in northern cities like Pennsylvania, Illinois, Indiana, and Ohio. The auto plants in Detroit and the meat packing plants in Chicago hired large numbers of blacks. Tobacco was the main industry in North and South Carolina. For most of the 1920s, migrants from the South beat a path straight to Detroit in hopes of getting a high-paying job in the auto industry. Henry Ford didn't hesitate in hiring blacks, feeling he would have their loyalty when the unions came to organize. The Ford auto plant became the largest industrial employer of African-Americans. Halfway into the decade, more than 10,000 blacks worked at the River Rouge Ford Plant. Blacks

A Reflection

also found work at the Packard and Dodge plants, and other factories that supplied raw materials to the car industry.

The Pullman Company was also one of the largest employers of African-Americans in the 1920s. Despite the higher wages earned by porters, they had to endure demeaning working conditions and unfair labor practices. Efforts to organize a union were unsuccessful in the first decades of the century, but in August of 1925, 500 porters met in Harlem and launched another effort to organize. The labor union called "The Brotherhood of Sleeping Car Porters" was then organized under the leadership of A. Philip Randolph and Milton P. Webster, their motto was "Fight or Be Slaves."

Social Clubs, Lodges and Fraternal Orders

Memberships in fraternal organizations multiplied and peaked in the 1920s. Rural black communities historically depended upon the benevolence and sacrifices of their relatives and neighbors to help families through hard times and meet economic needs. Social organizations were an important source of support in the black community. These secular organizations emphasized educational programs, helped find jobs and housing, offered insurance benefits, performed community service, and arranged social events and parties. Some supplied a regular menu of entertainment options. Fraternal orders attracted professionals as well as working-class men; many would have memberships in more than one organization. Weekly meetings provided a network of friends and connections.

Newly established in 1929, The National Ideal Benefit Society, and older Organizations such as Prince Hall Masons, the Odd Fellows, the Knights of Pythias, and the Elks offered black men the opportunity to build and apply leadership skills. Organizations such as the Order of the Eastern Star and various women's clubs and auxiliaries gave black women the opportunity to donate to their communities through philanthropy, promote the socialization of young girls, and to socialize with other women. In the South, these organizations additionally functioned as cooperatives that offered their members life and health insurance policies, aided widows and orphans of deceased members, and provided members financial services and opportunities to network and make business contacts.

The Young Men's and Young Women's Christian Associations, the YMCA and YWCA, were also important organizations in the black community. Although a Christian institution, the Y had been racially separated since the mid-nineteenth century. YMCAs organized athletic leagues, education classes, hosted lectures, and sponsored social affairs in the black community. By 1929, there were 34 thousand African-American members belonging to separate Y branches throughout the country.

Crime

This decade should have been called the turbulent twenties, every conceivable solution created a problem. Blacks migrated out of the South to escape oppression and abuse and discovered new troublesome predicaments. Whites and native blacks blamed them for the increase in crime rates. In as much as blacks were accused of perpetrating a disproportionate number of crimes, they were also more often the victims of illegal actions. The number of lynchings had been decreasing until 1926 when the trend was reversed. The Ku Klux Klan and other white racist groups were largely responsible for much of the lawlessness, but their crimes were rarely reported or investigated.

Blacks and specifically black males were labeled as genetically defective, prone to criminal behavior, unable to control their impulses, and lacking discernment. White individuals who participated in lynching, who bullied and intimidated, who raped and assaulted with reckless abandon, who pillaged and destroyed property, and raided black neighborhoods bent on destruction, were not labeled or judged. White criminal behavior has not been researched, their irrational behavior has not been dissected by social scholars, and they haven't been branded as social criminals or held responsible for their action by the criminal justice system.

Racial bias was prevalent in criminal justice, demonstrated in the arrest rates, incarceration, and sentencing of black people. Police brutality and discrimination were serious issues for blacks in every state of the country, but markedly so in urban areas. During 1925, in Detroit, 55 blacks were gunned-down by the police. In the following years, 1926 and 1927, more black men had been killed by police without a reasonable excuse than the total number of those lynched in the whole southern region of the nation for the same time period. Police officials tried to justify their actions by stating African-Americans were committing more felonies, noting that while blacks were only 7 percent of the population, they were guilty of 31 percent of the felonies.

Black people were always accused of being more inclined to criminal behavior than whites, but the comparison was not made from a level playing field. Blacks were more likely to be imprisoned for the slightest offense, where whites were protected by the law. During the 1920s, crime among blacks was decreasing year by year, especially in Georgia and South Carolina, but the crime rate among whites had doubled. An article

A Reflection

published in the *Pittsburgh Courier* reported from South Carolina, "Whites had gained the lead in the number of individuals committed to prison." Dr. W. Alexander, director of the Commission of Interracial Cooperation announced, *"In Georgia the Department of Welfare reports that there are fewer Negroes in the jails of the state in 1928 than in 1921, and 17 percent less than in 1924, Negroes provided 66 percent of Georgia's jail population in 1921 and 1928 only 55 percent."*

Homicide and robbery were the crimes most often committed by black people. During 1929, in New York, where blacks were 12 percent of the population, they were one-third of the victims. Homicide rates are higher for blacks in the South than in the North, with Birmingham leading Memphis as the top two murder leaders. The average age of criminals committing murder was 23 years.

A great portion of the increase in criminal activity for the 1920s can be attributed to prohibition. Alcohol thought to be the root of unlawful conduct, needed to be tempered, but making it illegal only led to more violence and higher crimes rates. Illegal bars, called speakeasies, sprung up throughout the country stimulating the growth of organized crime. This was the beginning of gambling networks under black controlled organized crime.

Black participation in organized crime was typically reserved to Bolito, the numbers game, illegal drugs, robbery, prostitution, and gambling. According to Francis A. J. Ianni, writer of *Black Mafia: Ethnic Succession in Organized Crime*, by 1925 there were thirty black policy banks in Harlem, several of them large enough to collect bets in an area of twenty city blocks and across four avenues. Quite a few blacks worked in the "policy racket" to compensate for rejections in other employment. At least 800 bet collectors spent their time running between betting customers and the policy bank each day. Bets were made in most Harlem businesses, beauty and barber shops, bars, pool halls, cleaners, most stores, and even at your home. The cash reward was high if you hit the number, odds were 600 to 1, and for blacks receiving the lowest wages or on relief it was a tempting proposition.

Health

The health of African-Americans in 1929 was very much neglected, more so than in slavery years. The black mortality rate was five times higher than that of whites. During the 1920s, blacks were still suffering more from tuberculosis, pneumonia and influenza than whites. Among these infectious diseases, tuberculosis was the most deadly. By the end of the decade, 1000 out of every 100,000 blacks in Chicago died from TB compared to 60 out of 100,000 for the white population. Black populations throughout New York were particularly susceptible to death from these diseases. In Harlem from 1923 to 1927, tuberculosis claimed the lives of 1839 black residents. Tuberculosis deaths for whites had decreased during this decade, but for blacks the epidemic was on the rise. The white rate of tuberculosis mortality was cut in half (to 55 per 100,000) during the 1920-1930 period, while the black rate of 263 (per 100,000) was less than a third drop for the same decade.

Blacks suffered from malnutrition and other diseases in higher rates than whites, with inadequate or no treatment being the rule. The infant mortality rate among black babies was double that of white babies, the unsanitary houses in unimproved districts were much to blame. Before, after, or while seeking treatment from medical practitioners, many migrants habitually took home remedies and patent medicines and received care from midwives and other lay healers. Public health officials in northern states believed that blacks were socially predisposed to bad health because of their southern background and destructive lifestyles. This theory became popular among northern medical and social authorities, supporting the stereotypical view of southern health authorities. During the 1920s, these northern medical opinions created race fears in the interpretations of the racial disparities in the mortality of infectious diseases.

In 1927, Charles S. Johnson did an in-depth research for the Urban League to examine the social needs of the black population in Buffalo. Johnson concluded that social and political circumstances were the cause of the black health problems in Buffalo. African-American physicians and social workers from within New York State's black communities traced the high black mortality to socioeconomic factors and inadequate medical services.

The number of beds available for patients in black hospitals was inadequate, with the number being virtually nil in some southern states. In 1928, a review of the hospital resources available to blacks in American cities was conducted by the Julius Rosenwald Foundation. Although they found several hundred hospitals throughout New York, only two hospitals were serving the health care needs of the densely populated black communities in the inner city, Harlem Hospital and Lincoln Hospital.

In the 1920s, larger numbers of black patients were looking for black doctors. At this time there are 3805 black physicians in the United States, 3719 male and 92 female. Black physicians and social workers then embarked on a quest to increase the medical facilities and personnel to improve the health of the black community. In this decade there were only two Black medical schools in the country, Meharry Medical College in

A Reflection

Nashville, Tennessee, and Howard in Washington, D.C., and only a small percentage of black students were being admitted to predominately white institutions.
The black doctor was well trained, but was unable to attend special society meetings, and for the most part was denied privileges at prominent hospitals. By the end of the 1920s, approximately 200 black hospitals and nurse training schools were established to provide health care services for African Americans in the South and the industrialized cities of the North.

Housing

Comfortable and affordable housing during the 1920s was still a significant problem for African-Americans in the United States affecting both their health and well-being. For the large numbers of blacks living in the South and sharecropping, housing was no more than shanties and shacks, shotgun houses, mostly two-room places without electricity, running water, and telephones. Payment for rent, seed, fertilizer, and the basic needs of the household were to be paid from the harvest, but in most cases the crops were insufficient to settle the debt, leaving tenants tied to the plantation.

The Great Flood of 1927 was the commencement of the disintegration of the Southern plantation system. Twenty-seven thousand square miles across seven states, including Arkansas, Kentucky, Louisiana, Mississippi, Tennessee, and Oklahoma, were devastated, destroying farms and their crops. Flood waters lingered for nearly six months in some areas. More than 130,000 homes were lost, and over 300,000 African-Americans were displaced, with tens of thousands migrating to Chicago.

By 1929, nearly 500,000 urban black families owned their homes. According to Census data, the median value for nonfarm homes owned by blacks was $1,341 compared to $4766 for native whites. Most homes in the metropolitan areas had modern conveniences; electricity, indoor plumbing, and sewer systems. Thousands of radio stations crossed the airwaves into family living rooms, but only 14 percent of urban black families and 0.3 percent of rural-farm black families had a radio set. Housing shortages for urban African-Americans continued on into the 1920s as black were continually pushed into overcrowded segregated neighborhoods. When financially secure middle-class blacks moved into white neighborhoods, their white neighbors would respond violently toward them, inciting riots in front of their homes, bombing the houses, and even murder. The Ku Klux Klan was known to burn fiery crosses in front of homes owned by blacks in the North and South.

1929

Racially restrictive covenants were contractual agreements among property owners that forbid the purchase, lease, or occupation of their property by a particular group of people. Racially restrictive covenants were rare before the 1920s and the Great Migration but were being used throughout the nation to maintain housing segregation and to isolate blacks in overcrowded slums. The covenants were used extensively in Chicago, resulting in two-thirds of Chicago's black residents living in neighborhoods that were more than 90 percent black. Blacks were more spread out in Detroit where the bulk of neighborhoods were between 10 and 20 percent black with only a few being over 50 percent black. Similar distributions in communities were found in Philadelphia, Baltimore, Washington, D.C., Birmingham, and New Orleans.

The black population of New York was concentrated in Harlem with high rents that forced them to be creative in keeping a roof over their heads. The median monthly rental for nonfarm homes rented across the country by blacks was $13.00, but one-room apartments in Central Harlem rented for $40 to whites and $100-$125 for blacks. Black households raised their monthly rent by taking in lodgers or hosting rent parties. Rent party hosts hired live jazz bands, supplied food and liquor, and collected money from their guests to pay the rent. In Harlem, nearly half of all households had lodgers, many were extended family members, some of no relation, and beds were sometimes occupied in shifts. Lodgers at times were disruptive to the household, having bad habits, erratic employment, and moving often.

The Urban League worked diligently during this time to eliminate overcrowding and the "lodger evil" in housing for blacks in urban cities. James H. Hubert, president of the Urban League at the time, initiated an aggressive campaign to encourage investors to construct affordable housing in Harlem. John D. Rockefeller, Jr. answered his call and built a large housing cooperative called the Dunbar Apartments. Opened in 1927, tenants paid $50 per room and then $14.50 per room each month which went towards a mortgage. Fulfilling the agreement, tenants would own the apartment within 22 years. The original tenants were mostly middle class, and childcare was provided on-site to support working mothers.

Family Structure

According to the 1930 Census, the overall marital conditions for blacks slightly declined in comparison to 1920. The percentage of black males recorded as married was similar to that of male whites. For black males 15 years and older, 60 percent were

A Reflection

married, equal to the number for white males. Blacks were still marrying at an earlier age than other races, and black males and females living on rural farms were marrying at higher percentages that those living in urban areas and rural nonfarm areas, at 86 percent and 75 percent respectively. In 1929, 75 percent of black families were still located in southern regions of the country. For all of the research that suggests the breakdown of African-American families, the 1930 Census classified 24 percent of black families as broken, but 90 percent of black rural-farm families were headed by a man, and 75 percent of urban black families were headed by a man. While the numbers were lower than white urban families headed by a man, the perception is much worse than the actual data, with less than 20 percent of African-American babies illegitimate or born to a single mother.

Southern families were usually larger than those in the North, and families in the North were becoming smaller as more black women gained access to information about birth control. The median family size for black families was 3.15, compared to native whites (3.40), foreign-born whites (3.74), and all other races (4.13), indicating that during the end of the 1920s blacks had smaller families. Fewer children under the age of 15 were gainfully employed, except in the Southern region of the country where twice the number of children 10 – 15 worked and contributed their wages to the household. The greatest percentages of children working were seen in South Carolina, Alabama, and Mississippi.

The responsibility for the financial stability of black families was increasingly falling on the shoulders of black women. Women comprised the greater part of black migrants, and most were raising a family and working outside of the home. For black females between 25 and 44, more than 55 percent were gainfully employed compared to 36 percent for native white females. Black males faced greater discrimination and hard times in seeking employment. Eighty-five percent of black females were employed in comparison to 63 percent of black males. Constant upheaval initiated by job instability and changing living arrangements brought up tensions within families and discord between husband and wife. Husbands became despondent when they were unable to find work; wives resented the responsibility of providing for the family, creating conflicts and recurrent arguments.

Some researchers have the opinion that black women challenge the patriarchal authority of their husbands and that is the common cause of violence and domestic homicide in black families. The institution of slavery, Frazier argued, supplanted the masculine authority of Black males with the authority of the master. This displacement, coupled with the privileging of the mother-child bond, from Frazier's perspective, is at the foundation of the evolution of

Black matriarchal families. Many agree that the socioeconomic position is a strong behavioral determinant, not only for black people, but for all people.

Entertainment and Artists

"But jazz to me is one of the inherent expressions of Negro life in America;
the eternal tom-tom beating in the Negro soul--the tom-tom of revolt against
against weariness in a white world, a world of subway trains, and work, work,
work; the tom-tom of joy and laughter, and pain swallowed in a smile."
--Langston Hughes, "The Negro Artist and the Racial Mountain"
(1926)

The decade of the 1920s was set to music, each characteristic had a melody all its own. The rhythm was mesmerizing and the people were compelled to dance. A mood of excitement and euphoria had spread across the country liked wild fire. Some were celebrating their good fortune, while others were trying to forget their troubles, the rest were caught somewhere in between. Prohibition was the catalyst that got the party started; nothing is more tantalizing than that which is forbidden. It was the jazz age, but liquor relentlessly vied for center stage. Entertainers who excelled high above the rest made the music that let our spirits soar, sang the songs that broke our hearts, and danced the movements that took our breath away.

The sounds of jazz migrated out of the South in the 1920s, traveling out of New Orleans with musicians like Jelly Roll Morton, Joe "King" Oliver, and Louis Armstrong making their way to Chicago. Musicians gravitated to the "Stroll" where large numbers of jazz talents flourished and speakeasies with a steady flow of drinks needed musical entertainment. Popular nightspots included the Deluxe Café and the Dreamland Cafe, where Lillian Hardin-Armstrong, the wife of Louis Armstrong led her own band.

Kansas City was also known for its version of jazz, with a host of cabarets, nightclubs, and dance halls, it became a sanctuary for jazz musicians in the Midwest. The jazz era created greater opportunities for musicians to work and the recording industry provided a chance for mass exposure through records. In 1927, 100 million phonograph records were sold. For the first half of the decade Chicago was the focal point for jazz, but for the latter half the center had shifted to New York.

The 1920s brought much needed leisure time to the masses, and black folks flocked to the movies with the rest of America. Blacks and whites were being seen together on

A Reflection

stage and movies screens for the first time. There were quite a few black-owned film companies producing movies for black audiences and by 1929, all-black movies with sound were playing. The big hits for blacks in 1929 were *St. Louis Blues* starring Bessie Smith and featuring W.C. Handy's hit song of the same name, *Jail House Blues* starring Mamie Smith, *Heart in Dixie* starring Lincoln "Stepin Fetchit" Perry, and *Hallelujah*, a film musical starring Daniel L. Haynes and Nina Mae McKinney. A host of black actors and actresses were featured in the movies during the 1920s, including Bill "Bojangles" Robinson, Ethel Waters, and John Lester Johnson. A few movie actors were able to cross between stage and screen; most memorable was Paul Robeson acting in Micheaux's 1925, *Body and Soul*, performing in Eugene O'Neill's "*All God's Chillun got Wings,*" and "*The Emperor Jones*."

During the 1920s, 20 plays with black themes were presented on Broadway, five were written by black writers with all-black casts. The first and most successful all-black musical was Shuffle Along in 1921, written by Noble Sissie and Eubie Blake, sparking a revival of black musicals presenting musical styles of ragtime, jazz, and blues. It had a run of 504 performances and gave breaks to future greats Josephine Baker and Paul Robeson. *Keep Shufflin*, a musical revue written by James P. Johnson and Andy Razaf, attempted to repeat the success of *Shuffle Along* but was not as successful. Johnson went on to compose another all-black musical, *Runnin Wild*, which gave audiences their first glimpse of the 'Charleston' starting a hot dance craze that spread across the nation. Other black musicals introduced popular dances; "Dinah" in 1924 introduced the Black Bottom to the public and quickly became all the rage. Triumphant Broadway musicals hits of 1929, *Hot Chocolate* and *Ain't Misbehaving* with music and lyrics written by Fat Waller and Andy Razaf featured the new musical idol, Louis Armstrong.

Musical revues and vaudeville acts were very lucrative during the "Jazz Age," and the longest running act was the family run Whitman Sisters. Mabel, Alberta, Essie, and Alice Whitman were a family of black women performers who were the highest paid act in "Negro Vaudeville," having the best black revue. Youngest sister Alice was a star-soloist in rhythm dance, known as the "Queen of Tap." Top performers in the Whitman Sisters revue were Leonard Reed and Willie Bryant who invented the Shim Sham Shimmy, and Bill "Bojangles" Robinson. Robinson performed his famous stair dance in *Blackbirds of 1928*, an incredibly successful music revue on Broadway, where he starred with Adelaide Hall.

The best jazz and tap dancers of the Renaissance era hung out at the Hoofer's Club in Harlem showcasing and trading dance moves 24 hour a day. The Nicholas Brothers,

Fayard and Harold, often seen there, were considered to be the greatest tap dancers of the time. Their act was full of energy and fast feet and acrobatic moves, described as having "high levels of artistry and daring innovations." The dance matched the music, with lively up-tempo "hot jazz."

The atmosphere of prosperity encouraged the masses to "let the good times roll." Folks dressed up in their "Sunday best" after payday and went out on the town for a temporary taste of the good life. Ballrooms, night clubs, and speakeasies sprung up in urban cities like New York, Chicago, Detroit, Kansas City, Philadelphia, and Memphis to satisfy the people's appetites for pleasure and other indulgences. Liquor and nightlife were courtesy of organized crime syndicates who featured the best musicians of the day. Three prominent venues for jazz and dancing were: The Apollo Theatre, the Savoy Ballroom, and the Cotton Club.

The Savoy Ballroom was a jazz club that catered to a mostly black clientele who desired to dance the night away. It opened for business on March 12, 1926, and was located in the center of Harlem. The Savoy featured bands that played Big Band and Swing music that moved the crowds all around the dance floor and became the most popular dance spot in Harlem. Dance fads that originated at the Savoy were: The Flying Charleston, The Lindy Hop, Jitterbug Jive, The Big Apple, The Stomp, Snakehips, Rhumboogie, the Shimmy, and the Mambo. A year later in November of 1927, another ballroom called the Savoy opened in Chicago, also featuring the country's hottest jazz bands, and became one of top night spots for that city. Both Savoy ballrooms had substantial dance floors, but the New York Savoy was more mainstream, a venue for the working-class to enjoy, whereas the Chicago Savoy was more refined and appealed to the more upper-class black in Chicago.

The illustrious Cotton Club in Harlem, originally called the Club De Luxe, was first opened by Heavyweight boxing champion Jack Johnson in 1920 on 142nd Street and Lenox Avenue in Harlem. The club was taken over by well-known gangster, Owney Madden in 1923, who changed the name to the Cotton Club. Blacks were denied admission to the Club as patrons, although supreme black musicians, blues singers, and dancers were eagerly sought after. The Club hired the best band at the time, led by Fletcher Henderson, who took his orchestra to a higher jazz dimension when he recruited Louis Armstrong. During the 1920s, the Cotton Club showcased Adelaide Hall, Bessie Smith, and Ethel Waters.

The legendary Duke Ellington's orchestra was the band at the Cotton Club for more

A Reflection

than three years beginning in 1927. Ellington and his band gained national exposure when the Cotton Club broadcasted his shows on the radio from coast to coast. During his tenure, Ellington explored and experimented with arrangements developing his repertoire and recording more than 100 compositions, elevating him to superstar status. The Cotton Club had other branches in Chicago and Culver City, California which showcased the performers from the Harlem branch.

In the 1920s, white record companies realized that African-American music audiences wanted to buy blues and jazz records or what they called "race records." Most blues singer at the time were women veterans of vaudeville, including Mamie Smith, Gertrude "Ma" Rainey, Bessie Smith, Ethel Waters, Clara Smith, and Victoria Spivey. Top musicians were booked to play for the recording, most sought after were Fletcher Henderson and Louis Armstrong, and premiere song writers W.C. Handy, Perry Bradford , and Clarence Williams composed the blues songs.

Fletcher Henderson's band was the most commercially successful band of the decade, and his protégé Louis Armstrong was the greatest jazz musician of the decade. Armstrong recorded 65 songs for Okeh Records with his bands, the Hot Five and the Hot Seven. In 1923, "Ma" Rainey made her first recording for Paramount Records, and in five years had recorded over 100 songs. Bessie Smith, "The Queen of the Blues," made her first recording for Columbia Records also in 1923, *Down Hearted Blues*, which sold 750,000 copies that year. During the decade, Smith was the leading recording artist in the world.

The only record label owned and operated by an African-American was Black Swan Records, founded by Harry Pace in 1921. The label struggled until he crossed paths with Ethel Waters. Waters' recordings of *Down Home Blues* and *Oh Daddy* were extremely successful, selling 500,000 copies in six months time and helped Black swan Records get out of the red. Pace followed up making a record a month with Ethel, and at its height put out ten records a month with other artists, but none reached the previous success of *Down Home Blues*.

Sports and Black Athletes

Most professional sports were still segregated, Jim Crow limited the competition for African-Americans and robbed gifted athletes of the glory and recognition they could have achieved along with the possible financial gains enjoyed by white athletes. Ora Mae Washington was one of the top black athletes who suffered this misfortune of being denied to compete outside of "Negro" organizations. Ms. Washington, born January

23, 1898, was raised in Northwest Philadelphia, in a section called Germantown. She was considered to be the best female athlete of the times and was known as the "Queen of Tennis." In 1929, she won her first American Tennis Association singles Championship, and went on to win seven more singles titles and 12 straight double titles of the next nine years. Helen Wills Moody, the reigning white female champion refused to play Washington in a tennis match. Ora Washington was a two-sport athlete, playing basketball for the Savoy Colts from 1928 to 1929, the Olivet Baptist Church Cosmopolitans, and the Germantown Hornets.

Great college football players were pushing past some blocks to integrate professional football. In 1922, the APFA and NFL merged into combined league known as the NFL. Over the next decade thirteen black players were signed to the league. Two notable superstar black athletes of the day were Frederick "Fritz" Pollard and Paul Robeson. Pollard was the first black quarterback, playing three years with the Akron pros, and went on to become the first black profession head coach in football at Milwaukee. In 1928, Fritz Pollard and Dr. Albert C. Johnson formed the Chicago Black Hawks, an all-black profession team that became one of the most popular teams.

At the end of the 1920s, there was still no organized black league in basketball, and the National Basketball league did not accept black players. All-black basketball teams were called "black fives," most teams were affiliated with athletic clubs, the YWCA, churches, social clubs, or businesses. Robert L. Douglas was the founder of the Harlem Renaissance Basketball Club, nicknamed the Rens in 1923. The Rens and the Harlem Globetrotters traveled across the country playing basketball, becoming top draws for white and black sports fans. In 1925, the New York Rens beat the champion Original Celtics, a critical turning point in the sport of basketball and racial interaction in the nation. The Renaissance Club was known as the best basketball team in the world.

Cumberland Posey was a phenomenal athlete, coach, and sports manager, a two-sport competitor; he played both professional basketball and baseball. He was the best African-American basketball player competing up until the mid 1920s. The sports press called him an "All-Time Immortal." Playing on the Loendi Big Five professional team, the most dominating team of the "Black Five Era," Posey maintained his star player status while managing, promoting and booking the squad. The Leondi Big Five won four consecutive colored Basketball World's Championships from 1920 to 1923. In no small feat Posey also found time to organize and coach the Homestead Grays football team in 1923, and also put together a Gray's basketball squad in 1927 that beat the New York

A Reflection

Celtics. Cumberland Posey ended his basketball career at the end of 1929 to fully focus on his baseball team, the Homestead Grays, which he had owned since the early 1920s.

Baseball was America's favorite pastime, particularly for urban black populations in larger cities. Professional baseball leagues remained strictly segregated. During the 1920's, there were three "Negro" leagues, the Negro National League, the Negro Southern League, and the Eastern League that would become the American Negro League. These leagues struggled with franchise organization during the first half of the decade, and with economic challenges during the latter half. The Negro National League was headed by Rube Foster, with eight teams: the Chicago American Giants, Chicago Giants, Cuban Stars, Dayton Marcos, Detroit Stars, Indianapolis ABC's, Kansas City Monarchs, and the St. Louis Giants. The Negro Southern League was organized by Thomas T. Wilson, owner of the Nashville Elite Giants, in Atlanta with teams out of Atlanta, Birmingham, Memphis, Montgomery, Nashville, and New Orleans. The Eastern League was organized in 1923 with teams, Bacharach Giants, Baltimore Black Sox, Cuban Stars (East), Hilldale Club, the Lincoln Giants, and Brooklyn Royal Giants who would be replaced by the Homestead Grays in 1927.

The Stock Market Crash

On October 24, 1929, later to be known as Black Thursday, the stock market began its downhill drop. The Stock Market Crash ended the jubilation of the celebration that was the "Roaring Twenties." The causes for the crash have been hotly debated with many finding the fault with the banking system and its overextended loans. The Binga State Bank in Chicago was the largest black-owned band in the country in 1929 with deposits of $1,500,000. It was built by Jesse Binga from an investment of $10. The Binga Bank was one of the casualties of the stock market crash that devastated public banks.

Analysis of the stock market shows that from 1925 to October 1929 common stocks had risen in value by 120 percent, in line with the growth of the national economy, but other data shows that stock investment had begun to decline. Some have the opinion that the economic decline began in 1928 with decreases in production, sales, and employment, but farmers had been in a depression since the end of World War I, unable to make a profit with lower demand and lower prices. Many industries had begun to recede including the auto industry, which laid off 140 thousand workers in 1921. Technological advances meant that fewer workers were needed on assembly lines. Co-dependency among industry employers brought down other businesses.

African-Americans were hurting from the declining national economy years before the stock market crash. Employment and economic situations for blacks had begun to deteriorate halfway through the 1920s. Industrial recessions in Philadelphia, Detroit, and Chicago had devastating consequences for blacks who were the last hired and the first fired. The fallout contributed to the suffering of black businesses, many were wiped out even before the crash. The underlying problem of the economy was the uneven distribution of wealth; the top 0.1 percent of the population had income equal to the bottom 42 percent. Although the 1920s had been a prosperous decade, it was reserved for just a few. Businesses profits grew by leaps and bounds but the worker received very little of the wealth they generated.

Memorable Moments

On October 2, 1925, Josephine Baker became a superstar when she opened in Paris at the Theatre des Champs-Elysees with her unique form of erotic dancing while practically nude.

Theodore "Tiger" Flowers defeated Harry Greb in 1926 and became the first African-American middleweight champion.

Black History Week, now Black History Month, was established in 1928 by Carter G. Woodson.

In 1929, the annual conference of the NAACP convened in Cleveland to mark the Association's twentieth anniversary. The NAACP had much to celebrate. It had launched a successful anti-lynching crusade; won important legal battles; and organized 325 branches. *The Crisis*, the Association's official organ, was the leading black periodical with a circulation of more than 100,000.

Reflections on a Decade

The more things change, the more they stay the same. The decade ending in 1929 began during a period of celebration after the end of World War I. Increased earnings and shorter work hours for factory workers left time for diversions, movies, baseball and other sports. The optimism and gaiety of the times was just a mask over the gloomy realities of poverty and unemployment for so many. While some blacks were reveling in the success and accomplishments of the Harlem Renaissance, enjoying the trappings of a little more money, living better, dressing better, eating better, entertaining themselves, dancing till dawn, life for the rest of black America, the majority still living in the South, was still hard as hell.

Catalyst for change during this decade was the continuation of the Great Migration out of the South, even though employment opportunities in major industrial companies were

A Reflection

tapering off in urban areas. Mass unemployment was probably the main contributor to criminal activity in the black community. Politically, African-Americans gained clout as their numbers became larger in northern cities where they had voting power. Blacks were being elected to local and state offices, and there was Depriest in Congress. The few steps that had been taken inspired blacks to climb higher. Greater percentages were staying in school longer; more were seeking college and professional degrees. There were organizations providing social and financial support in the black community, and the Urban League was working tirelessly to improve health and housing.

The Harlem Renaissance put a face on the 'New Negro', and a voice that shouted, the place you've designated for me is not my place, I'm taking my place. The connection with our African identity had given black people kinship with their misplaced heritage. The Harlem Renaissance was a critical point, a defining moment in the evolution of black people. For the entire world to witness was the exceptional intelligence, creativity, and talent displayed in literature, music, theatre, dance, and the visual arts. All the questions pertaining to racial inferiority, brain capacity, the lack of sophistication, had been answered.

The experiences of black life in the 1920s were filled with opposing dynamics and contradictions, like the negative image of a photograph, vacillating between light and dark, optimism and hopelessness, pain and ecstasy, defiance and defeat, dreams and doubts, and simply sadness and joy. African-Americans were straddling two worlds, one where they were isolated, but independent and self-sufficient, the one Marcus Garvey espoused to, where we reveled in our own power and beauty, and the world of white America where we were less than, unworthy of equal rights or pay, pointed to the rear, ordered to the back, always the least respected, and never good enough.

1939

Picture from the Franklin D. Roosevelt Library, courtesy of the National Archives and Records Administration.)
Resettlement Administration; Rural Rehabilitation; "Dave Mayberry"; Iredell Co., N.C. (Circa November 1933)

Any Human to Another

The ills I sorrow at
Not me alone
Like an arrow,
Pierce to the marrow,
Through the fat
And past the bone.
-- Countee Cullen

The Great Depression

It's impossible not to stare at the specter of the 1930's awestruck by the state of affairs. The decade preceding 1939 is characterized by the Great Depression, the worst economic decline in the history of the United States. The National income fell by close to 50 percent from $81 billion in 1929 to $40 billion three years later. Nearly 15 million workers had no jobs, unemployment reached 25 percent for all workers and 37 percent for farm workers. In states dependent on industrial jobs unemployment was even higher, in Cleveland it was 60 percent and 80 percent in Toledo, Ohio.

A Reflection

Thousands of businesses failed bringing down other businesses like dominoes. For those fortunate individuals who still had jobs, they suffered cuts in wages and lived in fear of losing work. Millions of Americans were homeless, migrating across the country in search of work to keep a roof over their heads and feed their families. Farmers had been in their own depression during the 1920s, and continued to lose land and farm equipment. African-Americans were already operating at a disadvantage before the Depression, trying to make something out of nothing, but their circumstances were exacerbated by the inability to find a day's work in farming or industry.

Bread line, 1937, Library of Congress

The statement later made by Malcolm X, "When white America catches a cold, black America gets pneumonia," spoke volumes on the plight of blacks during the Depression. White America had pneumonia and black America was on life-support. The black population suffered major setbacks due to the national Depression; unemployed white workers took jobs usually reserved for blacks, and employers fired black workers to replace them with whites who were out of work. Racist whites protested in southern cities carrying signs that said, "No Jobs for Niggers Until Every White Man Has a Job" and "Niggers, back to the cotton fields—city jobs are for white folks." In the industrial center cities like Chicago, Cleveland, and St. Louis, blacks were 50 percent of the unemployed.

1939

The shortage of available jobs meant possibly shifting back to sharecropping for survival for black families, but southern agriculture didn't offer solace to those in need, prices for crops were so low they were left in the fields to rot. Depressed prices for cotton, machines eliminating manual labor, and prejudice complicated the efforts of the poor black farmer who was barely able to survive. Twelve thousand more black sharecroppers left rural farm life and moved to cities in the South, North, and West. Job prospects in urban cities were less than dismal for black men and women, but they had a better chance of getting relief in the North than in the South. Disproportionate numbers of African-Americans lost everything and waited in bread lines, while many charitable organizations barred them from soup kitchens.

Desperation added force to racial tensions and violence erupted on work sites as competition for jobs between blacks and whites intensified. Some black workers were murdered by whites to get their jobs. Racial violence regained its momentum particularly in the South; lynchings had dropped to eight in 1932, only to surge to 28 in 1933. Hilton Butler, a contemporary observer concluded, *"Dust had been blown from the shotgun, the whip, the noose, and Ku Klux Klan practices were being resumed in the certainty that dead men not only tell no tales, but create vacancies."*

Demographics

The life expectancy for Black Americans is 53.5 years. Blacks now make up 9.8 percent of the population, with numbers around 12,866,000. More African Americans were still flocking to the cities, albeit at a slower pace, less than half of the 1920s migration total. During the 1930s, about 350,000 black people moved from southern states, 52.3 percent now live in urban areas, but only 22 percent live outside the Southern region. Black populations in northern cities grew by close to 25 percent, increasing the number of cities with 100,000 plus black residents from one in 1930 to 11 by 1935. The black population in New York State grew by 40 percent to 458,444 in the decade between 1929 and 1939, with half of the population on relief. The annual income for a black male was $547.45 compared to $1234.14 for a white male, and the annual incomes for black and white females were $331.32 and $771.69 respectively. The numbers of blacks migrating to the North and West diminished during the 1930s with no prospects for work. By 1939, blacks constituted 40 percent of relief rolls, and half of all black families relied on some government aid for subsistence.

A Reflection

Mood of the Black Community

Black people living in the four corners of the country had reached the point where they realized they had nothing more to lose and everything to gain. Things had to change if they were ever going to get rid of Jim Crow and receive their full rights as citizens of the United States. Small victories won by raising a united voice emboldened them to demand more; greater representation, more job opportunities, higher pay, better housing, and increased access to healthcare. Unfortunately African-Americans had not had the time to savor the experience of improved conditions or earning a decent living, having been the last hired before the setback of the Great Depression and now the first fired, nonetheless, returning to what went on before was not an option.

The distress and misery of the Great Depression was more devastating for blacks than it was for whites even though unemployment and homelessness were not new occurrences in the black community. Survival up to these years had always been a daily challenge Black people did what they had always done; they united and supported each other in the struggle. In urban cities, blacks watched each other's children, grew vegetable gardens, threw rent parties, and shared housing space, while the church fed, found housing, and clothed as many families as it could. The numbers game gave hope to some and employment to a lot more as runners and bookkeepers.

The hardships of the depression were exaggerated for blacks in the South with foreclosures of farms and low prices for crops; state and local agencies denied black farmers the relief given to white farmers. Black southern families grew what they could to survive, canned for the winter months, shared the fruits and vegetables with extended family members and neighbors, and they fished to eat and sell not allowing anyone to starve. Large numbers of whites who had never contended with this degree of adversity vented their anger and frustration on black people through vicious attacks and lynching.

Black consciousness developed during the 1930s, fueled by the growth of the black working-class, the support from the communist party, and strong black labor organizations. It was the beginning of the social protest movement. Voter registration drives dramatically increased the number of black voters in major industrial cities. Black people continued their refusal to patronize businesses that didn't hire blacks or showed them no respect. Dissatisfaction with discrimination and unemployment and tired of being victimized, a rumor in Harlem of a black youth beaten by the police set off a riot targeting white-owned stores. The looting and destruction continued on into the next day leaving three blacks dead and $2 million in property damage.

1939

In 1939, clothes gave identity and status, dressing up was often a way to offset degradation at work. Black and whites spent a lot time going to see movies, sometimes four or five shows a week. Overcrowded apartments and homes drove people out into movie theatres, stores, billiard rooms, speakeasies, and restaurants where they could relax and be comfortable. Friday and Saturday nights were times for leisure and pleasure, enjoying dances and parties.

Political Climate

The political climate was volatile during the depression; many states still denied or obstructed blacks from using their voting rights in efforts to limit their political power and to prevent them from receiving available benefits and representation. The patience of the people had worn very thin with President Herbert Hoover and his failure to solve the query of the economic downturn. Herbert Hoover offered no respite for the poor believing any government assistance or intervention would hinder self-reliance and the incentive for work. Hoover instead chose the "trickle down" theory, he supplied corporations with aid and federal loans with the rationale this would create more jobs. President Hoover's failed policies lead to his defeat in his re-election bid. Franklin D. Roosevelt became president in 1933, beating Hoover in a landslide.

The NAACP and prominent black leaders of the day, including Mary McLeod Bethune and Walter White, gave their support to Franklin D. Roosevelt in hopes that he would put an end to lynching. President Roosevelt focused his attention on the revival of the nation's economy and bringing an end to the Depression. As president, he put forth a series of domestic initiatives that would focus on giving the "forgotten man" a "New Deal." Roosevelt created a bevy of programs that included the Public Works Administration (PWA), the Civil Conservation Corps (CCC), the National Recovery Administration (NRA), Agricultural Adjustment Administration (AAA), and the Federal Emergency Relief Administration (FERA) to give relief during the economic recovery.

Initially Roosevelt was not the ally that black Americans had hoped for; he was opposed to civil rights legislation and the anti-lynching bill, not wanting to antagonize his political support from Southern Democrats while implementing his social programs. Most African-Americans got a "raw deal" instead of benefiting from the New Deal during Roosevelt's first term in office. The National Relief Administration along with Social Security barred 60 percent of blacks from receiving benefits. The AAA denied black farmers the compensation given to white farmers, and domestic and non-skilled workers were excluded from minimum wage protection.

A Reflection

At this time only 250,000, five percent of eligible blacks, were registered to vote. Blacks moved from parts of the country where they had limited political power to sections where there was the possibility of gaining political influence. These demographic changes gave strength to the black vote in national elections, their location making them a decisive factor. In 1936, Franklin Roosevelt received 76 percent of the Northern black vote. This trend shifted the balance of power in marginal states, so that by the mid-1930s black Americans were finally starting to reap some benefits of the New Deal. By the end of the decade income for the relief programs provided by the New Deal became the main source of income over agriculture and domestic service.

African-Americans had a strong ally in the White House, First Lady Eleanor Roosevelt, who used her influence to offset the protests of Southern Governors when conflicts related to integrating government appointments, programs, and benefits arose. Half-way through the decade of the 1930s, forty-five blacks had been appointed to Deal Agencies in addition to the "Black Cabinet" of advisors, which included Robert L. Vann, editor of the *Pittsburgh Courier,* Robert C. Weaver, an economist, and Mary McLeod Bethune, founder of Bethune-Cookman College in Florida. As Roosevelt became more outwardly supportive of African-Americans, signing the law that permitted blacks in the Army and Air Forces, and denouncing lynching as "a vile form of collective murder," white voters began to desert the Democratic Party.

More blacks were becoming aware of other political parties as varied agendas competed for the allegiance of African-Americans. The three major third parties during the 1930s were the Communist Party, the Socialist Party, and the American Labor Party. The Communist and Socialist parties became more attractive to some blacks who saw desperate times required radical measures amid the crisis of the Depression. Although these organizations were able to garner some support due to the discontent among black people by protesting lynching, challenging racial discrimination and segregation, pushing for more government relief, and the organizing of labor, the numbers were never large enough to effect much change. Furthermore, the black church was opposed to the atheism connected to the Communist Party.

1939

Leadership

Leadership in the black community was in transition in the 1930s, the numbers of the working class had grown over the last decade, along with their role and participation in the fight for civil rights. Their influence grew as they exercised their vote and voiced their social protests. During the active labor disputes of the Depression the NAACP lost some of the support and authority that they had become accustomed to from the black community, membership rolls were dropping and operating revenue was in short supply.

Many in the black community felt that the leadership of the NAACP and the Urban League had become too guarded and careful and viewed them as elitist dependent on white control. The NAACP was also suffering an inner turmoil as W.E.B. Du Bois and Walter White clashed over philosophical differences. Du Bois unimpressed by the New Deal and what it offered blacks began to speak out in favor of self-segregation, feeling the costs of integration were at times too high. His new stance went against everything the NAACP was founded on, integration and racial equality. White criticized Du Bois as being out of touch with the times. In June 1934, W.E.B. Du Bois, indignant and fatigued, resigned as editor of the *Crisis*, the NAACP journal, after 24 years of service.

A. Philip Randolph was the central figure in efforts to organize black workers and by 1933 the BSCP Union represented 35,000 Pullman porters. His finesse and success in the negotiation of labor and trade unions laid the foundation for the Civil Rights movement. Randolph understood the collective power of the organized union, the influence born from a strong independent voice that cannot be ignored. Blacks and whites in solidarity, with a common agenda in fair wages, and job safety and security were beneficial to both. The groups of unemployed and unionized workers were essential to the success of many movements. A. Philip Randolph said,

> "Salvation for a race, nation, or class must come from within. Freedom is never granted; it is won. Justice is never given; it is exacted. Freedom and justice must be struggled for by the oppressed of all lands and races, and the struggle must be continuous; for freedom is never a final fact, but a continuing evolving process to higher and higher levels of human social, economical, political, and religious relationships."

The Communist party played a large role in the battle for civil rights in the 1930s, viewing the racial conflict as part of a larger struggle between classes, the haves and the have-nots. Black workers in rural areas were also becoming more militant, and the Communist Party was instrumental in helping rural blacks in Alabama organize the

A Reflection

Sharecroppers Union, and the Socialist helped form the Southern Tenant Farmers Union (STFU). Militancy in labor practices increased participation in political issues. More radical and militant activists like John P. Davis, Ralphe Bunche, Robert C. Weaver, and A. Philip moved to the forefront forming the National Negro Congress (NNC) from six hundred organizations, and 1.2 million members, with A. Philip Randolph as its president.

The National Negro Congress brought a new game plan, organize and mobilize. The goal of the NNC was to bring political, religious, and fraternal organizations together in a concerted effort to lift the black community out of the Depression through trade unions. The NNC viewed the troubles of the black America from an economic perspective rather than political. Their approach was much more vocal, trying cases in the court of public opinion, nationally and internationally. The National Negro Congress was overwhelmed with Communist support, prompting moderates Randolph and Bunche to resign. The NNC was very effective until it was divided by cracks within the organization.

The Urban League did alter its stance on labor relations and discouraged black workers from breaking strikes and crossing picket lines, urging relationships between blacks and organized labor. They also joined the NNC in the formation of committees and councils to reveal the disparities in the New Deal programs.

The Black Church

Church memberships and attendance had gone down with jobs and wages. An article in the *Pittsburg Courier* (May, 1931) addressed the predicament, *"in this country where cash is God and credit is Jesus Christ, churches do not get very far with membership drives when there is a scarcity of money and a great army of unemployed."* The black churches in the North had been devastated, the majority had been stretched to their financial limits with large amounts of debt they accumulated from additions and purchases made to accommodate larger congregations. At the beginning of the Depression, 71 percent of urban churches were deep in debt. In the 1930s, the largest black church in the United State was Abyssinian Baptist, located in the largest black urban community, Harlem, with a congregation of a 14,000 members. During the Depression, their pastor, Adam Clayton Powell was very active in the community waging campaigns to improve city services, feed the hungry and create employment opportunities.

Our faith was truly in the Lord, and He would deliver and provide. Churches became not only centers for feeding and clothing during the Depression, but engines that powered the black community in the struggle for racial equality and civil rights. Reverend Adam C. Powell Sr. led a march on New York's City hall for Black relief. Powell was an effective leader and organizer at this time. He held the position of chairman of the Coordinating Committee for Employment. Powell organized a picket line at the 1939 New York World's Fair in protest of hiring practices. His efforts resulted in the increase of black workers from 200 to 732. He coordinated a bus boycott that led to the hiring of 200 black workers by the New York Transit Authority, and fought to have black pharmacists hired in Harlem drugstores.

***

Father Divine's Peace Mission had flourished over the last decade; over 150 Peace Missions had sprung up across the country. Twenty-five percent of the Missions were located in New York; the main one was situated in Harlem. During the depression years the followers multiplied, Father Divine estimated the size of his disciples near 10 million, but the New York Times in 1933 put the number of nationwide followers nearer two million. Political parties courted his favor in major elections to influence the vote of the African-American community.

The Peace Mission was also the largest property owner in Harlem; its businesses included hotels, restaurants, markets, dress stores, and auto garages. All of his enterprises provided high-quality goods and services, beating his competition with low pricing. Father Divine's guidelines saved his followers from the economic failures of the times. He prohibited the use of banks, his followers were not to deposit their money in banks, or borrow, and he insisted they get out of any debt.

The collapse of the Marcus Garvey's Universal Negro Improvement Association empowered father Divine's Peace Mission as the mass departure of members from the UNIA became Peace Mission followers. Members of the UNIA throughout the nation defected to the Peace Mission, from Newark, New Jersey to Los Angeles and Oakland, California. The two movements had some similar philosophies based on capitalism, economic independence, and racial uplift that encouraged African-Americans to become entrepreneurs.

Father Divine's Peace Mission was a godsend to the poor in the black community suffering during the Depression, providing food to tens of thousands, and creating jobs, much relief to those unemployed and struggling. Mission restaurants offered hot and hearty meals for only 5 or 10 cents, and insisted his followers refuse tips. The 1933 Easter service in New York was attended by up to 40,000 persons. By the end of the Depression decade, the Peace Mission had accumulated savings in excess of $15 million.

A Reflection

The Nation of Islam was founded in 1930 by Wallace Fard Muhammad in Detroit, Michigan. The doctrine teaches that W. Fard Muhammad is the Messiah of Christianity and the Mahdi of Islam, believing that he was Allah incarnated. Fard preached that Islam was the original religion of African-Americans. The creed is based on Suni Islam doctrine with a message of racial separatism, self-determination, black supremacy. Fard Muhammad recruited about 8000 members as he sold foreign goods door to door, calling them the lost tribe of Shabazz. He established a paramilitary force called the Fruit of Islam, the University of Islam, and the Muslim Girls Training Class for his followers.

The Black Press

The Great Depression was instrumental in the failure of many marginal black newspapers, while others like the *National News* and the *Negro World* in Harlem cut the number of pages in their tabloids to conserve costs. Surprisingly, several new newspapers were started in this decade, including the *Atlanta Daily World* in 1931, which was the nation's first black daily for the century, the *Cleveland Call and Post* in 1934, and the *Los Angeles Sentinel* in 1934, which became the largest black newspaper in the Western region of the United States. The Department of Commerce report of 1939 said: "Not less than 227 Negro newspapers and 105 magazines and bulletins were published by Negroes in the United States during the year beginning November 1, 1937 and ending October 31, 1938."

The power and influence of black newspapers was expanding with the migration and increased black literacy. In the early 1930s, the *Pittsburgh Courier*, with a circulation of 174,000, was the largest selling black newspaper. Robert Vann and the *Pittsburgh Courier* were largely responsible for reversing the black allegiance to the Republican Party and delivering the African-American votes to the Democratic Party and Franklin D. Roosevelt and his "New Deal." FDR, not ignorant to the influence wielded by the popular *Pittsburgh Courier* appointed Vann to a White House advisory post. African-American newspapers supported FDR for his second term in office, seeing the federal government as their only friend, as it was held to international scrutiny.

African-American newspapers continued to take the lead organizing campaigns to lift up black people. *The Norfolk Journal and Guide* and the *Cleveland Call and Post*, both led campaigns for the funding of the Scottsboro Boys' legal defense. National politics and raising black consciousness was a major emphasis, but black papers also focused on local issues to lift the black community, including a fairer distribution of public funds, better quality schools, street paving, and more black representation in jobs, particularly in white-owned retail stores operating in the black areas. "Don't buy where you can't work" campaigns were still being used by newspapers to pressure white business owners patronized by the black community to employ black workers.

Charlotta Amanda Bass, as publisher and editor of the *California Eagle* started "Don't Shop Where You Can't Work" campaigns in Los Angeles, and led a successful campaign to have blacks hired at the Southern California Telephone Company during the 1930s. A staunch soldier against racial injustice she formed the Industrial Council in 1930 to fight discrimination and encouraged entrepreneurship and black business. The *California Eagle* also began a 15-minute newspaper-of-the-air in 1938, broadcast on the KGF radio station six nights of the week.

The *Pittsburgh Courier* took a national leadership role in uplifting the black community and launched several campaigns to fight discrimination in sports; one initiative was to integrate baseball. The paper also ran a campaign against the most popular radio show in the country, "Amos and Andy," taking a stand against negative stereotyping of blacks portrayed on the show. Robert Vann and his *Courier* provided outstanding coverage of sports, traveling to Berlin, Germany to cover the performances of Jessie Owens in the 1936 Olympic Games. The *Courier* also took on the fight for the integration of professional sports. Wendell Smith, the sportswriter in 1938, denounced the segregation of the major leagues through his column.

The Afro-American, out of Baltimore, successfully campaigned to raise the salaries of black school teachers bringing them commensurate with that of white teachers, and also gained promises from the city to hire black policemen. *The Afro-American* additionally put forth "Clean Block Campaigns" in 1935 that were emulated in Philadelphia, Washington and Richmond, Virginia in 1937. These community improvement campaigns inspired competition among blocks in several neighborhoods on the cleaning and beautification of homes, yards, and streets. Prizes and recognition in the newspaper were awarded to the winners.

Black newspapers used their editorials to bring discussion on critical issues for blacks; the articles were talked about in barbershops, backyards, in the church, and in the pool hall. Photographs were used as symbols to incite emotions and action, Mary McLeod Bethune with Eleanor Roosevelt, Joe Louis, Jesse Owens, and the Scottsboro Boys. Their success was our success, their triumph was our triumph, their hurt was our hurt, and their injustice was our injustice.

A Reflection

Black Businesses and the Depression

Although black businesses and professionals suffered immensely during the Great Depression of the 1930s, there were still more black businesses per capita than there are today. In 1930, there were 70 thousand African-Americans businesses operating across the country, with 30,000 retail stores, which employed 43,000 workers with $71 million in sales. Jim Crow and segregation insisted that black people patronize their own establishments. Dependent exclusively upon black consumers and clients, black businesses endured fewer sales and lower profits due to the higher levels of black unemployment. At the end of the 1920s, total sales for 24,969 black retail stores in the United States was $98.6 million, by 1935, only six years later, the total sales had plunged more than 50 percent to $47.9 million and the number of black-owned retail stores had dropped to 22,756.

Chicago was the heart of black businesses going into the 1930s with 3000 black-owned businesses and two black-owned banks, including the largest, Binga Bank. Bronzeville, located on the South Side of Chicago, was known as the "Black Metropolis," the Midwest answer to the Harlem Renaissance. Bronzeville had thrived during the previous decade driven by the migration of blacks from the South. Black owned banks, insurance companies, restaurants, and nightclubs prospered there before the economic slowdown. During the Depression many black businesses and black-owned banks went bankrupt. By 1933, half of Chicago's black-owned business and its banks had been dissolved.

One of the survivors was the St. Luke Penny Savings Bank, the first bank founded by a black woman. Maggie L. Walker, the daughter of former slaves, started the bank in 1903 with $9430 among members of the Independent Order of St. Luke and African-American Benevolent Society in Richmond, Virginia, the foundation; *"Let us put our money together; let us put our money out at usury among ourselves, and reap the benefits ourselves."* Walker's savings bank survived the Great Depression by merging with two small black-owned banks in 1930, and was renamed the Consolidated Bank & Trust, which operates today with assets totaling $116 million. Richmond sometimes referred to as the Harlem of the South, was also the home to five more black-owned banks and scores of other African-American businesses.

The businesses of Arthur G. Gaston never missed a beat during the Depression, no small feat in Birmingham, Alabama, following his mantra of "Find a need and fill it." Gaston's Booker T. Washington Burial Society thrived from his connections with black clergy, and he expanded the business to include the Booker T. Washington Insurance

Company in 1932, offering life, health, and accidental insurance to his customers. He later added burial insurance, funeral services, casket manufacturing, and burial plots from company-owned cemeteries. His business acumen and proceeds supplied him with the funds to establish the Booker T. Washington Business College in 1939 to train black secretarial workers.

Above all others, the biggest and most profitable business in the black community was "the numbers" or policy game. Illegal lottery or numbers were the principal monetary force for blacks during the Depression, with annual revenue sometimes reaching $100 million and employing tens-of-thousands of black people nationwide. In Chicago, around 5000 blacks were employed by the policy business or running numbers in the 1930s. By 1938, Chicago's policy racket was bringing in $18 million a year. "Policy Kings" invested substantial amounts of the profits in the African-American community, provided monies for legitimate businesses, contributed to churches and hospitals, paid tuition for gifted students, and set up practices for black professionals.

Black Professionals

In 1939, there were 110,000 black professionals with the majority spread across five fields, the ministry, teaching, medicine, dentistry, and the law, with more than two-thirds being teachers or ministers. The largest numbers were concentrated in the ministry to the point of overrepresentation in the overall population. Most cities in the North and South were underrepresented in black professional physicians, dentists, and lawyers for the population. Chicago had more professionals than any other city, with New York and Philadelphia trailing close behind. During the Great Depression all professions suffered the ramifications of the black communities' economic devastation. The professional market of ministers was protected by segregation and the fact that black congregations preferred black preachers and their traditional form of worship. Black teachers suffered hardships due to the loss of revenue for education; those who kept their jobs received lower wages.

Black professionals benefited somewhat from the refusal of some whites to do business with black clientele, but this advantage was offset by many blacks who preferred a white doctor to a black one. Dentists were able to corner a market offering cosmetic work and gold teeth. In general, black doctors, dentists, and lawyers had to compete with white professionals for the African-American market, while the white market for them remained closed.

A Reflection

Extraordinary African-Americans

Mary McLeod Bethune was one of the most influential black leaders in American History. Born to former slaves in South Carolina, the fifteenth of seventeen children, she grew up on the land of her parents' former owners. Having shown an early desire to learn to read and write, she attended Trinity Mission School, a one-room school house, where she met her long-time mentor and teacher, Emma Jane Wilson. Bethune attended college with the hope of becoming a missionary in Africa at Scotia Seminary and Dwight Moody's Institute for Home and Foreign Missions in Chicago. Finding few opportunities for black missionaries, she decided to teach. Mary McLeod began her teaching career at Haines Normal and Industrial Institute in Augusta, Georgia in 1896. She patterned the philosophy of her pedagogy after Lucy Craft Laney, the founder of the school, with a Christian base emphasizing moral character and practical education for young ladies, stating "*I believe that the greatest hope for the development of my race lies in training our women thoroughly and practically.*"

After a few years of teaching and social work, Bethune relocated to Dayton, Florida to start her own school. She rented a small house for $11.00 per month, making desks and benches out of discarded items and whatever charity she could get. In 1904, with $1.50 and only six students, including her own son, she formed the Literary and Industrial Training School for Negro Girls. The early curriculum was based on a Christian life, home economics, and industrial skills like cooking, dressmaking, millinery, along with other abilities that assist in self-sufficiency. Later, additional courses of science, business, and then high school English, math, and foreign languages were included. By 1920, the enrollment was 102, and in 1923 the school was merged with the Cookman Institute for Men, with Mary McLeod Bethune as president.

Mrs. Bethune served in leadership capacities in a host of organizations. In 1896, she was the Florida chapter president of the National Association of Colored Women, before becoming the national president in 1924. From 1920 to 1925 she was the president of the Southeastern Federation of Colored Women's Clubs. Bethune was also the founder and president of the National Council of Negro Women in 1935, bringing more than 28 organizations together to forming a council, stating the mission:

> "It is our pledge to make a lasting contribution to all that is finest and best in America, to cherish and enrich her heritage of freedom and progress by working for the integration of all her people regardless of race, creed, or nation origin, into her spiritual, social, cultural, civic, and economic life, and thus aid her to achieve the glorious destiny of a true and unfettered democracy."

The NCNW hosted the White House Conference on Negro Women and Children in 1938, and during World War II they were successful in opening doors for African-American women to military officer roles in the Women's army Corps. By 1955, the membership of the NCWW had reached 800,000.

Consecutive presidents of the United States recognized Mary McLeod Bethune's authority, President Coolidge invited her to the Child Welfare Conference in 1928, and President Hoover appointed her to the White House Conference on Child Health in 1930. A strong supporter for the election of Franklin D. Roosevelt in 1932, Bethune also developed a close relationship with Eleanor Roosevelt, a friendship that afforded her clear access to the White House. She formed an alliance with prominent leaders of other black organizations called the Federal Council on Negro Affairs, which evolved into the "Black Cabinet," serving in an advisory role on issues concerning black Americans.

During President Roosevelt's second and third terms Bethune served as his special advisor on Minority Affairs, and was also appointed as his director of the Division of Negro Affairs of the National Youth Administration, becoming the first African-American to head a federal agency. The Director position in the NYA afforded her the opportunity to fund black students in school programs at every educational level as well as black colleges. Her assistance was pivotal in graduating the first black pilots in the civilian pilot training program.

Bethune's post in the NYA was helpful in getting appointments for additional black officials to positions of political power, hiring large numbers of administrative assistants on the state and local level to work between the two federal agencies she commanded, leading to the highest number of blacks working within federal agencies in the history of the country. Bethune was successful in convincing government officials of the need to improve employment opportunities for young black men and women. The NYA was beneficial to more than 300,000 black youths, providing projects that supplied them with work training and employment, making it possible for most of them to gain skills that qualified them for jobs previously out of their reach.

Stretched between Bethune-Cookman College, leadership in women's organizations, and her demanding role in President Roosevelt's administration, her health began to fail, forcing her to relinquish her presidency at the college. Mary McLeod Bethune was a dedicated educator committed to educating blacks and whites about the endeavors of African-Americans, stating *"Not only the Negro child but children of all races should read and know of the achievements, accomplishments and deeds of the Negro."*

A Reflection

Ernest Everett Just

In 1939 Dr. Ernest Everett Just, known as the Black Father of Scientists, a professor of embryology and cell biology published the culmination of his research work in Europe, *The Biology of the Cell Surface,* which became one of the most important textbooks in the world of science. Dr. Just believed that the cell had a central role in the development, inheritance, and evolution of life. His book challenged all scientific theories relating to the role of the cell surface in the structure and development of the cell; convinced that the cell surface is an active determinant of essential cellular processes with a complex design, not merely an encasement. Ernest E. Just was described by Dr. Charles Drew as "a biologist of unusual skill and the greatest of our original thinkers in the field." Just's research studies demonstrated that all fragments and subdivisions of a cell influence the cell's activity, and his contributions to fertilization and embryo research are still significant in the 21st century.

> The egg cell...is a universe. And if we could but know it we would feel in its minute confines the majesty and beauty that give us the story of all life from the first moment when somehow out of chaos came life and living. That first tremendous upheaval that gave this earth its present contour finds its counterpart in the breaking up of the surface of the egg which conditions all its life to follow (Just, 1939)

Ernest Everett Just was born in Charleston, South Carolina in 1883. His parents were Charles Frazier Just Jr., a dock builder, and Mary Matthews, a school teacher. Just's father died when he was only four years old, and his mother, dedicated to education, hoped he would become a teacher. Feeling that northern schools were superior to those in the South, he was sent north to attend Kimball Union Academy in New Hampshire, and then on to Dartmouth College, where he graduated magna cum laude. More than aware of the limited prospects of highly educated African-Americans in the nation Just accepted a faculty position at Howard University, and earned his doctorate from the University of Chicago.

E. E. Just, overloaded with teaching responsibilities and inadequate laboratory facilities with a desire to pursue research in experimental embryology, contacted Frank R. Lillie at Woods Hole, the head of the Marine Biological Laboratory. He spent the next twenty summers at Woods Hole, Massachusetts, producing most of his eighty scientific papers. Just explained, *"To fully understand how a living thing works, you have to study it under conditions like those in which it lives. And that applies down to the level of individual cells."* He became the international authority on the process of fertilization and egg development.

He was a member of the Corporation of the Marine Biological Laboratory at Woods Hole, a vice-president of the American Society of Zoologists, and was on the editorial boards of "Protoplasm" and the "Biological Bulletin." He was the only African-American with a star in the "American Men of Science" publication, marking those esteemed with the highest achievements in research. Although the National Academy of Sciences would not admit blacks as members, Just was often consulted about the qualifications of other potential inductees.

Dr. Just received invitations to conduct his research at several European laboratories; segregation in the Unites States denied him invitations to prestigious laboratories in his own country. Invitations came from various Russian research facilities, the Naples Zoological Laboratory, the Sorbonne in France, and the Kaiser Wilhelm Institute. Just made nine trips to Europe to further his research interests, and in 1930 exasperated with obstructions of racial discrimination hampering his research he left the country in a self-imposed exile.

World War II was raging in Europe and Just was working in France. The French government had advised foreign citizens to leave the country, but Ernest chose to stay and finish his writing. In 1939, Hitler invaded France, Just was captured and spent time in a Nazi concentration camp where his ill-health declined further. The assistance of friends and the U. S. Department saw to his release and he returned to Washington where he died in 1941 of pancreatic cancer. On a side note, Ernest Just along with three Howard University established the Omega Psi Phi fraternity in November of 1911.

Employment

In terms of black America, the Great Depression made a bad situation worse. Having always been the "last hired and first fired" blacks were out of work in large numbers before the full impact of the economic crisis had taken effect. Unemployment levels for African-Americans averaged near 60 percent across the country and the number of employed skilled workers dropped by 50 percent. Black workers were also being discriminated against by New Deal agencies like the Agricultural Adjustment Administration, the Works Progress Administration, the Farm Credit Administration, and the Resettlement Administration, receiving much less than their fair share of work relief assistance.

A Reflection

Competition for jobs between blacks and whites became even more fierce, outbreaks of violence in the North between unionized whites and nonunionized black workers were commonplace, and in the South, black workers were attacked and murdered for their jobs. Public utility and public service jobs, like policemen and firemen were reserved for whites, in the South, black firemen were attacked, intimidated, and some even murdered for their jobs. Black workers had already been shifted from factory jobs after World War I ended, new technology and the use of machines had decreased the need for many laborers, and now they faced the loss of work in agriculture and domestic service. The small numbers of jobs available were temporary or seasonal work, such as farm labor or construction.

The Depression transferred the burden of supporting the family to women as job opportunities for men became scarce. Lower wages and unemployment for black men increased the number of black women in the work force by nearly 77 percent. Black female employment levels were higher than black males in non-relief city jobs, and unemployment for young blacks was also much higher than the adult average.

The economic upheaval changed domestic service in many ways. Black housekeepers were greatly impacted with higher levels of unemployment; large numbers of white women were compelled to enter the work force, competing for their jobs as maids and cooks. Hours were cut and domestic workers had to rely on part-time work. Households whom under normal circumstances could not afford a maid would pay 10 cents an hour for housekeeping. More black women were forced into the "slave market" as housekeepers earning a mere five dollars per week, others made next to nothing or were even cheated out of their wages.

Black leadership organizations had not developed a satisfactory economic policy to address labor issues for black industrialized workers like longshoremen, steel and railroad workers, woodworkers, metal miners in Alabama, or coal miners in West Virginia. In 1935, after twelve years of great effort, A. Philip Randolph's organization of the Sleeping Car Porters' Union, composed of 35,000 black Pullman porters and maids, one of the most powerful unions admitted into the American Federation of Labor (AFL), was finally successful in negotiating an agreement with the Pullman Company, the first between a company and an African-American union, a landmark achievement in American civil rights history.

The onset of the Depression produced a dichotomy within the labor force; while vast numbers of industrial workers were unemployed, those that were fortunate enough to have jobs were gaining power through the organization of labor unions. In 1935, the interracial Congress of Industrial Organizations (CIO) was successful, after extended efforts, in organizing Chicago's Steel Industry, the United Auto Workers in Detroit, and the United Meatpacking Workers of America. Additionally they were effective in removing segregation of job positions, allowing blacks to advance to management and supervisory positions.

Black workers who were basically company loyal began joining labor unions for protection of their rights on the job. Black women in the dress industry joined the International Ladies Garment Workers' Union. Labor unions in their quest for organized labor, better working conditions and higher wages, essentially provided a "New Deal" for African-American workers by reducing racial and economic inequalities in the workplace before the beginning of the civil rights movement.

As a result of organized labor more black workers were hired in Detroit Auto plants, meat packing plants in Chicago, and in tobacco plants in North and South Carolina. A black working class was developed, working in Pennsylvania, Chicago, Indiana, and Cleveland. The CIO made all the difference for African-American workers, earning them a living wage with benefits, creating the blue collar middle-class, and raising the quality of life for so many African-Americans. Unfortunately the CIO was unable to effect equitable re-hiring of workers during the late 1930s as the nation slowly recovered from the depression.

Education

The Depression of the 1930s did nothing to improve the education of African-Americans, and was a catastrophe for southern black schools that remained racially segregated. Funding disparities between black and white students grew even further apart. Blacks were not represented on school boards to demand increased funding, and school boards with all white members were unwilling to distribute the limited funds of the day to black schools. On average, for every $80 paid in support of the education of a white child, only $15 was spent on each black child each year.

Nationwide blacks made up 25 percent of students, but received only 3 percent of the budgeted funds for transportation, and students could not ride buses. The powers that be were determined that black children and youth would not receive an equal or adequate education. A commission on education by Herbert Hoover in 1931 stated that black students were "by far the most heavily disadvantaged group of children in the entire field of education."

A Reflection

Black communities worked hard to combat limited resources and minimize inequities between the educations offered in black and white schools, but the depression inhibited their ability to raise funds. Southern communities of sharecroppers which had been building and supporting their own elementary schools could no longer afford to eat, much less donate monies for teacher salaries, books, and supplies. Many black southern schools could not afford heating or electricity. Blacks in rural communities like those in Louisiana donated labor to support their schools. Teachers taught more than the curriculum dictated and skilled laborers in the community volunteered to teach trades like carpentry and brick masonry to male students.

Transportation for black students to get to school was basically non-existent; some students had to walk long distances past white schools plagued by the harassment and torment of whites along the way to get to segregated schools. W.E.B. Du Bois had begun to question whether the pursuit of integration in the South was worth the fight, being that there were no public high schools available. He began endorsing segregated schools for black children where they could retain some self-respect and be treated decently.

School attendance had continued to increase over the last decade by more than 5 percent, according to Census data, black students 10 to 13 years of age attend school at comparable levels of white students in the same age group. Levels of attendance for black students started decreasing at higher grade levels as the age group rises. For students 16 to 17 years of age school attendance went down to 60 percent in urban locales, to 48 percent in rural-nonfarm areas, and to 47 percent in rural-farm communities. The median number of school years completed also varied with the community, for urban populations 6.8 years completed, 5 years in rural-nonfarm, and 4 years in rural-farm communities. The median number of years completed by white students in urban, rural-nonfarm, and rural farm were, 9.6 years, 8.6 years, and 8.0 years respectively. Black males were attending school in lower numbers than black females in every age group.

Although the number of southern blacks graduating from high school and college was growing, Census records show only four percent of African-Americans finishing high school in comparison to 20 percent of white persons over the age of 25 years, for those living in rural-farm communities only one percent graduated from high school. College attendance followed a similar pattern. Only 1.2 percent of black students graduated from college compared to 5.4 percent of white persons in the same age group. With large numbers of black families still living in rural and rural-farm communities in the South this in itself explains the perpetuation of the black struggle to raise socioeconomic status, without a competitive education you can't gain access to higher-skilled and higher-paying jobs.

By the end of 1939, there were 80,000 black college graduates over 25 years of age, but problems in higher education for black students and professors persisted. There were conflicting opinions on the state of black colleges during the Depression, some were able to prosper and move forward during the Depression, recipients of generous donations by northern white philanthropists, while others suffered deep financial problems. Black students were still being discriminated against in gaining admission into white colleges.

The National Youth Administration, a New Deal agency, assisted in providing African-Americans instruction in industrial arts and domestic services. The Legal Defense and Education Fund, created to fight discriminatory laws obstructing the education of African Americans, was lead by Thurgood Marshall, who worked in conjunction with the NAACP to challenge the exclusion of blacks in public colleges. Together they brought forward nine court cases. In 1935, a decision by the Maryland Court of Appeals ordered the University of Maryland to admit African-Americans to the state law school or establish a new separate but equal facility for black students. Reluctant to expend the great cost of establishing a new all-black law school, officials in the university dropped the racial barriers and admitted black students to the institution.

Crime

Bernard Shaw said, *"that poverty is the greatest crime in the world, that it is the root of all other crimes..."* The crimes committed by blacks during the 1930s are characterized by personal violence, offenses against property, gambling, and prostitution, rape was very rare. Homicide among blacks increased during the Depression, statistics for the end of the decade show about 100 murders per year in Harlem. The homicide arrest rate for blacks was more than six times that for whites at 36 per 1000. Associated with problems of poverty and southern culture, rates of violence and homicide were high. Some women resorted to prostitution to survive.

An article in the Norfolk Journal in July of 1932 reported on the 30 most murderous cities in the United States, surprisingly none of the ten largest cities are in the infamous thirty, Memphis, Atlanta, Lexington, KY and Birmingham are the top four. The killings in Birmingham are, "on average, at a rate seven times greater than New York City, more than three times that of Chicago, and 26 times that of Boston, or bluntly stated, every time a person is murdered in Boston, 26 are killed in Birmingham." It was also stated that in the

A Reflection

same year half the total number of victims were killed by policemen for resisting arrest.

Juvenile delinquency was the major crime dilemma in large urban cities, growing as the black populations increased. The problem of juvenile delinquency was higher among blacks than whites in New York, with five times the number of black youths in state and local prisons relative to their portion of the population. Juvenile gangs were becoming a serious problem in urban areas, as gang violence increased other criminal activities followed suit. The notorious Forty Thieves juvenile gang in Philadelphia terrorized the community with countless robberies. The subject of "Negro Delinquency in New York" by Paul Blanchard explained, "A Negro boy may become a burglar because his mother is working every afternoon and evening, and must leave him neglected, and the mother may be compelled to work because some white employers discriminate against the boy's father by refusing to employ Negroes."

During this time in history there were extenuating circumstances that exaggerated the disproportionate number of crimes committed by blacks; racial prejudices were pervasive in the criminal justice system. Blacks were more likely to be suspected, accused, arrested, and physically coerced into confessions by law enforcement officers without evidence. Blacks were more likely to be convicted by white juries, guilt or innocence was irrelevant, and sentenced to longer sentences by white judges, while criminal acts perpetrated by whites against blacks went undocumented. Nevertheless increased incidents of crime were being committed by blacks against other blacks. Causes for increased criminal activity were attributed to "illiteracy, poverty, bad neighborhoods, and low standards of morals." Sociologists concluded that homicides would decrease as education continues to increase.

Scottsboro Boys

Miscarriages of justice against African-Americans in the first half of the twentieth century were commonplace and widespread across the United States. The civil rights of black persons accused of a crime were particularly immaterial when up against the criminal justice system in the South. The Southern atmosphere during the 1930s was filled with the tension and angst of the Depression mixed with hatred and indignation for black people. White mobs would gather without much provocation to exact their own brand of injustice on black alleged law breakers. The motivation for some was racial hate, others to vent the frustrations from their own lives, and to some for the sheer recreation of killing. To describe the convictions of the "Scottsboro Boys" as a miscarriage of justice would be an understatement of epic proportions.

1939

Scottsboro Boys and Attorney Samuel Leibowitz (Image Ownership: Public Domain)

During the Depression years thousands of out-of-work men, black and white, young and old, rode the rails hoboing and looking for jobs. On March 25, 1931, a group of young whites and blacks were riding the Southern Railroad freight from Chattanooga to Memphis. Some of the black youths were headed to Memphis looking for work hauling logs on the river, while some of the whites were returning from a fruitless trip to Chattanooga to work in the cotton mills. One white teenager stepped on the hand of a black teen named Haywood Patterson, who recounted, *"We was just mindin' our own business, when one of them said, "This is a white man's train. All you Nigger bastards unload.' But we weren't goin' nowhere so there was a fight. We got the best of it and threw them off."*

A Reflection

Several of the whites reported to the stationmaster in Stevenson that they had been assaulted by a gang of blacks; he sent a wire forward to Paint Rock, Alabama where a posse gathered and stopped the train. The mob of armed white men rounded up all the black males on the train, nine youths ranging in age from twelve to twenty-one, and two young white women from Huntsville, dressed like men in overalls. One of the women told the gang of white men, *"We've been raped. All those colored boys raped us."* The young men were arrested and taken to Scottsboro.

The lynch mob carrying guns and rope grew larger demanding the boys be brought out, but the governor of Alabama, B.M. Miller, ordered the National Guard to the jail to protect the suspects. The first trial began April 6, 1931 with a crowd of thousands from miles around in attendance, most armed with shotguns, even a brass band came to play. The NAACP hesitated to get involved in the controversy; initially not sure of the innocence of the boys.

The families of the youths had no money, barely able to raise $60 to pay a Chattanooga real estate attorney to represent them, who then advised them to plead guilty. Only four of the young men knew each other before this incident, fearful for their own survival, and knowing they would not be believed they began to blame each other. The trial lasted only three days and all nine were found guilty of rape. All but thirteen year-old Roy Wright were sentenced to death in the electric chair. The Communist Party's League of Struggle for Negro Rights (LSNR) with the International Labor Defense took on the defense of the Scottsboro Boys appealing to the United States Supreme Court and preventing their probable execution.

The second trial had one of the alleged rape victims confessing that she had lied, but to no avail, the jury found the nine youths guilty again. However on June 22, 1933, Judge James Horton set aside the guilty verdict and ordered the third trial. Found guilty again, appealed again, the Supreme Court ruled that Alabama had deliberately excluded blacks from juries, and again overturned the verdicts of guilt. Before the fourth trial, charges were dropped on four defendants, Olen Montgomery, Willie Roberson, Roy Wright, and Eugene Williams after six years in jail, but the remaining five were found guilty again. Eventually, four of those left were paroled, now grown men, Charlie Weems, Andy Wright, Clarence Norris, and Ozie Powell. The last of them, Haywood Patterson escaped in July, 1948, wading through streams by day, protected by compassionate black families at night. He finally hopped on a train to Detroit and was met by his family, free after more that seventeen years.

No other crime in American history had the number of trials, conviction, reversals and retrials as that of the Scottsboro Boys. The case garnered national as well as international attention and protests. Letters of support were written to the President, the Supreme Court, and the governor. The American criminal justice system was actually put on trial and found to be racially biased against African-Americans. These events helped motivate the formation of the NAACP Legal Defense Fund.

Health

Tuberculosis was still the number one cause of death among African-Americans and mortality rates from the disease had began to creep up again during the Depression after declining in the previous decade. Deaths from tuberculosis and pneumonia accounted for more than 30 percent of the total deaths of New York City blacks. Work and living environments contributed to the spread of the disease, ramshackle housing, insufficient nourishment, and having to work while sick without money for medical care added to morbidity rates for black people. Diets were inadequate, consisting mainly of molasses, fatback, and cornbread. The *Report to the President on the Economic Conditions of the South* (1938) estimated that of the employed workers in the South's largest cities, more than half could not afford "an adequate diet."

Private physicians were a luxury that black working-class migrants could not afford, most depended on clinics or went without medical care. Others relied on home remedies or visited spiritualist mediums who worked in black neighborhoods. It wasn't until the 1930s that Harlem Hospital had an integrated professional staff, and they were still overwhelmed by the sheer volume and degree of the health needs of the black community.

Lincoln Hospital's nursing school was one of the best nurse training facilities for blacks in the nation, but once trained, they were still restricted to segregated units in the New York municipal hospital network. Black physicians dealing with racism and segregation found it difficult to acquire internships in hospitals for residency training.

During the 1930s, malaria was infecting African-Americans in the South at higher rates as laborers moved back to the land to scratch a living from the earth. Mosquitoes bred near the moist rich bottom land and transmitted the disease to farm laborers. Dilapidated shacks, inadequate nutrition, and the lack of medical treatment continued to leave blacks at a disadvantage. Public health departments during the Depression lacked the revenue to spray insecticides or purchase the quinine to treat malaria. There were few rural clinics, hospitals, or health care workers. Some counties had no health facilities at all.

A Reflection

Pregnancy and childbirth were to blame for the deaths of more black women between the ages of 15 and 44 years than any other disease with the exception of tuberculosis, and most could have been prevented with basic prenatal care. During the 1930s, over half of the black infants born were delivered by midwives, but in the South about 80 percent of births were attended by midwives. Syphilis was the cause of more than 4000 stillbirths each year.

Infant mortality in New York for blacks was nearly double that of whites; 100 to 59 per 1000 live births, with pneumonia alone accounting for 20 percent of the state's black infant deaths. The maternal mortality in New York during the Depression was the highest among northern states. Poverty and poor health contributed to black mothers dying at twice the rate of white mothers. African-American women had less access to contraceptive services or birth control during these years, with quite a few health professionals believing that African-American women lacked the intelligence to use varied forms of birth control, consequently more black women relied on home remedies and resorted to illegal abortions.

Incidents of venereal diseases were a serious health problem and rising in the 1930s with African-Americans being infected and dying at much higher levels than whites. A 1930 venereal disease survey over six southern states identified Macon County, Alabama as having the highest occurrence of syphilis, 35 percent of the people were infected, with a population that was over 82 percent black. Beginning in 1932, the federal government funded a study of the venereal disease syphilis by the U.S. Public Health Service in Macon County. The Tuskegee Syphilis Study is still considered as one of the most egregious biomedical research experiments in American history.

The U.S. Public Health Service in conjunction with the Tuskegee Institute recruited 399 poor black sharecroppers diagnosed with syphilis and 201 healthy men to be used as human guinea pigs to chart the untreated progression of the disease. The experiment was carried out from 1932 to 1972; the human subjects were told they were being treated for "bad blood," none of the men were told they had syphilis. It's inconceivable that when penicillin was determined to be an effective cure for the disease that researchers withheld treatment from the men, continuing to cruelly exploit the participants for another twenty-five years. By the time the study was shut down in 1972, 28 had died of syphilis, 100 more died of complications related to the disease, 40 of the men's wives had been infected with syphilis, and 19 children were born with the disease.

During the Depression, the Negro Health Movement worked diligently to address the critical health issues in black communities, composed of black health professionals and black laywomen, they educated the communities about health concerns, and conducted health clinics offering physical examinations and inoculations. Their organization of the National Negro Health Week was expanded by the United States Public Health Service with assistance from the Julius Rosenwald Fund to a year-round undertaking called the National Negro Health Week.

Housing

Housing for African-Americans and the poor in the 1930s was at a crisis point across the country with major cities having large numbers of rundown homes and shacks. In 1931, a study ordered by President Hoover concluded that less than half of the homes occupied by African-Americans met modern standards. The typical home on a southern farm had no electricity, no running water, and no indoor bathroom. Black farmers in the South who had lost their land or tenancy became migrant workers living in warehouses provided by the employer or in their cars or tents. Black migrants continued to move north for more sanitary and higher quality dwellings, but housing conditions in urban cities were just as deplorable.

Railroad tracks were still the dividing line of black and white neighborhoods; middle-class blacks who could afford to buy homes outside of urban areas designated for blacks were met with hostility. Incidents in Kansas City, MO where racist whites were using dynamite and fire to destroy the homes of blacks who moved into white neighborhoods were becoming common throughout the nation with the fear that black residents diminished home property values. As overcrowded black communities began to spill over their boundaries, suburban communities began to develop. These all-white towns attracted industry away from the inner cities and stimulated the mass exodus of whites from metropolitan areas. Inflated prices, "redlining," and racism overlooked by government authorities prevented minorities from relocating. Homeownership among blacks continued to fall during this decade, and predominately black neighborhoods were valued at 75 percent less than their white counterparts (Federal Home Loan Bank Board, 1940).

Landlords in large urban cities in New York charged black tenants a premium for the most decrepit residences. Adam Clayton Powell Jr. was quoted on the living conditions of 10,000 Harlem residents; he described them as *"dark, damp dungeons in squalor worse than that of the Arkansas sharecroppers."* In the Bronx, three-room apartments rented to whites for $28 per month were raised to $38 when black tenants moved in. In the mid-1930s, the Public Works Administration, one of the New Deal Agencies, began building large-scale

A Reflection

housing projects as a solution to urban slums and unemployment. Initially public housing projects were to temporarily provide affordable housing to middle-class families who were financially stressed because of the Depression, preferably married couples, with occupancy restricted to persons without criminal records.

The United States Housing Act of 1937 laid the groundwork for 184 housing projects that would encompass 71,699 dwelling units. Housing projects to eradicate slums and overcrowding in urban neighborhoods sprang up in inner cities throughout the nation. The first two public housing projects built in Harlem were the Harlem River Houses in 1936. The second federally funded housing built in the South after projects in Atlanta was the Liberty Square Housing Projects, built for low-income African-Americans in Miami, Florida. The first federally-funded housing project built in Detroit designed for African-Americans was the Brewster Homes, which had 701 units occupied by 1938. In Chicago, there were the Jane Addams Houses, the Julia C. Lathrop Homes, and the Trumbull Park Homes. The PWA constructed 49 low-income housing projects with 14 exclusively for African-Americans. These projects had unintended consequences and contributed to overcrowding by building less units than those demolished.

Family Structure

The majority of African-Americans were still living in stable two parent homes, although there was a slight decline in the number of husband-wife headed families from 80- to 77 percent, and the number of female headed households went from 15- to 18 percent. According to Census data, marriage rates were showing small decreases particularly among black females from the previous decade. Marriage rates are higher in the South than in urban cities in the North, for black males in the age group 40 to 44 years marriage rates were 83 percent in South, 75 percent in the North, and 67 percent in the West, for black females the numbers were 72 percent, 70 percent, and 78 percent respectively.

The difference in the marriage rates between black males and black females reflects the higher mortality rate of black males, with 24 percent of black females over 45 years of age being widowed. Black males were delaying marriage to an older age in comparison to the 1920s, less than 3 percent under the age of twenty years were married, and the adverse labor market was probably a major factor.

The number of illegitimate births rose during the 1930s, up to 16.8 percent after declining during the 1920s. The number of black children living in a home with two parents was close to 76 percent, but black families across the country were having fewer children. Research by Franklin Frazier found that black families with no children under the age of ten ranged from 52.3 percent among those who migrated to the North in cities with populations of 250,000 and 28.5 percent in rural-farm areas. Black farm families were on average 65 percent larger than urban families, and both struggling to feed themselves made conscious choices not to have children.

The Depression wrecked havoc on African-American families throughout the 1930s, between 66- and 75 percent of southern black families needed public assistance to survive, and by the end of the decade the poverty rate among black families was 87 percent. Households needed more income and employers didn't have the money to pay. Southern state and local officials ignored New Deal federal guidelines and paid blacks on relief less than the amount whites were given; in Atlanta blacks were given $19.29 while whites were given $32.66 per month.

Ten percent of black urban households had lodgers and another 10 percent had a grandparent or other relative living in the home. The numbers were less for black rural-farm households with less than four percent having lodgers and around eight percent having a grandparent or other relative living in the home. In black rural-farm households only 1.4 percent had a lodger but over eight percent had other relatives living in the home.

Black family stability was continually challenged by poor living conditions, traditional roles in the family had changed for so many, black men had to depend more on their wives, and children also worked and contributed their wages to the household. In Harlem, family income declined 44 percent. In 1933, a survey found that in 61 percent of the black families sampled, women maintained some sort of employment. In large urban cities in the North with populations over 100,000; 29.5 percent of black households were headed by women compared to 21.7 percent in rural non-farm and 11.5 percent in rural-farm households.

In 1935, the Social Security Act established the Aid to Families with Dependent Children (AFDC) program to allow the states to provide welfare payments for children with a parent absent from the home, unemployed, disabled, or deceased. Some black men were compelled to leave their families in search of work; some joined the military, most with the intention to return. Critics of the AFDC program claimed it contributed to black fathers deserting their families.

Land ownership had risen among farmers to 21 percent, reducing the number of sharecroppers in the South, but acquiring and maintaining credit was still a major

A Reflection

challenge to earning a decent living. Poor and rural communities survived with the support of community churches, lodges and fraternal organizations.

Entertainment

The most chronic side effect of the Great Depression of the 1930s was unemployment. New Deal programs had been implemented to relieve the loss of jobs for those fields strongly impacted by the economic slump. Federal initiatives to address unemployment in cultural fields were under the Works Project Administration (WPA), which established a group of projects under the arts programs, Federal Project Number One, to employ professional artists, writers, and performers. The five components of the project were the Federal Art (FAP), Federal Writers (FWP), Federal Theatre (FTP), Federal Music (FMP), and the Historical Records Survey Projects (HRS). The Federal Arts Project breathed new vitality into the Harlem Renaissance as the Depression sucked the life out of the black community, providing funding and opportunities for black professional artists to develop and create. Projects chronicling the lives of former slaves were also initiated under the sponsorship of these programs.

The Federal Arts project (FAP) was created in 1935 to provide work relief for graphic artists, painters, sculptors, and muralists. Black artists received the same opportunities as others artist, racial discrimination by project administrators was minimal. Sargent Johnson, one of the most prominent artist and sculptors of the Harlem Renaissance, served as a supervisor on the Federal Arts Project. The Art project offered arts education in black communities and blacks contributed significant works during the Depression era. The New York City Project listed 115 black artists in July of 1937, of which three were supervisors. Most of the artists participating were anonymous and little is known about how their careers were affected by the Project, but several gained new audiences including Dox Thrash, Ernest Crichlow, Allan Rohan Crite, Aaron Douglas, and Archibald J. Motley, Jr. Tennessee folk artist and stone carver, William Edmondson, was honored with a one-person exhibition at New York's Museum of Modern Art in 1937, the first African-American artist to receive that merit.

1939

William H. Johnson, Street Life, Harlem, about 1939

William E. Smith, No Body Knows 1930s

Allan Rohan Crite (American, 1910-), Beneath the Cross of St. Augustine, 1936

A Reflection

The Federal Writers' Project funded written works and supported writers during the Depression years. Gifted poet Robert Hayden began working for the Writers' Project researching black history and folk culture in 1936, and Richard Wright wrote and edited projects for the FWP in Chicago. Wright's first book, *Uncle Tom's Children* (1938) was the first prize winner in a writing competition sponsored by the Federal Writers' Project. The FWP strengthened the flood of fiction from black authors that began during the Harlem Renaissance moving it to a higher level as more writers found their voice in protest literature.

Quite a few black writers of the time were influenced by the communist party, subsequently much of the subject matter turned to issues of race, class, and capitalism. Other black authors completing successful works in this decade includes, Langston Hughes, *Not Without Laughter* (1930), George Schuyler, *Black No More* (1931), Sterling Brown, *A Southern Road* (1932), Rudolph Fisher, *The Conjure Man Dies: A Mystery Tale of Dark Harlem*, (1932), Arna Bontemps, *Black Thunder* (1936), and Zora Neal Hurston, *Jonah's Gourd Vine* (1934) and the novel for which she is best known, Their Eyes Were Watching God (1937).

The theatre suffered devastating blows not only from the economics of the depression, but from the growth of the film industry and radio broadcasts. The Federal Theatre Project had black divisions set up in 23 cities called the Negro Theatre Project (NTP) to keep black theatre actors working through the depression. The "Negro Units" were headed by Rose McClendon, a popular black actress and John Houseman. One spectacular production by the New York unit was *Voodoo Macbeth,* which brought real witchdoctors from the Caribbean. Productions from the NTP were credited with the reduction of stereotyped images, bringing live theatre to millions who had never seen it before, and with putting more African-Americans to work in the 1930s than ever before.

Although vaudeville circuits and local theatre were disappearing, all-black theatre productions were popular on Broadway during the Depression. Two plays written for black performers were Marc Connelly's *"The Green Pastures"* which won a Pulitzer Prize, and George Gershwin's *"Porgy and Bess"* which was "one of the most important American operas of the twentieth century." Successful plays written by African-American authors appeared on Broadway, *"Run Little Chillun"*(1933) a folk musical by John Hall and *Mulatto* (1935) by Langston Hughes. *Mulatto* became the longest running black play on Broadway until the 1950s. Hughes interested in "serious colored theatre" founded several black theatre groups in Harlem, Chicago, and Los Angeles, where black stories could be told for the black audience, making social and political statement without fear or embarrassment. He used a variety of subjects for nearly 100 theatrical plays. Later in the decade Hughes became a reporter for the Baltimore *Afro-American*.

The Apollo Theatre purchased by Sidney Cohen in 1932 became a black vaudeville house offering a variety of live entertainment seven days a week during the Depression, top black performers and comics in blackface make-up were regularly featured. In 1934, the Apollo was renovated and a new format geared for black audiences was implemented, "Amateur Night at the Apollo." Ella Fitzgerald was one of the winners in the first year. Billie Holiday also gave her breakthrough performance there that set her apart from other blues singers featuring her own unique style and musical interpretations.

Across the United States more than 70 million movie tickets were sold every week. All-black theatres sprung up in urban cities of the North like Chicago, Detroit, and New York to accommodate black audiences. In the South, balconies were designated for "Negroes" or the theatre was reserved one day for black films and movie-goers. By 1939, there were 400 black theatres. Genres of black films resembled those of Hollywood; musicals, westerns, gangster, and mysteries. The most prominent black producer-director-writer teams of the decade were Oscar Micheaux and Spencer Williams and George and Noble Johnson.

Moving through the 1930s movie audiences wanted higher quality filming and Micheaux's reputation was dwindling. Million Dollar Productions took the next step forward moving black films into the mainstream with an integrated corporation where blacks had control over production. Formed by Ralph Cooper, a musical entertainer, and Harry and Leo Popkin, the quality and style of Million Dollar films were on par with the top Hollywood B studios, finally making black films that were polished productions. Writing and starring in most of the pictures, Ralph Cooper became the first black matinee idol, earning him the title of "the bronze Bogart." The highly successful Million Dollar Productions released twelve films between 1937 and 1940.

Although the movie industry refused to acknowledge African-Americans as equals, they realized that their money was green and had no qualms about pursuing it. The deep pockets of Hollywood began producing all-black movies drawing the audiences of blacks who wanted to watch the more technically advanced productions. African-American actors breaking into Hollywood were limited to maid and butler roles or savages in the jungle during the 1930s. Successful black actors of the period were Louise Beavers, Lincoln "Stepin Fetchit" Perry, Clinton "Dusty" Fletcher, Hattie McDaniel, Herb Jeffries,

A Reflection

Bill Robinson, and Butterfly McQueen. Hattie McDaniel, the first African-American to win an Academy Award answered the criticism of her playing a subservient role saying, "I'd sure rather play a maid than be one."

The 1930s furthered the "golden age of radio," with news broadcasts, comedies, dramas, quiz shows, and lots of music streaming through the receivers of 80 percent of the population that informed and entertained. Radio was a big business with advertisers sponsoring the programming, but with less than 18 percent of black families having a radio in their homes little investment went into black programs except for African-American singers and musicians.

Paul Robeson was a featured singer on a number of programs in 1932 and 1933, while Ethel Waters had her own program. Duke Ellington, Fats Waller, the Mills Brothers, and Cab Calloway were also among the many talented artists who had regular network series. Along with secular music, black gospel music and spirituals were also significant elements of radio programming with choral groups appearing regularly in their own shows or as background singers. The most popular show on the American radio in the 1930s was the Amos and Andy Show even though it was widely protested for its racist stereotypes and negative images from minstrel shows.

The Depression nearly wiped out the music industry with the bulk of record companies going out of business. Kansas City was an oasis during the hard times with jobs and wealth, with more than 100 night clubs and dance halls featuring jazz music, gambling houses, brothels, and the fact the alcohol flowed freely there during prohibition didn't hurt. Kansas City's jazz was bluesy with a freer style and up-tempo beat. Legends playing in the jazz clubs there included Louis Armstrong, Count Basie, Joe Turner, and Charlie Parker. The repeal of prohibition created more night-clubs where jazz musicians had opportunities to work.

In New York, the Harlem Renaissance had lost some of its jauntiness with the Depression, but jazz continued to change and evolve. The restlessness of the people was expressed in the music; synchronized tempos gave way to improvisation and free style play called "hot" jazz. As the decade moved forward orchestras grew larger, and arrangers were necessary to blend the musicians in big bands, lessening the amount of improvisation. This style of jazz music was called swing and it ignited new dance crazes like the "lindy hop" that served to increase its popularity in ballrooms and dancehalls. African-American orchestra leaders included Duke Ellington, Count Basie, and Chuck Webb. Bands alternated playing at the Savoy Ballrooms in Chicago and New York for all-night continuous music. Expressed best by Duke Ellington's hit song, *"It Don't Mean a Thing If It Ain't Got That Swing."* The recording industry was revived with Swing by the end of the decade, in 1939, 50 million records were sold, tremendous growth from 10 million sold in 1932.

Black Athletics

Most professional and amateur athletics were still segregated during the 1930s. Two sports that had always been integrated, albeit at a disadvantage, were boxing and track and field. The premier competitive event in track-and-field was the Olympic Games. Louise Stokes and Tidye Pickett, two African-American women from the Tuskegee Institute, qualified for the 4 x 100- meter relay in the 1932 Olympic Games in Los Angeles. Pure racism kept them from competing; before the race they were substituted on the relay team with two white runners who had not qualified. Two African-American sprinters, Eddie Tolan and Ralph Metcalfe dominated the field in the 1932 games, with Tolan winning the gold in the 100-meter race with a new world record granting a preview to the spectacular performance to come four years later.

In the 1936 Olympic Games Jesse Owens destroyed Hitler's notion of the Germans being the "master race" when he claimed the victory in the 100-meter race before a crowd of 100,000, and earned the crown of the "world's fastest human." Owens continued his conquests winning four gold medals, tying the world record 100-meter race, setting the Olympic record in broad jump, the Olympic record in the 200-meter race, and the Olympic and world record in the 400-meter relay. Sportswriters dubbed Owens as the "greatest track-and-field athlete of all time." Jesse Owens considered his triumph as "the greatest moment of my career," but noted he was offended that President Roosevelt did not acknowledge his performance with an invitation to the white House, a telephone call, or even a telegram of congratulations. Cornelius Johnson, another black U.S.A track-and-field team member broke the Olympic record for high jump.

Two black men reigned supreme in the boxing ring during the 1930s, Joe "the Brown Bomber" Louis and "Hammering" Henry Armstrong. For ten months between 1937 and 1938, Hammering Henry, only 24 years old and an unparalleled boxer, gained and held three titles simultaneously, the featherweight, welterweight, and lightweight championships. Pushed by his manager, Armstrong fought 17 bouts in seven months. His exceptional record had 175 bouts recorded, although the number of actual fights was much higher, closer to 300 bouts.

A Reflection

Joe Louis held the world heavyweight title longer than any other boxer, eleven years, eight months and seven days. Louis became a symbol of strength, invincibility, and pride as a champion for black people throughout the United States. He was able to accomplish what most black people dreamed of; challenging white America and coming out a winner. His first professional fight took place July 4, 1934, and he amassed a record number of victories until June 19, 1936 when he fought Max Schmeling and got his first defeat. The Brown Bomber regained his focus and worked on his comeback, and became the Heavyweight champion after demolishing Jimmy Braddock on June 22, 1937. His prowess in the ring elevated him to hero status. Louis's triumphs in 25 championship fights were not his alone; they became triumphs of all black people, lifting their hopes and spirits during the miserable years of the Depression.

In 1939, Kenny Washington was football's "almost perfect player," gaining 863 yards in 141 carries, completing 32 of 76 passes for 497 yards from his tailback position, leading UCLA to its greatest season in history up to that date. Washington had also been the All-Pacific Coast choice of the previous season. His dreams as a professional player in the NFL would be put on hold where after 31 years of limited integration; African-American athletes were banned in 1933 from participating in the National Football League.

The 1930s were considered the "Golden Years" of black baseball in America. Despite the growing popularity of the Negro Baseball Leagues, they experienced some difficult times during the Depression. The East-West League was formed in 1932 but didn't last the season. The Negro Southern League was the only league left until the National Negro League was formed by Gus Greenlee in 1933. The Southern League merged with some Midwest teams and became the Negro American League.

An all-star game played at Chicago's Comiskey Park, known as the East-West game, was more popular than the World Series and black baseball's biggest payday, drawing between 20,000 and 50,000 fans each year. Greenlee's Pittsburgh Crawfords were the premier team in the 1935 with future Hall-Of-Famers, Satchel Paige, Josh Gibson, Cool Papa Bell, Oscar Charleston, Judy Johnson, and "Double Duty" Radcliffe. By the end of the decade, Cumberland Posey's Homestead Grays had taken over as the team to beat, winning the Negro National League title nine years in a row.

Professional basketball was limited to the New York Rens or the Harlem Globetrotters in the 1930s. The Rens drew crowds of 15,000 wherever they played. Their 1938-1939 season ended with 112 wins and 7 loses priming them for the first world championship basketball tournament. The Rens swept their opponents to victory.

1939

In the women's league, Ora Washington was referred to as "the best Colored player in the world." She earned the national female title in 1930 after a 22-1 record with the Germantown Hornets and led them to win the 1930-1931 Colored Women's National Championship. Washington joined the Philadelphia Tribunes in 1932 as the team's center and coach, and became their leading scorer playing men and women. The Tribune Girls won 11 straight Women's Colored Basketball World's Championships, rarely losing to black or white teams.

Ora Washington, a two sport athlete, played tennis at world class level before she began playing basketball. In the 1930s she competed in both sports, winning the American Tennis Association's national singles title eight times in nine years between 1929 and 1937, and 12 straight double championships between 1924 and 1936. She also won mixed doubles championships in 1939. Helen Moody, the white tennis champion continued to dodge Washington refusing meet her on the court. The quintessential athlete, Washington also became a first-class swimmer and superior baseball player. Unbelievable for an athlete of her caliber Ora Washington had to supplement her income during her playing careers as a housekeeper.

Memorable Moments

James W. Ford was the first African-American to appear on a presidential ticket as a candidate for Vice President for the Communist Party in 1932 and 1936.
"Precious Lord, Take my Hand" was written by Thomas A. Dorsey in 1932.
In 1932, the Black professional basketball team, the Rens, won the first World Championship by beating the Boston Celtics.
Harlem is Heaven was the first all-black film ever made in 1933.
Arthur W. Mitchell of Chicago was the first black democrat elected to Congress in 1934.
Bill "Bojangles" Robinson organizes the Black Actors Guild in 1936.
In 1936, Josephine Baker and the Nicholas Brothers were featured in the Ziegfeld Follies.
Bessie Smith was killed in a car accident on September 26, 1937.
In 1937, in a move that stunned the nation, Roosevelt appointed the first black federal judge, William Hastie.
In 1938, Crystal Bird Fauset was the first African-American woman elected to State Legislator (Pennsylvania) in the United States.
Ethel Waters became the first African-American to star on Broadway in *Mamba's Daughters* in 1939.

A Reflection

In 1939, Billie Holiday recorded her biggest selling record "Strange Fruit."
Lena Horne made her first movie; The Duke is Tops in 1939.
"From Spirituals To Swing," the title of two influential concerts presented by John Hammond to sold-out houses in December of 1938 and 1939, were the first major concerts in Carnegie Hall starring African-American performers in front of an integrated audience. The concerts, sponsored by '*New Masses*', the journal of culture for the Communist Party, showcased African-American music from its raw beginnings in Africa through spirituals and gospel, to the blues, and from jazz and to swing.
Jane M. Bolin became the first African American woman judge in the U.S. domestic relations court of New York City in 1939.
When the Daughter's of the Revolution refused to allow Marian Anderson to sing in Constitution Hall, Eleanor Roosevelt arranged a concert in front of the Lincoln Memorial where on Easter Sunday in 1939 more than 75,000 gathered to hear Marian Anderson sing, and millions more heard her on the radio. She sang Negro spirituals.
In 1939, Augusta Savage's sculpture "Lift Every Voice and Sing" is shown at the New York World's Fair, it is destroyed after the fair, Savage lacked the funds to finish the piece.

Augusta Savage (1939) Lift Every Voice and Sing

1939

Reflection of a Decade

White Houses
Your door is shut against my tightened face,
And I am sharp as steel with discontent;
But I possess the courage and the grace
To bear my anger proudly and unbent.
The pavement slabs burn loose beneath my feet,
A chafing savage, down the decent street
And passion rends my vitals as I pass,
Where boldly shines your shuttered door of glass.
Oh I must search for wisdom every hour,
Deep in my wrathful bosom sore and raw,
And find in it the letter of your law!
Oh I must keep my heart inviolate
Against the potent poison of your hate.
---Claude McKay, 1932

The decade leading to 1939 served as a wake-up call after the emotional exuberance of the 1920s. The reality that a change in geographical location doesn't necessarily bring changes in the social and economical situation would not be ignored during the Great Depression. Large numbers of black migrants who had found employment in the Northern and Midwestern urban cities now suffered through joblessness and deprivation in several categories. Nevertheless, with increased racial consciousness African-Americans strengthened their resolve, became more pro-active through organized protests for political representation, employment opportunities, and improved housing. By 1939, thousands of blacks in large southern cities were registered to vote.

The strong leadership of A. Philip Randolph and the National Negro Congress, supported by the black press and black churches, were pivotal in continuing progress for African-Americans economically during this decade despite the setbacks of Depression. Small gains were made in education, health, and housing but the wide disparities between whites and blacks remained intact. Black families were negatively impacted by the intensified poverty and unemployment, and the relief program did nothing to hold poor families together. More responsibility for maintaining households were shifted to

A Reflection

the shoulders of black women, and children left to their devices while parents worked sometimes drifted into juvenile delinquency.

The Depression acted as a catalyst encouraging black workers to unite in labor unions that fought for higher-pay and better working environments. New Deal programs in the latter-half of the decade were more effective in opening doors and creating jobs. A black working class developed that was more educated and made enough money to buy homes. Research conducted by E. Franklin Frazier documented changes among African-Americans that showed upward mobility, increased home ownership, higher education attainment, better jobs, and less segregation in northern states. Unfortunately these changes were not seen for the majority of black people, specifically those living in the South.

Although Black people were united by race, history, culture, and in their battle against Jim Crow, they were beginning to become stratified by income, education, and generational lines. As the economy improved, re-employment for black workers trailed far behind leaving many dependent on relief and public service programs. There was still much work to be done towards racial equality and civil rights.

1949

Observation of the decade leading up to 1949 reveals critical points in the evolution of black people in America. As the Depression years drew to a close, new winds of optimism about the future began to blow, northerly winds that beckoned black people to search for opportunities in the "promise land" they'd heard so much about. Several monumental events served to chart the course for the next phase in the journey altering more than a few aspects of black society. World War II was the fundamental catalyst that restored the momentum of the African-American exodus out of the South. The United States' entrance into war created a massive labor shortage in the defense industry; workers were desperately needed in shipbuilding, munitions plants, and military aircraft factories. African-Americans languishing in the South were more than anxious to answer the call, wanting a respite from the horrors of racism, inadequate education for their children, and trying to improve their lives with next to nothing.

Blacks stepped up to fight for democracy in foreign lands, notwithstanding the fact they were short of equality in their own homeland. More than 2.5 million African-Americans registered for the draft and more than one million served in the military. Before World War II, blacks were excluded from flying for the U.S. military; The Tuskegee Airmen

A Reflection

were the first African-American military pilots after 20 years of effort to obtain funding for training. The Tuskegee pilots provided escorts for bombers over Germany, winning glory for never having lost any plane they guarded.

Even as more doors were opened, segregation still ruled the day. Black soldiers and civilians in war-related industries were relegated to the lowest level of service in menial positions, but for many that was a large step forward. Industrial jobs paid Blacks more money than they had ever earned and many moved up to middle-class status.

The Second Migration created more conflict and frustrations among whites and native blacks who felt overwhelmed by overcrowding. This phase of migration had similar destinations from the first beginning in 1910; Chicago, Detroit, New York, Philadelphia, but larger numbers were heading out west to California. As the numbers of blacks migrating to urban American regained steam, whites were leaving metropolitan areas for outlying suburbs with manufacturing and retail facilities following close behind them. This de-industrialization of cities had devastating ramifications for the African-American community and led to more racial segregation. Racial tensions were aggravated during the War and race riots exploded in Detroit, Harlem, and Los Angeles.

Demographics

Figure 16.—PERCENTAGE OF NEGROES IN THE TOTAL POPULATION, BY STATES: 1950

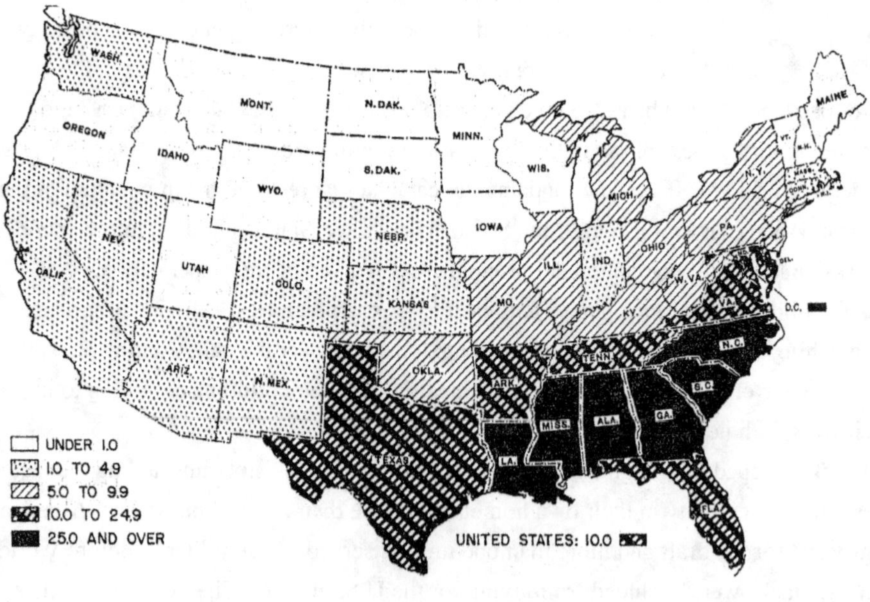

UNDER 1.0
1.0 TO 4.9
5.0 TO 9.9
10.0 TO 24.9
25.0 AND OVER

UNITED STATES: 10.0

1949

By the end of 1949, the life expectancy for African-Americans is 62 years, with the median age being 26 years. There are 94.3 black males to every 100 females, with the ratio even lower in urban areas with 90 males to 100 females. The black population in America was expanding from the last decade; blacks made up 10.0 percent of the population, with numbers around 15,042,286. Although 68 percent of blacks lived in the Southern region of the country, the population of black people living in urban areas continued to rise with 62 percent living in cities, 17 percent in rural-nonfarm communities, and 21 percent in rural-farm areas. Georgia led all the states with the largest black population of 1,084,927, with Mississippi being a close second, but the top five cities with the largest black population were all above the Mason-Dixon Line, New York, Chicago, Philadelphia, Baltimore, and Washington, D.C.

The calamities of the Southern agricultural industry in the previous decades devastated farmers, tenant-farmers and sharecroppers, fewer were needed in the advent of mechanized farming, displacing growing numbers to the North, Midwest, and towards the Pacific coast. Between 1940 and 1949, about 1.5 million African-Americans relocated out of the South. During this second wave of the Great Migration, blacks traveled from Alabama to Cleveland and Detroit, from Mississippi and Arkansas they ventured to Chicago, from Georgia and the Carolinas that went north to Philadelphia, New York, and Boston, and increased numbers from Louisiana, Arkansas, and Texas made the long journey out to California. In total, 450,000 African Americans moved to the Western region of the country during the 1940s, compared to barely 49,000 in the previous decade. Migrants were concentrated in Nevada, California, Washington, and Oregon.

According to the 1940 Census, there were nearly 7.5 million blacks of voting age in the country, but more than 5 million are still living in the South where voting rights were restricted by law or threat of reprisal. With such large numbers unable or unwilling to vote, black majority populations in over 100 counties were not politically represented.

The annual income for a black male at the end of the decade was $1761.06 compared to $2984.96 for a white male, and the annual incomes for black and white females were $992.35 and $1781.96 respectively. Income levels for blacks in urban areas were more favorable than in rural areas, with the median farm income being $600.00 annually. The buying power of blacks in the Southeast region of the country was $3.5 billion, having increased 250 percent over 1939. The key factor was the shift from farm jobs to industrial labor.

A Reflection

Mood of the Black Community

"We're mad as hell, and we're not going to take this anymore," a quote from the movie Network, describes the emotions running through black communities across the country. African-Americans were frustrated, becoming more militant, and less accommodating. The deepened hatred and aggravation of white society was answered by black people with grievances of their own. The black population began to take America to task for the hypocrisy and contradictions evident throughout the nation concerning freedom and social equalities in other countries. They became cognizant of the American government extolling the virtues of democracy around the world while denying their own citizens equal rights and participation in the political system. Blacks wanted more power and security prompting 1.5 million to join labor unions.

Black war veterans had no desire to return to the Southern farms, portrayed by some as restless and ambitious, they were ready to reap the benefits of their service to the country. Feeling they had a right to more of the American dream, they were working for it, fighting for it, and dying for it. Resentment over the lack of acceptance and continued discrimination, police brutality, and racist attempts to put veterans back "in their place" exploded into destructive race riots in 1943. The decade's worst riot took place in Detroit provoked by disputes over housing.

The year 1943 saw the second Harlem riot. A black soldier knocked down a policeman who then shot him. An onlooker shouted that the soldier had been killed, and this news spread throughout the black community and provoked rioting. A force of 6,600, made up of city police, military police and civil patrolmen, in addition to 8,000 State Guardsmen and 1,500 civilian volunteers was required to end the violence. Hundreds of businesses were destroyed and looted with the property damage approaching $225,000. Overall, six people died and 185 were injured. Five hundred people were arrested in connection with the riot.

The race riots were followed by a resurgence of the Ku Klux Klan and violence against African-Americans in the South, and there was additional retaliation in response to anti-discrimination legislation. African-Americans had declared their own war against discrimination. Boycotts, sit-ins, marches, and freedom rides were spreading like brush fire fanned by the impatience and energy of black youths who felt their time had come.

World War II brought a host changes, money from better jobs gave black people more stability and financial security, they were able to buy the food and clothes they needed and became healthier, but the effects weren't all positive. Segregation in the workplace had ebbed, but became more overt in places of entertainment, restaurants, theatres, dancehalls, and even at hospitals. Poverty had once unified the black community, personal identity was in the shared struggle, but factions began to drift apart, and church attendance decreased. As more blacks prospered intra-racial tensions between the classes surfaced. The black middle-class regarded the poor as lazy, self-destructive, and criminal. New migrants were seen as additional competition that lowered wages for the limited unskilled and domestic jobs available for black people.

The Second Great Migration

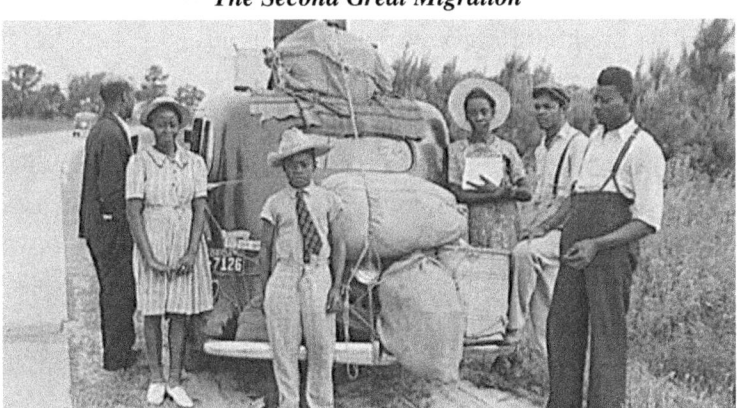

Library of Congress, Prints and Photographs Library of Division, FSA/OWI Collection

The 1940's were marked by World War II and the second Great Migration. The proportion of African-Americans living in urban areas expanded to roughly 50 percent. Several factors contributed to the revival of the mass departure of blacks out of the South. The cotton economy was still in decline, and nearly all new southern industries and factories wouldn't hire unemployed blacks, and relief payments were insufficient in sustaining a family. The North and West offered solutions to these troubles in the form of wartime jobs. This second migration was much larger, more blacks migrated during the 1940s than all three previous decades combined.

Newer black migrants tended to be already urbanized coming from southern cities and towns. Travel in this phase was more often by automobile or buses than by train as with the previous migrants beginning in 1910. The latter were more ambitious, better educated, with more urban skills to apply in their new homes. The principal problem of the second flow of migrants was not discrimination in employment; their major issue was inadequate housing.

A Reflection

Greater numbers of migrants headed into Chicago, at one period in the 1940s, over 3,000 blacks arrived by train in the city each week. Chicago had become the black capital of America. An editorial in the *Chicago Defender* acknowledged Robert Abbott, its late publisher, as the Moses of the first Great Migration and applauded his efforts, but then objected to the second migration, seeing it as an unbefitting solution to the problems of black people. The article conveyed that the North was not the "promised land" or the final road to freedom, the problems of African-Americans were more economical than regional (Chicago Defender, Dec.18, 1943). In all their efforts black people couldn't escape segregation, overloaded schools, or job discrimination.

Racial animosity was attributed to overcrowded black ghettos bursting at the seams and spilling out in white areas. A process referred to as decentralization was beginning in urban centers. As the numbers of blacks migrating to urban American regained steam, whites were leaving metropolitan areas for outlying suburbs with manufacturing and retail facilities following on their heels. This de-industrialization of cities had devastating implications for the African-American community and led to more racial segregation. The reduction in industry translated into diminished employment opportunities and the deterioration of living conditions with more poverty.

Political Climate

Franklin D. Roosevelt won a third term in 1940 and a fourth term in 1944 as president of the United States with the support of the Southern Democrats, labor unions, and African-American voters. Roosevelt continued to ride the fence between supporting civil rights and anti-lynching legislation and alienating racist southern Democratic supporters, but as the nation prepared for war black soldiers and civilians were no longer willing to accept the status quo. Black leadership took this opportunity to focus the fight for equal treatment and opportunities in the military services. President Roosevelt, wanting to stay neutral between the armed services and civil rights leaders, advised the army to institute a quota system and accepted a compromise that admitted black soldiers in numbers proportionate to their numbers in the national population. However, black enlisted men would continued to be segregated in all-black units in each branch, classified as unfit for combat, and restricted to menial and support duties of cleaning and serving food to officers.

In September of 1940, A. Philip Randolph, the NAACP, and the Urban League, unsatisfied with these concessions, joined forces to urge President Roosevelt to desegregate the military, allow black soldiers to serve in combat, and eliminate discrimination in defense industries, but he was not persuaded. Randolph advised black men to ignore the draft until Truman integrated the armed forces. Randolph also proposed a March on Washington, scheduled on July 1, 1941, to pressure the White House to integrate the armed services and eliminate discriminatory policies in the federal government. One week before the march was to commence; Roosevelt issued the Executive Order 8802, which established the Fair Employment Practices Committee (FEPC). The order prohibited discrimination in hiring by the federal government and defense industries based on race, color, creed, or national origin. Unfortunately, military services evaded his order and remained segregated until1943, and banned black soldiers from combat until 1944.

Harry Truman succeeded to the presidency in 1945, after Roosevelt died four months into his fourth term, and presided over the end of World War II on August 14, 1945. Truman, born and raised in Missouri, adopted the racist attitudes of those around him, but after coming into public service he recognized the U.S. Constitution protected the rights of all Americans. Campaigning for senator he stated,

> "I believe in brotherhood….of all men before the law….if any (one) class or race can be permanently set apart from, or pushed down below the rest in politics and civil rights, so may any other class or race……and we say farewell to the principles on which we count our safety…….The majority of our Negro people find but cold comfort in our shanties and tenements. Surely, as free men, they are entitled to something better than this."

Truman became the first president to address civil rights issues of African-Americans since Lincoln, and the Ku Klux Klan voiced their disapproval of Truman and his civil rights stand. Truman stated his reaction to the escalation of racial violence in the nation, *"My forebears were Confederates… but my stomach turned over when I learned that Negro soldiers, just back from overseas, were being dumped out of Army trucks in Mississippi and beaten. Whatever my inclinations as a native of Missouri might have been, as President I know this is bad. I shall fight to end evils like this"*

In 1946, Truman formed the Committee on Civil Rights to investigate the status of civil rights in the U.S. and provide recommendations to advance and protect the civil rights for American citizens. The final report issued in 1947, called "To Secure These Rights," admonished the country for their treatment of African-Americans while claiming to be the world leader of democracy. The committee advised strengthening civil rights laws,

A Reflection

establishing a permanent federal organization to monitor civil rights, declaring lynching a federal offense, and eradicating poll taxes.

In 1948, President Harry Truman declared that all the recommendations should be implemented and issued two executive orders that banned segregation in the armed forces and racial discrimination in civil service. As a result, Truman received the black vote in the 1948 election, winning the close race, and celebrated with an integrated inauguration. Segregation still reigned at the end of Truman's presidency, the laws were in place, but the states had no intention of implementing them.

During 1949, only 750 thousand blacks are registered to vote, but the black vote was very influential in the North. In this decade, 24 blacks were serving in state legislatures in northeastern states. William L. Dawson, the most powerful black politician in America, was elected as a Democratic Representative from Illinois in the seventy-eighth Congress, serving from January 3, 1943 until his death in 1970. Ralph Bunch, as a diplomat and ardent mediator was able to accomplish the seemingly impossible by negotiating the 1949 armistice between one-year-old Israel and its Arab neighbors.

Leadership

Leadership for African-Americans during this decade converged from a number of varied sources. There was the NAACP, A. Philip Randolph, CORE, the Urban League, the CIO, politicians on the local, state, and national levels, and the Clergy. Military spending for war created industrialized jobs and lifted the nation out of the Depression, changing the focus of the struggle from the economic disadvantages of the 1930s to racial prejudice, the fight was no longer against corporations and the federal government, but against morality and injustice. The most significant organization to emerge to the forefront in the 1940s was the Congress of Racial Equality (CORE). This racially mixed group was formed by the pacifist Fellowship of Reconciliation. James Farmer a divinity graduate from Howard University was one of the black charter members.

The NAACP regained its position of major influence during this time with its membership growing from 50,000 at the beginning of the decade to over 500,000 by the end of the war. The second migration afforded the NAACP with a new weapon in their battles for justice; the concentration of the black vote in urban cities. This newfound political strength that swung the close presidential election in 1944 and 1948 enabled the NAACP to widen their field into political activism. The NAACP persisted in their use of legal tactics and lobbying to address discrimination and inequality with Thurgood Marshall as their Chief Counsel, attacking the foundation of the Plessy v. Ferguson doctrine of "separate but equal" before the Supreme Court, and Clarence M. Mitchell, the chief lobbyist for the NAACP, was instrumental in the integration of the armed forces in 1948.

A. Philip Randolph kept his focus on economic justice, addressing the exclusion of blacks from defense industry employment. After an unsuccessful meeting with President Roosevelt that included Walter White, president of NAACP, and a representative from the Urban League, Randolph ramped up his use of Gandhian techniques in his mass direct-action campaign to march on Washington in 1941. Members of the Brotherhood lobbied the march in national defense factories, mines, and mills. The goal of the March on Washington for Jobs and Equal Participation in National Defense was to pressure the FDR administration to eliminate racial discriminatory hiring practices in defense industries. The notion of the march was enough to persuade Roosevelt to establish the Fair Employment Practices Commission (FEPC), and Randolph in turn canceled the march.

The Congress of Racial Equity (CORE) was founded in 1942 in Chicago by a group of college students with a desire to change racist attitudes, and functioned as a Civil Rights organization. CORE was a pioneer of non-violent direct action protests in the 1940s, using small groups to conduct "sit-ins" to desegregate public accommodations, housing, and the workplace. Near the end of the decade, there were 13 CORE chapters, with each raising funds that were primarily used at the local level. CORE chapters organized several non-violent "sit-ins," picket lines, and boycotts in the North and Midwest in efforts to desegregate schools and lunch counters, and were successful in integrating public facilities in the North.

The Congress of Industrial Organizations was open to blacks and was the leader in organizing labor unions. The Civil Rights struggle and the (CIO) had some common agendas in the 1940s that were implicitly intertwined. The CIO pledged their full support behind the fight against terror in southern states. Expansion of the CIO into the South was essential to their future success, and the South was home to the largest number of organized workers and African-Americans. The mobilization of the black workers in the South was invaluable in the fight for civil rights. In 1944, black union membership totaled more than 1,250,000, with most in large CIO unions. John White explained, *"The labor movement gave black people the opportunity to do things that the civil rights movement gave them the right to do."*

A Reflection

William L. Dawson, the third black elected to Congress after the turn of the century and the only African-American serving in Congress during this time, spoke out against the poll tax, which discriminated against poor voters, and prevented many blacks from voting. Dawson was also opposed to the Winstead Amendment, which would have allowed military personnel to decide whether they would serve in racially integrated units, and he was credited with its legislative defeat. In 1949, Dawson became the first African American to chair a regular Congressional Committee on the House Committee on Expenditure in Executive Departments.

Adam Clayton Powell Jr., a civil rights activist, succeeded his father as pastor of the Abyssinian church in Harlem. Powell Jr. built the church membership up to 13,000 forming a power base that he used to attack racism in the military and at home during the war. In 1941, Powell organized the bus boycott against the Fifth Avenue Bus and New York Omnibus companies for their refusal to hire black drivers. In collaboration with the Harlem Labor Union (HLU) and the National Negro Congress (NNC), Harlem residents boycotted the buses of these companies for close to a month. Their successful campaign led to the hiring of 200 black bus drivers and mechanics by the two transit authorities.

Powell also led a fight for black pharmacists who could not get employment in Harlem drugstores. Popularity from his work in the community moved him into politics and he was elected to the New York City council in 1941. Adam Clayton Powell Jr. was elected to the U.S. House of Representatives in 1944, winning the Harlem seat created in 1942, becoming the first African-American to represent New York, and the second black member of congress.

Civil Rights Movement

The birth of the Civil Rights Movement was after a long gestational period that included the formation of a mindset that could wait no longer. Tolerance and conciliation towards racism, second-class citizenship, and injustice had run its course. The courage and boldness of black war veterans was contagious, and black people were ready to demand equality and their civil rights. They would no longer be passive victims of oppression in a country they had defended. A. Philip Randolph realized that traditional methods of negotiating were ineffective and proposed the March on Washington Movement.

> "In this period of power politics, nothing counts but pressure, and still more pressure, through the tactic and strategy of broad, organized,

aggressive mass action behind the vital and important issues of the Negro. To this end, we propose that ten thousand Negroes MARCH ON WASHINGTON FOR JOBS IN NATIONAL DEFENSE AND EQUAL INTEGRATION IN THE FIGHTING FORCES OF THE UNITED STATES."

Using the power of the Brotherhood of Sleeping Car Porters, Randolph helped to mobilize masses of black working people as well as middle- and upper-class blacks who would protest on their own behalf. The movement was joined by the NAACP, the Urban League, fraternal organizations, and the churches. The march was scheduled for July 1, 1941 with estimates of 100,000 people participating. After Roosevelt made concessions and the march was cancelled, the MOWM organized rallies throughout the summer of 1942. The MOWM symbolized the power of a mass movement and its ability to effect change for achieving civil rights that could not be achieved in the courts or with lobbying.

PROGRAM OF THE MARCH ON WASHINGTON MOVEMENT

1. We demand, in the interest of national unity, the abrogation of every law which makes a distinction in treatment between citizens based on religion, creed, color, or national origin. This means an end to Jim Crow in education, in housing, in transportation and in every other social, economic, and political privilege. Especially, we demand, in the capital of the nation, an end to all segregation in public places and in public institutions.
2. We demand legislation to enforce the Fifth and Fourteenth Amendments guaranteeing that no person shall be deprived of life, liberty or property without due process of law, so that the full weight of the national government may be used for the protection of life and thereby may end the disgrace of lynching.
3. We demand the enforcement of the Fourteenth and Fifteenth Amendments and the enactment of the Pepper Poll Tax bill so that all barriers in the exercise of suffrage are eliminated.
4. We demand the abolition of segregation and discrimination in the army, navy, marine corps, air corps, and all other branches of national defense.

Significant gains were made in the civil rights battle during the 1940s. The Supreme Court ruled that state laws calling for segregated buses traveling interstate were unconstitutional. Voter registration in Texas and Georgia was rising.

A Reflection

Race Riots

There were more than 200 race riots recorded during the 1940s, severe riots erupted in New York, Detroit, and Los Angeles. The demands of World War II and the added competition for jobs and housing stressed the limits of tolerance for everyone. Tempers flared and violence erupted with little provocation. Much of the unrest was instigated by rival gangs of black and white youths, but increasing reports from Texas, Mississippi, and Georgia told of black soldiers in uniform being shot and killed by policeman and civilian whites in cold blood. White women giving false accusations of rape have been the motivation behind scores of lynchings and sit at the base of quite a few race riots including the incident in Beaumont, Texas during this same year. After two days of violent mayhem by white hoodlums who looted and burned 200 homes of black residents, two people were left dead without cause.

The most brutal riot took place in Detroit, Michigan. Dating back to the 1920s, Detroit had been a stronghold for the Ku Klux Klan, and the growing population of blacks in the city stretched the racial tensions to a breaking point on June 20, 1943. It began at Belle Isle, an amusement park and picnic area. Fist fights between teenagers were not unusual, but white sailors jumped in the melee on the side of the white youths. While the conflict spread, a mob of 5000 whites gathered at the entrance to attack black patrons of the park. Rumors of the root of the riot incensed both blacks and whites and the slugfest escalated to the looting and bloodshed in the black part of town called "Paradise Valley" and then spread to other sections with white-owned stores. Blacks exiting a movie theatre downtown were attacked as the mob traveled; more were attacked on street cars riding to work. By the end of the next day, 6000 U.S. Army Troops had to be called in to subdue the pandemonium. Over the course of two days, 25 blacks and nine whites had been killed, 17 of the blacks had been killed by white policemen. Around 700 were injured and property damage was estimated to be above $2 million.

One month later another race riot broke out in Harlem, New York on August 1, and 2, 1943, incited by a rumor that a black soldier had been killed by a white police officer. The U.S. Army was called again to end the chaos. In the aftermath of 16 hours of rioting, six had been killed, 500 injured, and 359 had been arrested. U.S. troops occupied the city of Detroit until January of 1944; it was six months before President Roosevelt felt it was safe to pull them out.

1949

Black Churches

Black churches maintained their leadership role as the center of the African-American community in this decade. According to Census data, there were 34 predominately black denominations. The National Baptist Convention of America was the largest with 4.4 million members. Urban churches continued to grow larger, as did their resources, increasing their stability and financial independence. The Federal Council of Churches proposed the merger of various denominations to pool resources for a concentrated effort to tackle the serious issues of the black community. A number of these interdenominational groups were formed, the Council of Negro Churches, the Federal Council of Churches, and the Fraternal Council of Negro Churches which had 5 million members. The primary responsibilities of these groups were to address the economic conditions, crime, and educational shortcomings of black people. E. Franklin Frazier (1993) characterized the black church: *"for the Negro masses in their social and moral isolation in American Society, the Negro Church has been a nation within a nation,"*

Midway through the 1940s, racial conflicts became more severe. Leadership in black churches was committed to the fight for anti-lynching legislation and civil rights, pastors preached for victory over racial hatred and discrimination, and members provided the numbers for mass action campaigns and protests. The greatest force in membership was in the Baptist and Methodist churches of the South. During the war, black churches joined in the movement for greater participation in defense programs. Letters were written to the president and secretaries of the Navy and Army voicing church opposition to the segregation of armed forces. A spokesman for the CME church gave a statement to the *Defender*, Feb. 1941, *"We condemn with all possible emphasis the widespread discrimination, prejudice, and unfair treatment which is afforded Negro citizens in the National Defense Program."*

Black churches supplied a communication network for organizations like the NAACP, the Urban League, and smaller local groups, donating revenue and opening their buildings for meetings. A united call for justice after the end of the war resonated from churches throughout the nation. Church youth groups were involved in direct-action protests in their communities against discrimination during these years; precursors for the youth-led protests yet to come. These protests during the war and after were interpreted as a lack of loyalty. Rev. Ray testified before the House Committee on un-American activities in July 16, 1949: "Race Dissatisfied, Not Disloyal"

"As religious leaders we have no sympathy with any movement which

A Reflection

seeks to overthrow this government by violence. We do, however seek to over throw an intangible empire which exists within our government and many of our land. It is the empire which shelters injustice, oppression, exploitation, segregation, discrimination, ill-will, and all the inconsistencies which make for separation, tension and strife. It is against that empire that we wage war." (New York Amsterdam News)

The Black Press

The Negro Newspaper Publishers Association (NNPA) was founded at the beginning of the decade. Their mission was to *"promote the interest of the Black Press by securing unity and action in all matters relative to the profession of journalism and the business of publishing,"* they soon became the most effective national trade association for black publishers. By 1949, the black press had become a powerful force in the African-American community in the struggle for civil rights and social equality.

The numbers of black newspapers multiplied and grew stronger through their monopoly of black readers. In this year there were 210 newspapers with circulations over two million, and an additional one hundred religious and general magazines. The top four black newspapers of the day were the *Pittsburgh Courier*, the *Baltimore Afro-American*, the *Chicago Defender*, and the *Norfolk Journal and Guide*. The *Baltimore Afro-American* had the highest circulation on the Atlantic coast in the 1940s, and was the first black newspaper to have foreign correspondents reporting on World War II. The *New York Amsterdam News* achieved its greatest readership during the war pushing for the desegregation of the U.S. armed forces, as did the *Norfolk Journal and Guide*.

Black newspapers had waged aggressive crusades against Jim Crow in the South that included "Don't Buy Where You Can't Work" campaigns, nationwide protests of lynching and police brutality, integration of professional baseball, and many forms of racial injustice through the press. The inception of World War II created a quandary for black newspapers, on one hand they supported the fight for democracy, but on the other had they objected to the discrimination in the military. Most papers encouraged blacks to enlist and printed representations of the dedication and bravery they exhibited in the war, but black editors were also liberal in their criticism of federal policies that discriminated against black soldiers and civilians.

The *Pittsburgh Courier* waged a campaign called "Double V" during World War II, standing for "victory overseas and victory at home" over racial prejudice. A number

1949

of other black newspapers united in the campaign and circulations escalated, and the *Couriers'* reached 270,000. The "Double V" campaign was very popular in the black community and had a theme song, pens, and badges.

Some official viewed the "Double V" campaign as un-American, and accused the black press of spreading discontent and encouraging violence. The Houston Informer printed *"....since the Black man fought to make the world safe for Democracy; he now demands that American be made safe and maintained safe for black Americans."* J. Edgar Hoover's Federal Bureau of Investigation (FBI) had been monitoring black newspapers since World War I and was worried about the increased militancy voiced in the black press. During the War, black editors were monitored and investigated by seven government agencies, the FBI, the War Department, the US Post Office, the Justice Department, and the Office of Censorship. More so, the War Production Board was accused of restricting newsprint supplies to black newspapers.

President Roosevelt was being pressured by J. Edgar Hoover and his FBI to bring sedition charges against the black press, but Frances Biddle, the Attorney General, was a staunch advocate of freedom for the press, and put a halt to the FBI court actions. Charlotta Bass, publisher of the California Eagle, was one of the black editors targeted for investigation by the FBI as a member of the communist party. Bass had been an avid fighter against the criminal justice system and their unfair treatment of minorities and used the Eagle to expose the rampant police brutality in the city, some readers wary of being associated with the paper chose the more conservative Los Angeles Sentinel.

***

John H. Johnson, a poor college student, prepared a monthly digest of newspaper articles for his employer Supreme Life Insurance. This digest inspired him to replicate the "Reader's Digest" for African-Americans, the publication was to include history, literature, arts, and cultural issues. Johnson offered subscriptions to policyholders of Supreme Life and three thousand signed up. He published the first Negro Digest in 1942 and in six months the circulation was 50,000.

Johnson's next venture was to create a magazine that would *"show not only the Negroes but also white people that Negroes got married, had beauty contests, gave parties, ran successful businesses, and did all the other normal things of life."* The new magazine was called "Ebony" and its first run of 25,000 copies was completely sold out. Johnson's magazines were among the first publications that attracted corporate advertising.

A Reflection

The unprecedented circulation of black newspapers attracted large corporations wanting to place ads in the papers; however, the papers soon discovered that the lucrative ads for cars and department stores would be withdrawn if the editorials were too confrontational or radical. Some black newspapers dependent on the revenue from ads used a more restrained tone.

Employment

The employment picture of 1949 had not changed much from the previous decade. Seventy-five percent of black men were still employed in unskilled jobs as janitors, porters, cooks, and laborers. Fifty percent of black women worked as maids or domestics, and 20 percent were employed in service work. At the beginning of the 1940s, the job market rebounded from the dearth of employment during the Depression to a surplus of industrial jobs prompted by the demand for war-related supplies. Despite Roosevelt's Executive Order 8802, many large industrial corporations still refused to hire blacks. Even black skilled workers were continually refused work in defense industry companies. Some companies gave flimsy explanations citing the safety of the workers, while governmental agencies claimed they had no legal recourse to force private companies to employ blacks.

The aircraft industry was particularly egregious in their prejudice against African-American workers; several were investigated for the racial discrimination in hiring. The Consolidated Aircraft Company allegedly stated to the NAACP that they would not hire blacks in skilled or semi-skilled positions. Edgar Gott, vice president of the company, stated his belief that his white skilled workers would not work with blacks, denying the allegation he also said, *"We have in the past employed Negroes in positions which they as individuals were capable of filling and will continue to do so."* The positions that Gott spoke of were nine lavatory janitors out of 16,000 employees. The president of North American Aviation stated, *"Under no circumstances will Negroes be employed by his company except as janitors, regardless of their training as aircraft workers."* Republic Aviation had only one black employee out of 2400, classified as a chauffeur.

African-American workers had gained two allies in the fight for equality in hiring practices, the CIO and the federal government. Powerful labor unions admitted black workers and challenged workplace discrimination, and the federal government had been pressured to ban discrimination in the hiring and promotion of black workers in war-related factories. The UAW was racially progressive and partnered with many industrial union movements seeking equality in the workplace. The labor movement had advanced further in desegregation and equality than the rest of American society. The United States was then in the challenging position of having to practice what she preached. The median income of employed black workers rose from 41 to 60 percent of the median white income from the beginning of the decade.

By 1949, high unemployment was still an issue. Layoffs came after the end of World War II, along with cutbacks in hours for most workers. War contracts valued close to 2.4 billion dollars were cancelled, and price controls were lifted. Unemployment was a persistent problem in urban areas where competition for jobs was high. Black unemployment was double that of whites, approximately 28 percent, and even higher for black youth, around 40 percent, and pay for white youths was $17.90 per week nearly double the $9.70 for blacks.

The standard of living for many in the black community began to deteriorate. Only 32 percent of the jobs held by blacks paid a living wage, 60 percent earned incomes less than $3000 per year. Unexpectedly at the end of the decade, 70 percent of blacks worked in service jobs, not in manufacturing or industrial work. More jobs were reserved for whites and factories were being built in suburban communities in efforts to escape union organization in the cities and large black populations.

The CIO and labor unions helped African Americans advance into more skilled jobs and supervisory positions, by mid-decade there were 500,000 black members in CIO unions. However most of the improvements in labor movement were in the Northern states. The Southern white employers stood obstinate against any progressive change, refusing to hire any qualified African-American veterans in white-collar positions. Although they were to receive preference, black veterans made up the majority of the unemployed in most cities.

Black Businesses

The buying power of blacks in the Southeast region of the country was $3.5 billion, having increased 250 percent over 1939. The key factor was the shift from farm jobs to industrial labor. Black businesses began to prosper again in the 1940s with the expanded markets from the second migration, increased incomes, and greater purchasing power of African-Americans. Hotels, restaurants, retail stores, movie theatres, and a host of public places remained segregated by law in the South and by custom in the North. Black businesses provided services and filled the needs of black clientele that were shut out

A Reflection

of white establishments. Businesses included restaurants, rooming houses, barber and beauty shops, retail shops and nightclubs.

By the end of the decade, there were about 57,195 black businesses operating across the country with a total income of $108,119,000. Some blacks operated businesses out of their residences or hired themselves out, providing services like catering, sewing, or delivery. Black business districts or streets served a double purpose, a central location or network for business and as social sites purveying a sense of pride where many gathered information from the community and interacted with one another. The golden era of black businesses took place during this decade; Auburn Street in Atlanta was home to blocks of black businesses, churches, beautiful homes, and entertainment venues, and was referred to as "the richest Negro street in the world."

Negro baseball leagues and Insurance companies were among the most successful and largest black businesses operating. The largest surviving insurance companies were Atlanta Life, North Carolina Mutual, Supreme Life, and Golden State. North Carolina Mutual Insurance grew assets from $6,419,786 in 1940 to $26,250,000 by 1949. Dr. Theodore Roosevelt Mason Howard, a surgeon, banker, and farmer, formed an insurance company and launched several businesses in Mississippi during the 1940s and was one of the riches blacks in Mississippi.

Black women played significant roles in growing black businesses. Women operated restaurants, groceries, clothing stores, and laundries. Sarah Spencer Washington, a self-made millionaire grew her business from a small one-room beauty shop to the Apex News & Hair Company and the Apex Beauty Products Company, worth more than $500,000 in 1944. Spencer manufactured and marketed her line of high quality cosmetics with 200 employees and 35,000 agents across the country. She operated eleven beauty schools that graduated 4000 students each year.

In 1942, Rose Morgan and Olivia Stanford co-owned and operated the largest African-American beauty parlor in the world, The Rose Meta House of Beauty in New York City having 20 hair stylists, 3 licensed masseurs, and a registered nurse. Morgan also sold a line of beauty products, Rose Meta Cosmetics.

Most of the black-owned banks and insurance companies were devastated by the Depression and their financial recovery was slow in the making, by the mid-1940s, Chicago still did not have a bank owned by an African-American. By 1947, there were only 13 black-owned banks in the U.S., eleven were survivors of the Depression and two were new established banks. During this period of intense racial prejudice white banks were unwilling to lend to blacks, with only a few black banks, and many without a strong footing, black business owners and entrepreneurs resorted to black policy or numbers bankers for loans and support. After the war, income from the numbers game tripled and numbers bankers were held in high esteem in the communities. They provided the seed money for funeral homes, hotels, insurance companies, newspapers and various other enterprises.

Black Professionals

Black professionals prospered after World War II along with other black businesses in urban cities. The numbers of black men and women in professional services and trades grew over the last decade, but their proportion in relationship to other professions remained small. Black professionals made up only 3 percent of the black community, and business markets outside of the black community were closed to them. The federal government was the primary employer of black professionals in the 1940s after the ban on employment discrimination by federal agencies.

Segregation provided the black professionals with an initiative to form strong organizations and associations they controlled and used for support and in the fight against unequal access or restrictions that limited their practices. African-American lawyers, educators, physicians, and black professionals in various fields were on the forefront of the struggle for equal opportunities.

During the war, black professionals in conjunction with civil rights groups pushed for the training of black pilots equal to that of whites which led to the Tuskegee base where the African American fighter pilots that were later a part of the Army Air Force were trained.

The majority of black male professionals were ministers, teachers, and musicians. Black female professionals were teachers and nurses. Insufficient numbers of doctors, lawyers, and nurses were seen in northern and western states, but severe shortages were seen in the South. During the 1940s, there were a mere 27 black physicians for every 100,000 blacks throughout the country, and three physicians in San Francisco. In Georgia, there were eight black lawyers to serve a population of 800,000, three in South Carolina to serve a population of 3 million, one in Louisiana for a population of 800,000, and in Mississippi only three black lawyers in the entire state.

Extraordinary African-American

Charles Drew was an extraordinary researcher, medical doctor, and surgeon who is best

A Reflection

recognized as the creator of the blood bank. Charles Drew, the eldest of five children, was born on June 3, 1904 in Washington, DC to Richard Thomas Drew and Nora Burrell. He attended Dunbar High School in 1918, the first black high school in America, renowned for its high academic excellence. A standout athlete as well, winning the James E. Walker Memorial medal as the school's best all around athlete, Drew was an award winning swimmer, excelled in football, baseball, basketball, and track and field.

In 1920, his sister Elsie, sick with tuberculosis, died from the influenza pandemic. Drew deeply affected by her death was compelled to study medicine. He was admitted to Amherst College in Massachusetts in 1922 on an athletic scholarship with a major in Chemistry. There he was the captain of the track team while starring as a halfback on the football team. In his junior year, Charles was the most valuable player and was named to the All-American team. In 1926, he graduated from Amherst and was awarded the Howard Hill Mossman trophy having been the ultimate athlete during his attendance.

Charles Drew taught biology and coached at Morgan State College in Baltimore before attending McGill University School of Medicine in Montreal. An exemplary student, he was an Alpha Omega Alpha Scholar and winner of the J. Francis Williams Fellowship. At McGill University, Drew studied blood transfusions under Dr, John Beattie as an intern and had the experience of saving the life of a patient with a blood transfusion. Graduating in 1933, Drew received his M.D. and a Master of Surgery degree besides ranking 2nd in a class of 127 students. He served as a faculty professor in pathology at Howard University for two years, and then became a professor of surgery and assistant surgeon at Freedman's Hospital before being awarded the Rockefeller Fellowship at Columbia University in 1938.

Drew's post graduate study focused on the development of a technique for long-term preservation of blood plasma, which could not be stored for more than two days, and blood transfusions. He discovered that if the whole blood was separated from the plasma and then refrigerated they could be recombined for a transfusion up to a week later. He also determined that plasma is the same for everyone regardless of the blood type, meaning that it's possible to give plasma transfusions to anyone. His accomplishments gained him worldwide recognition. In 1939, Charles Drew married Minnie Lenore Robbins and they had four children. In 1940, he completed his doctoral thesis titled "Banked Blood: A Study in Blood Preservation." There at Columbia, he became the first African-American to earn the Doctor of Medical Science degree.

Charles Drew was the founder of two of the world's largest blood banks. He encouraged Columbia University to establish a blood bank, and was sought by England to set up blood banks during World War II. Drew was appointed medical supervisor of the "Plasma for Britain" program through which he collected 14,500 pints of plasma, and the storage of this plasma saved the lives of hundreds of wounded soldiers in Britain. In 1941, he established the blood bank of the American Red Cross for the U.S. Army and Navy, and as its first director insisted that the race of donors and receivers be ignored, the armed forces ruled that the blood supplies would be segregated, to which Drew resigned from his position.

Drew returned to Howard University in 1942 as the head of the Department of Surgery and the Freedman's Hospital as the chief of Staff. In 1944, the NAACP awarded the Spingarn Medal for his work in establishing the blood banks. He received the E.S. Jones Award for his research in Medical Science, and was the first African-American surgeon to serve on the American Board of Surgery in 1943. He was also presented with honorary Doctor of Science degrees from Virginia State College in 1945 and Amherst College in 1947. Drew was appointed Surgical Consultant for the United States Army's European Theater of Operations in 1949.

Charles Drew was killed in a car accident on April 1, 1950 when he fell asleep while driving with three colleagues to a meeting in Tuskegee, Alabama. He suffered massive injuries and the blood transfusion he received was not enough to save his life. Charles Drew has remained one of the most honored and respected individuals in the field of medicine. His establishment of the blood plasma bank has saved the lives of millions all over the world.

Education

School attendance and education attainment for African-Americans continued to increase during the 1940s, although attendance was lower in rural farm areas in the South. Illiteracy, which was also more concentrated in the South had been reduced to a range between 9-12 percent. Early childhood education or kindergarten had decreased during the Depression and was not attended in high numbers. Children in urban regions were more likely to enroll in kindergarten than in rural areas, with numbers approaching 30 percent. More than 90 percent of black children enrolled into school at 7 years of age. Attendance in elementary school for ages 5-9 were about 69 percent, secondary school attendance for ages 10-14 was over 93 percent, but for ages15-20 attendance fell to 45 percent, where high school attendance among blacks dropped

A Reflection

drastically. The average years of school attendance was 6.8 for black males, and 7.8 for black females, a difference of three years less between white males and females.

The migration out of the South to urban cities in the North and Midwest contributed to gross overcrowding in schools. In some Chicago elementary schools, 2 and 3 children had to share one seat. State expenditures per pupil remained disproportionate between blacks and white students in every state, Mississippi ratios were by far the worst at $22.29 to $71.00. Black public school teachers began campaigns to achieve equal salaries in several cities and states, some teachers were successful in lawsuits filed in federal courts, but parents were not as fortunate in raising state allocations for segregated public schools.

The number of high schools for black students reached 1000 in the 1940s, and according to U.S. Census data, at the end of the decade, 14 percent of African-Americans over the age of 25 years had a high school diploma, and 2 percent had a bachelor's degree. College enrollment surged in this decade, at the start of the 1940s, 23,000 black students were enrolled in college and by the close of the decade, 88,000 black women and men between the ages of 18 to 24 were enrolled in universities, about 4.5 percent of their age group. College student numbers in the South were lower than those in other parts of the country.

Forty-nine percent of black veterans had used the G.I. Bill for education or training, 12 percent entered colleges with most entering vocational schools. Unfortunately, African-American veterans had not received adequate academic preparation for college level studies. Black veterans in the North attended integrated institutions, but the bulk of them attended Historically Black Colleges and Universities in the South. Most of the HBCU's curriculums were geared to teacher training or religious studies for future clergy with limited space, up to 50,000 black veterans were turned away.

By the end of 1949, HBCUs were responsible for educating 90 percent of the black students in post-secondary institutions. Furthermore, HBCUs produced 75 percent of all black army officers, 80 percent of all black federal judges, 85 percent of all black physicians, and 75 percent of all black PH.D.s. African-American applicants were admitted to most public institutions, and 40 private white colleges had begun admitting black students. Nearly 50,000 black college students were located in southern institutions. Many of these southern black students participated in sit-ins.

Quite a number of educated blacks had some difficult in gaining employment stirring the old debate as to whether extra education was a benefit or a hindrance. Incredibly, half-way through the decade, 40 percent of whites still believed that blacks were less intelligent and less able to learn even with equal education and training. However, less education meant no upward social mobility, and that would make sure black people stayed in their place. Educators advised that education should be valued, not just as a solution to unemployment. Education is to benefit the youth not help labor market.

Black on Black Crime

African-Americans were still arrested and sentenced to prison at rates disproportionate to their numbers in the population. Higher incidences of crime in cities with large black populations more often than not were 'Black on Black' crimes. In Michigan, blacks make up only 7 percent of the population but comprised 40 percent of the prison population in 1949, with most of the inmates coming from Detroit and other industrial regions of the state. Most of the black prisoners were migrants from Georgia, Alabama, Michigan, Tennessee, Mississippi, and Arkansas. The majority of blacks and whites were arrested for burglary and robbery in this decade, but blacks committed more aggravated assaults and homicides.

In the 1940s, the prevalence of black crime, specifically juvenile delinquency among poor blacks in lower-class communities seemed to be out of control. Black youth gangs in urban areas roamed the neighborhoods aimlessly looking for trouble, preying on random victims. Most of the criminal activities were physical assaults, robbery, and crashing private gatherings. Members of youth gangs usually came from homes where either both parents worked or single-parent homes. The blame for the increases in black crime ranged from the lack of parental guidance, the lack of recreational facilities, segregation and overcrowding of black slums, disregard of white police officers towards crime in black communities, but the bulk of the blame lies with the insufficient education, unemployment and abject poverty. Community leaders were frustrated with their inability to make any progress reducing the level of criminal activity and pastors pleaded with parents in the congregation to gain tighter control over their children.

The criminal justice system during this time was overrun with individuals who brought their prejudices and hostilities to the job. Fuel to the fire was the distrust of law enforcement felt by blacks, having had no history of fair treatment. Police brutality and their lack of concern for 'black on black' crime was a continual matter for contention in black neighborhoods. Conflicts with racist white law enforcement were endemic from large metropolitan cities in the North to small rural towns all through the South after the war ended. Tensions between African-Americans and

A Reflection

white police officers who viewed them as criminals exacerbated the fears of white residents who saw increasing black populations as further competition for jobs and housing. Police harassment and incarceration were also used to control the growing numbers of migrants.

Skirmishes between white law enforcement were apparent in cities with large black populations including Chicago, Detroit, New York, and Philadelphia. Allegations of excessive force when dealing with black youths and peaceable citizens were widespread along with accusations of police corruption. In 1949, 80 percent of those arrested in Philadelphia were black youths. In southern cities the police brutality escalated to higher levels of egregious behavior, in Memphis, police routinely stopped black women and sexually assaulted them. In 1945, two white police officers raped two young black cafeteria workers; an enraged public reaction finally covered by local newspapers initiated the call for an end to police brutality.

The majority of crimes committed in America were intra-racial. The lack of black police to patrol their own communities versus the white officers who ignored black-on-black crime and white-on-black crime was a source of frustration for black leadership. Cocaine and heroine were pouring into black ghettos, and while small-time dealers and users were readily arrested, white officers turned their heads and protected the drug lords and allowed other illegal activities.

After World War II ended, there was more economic mobility in the African-American communities across the country and the rate of crime among blacks began to diminish. During the 1940s, the number of black homicides declined along with arrests for other serious offenses, less than half of those arrested were charged with murder, manslaughter, rape, robbery of burglary, but the number of blacks arrested for minor offenses jumped from just over 22 percent to 34 percent of total arrests.

Health

Among the most confounding issues before government officials, healthcare providers, medical policy makers, and social scientists are the constant inconsistencies in black and white American health. Communicable diseases, childhood illnesses, poor nutrition, and the lack of preventable healthcare weighed heavily on the black community. During this decade the life expectancy for blacks became considerably longer, but disturbing disparities in mortality and morbidity between specific age ranges in comparison with whites continued. Deplorable housing and working conditions compromised the health of blacks exacerbating the containment of contagious and transmittable diseases.

At the beginning of the decade, tuberculosis led as the primary cause of death among African-Americans between the ages of 25 to 44 years, dying at range of three to five times the rate of whites in the same age category depending on the city. Black morbidity was also rising above whites among other chronic illnesses associated with infections, as well as heart disease and cancer. In 1945, after medical discoveries such as antibiotics began to successfully combat the tuberculosis problem, the leading cause of death for blacks was heart disease with stroke being the second, and tuberculosis dropped to third. Improvements in sanitation, nutrition, living conditions and scientific advances had begun to reduce the morbidity and mortality for a number of diseases. The availability of treatment for venereal diseases may have had an adverse affect, the cases of syphilis among blacks were rapidly multiplying, selective service records showed 32 percent of black soldiers were infected.

Infant mortality was still at unacceptable levels, nearly 10 percent of African-American babies born in the 1940s died in the first year of life. Federal maternal-child health clinics were established to address black infant mortality rates through the education and training of midwives to reduce the deaths of black women in pregnancy and childbirth. Maternal deaths among black mothers were double those among whites due to the absence of adequate clinics and hospitals for African-Americans providing pre-natal and post-natal supervision. In the 1940s, 75 percent of the births of black infants were attended by midwives.

There were insufficient numbers of black physicians and nurses to care for the black community. During the 1940s, there were 1,751 black physicians, a mere 475 black public health nurses, and 644 black dentists practicing in the Southern states. In South Carolina, there were only 100 black physicians to care for more than 800,000 blacks in the state. White doctors who cared for black patients saw them in separate offices or different days.

Black doctors, nurses, dentists, and pharmacists were essentially barred from white hospital staffs and denied membership in medical associations. Qualified young black women were trained in only 275 of the 1200 nursing schools in the nation, and were unable to enroll in nurse training courses in white hospitals. World War II only added to the nursing shortages for blacks, after the war there were about 8,000 black nurses in the United States. Racial disparities in healthcare were the greatest in Mississippi where blacks have only a fraction of the number of beds available to white patients. In Jackson, the capitol of Mississippi, only 10 percent of babies were born in a hospital, compared to 69 percent of whites, the national average was 45 percent of black babies versus 87

A Reflection

percent of white babies.

Black patients throughout the nation were treated in all-black hospitals by black physicians, Jim Crow kept them segregated in the South, admitting a few black patients in black wards usually located in the basements of hospitals, while hospitals in urban cities in the North with large black populations reserved training and staffing for white doctors. There were only 79 hospitals in 16 southern states to serve nearly 10 million blacks. The count at the beginning of the decade was 10,000 beds nationwide, and by 1944, there were only 124 black hospitals across the country, most were unaccredited, substandard, and struggling to afloat. Some fraternal organizations provided hospital services as in the Taborian Hospital in Mound Bayou, Mississippi.

After the war a new public policy approach to health care and civil rights began to emerge. Carl V. Reynolds, the state health care officer in North Carolina declared in May 1946 *"that the influential are determined to make available adequate medical, surgical, obstetrical and hospital care,--certainly for the underprivileged citizens--regardless of race, creed or color."*

Housing

The exodus out of the South regained its momentum in the 1940s putting further pressure on urban cities to answer the demand for additional housing. Job opportunities had multiplied, but housing hadn't kept up with the pace. Black migrants were restricted by segregation to crowded neighborhoods with no plans for additional housing. Most blacks were living in substandard housing while paying premium rent; landlords took advantage of housing shortages by overcharging.

Families doubled up to cut living expenses. Single-family houses were turned into tenements that lodged several large families. A city-wide survey taken in Philadelphia showed that "one out of every five Negroes lives in dwelling units was occupied by eight or more persons." In New York, 40 percent of black families in Harlem were taking in lodgers. According to Census data, nearly 280,000 black households contained two or more married couples living doubled up. Overcrowding and the lack of enforcement of housing and sanitation codes resulted in unsanitary conditions. In Detroit, half the dwellings rented to black tenants were unsafe, whereas only one-fifth of those occupied by whites were in poor condition.

The Public Works Administration had begun building low-cost housing projects during the 1930s to provide relief from the decrepit shacks in the ghetto. The United States

1949

Housing Administration was also working to supply housing for new migrants, but their efforts were insufficient. In Detroit at the start of the decade, 9,000 families had placed applications for public housing where there were only 2000 available apartments in the housing project. The elimination of dangerous and unsanitary slums in favor of public housing was referred to as "urban development" or "slum clearance," unfortunately some decent neighborhoods and good buildings were demolished in the process. The public housing projects like the Ida B. Wells homes in Bronzeville, Chicago were clean and safe alternatives for working families.

In Detroit, blacks were excluded from all public housing projects except for the Brewster-Douglas homes. The Sojourner Truth Housing project was built in a white neighborhood, and blacks and whites began to clash in major disputes over who would get to live in the homes. Initially the federal government informed the Detroit Housing Commission that the project would be designated for whites and an alternate location would be designated for blacks, but without a new location found, federal housing authorities gave notice that the Sojourner Truth projects would be accessible to blacks. Angry whites protested, the projects were picketed, and crosses were burned to intimidate black tenants, nevertheless two dozen black families under guard of 800 state police moved into the project. Even the UAW militants organized thousands of members to defend the African-American occupancy of Sojourner Truth Projects.

Halfway through the decade, the Chicago Housing Authority (CHA) attempted to lessen the crowding of inner-city ghettos and proposed locating public housing sites in other less congested communities. This proposal was hotly disputed by white residents, the CHA acquiesced, and the development of future high rise projects would be kept in the Black Belt and the West Side of Chicago. Slums proliferated across the cities with the number of new migrants; blacks with varied income levels, skills, and education were all packed together by the limitations of segregation. Middle-class blacks found themselves in a quandary, their income was above qualifications for housing projects yet home builders would not build for them in the suburbs. They wanted better housing and pushed to move out of the confines of the ghettos, but racial housing restrictions were still in place and white resistance came in the form of thousands of racial incidents including house bombings and burnings nationwide. Arnold Hirsch's book *"Making the Second Ghetto"* contained a case study of race and housing in Chicago where he cited over 350 incidents of racial violence related to housing conflicts reported to the

A Reflection

Chicago Commission on Human Relations between 1945 and 1950.

Results of a survey done by the Southern Regional Council on housing conditions in the South found that *"Negroes as a group are the poorest-housed citizens in the South and the entire country."* The *Atlanta Daily Word*, May 25, 1948 reported that 40 percent of southern blacks live in rural areas in the Cotton Belt where housing is the worst in the nation. Data from the survey showed only one out of ten black people had a home that met minimum requirements, and one out of three live in homes that have no modern improvements and need extensive repairs.

In another 1948 study done by Housing and Home Finance Agency it was found that housing for blacks had made some improvements; better incomes were reflected in the enhanced condition of homes and a greater proportionate increase in home ownership. In the first half of the decade homeownership climbed from 500,000 to 719,771. However, even with these gains, blacks were still below whites in the quality of housing and the amount of space occupied per person. The study also concluded that many blacks could financially afford to live in better houses if they were available to them. The GI Bill was to assist all veterans with loans to buy homes, an Ebony magazine survey determined that out of 3000 VA home loans approved in Mississippi during the summer of 1947, only two loans went to black veterans.

Further into the decade, the ghettos and the "black belts" of Northern and Midwestern cities overflowed their boundaries causing turnovers in white residential areas. Whites fled to the suburbs to escape the influx of migrants, taking retail and manufacturing businesses in tow, and concentrating the number of blacks in metropolitan areas. This shift perpetuated the decline of inner-cities across America as "deindustrialization" took hold. The National Housing Act of 1949 provided funding for the renewal of urban areas by the elimination of slum neighborhoods and the construction of 810,000 subsidized public housing units to redevelop central cities.

Family Structure

Employment and economic gains had eased some of the pressure on African-American families by 1949. Job opportunities were once again inspiring families to pack their bags and search for a better life. Similar paths were taken in this second phase of departure out of the South as in the first Great Migration. Black people left in a variety of ways; sometimes the entire family went together, for others the parents went ahead leaving children in the care of grandparents or other family members until they got on

1949

their feet. Wives followed husbands, and even single black men and women went alone joining relatives in the North, Midwest, and larger southern cities. Lodges and Fraternal Organization continued to be a base of support for poor and rural communities as they transitioned to new environments.

E. Franklin Frazier reported to the American Youth Commission at the beginning of the decade that migration caused undue stress on the black family, and thus had a marked effect on black youth. In his opinion these youth could not identify with family from the South or North stating, "He lacks the former's spirit of submission and the latter's sense of racial dignity and solidarity." Contrary to the opinions and assertions of the uncivilized nature of migrants from the South who were unable to adapt to an urban lifestyle, migrants were more likely to be married with stable families than native blacks.

Young people enjoyed going to movies for recreation and began to date around 16 years of age. Approximately 63 percent of black males and females were married at the end of the decade, with 21 percent of black females 15 years and older having never been married. The problem of fathers and husbands abandoning their families in the 1930s because of financial hardships were somewhat alleviated by the demand for workers during the 1940s. There was actually a rise in the proportion of married adults living with their spouses at the beginning of the decade, with numbers reaching their peak of 72 percent in 1947, and then the decline began again.

The average number of children in a family was 3.78, with black birth rates in the Southern rural areas being the highest in the nation. According to Census data, the decline in the birth rates that began in the last decade had begun to stabilize; the results were a smaller percentage of children between the ages of 5- and 17 years of age. More than 74 percent of black children up to the age of 14 were living with two parents, but the number of black families headed by a female had grown close to 20 percent.

At the beginning of the decade, the poverty rate for black families was shockingly near 80 percent, but dropped to 70 percent by the end of the decade. Black families in 1949 had an average income of $1869.00, a mere 54 percent of the $3345 average income earned by white families. What is more upsetting is that greater percentages of black families had two incomes and still fell short in comparison with white male incomes. Thirty-four percent of black married couples both worked compare to 21 percent of white couples. In urban cities, four to five families often shared one dwelling which had adverse consequences of juvenile delinquency and absenteeism in school and on jobs. Black youths were becoming skeptical of their opportunities as they watched their parents get

A Reflection

the short end of the stick every time.

Black Athlete and Sports

The return of prosperity renewed the peoples' appetite for spectator sports. Prior to World War II, nearly all competition in professional sports was segregated, and only a few black players were participating in major college programs. In the South, black athletes were restricted by Jim Crow laws, in the North, it was by "gentlemen's agreement." However, the 1940s ushered in the ground-breaking re-integration of sports in the United States, specifically baseball which was the great "National Pastime."

Wendell Smith, an editor and sportswriter for the *Pittsburgh Courier,* used his column as a vehicle to push for the integration of baseball years before the start of World War II. Inspired by his own personal experience as a baseball player who had been excluded just because of the color of skin, Smith spent much of his career fighting for the inclusion of black Americans in Major League Baseball. As a sportswriter following the careers of black phenomenal players like Satchell Paige and Josh Gibson, Smith applied the unrelenting pressure of his pen to fulfill his quest to see the desegregation of baseball. He systematically cross-examined every level of organized baseball on their opinion of blacks playing in the major leagues, Ford Frick the President of the National League, owners, manager, players, and Judge Kenesaw Landis, the Czar of organized baseball, placing them on record as having no objections to the removal of the color-ban. Smith also solicited prominent public figures to speak out in support of black ball players in hopes of influencing public opinion.

Branch Rickey, under the pretext of starting an all-black ball club began scouting for the ideal entrant to break the color barrier. Rickey wanted a strong-minded, independent, and confident black player with superior athletic talents who was also above reproach with a stable temperament. Wendell Smith recommended Jackie Robinson as the *Couriers* number one candidate to Brooklyn Dodger's coach, Branch Rickey, for the "great experiment" of integrating the League. Robinson had been an all-star athlete with varsity letters in four sports at UCLA, he played basketball, baseball, and had a 12-yard ball carrying average in football, and starred on the track team.

In 1945, Jackie Robinson signed a contract with the Brooklyn Dodger's farm team, the Montreal Royals. After only one season with Montreal, Robinson moved up to the majors and helped propel the Dodgers to a National League pennant. Robinson's impressive performances on the field earned him National League Rookie of the Year honors, and in 1949, he was named the National League's most valuable player.

1949

Robinson batted .347 and stole 37 bases. Robinson's success made a path for other black players from the Negro Leagues to follow into the majors. Stars like Roy Campanella and Don Newcombe joined the Dodgers and Larry Doby joined the Cleveland Indians as the first black in the American League.

The entrance of blacks in the major leagues was the beginning of the end for Negro baseball leagues. Just a few years earlier they had been at their pinnacle packing the stands in every league during the war, now they were losing their life's blood, their most talented players. Some players went into the majors, more into the minors; others had already played past their prime. As a result, attendance waned in the black leagues and the Negro National League split after the 1948 season. Formerly one of the most financially successful African-American enterprises in the country, the Negro baseball leagues became a casualty of integration.

The National Football League was actually the first to re-integrate in 1946, while Jackie Robinson played on the Dodgers farm team. The Cleveland Rams organization in a move to Los Angeles was required by contract to integrate and signed the first two African-Americans and former teammates at UCLA, Kenny Washington and Woody Strode. In 1944, the All-American Football Conference publicly announced that race would not prevent them from recruiting the best players. The league rivals of the NFL, followed with the integration of teams in 1946, but the Cleveland Browns had a much different motivation for signing black college football stars, they wanted the best players to win games. Former college players of Paul Brown at Ohio State, Bill Willis and Marion Motley were recruited and the team won the AAFC's first championship with a 12-2-0 record, leading their teams in rushing, passing, and receiving.

In 1947, a bidding war ensued in the AAFC over Claude "Buddy" Young, known as the "Bronze Bullet." Young had been a track star at the University of Illinois, having won the NCAA championships in the 100 and 220-yard dash, tied the world record for the 45- and 60-yard dashes, and reigned as the Amateur Athletic Union's 100-yard champion. After a stint in the Navy, Young returned to lead Illini to the 1946 Big Ten Championship, and a spectacular 45-14 victory over UCLA in the 1947 Rose Bowl game. Despite being one of the shortest men to play football, at 5'4," Young was one of most sought after rookies, and signed with New York Yankees. By 1947, the NFL had signed seven African-American players and the AAFC had signed twelve, and even though it was obvious that integrated teams won more games than segregated ones, seven teams of the NFL refused to sign black athletes. The only other NFL teams to recruit black players during the 1940s were the New York Giants signing

A Reflection

Emlen Tunnel in 1948 and the Detroit Lions signing Wally Triplett in 1949.

Basketball was not as popular in the 1940s as some of the other sports, at the beginning of the decade there were several small leagues operating around the country, but no national league. Black players in college basketball were barred by the gentlemen's agreement from playing in the Big Ten Conference, and few played at predominately white universities, most played in historically black colleges and universities. Exceptionally players like Don Barksdale were able to play in the Amateur Athletic Union (AAU). The YMCA continued to sponsor basketball teams where black players could compete; they played against other black teams including soldiers in the Army. Several all-black teams like the Washington Bears played white local and professional teams and competed in a host of tournaments including the World Professional Basketball Tournament.

The National Basketball League (NBL) broke the color barrier in 1942, with the Toledo White Huts signing four black players and the Chicago Studebakers signing six black players. In 1946, the Basketball Association of America (BAA) was formed, and cognizant of the draw of black teams, also began to sign black players. Black professional teams like the New York Rens and the Harlem Globetrotters had a huge fan base. During the 1940s, the Harlem Globetrotters dominated the game and the stands playing serious ball. The National Basketball League, not much of draw, arranged games with the Harlem Globetrotters to stay afloat. The Globetrotters beat the premier team of the NBL, the Minneapolis Lakers, twice in 1948 and 1949 demonstrating their basketball prowess. The integration of the white professional basketball teams ended the Black Fives era when the New York Rens, who had compiled a 2318-381 record, joined the NBL and became the Dayton Rens. The NBL and the BAA merged in 1949 to become the National Basketball Association.

Don Barksdale was the first black all-American basketball player. In 1948, he joined the U.S. Olympic team as the first black to play on the basketball squad in the 1948 Summer Olympics. Barksdale was the first African-American to win an Olympic gold medal in the sport of basketball. He would also become the third African-American to sign a contract with the NBA and the first to play in the NBA All-Star Game.

***

The international inclusiveness of the Olympics allowed blacks to compete unimpeded by racial hindrances. After the spectacular performance of Jesse Owens in the 1936 Olympics, the games were canceled in 1940 and 1944 due to World War II. In track and field, Tuskegee Institute continued to dominate the women's field winning eleven out of twelve AAU outdoor championships.

1949

Alice Coachman, their star athlete, competed for Tuskegee from 1940 to 1946. Coachman won track and field championships in 50 and 100-meter dashes, the 4 X 100 meter relay, and the running high jump. She was also a standout player in basketball as a guard, leading the Tuskegee basketball team to three consecutive championships. Alice Coachman joined the U.S. Olympic team in 1948 competing in the high jump. In the finals, Coachman jumped 5 feet 6 1/8 inches on her first try and became the first African-American woman to win a Gold medal and the only American woman to win a gold medal in the 1948 Olympic Games. Coachman had won 25 AAU indoor and outdoor titles before retiring in 1948.

The sport of boxing went through a quiet period during the war, Joe Louis was still the heavyweight champion, but most of his fights were exhibitions. Louis kept his title until his retirement in 1949. The decade saw the emergence of Sugar Ray Robinson, born Walker Smith, and his dominance in the boxing game. Having won the Golden Glove championships in both the lightweight and the welterweight classes in 1939, in 1940, Sugar Ray was ready to turn professional. Robinson began his pro career powerfully, accumulating 38 consecutive wins, 27 by knockout, until losing to Jake LaMotta after 10 rounds. Sugar Ray came back with a vengeance, winning 96 straight bouts including the World Welterweight title form Tommy Bell, and on February 14, 1949 he knocked out Jake LaMotta winning the World Middleweight title. Sugar Ray Robinson was considered by to be the greatest pound-for-pound fighter of all time, if not the greatest fighter who ever lived by many during his time.

Cultural Expression

The Federal Arts Project propelled a number of African-American artists into the national spotlight. Art exhibits featuring black artists spread across the country, Jacob Lawrence was the most renowned of the select group. At the youthful age of 24, he became the first African American Artist included in the permanent collection of The Museum of Modern Art.

A Reflection

2013 The Jacob and Gwendolyn Lawrence Foundation, Seattle./Artisy Rights Society (ARS), New York

Richard Wright moved to the forefront of African-American literature at the start of the 1940s with his book Native Son. Written in the protest genre, Wright's radical novel garnered international attention through its controversial illustration of the destructiveness of racism and poverty in America. Through his protagonist, Bigger Thomas, Wright depicts the consequences of generations of slavery and segregation and how they dehumanized both races, while giving justification for the character flaws developed in the poor and victimized.

> "You're trying to believe in yourself. And every time you try to find a way to live, your own mind stands in the way. You know why that is? It's because others have said you were bad and they made you live in bad conditions. When a man hears that over and over and looks about him and sees that his life *is* bad, he begins to doubt his own mind.... The job in getting people to fight and have faith is in making them believe in what life has made them feel, making them feel that their feelings are as good as those of others." Native Son (390-391).

Additional themes in the book were the hatred of whites and the self-hatred felt by black people. Native Son was an instant bestseller, selling 250,000 copies in the first three weeks, and was subsequently the first book authored by an African-American to be chosen by the Book of the Month Club. Not only did Wright receive the Spingarn Medal for his worthy achievement, the book also made him the wealthiest black writer of the period. One year after the book's release the stage production of Native Son opened on Broadway.

Wright followed his triumph with another masterpiece, *Twelve Million Black Voices: A Folk History of the Negro in the United States*, which was a narration of black life in America inspired by pictures from the Farm Security Administration files. The photos were representative of the conditions and experiences of black people during the Great Depression in the 1930s. Wright wraps his words around the misery and oppression, the degradation and the resignation, to the strength and determination, faith and optimism that are the struggle of being black in America. He charted each stage of the journey from slavery to freedom through migration to the ghettos of the North. In 1945, Richard Wright published his autobiography, *Black Boy*, describing his childhood in the racist South, his move to Chicago and his involvement with the Communist party. *Black Boy* was too an overnight bestseller selling 195,000 copies in its first edition and 351,000 additional copies through the Book-of-the-Month Club.

The cultural expression of black people is often exhibited in their style of dress and in different forms of dance. In the 1940s, for young blacks, the zoot suit and the jitterbug ruled the day. The "zoot suit" or the "drape" was very loose fitting except for the narrow cuffs on the pants; the coats were long, sometimes even below the knee with thick shoulder pads. The zoot suit was usually worn with a long watch chain and a wide-brimmed hat and a long feather, with some wearing "process" or "conk" hairstyles. The drape was the favored style of the hip black man, jitterbug dancers, and jazz entertainers. The baggy pants gave dancers freedom to move and the narrow cuffs kept the shoes of dancers from getting caught in the pants.

Bans against the fashion came from the War Production Board in a declaration that "they must go," the rationale being the suits wasted fabric during wartime when there was a shortage of wool. The outfit was seen as rebellious and identified with juvenile delinquency and crime. Countless incidents of individuals being attacked and even causing riots for wearing the zoot suit were reported across the country. Some government officials even tried to stop the jitterbug, which many felt encouraged interracial dancing, by levying taxes on dance halls. Some suspected this was the root of the close of the Savoy Ballroom.

Entertainment

Black stage and theatre productions reflected the attitude and mood of African-Americans after World War II. Playwrights were more militant and radical in their themes, their works sought to express black culture without the usual stereotypes in characters so often seen in plays by white writers. Black theatre was dominated by two groups, the American Negro Theatre and the Negro Playwrights' Company. These black-owned community theatre organizations trained a number of the most gifted actors, playwrights, and technicians of the stage in the 1940s. Sidney Poitier, Ruby Dee, Ossie Davis, Harry Belafonte, and Alice Childress were among the many outstanding actors and actresses who studied in the American Negro Theatre.

The Negro Playwrights' Company was formed by Abram Hill, who united several playwrights who came out of the Federal Theatre Project of the 1930s, including Langston Hughes, Theodore Ward, and Richard Wright, to bring quality theatre to Harlem. Protest dramas criticizing the conditions for blacks in America like the stage adaptation of Wright's Native Son flooded the black theatres. In 1947, the play, *Our Lan,* written by

A Reflection

Theodore Ward, centered on the Reconstruction period in the South, opened at the Henry Street Settlement Playhouse before its 42 performance run on Broadway. More of an artistic achievement receiving critical acclaim than a commercial success, it earned Ward a Guggenheim Fellowship to write about John Brown the abolitionist.

The American Negro Theatre, the more accomplished of the two, was founded by Abram Hill and Frederick O'Neal, after Hill's decision to leave the Negro Playwrights' Company. Motivated by his desire to elevate the artistic focus of his works rather than making political statements, Hill used more universal themes. Throughout the 1940s, a host of ANT plays were performed at the Harlem Library Theatre with some transferring to Broadway. Their first play, *On Strivers Row,* in 1940 was a success, but their greatest triumph was, *Anna Lucasta*, in 1944, having a run of 957 performances before a nationwide tour and traveling overseas to London, England.

All-black musicals during the 1940s, *Cabin in the Sky* (1940), *Carmen Jones* (1943) and *St. Louis Woman* (1946), were white-directed and produced, competed for black audiences, and satisfied white audiences who wanted to see black entertainers perform without the social commentaries. Katherine Dunham and her dance company were featured in *Cabin in the Sky* and Dunham played the sexy siren, Georgia Brown, which led to the successful Broadway musical *Tropical Revue* in 1943.

The first grand opera composed by an African-American, William Grant Still, was presented by the New York City Opera in March of 1949. The *Troubled Island* premiere received 22 curtain calls from a packed theatre, an obvious success, but New York critics disparaged it, assuring its demise and the production was shut down after just three performances. Many believe the opera was sabotaged in a conspiracy to diminish the accomplishment of a talented black composer.

The movie industry continued to grow in popularity after the war, and Black cinema also thrived in this decade with thanks to Jim Crow. Black writers, stars, and directors who found the doors of Hollywood closed to them had opportunities in the production of all-black movies or "race films." The number of films produced for black movie theatres approached 700 in this era. Similar genres were recreated in black movies as those represented in Hollywood, except, by the 1940s, black actors were becoming disgruntled with the limited roles they were offered. Clarence Muse was overt in his criticism of parts available in major films and took matters in his own hands by writing a script that would be void of any offensive stereotypes of blacks. In 1940, his venture *Broken Strings*, was released. Muse in the starring role, shot in only four days, portrayed a distinguished professional concert violinist who was critically injured in a car

accident which left him unable to play. A review appeared in the *Pittsburgh Courier*;
> "The motion picture "Broken Strings" is an artistic triumph! Here is a Negro movie that tops anything and everything that has been done… Mr. Muse's portrayal of a concert violinist who thought that swing music desecrated the very word "music" is indeed masterful. Probably for the first time, women will shed a tear viewing an all-colored cast."

The major studios in Hollywood kept black actors in demeaning roles as servants, nannies, and janitors, catering to racist audiences, yet the salaries paid for these parts were far above the amounts that a black actor could earn in an all-black production. However the success of all-black movies did not go unnoticed by the major studios that rushed to capitalize on the success of the stage version of *Cabin in the Sky* making it into a film. Black movie stars featured in the film were Ethel Waters, Eddie Anderson, and Lena Horne.

Katherine Dunham was very influential in the dance styling in musicals on the big screen choreographing dance routines in *Carnival of Rhythm* (1942), *Stormy Weather* (1943), and *Casbah* (1947). By the end of the decade, independent black films began to illustrate social issues and discrimination with commercial success, prompting Hollywood to follow suit with its release of *Pinky* in 1949 which depicted race relations in America and the subject of interracial relationships.

The Apollo Theatre in Harlem served up a cornucopia of entertainment during the 1940s, from comic throwbacks from vaudeville, to gospel revues, Amateur Night, jazz and blues singers, the greatest tap dancers, a chorus line of beautiful ladies, and the latest styling of the hottest musicians and bands. It was at this time that African-American comics said no more to blackface makeup. Amateur Night winners in the 1940s included Sarah Vaughn, Billy Eckstine, and Ruth Brown, and Sammy Davis Jr. and Dinah Washington. Charles "Honi" Coles and Charles "Cholly" Atkins were featured dancers with best of the big bands, Cab Calloway, Louis Armstrong, Count Basie, and more.

The Las Vegas Strip in Nevada established itself as an entertainment mecca in the desert in the 1940s. Black entertainers went west to perform in these venues, but Jim Crow was never far behind. Even Louis Armstrong was required to come in the back doors of the hotel-casinos. African-American superstars such as Sammy Davis Jr., Louis Armstrong, Lena Horne, Nat King Cole, and others could not stay in or eat at the hotels where they performed. Black entertainers stayed at all-black hotels or in private homes on the Westside of Las Vegas. The segregation practices earned Nevada the title "The Mississippi of the West" from black performers. Josephine Baker challenged the discrimination in Las Vegas

A Reflection

by using her position to allow local blacks to attend her show at the El Rancho.

Music styles evolved with each generation of musicians and singers. Jazz was again transformed by younger contemporaries who rejected the constraints of swing music with its controlled arrangements and large bands for the free expression of "bebop." The origination of bebop depends on who you ask, but two are credited with its conception, Dizzy Gillespie, trumpet player, bandleader, singer, and composer and Thelonius Monk, pianist and composer. It took exceptional talent to sing with bebop and the best were Ella Fitzgerald the "First Lady of Song" and Sarah Vaughn the "Divine One."

In 1945, Dizzy Gillespie and Charlie Parker and their innovative band elevated jazz to a greater height of creativity with faster tempos, intricate melodies, and lengthy improvisational solos. *"If you really understand the meaning of bebop, you understand the meaning of freedom."*—Thelonious Monk.

Bebop was not as popular as swing for record companies and they began to steer jazz artists such as Nat King Cole, Ella Fitzgerald, Billie Holiday, and Sarah Vaughn towards singing pop-oriented songs that appealed to mainstream audiences. The record sales of Nat King Cole and his trio single-handedly rescued Capital Records from failure. By the end of the decade another metamorphosis of black music brought forth a new genre called rhythm and blues. Boosted by the blues originating in the Mississippi Delta from musicians like Robert Johnson, this popular style of music recordings had been promoted as "race records." A blend of jazz, blues, gospel, and boogie-woogie, R & B took black music in a distinctive direction. The Aristocrat record company led the pack signing Muddy Waters and Bo Diddley.

The first all-black radio station with an all-black on-air staff, WDIA, was established in Memphis, Tennessee with programming designed for African-American listeners in 1948. The first black-owned radio station, WERD, was purchased in Atlanta by businessman Jesse B. Blayton Sr. in Atlanta, Georgia in 1949. In the beginning they were only on the air from sunrise to sunset, but they filled the time with a mix of popular black music: jazz, R & B, and some gospel. The station also offered public service programs, news that blacks couldn't hear on other stations, church services, and educational shows. WERD was also the radio home of "Jockey Jack" Gibson.

Memorable Moments

In 1940, Hattie McDaniel made history becoming the African-American to win an Oscar for her role as Mammy in Gone with the Wind.

1949

In 1943, Charles Drew was selected as the first black surgeon to serve as an examiner on the American Board of Surgery.

In 1944, Frederick Douglass Patterson establishes the United Negro College Fund on April 25 to help support black colleges and black students.

Althea Gibson won the first of ten consecutive American Tennis Association national championships in 1947.

John Hope Franklin publishes his monumental book of African-American history "From Slavery to Freedom" in 1947.

In 1948, Dr. Ralph Bunche became the UN mediator for Palestine.

Satchel Paige at last joins the baseball major leagues in 1948.

In 1949, Wesley A. Brown was the first black to graduate from the US Naval Academy, Annapolis.

William Hastie became the first African-American Federal Appellate Court judge in the history of the United States in 1949.

Heavyweight Champion Joe Louis retired from the sport of boxing in 1949.

Reflection on a Decade

The wide view of the 1940s shows this was a pivotal decade as African-Americans attempted to regain the momentum from the 1920s. Progress achieved over the decade empowered blacks to push further and renewed the trek out of the South. The greatest catalyst for this second migration was economic. World War II had created a mass of employment opportunities; workers as well as soldiers were needed. This wave of migration to urban areas in the North and West of the country greatly impacted the lives of African-Americans; many were lifted out of the Depression with industrial jobs that were plentiful during the war.

Changes in attitude were evident as black people fought back and even took the offensive in racial conflicts. Newfound political leverage was exercised resulting in the desegregation of the armed services. Black newspapers, churches, and politicians echoed the militancy of the people during this decade of protest, and the unified front increased the energy in the journey toward equality.

The Civil Rights Movement was emboldened by the courage of black war veterans who returned home determined to continue to fight for democracy within the United States. New Jersey was the first state to end discrimination in all public accommodations, and by 1949, 18 states had disallowed segregation in public

A Reflection

transportation, restaurants and hotels, educational institutions, parks, libraries, and entertainment venues, but resistance from white America also had grown stronger.

A number of factors were contributing to the changes throughout the decade. The importance of the black church was renewed as it took a central role in the struggle for social equality through its support of leadership organizations. The black press flexed their muscles in the initiation of campaigns that advanced the interests of black communities. The organized labor unions were vital to black workers acquiring higher wages, eliminating discriminatory hiring practices, and providing some job security.

The economic situation of black America was much improved; more black farmers owned their land and homeownership in urban areas increased. Certainly the employment picture looked brighter, but behind the lower unemployment numbers was the reality that blacks had not gained much ground in accessing skilled or managerial positions. Black workers realized that they need more than the menial jobs to take them to the next level. Progress for the race was directly related to education, and for that reason education should be valued, not merely as a solution to unemployment, but as a benefit to the viewpoint of the growing number of disenchanted black youths. However in 1949, education didn't guarantee a good job, segregation and prejudices remained strong adversaries. The disparities between blacks and whites in so many aspects had been narrowed in the 1940s but the gap remained very wide.

Magnification of the image of black society at the end of the decade showed divisions cropping up that stratified the masses and moved them in different directions. Blacks that were privileged enough to gain sufficient education and training were able to advance beyond the majority, others were able to progress on jobs and earn better than average pay, while most were locked in situations where they lacked the money and preparation for more education and the skills to ask for better employment. More well-off blacks wanted better housing and education for their families and branched off to seek a higher quality of life away from the slums and ghettos, some subsisted on the fringes, while those who couldn't escape the poverty and hopelessness resorted to criminal activity to survive or at least dull the pain.

In the dark room of racism and discrimination the door was cracked, the opening slight, but enough light to change the perspective, to remove apprehension and regain confidence, the path through the door had been made clear. Each step forward allowed black people to move closer to true freedom. Unfortunately there was still a lot of distance between this point and racial equality, but for those having nothing and getting a job, it was a major achievement. Each step in an atmosphere of severe bigotry and injustice was an accomplishment. One might be tempted to say they should have reached higher, focused more on education, but the context of the times requires us to understand what was available and to congratulate the exceptional. Every opportunity was taken, none were given. The reality is that black people were grabbing everything they could get their hands on.

Frederick Douglass
When it is finally ours, this freedom, this liberty, this beautiful
and terrible thing, needful to man as air,
usable as earth; when it belongs at last to all,
when it is truly instinct, brain matter, diastole, systole,
reflex action; when it is finally won; when it is more
than the gaudy mumbo jumbo of politicians:
this man, this Douglass, this former slave, this Negro
beaten to his knees, exiled, visioning a world
where none is lonely, none hunted, alien,
this man, superb in love and logic, this man
shall be remembered. Oh, not with statues' rhetoric,
not with legends and poems and wreaths of bronze alone,
but with the lives grown out of his life, the lives
fleshing his dream of the beautiful, needful thing.
---Robert Hayden

from Collected Poems of Robert Hayden.
Used by permission of Liveright Publishing Corporation

A Reflection

1959

Montgomery Bus Boycott

The 1950s were tumultuous years for African-Americans as the fight for civil rights amplified in fervor. At the start of the decade, the battle for civil rights had waned among all the other troubles that black people were focused on. The social problems from the 1940s had only intensified; racial conflicts, inadequate housing, increased crime rates in the black community and the problem of juvenile delinquency had become epidemic. The impatience and tenacity within young black men and women participating in the struggle injected a burst of energy that sparked a current of protest demonstrations, sit-ins, and direct-action campaigns across the Southern states.

The year 1952 was remarkable in that it was the first year without a lynching since they were first recorded in the late 19th century, but this is not to say there was not a white backlash to the surge in momentum of the Civil Rights Movement. The Ku Klux Klan was revived and swiftly began to recruit additional members. White Citizen Councils were formed in 1954, composed of business and professional white people who sabotaged civil rights supporters through the loss of jobs and the denial of credit. Cross burnings and bombing of homes, churches, and schools had become usual occurrences. Even though the number of blacks registered to vote in the South had reached 1.2 million that was only 20 percent of the voting-age population. Cities in the Deep South were relentless in their fight to keep black people from registering and voting. Potential voters were terrorized, some physically attacked, and even others were killed.

By 1959, the wave of the Great Migration had begun to recede. Unskilled jobs in the Northern cities had dried up, and the South was becoming industrialized benefiting from large companies evading the higher taxes of the North. Black populations in inner cities were beginning to be displaced by urban renewal and limited housing was exacerbated by the commitment to residential segregation. De-industrialization and "white flight" out of the inner cities left black people isolated and further from the resources and opportunities they required for economical and educational growth. The upheaval produced an atmosphere of uncertainty throughout the nation as African-Americans bucked against government supported racism that confined them in second-class citizenship.

Television made the crucial difference in the fight for Civil Rights. Through the clear lens of a camera the cloak had been pulled away. The violence and brutality that ran rampant in the dark of night burst out into the light of day without shame. Southern whites had always harbored an irrational justification for the hideousness of their actions. Only when they saw themselves in an honest portrayal outside of their own deceptive filter did they begin to realize their transgressions.

Demographics

The life expectancy for African-Americans had improved, for black men it had risen to 60.7 years and for black women 65.9 years. The median age in 1959 is 23 years overall, but only 17.4 in rural farm regions. The ratio of black men to black women continues to decline; now 93.3 black men for every 100 black women. Blacks then made up 10.5 percent of the population, with numbers around 18,872,000. The black population had increased by more than 25 percent over the last decade. Close to 60 percent of blacks still live in the South, but 75 percent of the black population resides in urban areas. The number of black farm owners has decreased to 272,541, down from 926,000 in 1919. New York has the largest black population with Texas, Georgia, North Carolina, and Louisiana following in numbers. Washington, D.C. has the greatest proportion of blacks, making up over 53 percent of the city's population. Black populations in the West and

A Reflection

Pacific coast have grown by 89 percent over the decade.

During the 1950s, wider use of the mechanical cotton picker initiated another wave of black rural farm workers out of the South. An additional 1.5 million moved north in this period. Between 1940 and 1960, Chicago was the most selected destination for migrants from the South. Its black population grew from 278,000 to 813,000, with 2000 more arriving every week. As white flight to the suburbs gains steam, fears of major cities like New York, Chicago, Detroit, and Los Angeles being controlled by majority black populations were fueled.

The median income for black workers was 60 percent of the median for white workers. According to U.S Census data, the average annual income for a black male is $2300 up from $910 in the previous decade, compared to $4300.00 up from $2600.00 for a white male. The average annual incomes for black and white females are $1412.16 and 2371.80 respectively. Gross expenditures by African-Americans in 1959 were nearly $30 billion, with the number of middle-class blacks having grown significantly, but the majority of blacks were still poor. Only 10 percent of the black population is classified as middle-class.

Mood of the Black Community

The respite from the horrors of lynching was short-lived as the murder of black men and women picked up steam in the 1950s. The vicious attacks and the surge in Ku Klux Klan activity was most likely aroused by the aggressive push by blacks to move to an equitable position in American society. The brutal killing of Emmett Till and the acquittal of his murderers furthered the realization for Southern African-Americans that they could not rely on the legal system for justice. Black people were ready to take the initiative for the changes they wanted see. Black clubs or groups were formed to defend the black community from the white violence that was plaguing them as they fought against racial segregation.

Martin Luther King, Jr. said, *"There comes a time that people get tired of being trampled by the iron feet of oppression. There comes a time when people get tired of being plunged into the abyss of exploitation and nagging injustice."* Black people were beyond tired of waiting for justice to roll down like water as written in Amos 5:24, they were ready to push for the righteousness that should have flowed like a mighty stream. A host of boycotts, pickets, and sit-ins mushroomed throughout the country forcing the acknowledgment and acquiescence of their demands. Any business that treated black clientele second rate was subject to protest. The economic power of black consumers in boycotts was devastating for companies that relied heavily on black patronage.

The determination was evident beginning with the Baton Rouge Bus Boycott in 1953 and then later with the Montgomery Bus Boycott. Black people carpooled, took taxis, and walked, hitting white businesses where it hurt the most, in the pocketbook. A heightened resolve was spreading within the black community. As a challenger who senses vulnerability in his opponent, as a boxer who sees an opening for his knock-out punch, efforts were intensified. As the runner who spots weakness or fatigue in the field and realizes there is a chance to win, that hope strengthens the fortitude to push forward towards victory. We shall overcome!

Legal Victories against Segregation

Many view the 1950s as the beginning of the Civil Rights Movement, but it was more of a continuation of the struggle that began even before the Plessy v. Ferguson decision in 1896 established a legal precedence for racial segregation. Working in concert with the NAACP chief counsel, Thurgood Marshall, the lead attorney, won 29 of the 32 cases he brought before the Supreme Court with a unanimous ruling in his greatest triumph, Brown v. Board of Education. The bulk of his challenges were based on the constitutionality of racial discrimination and segregation. Marshall's efforts garnered the legal victories that led to the defeat of the deep-seated segregation in the South. The 1950s marked the reversal of this racist "separate but equal" doctrine starting with two U.S. Supreme Court decisions decided on the same day, June 5, 1950.

The first case was the Sweatt v. Pointer, where Herman Marion Sweatt had been denied admission to the University of Texas Law School. The court had delayed the decision six months until a separate law school for blacks could be established, Texas Southern University, but Thurgood Marshall had effectively proven the lack of equality, and the courts ruled "saying that the separate school failed to qualify, both because of quantitative differences in facilities and intangible factors." The second case was McLaurin v. Oklahoma, where George McLaurin was denied admission to the University of Oklahoma to pursue a Doctor of Education degree. The U.S. Supreme Court ruled that a public institution of higher learning could not discriminate against a student because of race, as doing so would be in violation of the Fourteenth Amendment.

In the early years of the 1950s, the NAACP combined five cases challenging the

A Reflection

"separate but equal" doctrine supporting segregation of public schools. In May 1954, the U.S. Supreme Court ruled that "separate educational facilities were inherently unequal" and violated the Fourteenth Amendment, reversing the Plessy v. Ferguson decision of 1896. Jim Crow had finally been defeated. The Supreme Court ruling in Brown versus the Topeka Board of Education was to desegregate America's school system, but despite the Supreme Court ruling for the desegregation of schools, Federal Troops were required to be present to enforce the integration of Little Rock High School in Little Rock, Arkansas in 1957. This progress was the beginning, not the ultimate goal, blacks were still not able to attend adequate and equal educational and school facilities or receive equal pay for equal work.

Mary Mcleod Bethune responded to the Brown v. Education Supreme Court decision, the legal victory that turned over the Plessy V. Ferguson ruling with this note in the *Chicago Defender*:

> "There can be no divided democracy, no class government, no half-free county, under the constitution. Therefore, there can be no discrimination, no segregation, no separation of some citizens from the rights which belong to all... We are on our way. But these are frontiers which we must conquer... We must gain full equality in education ...in the franchise... in economic opportunity, and full equality in the abundance of life."

In the Hansberry v. Lee decision the NAACP won a victory against residential segregation. The case was initiated after an incident surrounding the Hansberry family moving to a white neighborhood near the University of Chicago. The attack on the family, inspired daughter Lorraine Hansberry to write the play, "A Raisin in the Sun"; the first play of a black woman to be produced on Broadway.

Political Climate

Dwight D. Eisenhower was elected president of the United States in 1952 and again in 1956, even with 75 percent of blacks voting for Adlai Stevenson. The 1950s marked a period of transition that began in the 1940s and continually gained momentum throughout the decade. Eisenhower was not an advocate of swift social change; he believed that rapid transformation precipitated high levels of violence, and that the Federal government should refrain from intervening in the state politics. However, Eisenhower was concerned with the perception of the U.S. by other non-white nations and took measures to eliminate overt or visible instances of discrimination or segregation that would serve as an embarrassment to the nation. As a result, he completed the integration of the military which had been ordered by President Truman in 1948, and by 1953, 95 percent of the combat troupes serving in Korea were integrated. Eisenhower also integrated public schools, public transportation, and public accommodations in Washington, D.C. where foreign dignitaries would not witness the segregation seen in the rest of the nation.

President Eisenhower appointed Earl Warren as Chief Justice in 1953, a choice he later regretted. In 1954, when the Brown v. Board of Education of Topeka case was being reheard, Eisenhower met with Chief Justice Earl Warren at the white house to confer over the case, he told Warren: *"[Southern whites] are not bad people. All they are concerned about is to see that their sweet little girls are not required to sit in school alongside some big overgrown Negroes."*

Despite the hesitation on the part of some justices who feared that an order of desegregation would create chaos in the South, the Supreme Court unanimously ruled that "separate educational facilities are inherently unequal." Eisenhower responded, *"The Supreme Court has spoken and I am sworn to uphold the constitutional processes in this country; and I will obey."* In what is referred to as "Brown II" the Supreme Court heard arguments by schools looking for a reprieve in the undertaking of desegregation. In 1955, Chief Justice Earl Warren rendered the decision that schools should be integrated with "all deliberate speed."

The watershed for Eisenhower was his reluctance to enforce the Brown decision which gave license to other opponents who sought to avoid any form of desegregation. In 1956, Southern states declared the Supreme Court decision void and some went as far to impose penalties on those who complied. However, President Eisenhower did put forth the first civil rights legislation since reconstruction, some 82 years prior, in the Civil Rights Act of 1957. The goal of the bill was to ensure that African-Americans would have their right to vote. Although less than enthusiastic in his support of the fight for racial equality, he did push the voting bill through Congress. The Civil Rights Act of 1957 also established a permanent civil rights office and permitted the U.S. Department of Justice to intercede in local law enforcement cases when the civil rights of individuals were violated. In some part this may be attributed to the handling of the Emmett Till murder case.

In response to the bill, a young Martin Luther King, Jr. implored Eisenhower to use *"the weight of your great office to point out to the people of the South the moral nature of the problem"* in answer to the violence and horrendous acts perpetrated against African-

A Reflection

Americans. Eisenhower saw no need to use his influence as president to lead the nation in acceptance of blacks as equals, he conveyed to reporters in July of 1957, *"I can't imagine any set of circumstances that would ever induce me to send federal troops into any area to enforce the orders of the federal court, because I believe the common sense of Americans will never require it."* He would not have the luxury of sitting on the sideline much longer.

The "Little Rock Incident" began with the ensuing integration of the Little Rock Central High School by a group of nine African-American students in 1957. On their first day at school, September 4, the Arkansas National Guard had been deployed by Governor Orval Faubus to prevent the "Little Rock Nine" from entering the school. An injunction against the Governor's use of the National Guard was granted by a federal judge, and on September 23, 1957 the black students were escorted by police into the building. An angry mob surrounded the school and the Mayor of Little Rock, Woodrow Nilson Mann, petitioned President Eisenhower for federal troops to protect the students. Eisenhower under Executive Order 10730, federalized the Arkansas National Guard, and on September 26, 1957 the "Little Rock Nine" entered the school under the protection of 1000 members of the 101st Airborne Division.

In New York and Chicago, blacks wielded the political clout gained from their concentrated populations and elected blacks candidates to serve in Congress. In 1954, Charles C. Diggs, Jr. from Detroit joined William Dawson of Chicago and Adam Clayton Powell, Jr. from Harlem in the U.S. House of Representatives. Despite increases in the registered voter rolls, most blacks in the South remained disenfranchised, especially in the lower south. By 1957, only about 20 percent of African Americans had registered to vote.

Black Leadership

Theodore Roosevelt Mason Howard was one the less recognized civil rights leaders of the 1950s. Born on March 4, 1908 in Murray Kentucky, he was a surgeon by profession, an entrepreneur, and a leader in the state of Mississippi. A political and civil rights activist while in medical school, Howard wrote a column for the California Eagle. In 1951, he founded the Regional Council of Negro Leadership (RCNL), the leading civil rights organization in Mississippi. The mission of the RCNL was to "reach the masses through their chosen leaders," with most of the leadership being businesspersons or professionals.

Medgar Evers joined the RCNL right after graduation from Alcorn State University in 1952 becoming its program director. The RCNL demanded equality within the school system for both races and unrestricted voting rights. Howard spoke out emphatically around the country condemning the acquittal of the murderers of Emmett Till. One such speech given was hosted by Martin Luther King, Jr. at the Dexter Avenue Baptist Church. Howard left Mississippi in 1956 and the RCNL slowly began to lose its status as the struggle center moved to Montgomery, Alabama.

Martin Luther King, Jr. was born on January 15, 1929 into a family lineage of pastors in the Ebenezer Baptist Church in Atlanta, Georgia, in which he continued the family tradition. Educated at Morehouse College and Crozer Theological Seminary, it was in 1953 that he completed the residence for the doctorate at Boston University. King then became pastor of the Dexter Avenue Baptist Church in Montgomery, Alabama in 1954. The following year King was serving on the committee of an African-American Birmingham Community group that had decided to protest the segregation of the city's public bus transit system. On December 1, 1955, Rosa Park's refusal to give up her seat supplied the group with an ideal representative. They formed the Montgomery Improvement Association, established Martin Luther King, Jr. as the leader, and proceeded with the Montgomery Bus Boycott.

From this point Martin Luther King, Jr. was drawn to center stage as a leader during the civil rights movement. He took his philosophy from many places, but based his nonviolent approach on Gandhi's. He felt the church should be concerned with all the needs of the people, not just the spiritual ones; "people lift their souls after they lift their social condition." King recognized the effectiveness of mass movements in protest after the success of the Montgomery bus boycott and organized the Southern Christian Leadership Conference (SCLC) to equip himself with a base for future campaigns throughout the South.

The leadership in the late 1950's was generally dominated by the NAACP and the SCLC in spearheading the Civil Rights Movement. Initially there were misgivings on the part of the NAACP causing tension between the two groups. The NAACP saw the SCLC as a financial threat in competition for the control and support of church congregations. The two groups had different approaches in the quest for desegregation and equality. The SCLC had a strategy of non-violent direct action by the people, where the NAACP used a legal approach. At this time the membership for the NAACP was only one percent of the total black population; their sequestered fights within the courts separated them from the masses. The black community preferred the direct approach; it seemed more effective in getting their desired results. It gave them a sense of power through participation, the chance to do

A Reflection

something, to act in their own behalf. The SCLC had the ability to mobilize a mass base for boycotts and sit-ins. Social protest captivated the minds of young adults and teenagers.

Martin Luther King, Jr. worked to ease the stress between the two groups and appeased the NAACP by praising their accomplishments and encouraging NAACP memberships. To further avoid conflict, money was raised jointly and divided between the two groups. Their association was mutually beneficial, providing the SCLC with the network to organize rallies for fund raising, and arming the NAACP with the magnetism and charismatic leadership of Martin Luther King, Jr. The more militant members of the NAACP borrowed a page out of the SCLC strategy book and began organizing sit-ins at local stores in Oklahoma.

***

Malcolm X, formerly Malcolm Little, was born on May 19, 1925 in Omaha, Nebraska. Malcolm was an intelligent child, but lost interest in school and dropped out. Living in Boston, Massachusetts he worked a few odd jobs while delving in some criminal activities before moving to New York. In Harlem, Malcolm got involved in drugs, gambling, and prostitution, and in 1946, he was convicted on burglary charges and sentenced to 10 years. In prison he began to read and educate himself and became a member of the Nation of Islam before he was paroled in 1952. *"I am not educated, nor am I an expert in any particular field... but I am sincere and my sincerity is my credential."* An eloquent speaker, Malcolm became the national spokesman for the Nation of Islam and the Assistant Minister of the Detroit Temple in 1953.

Malcolm X was a force to be reckoned with; his presence and articulation elevated him among other leaders. His philosophy was influential in forming the black power movement following in Marcus Garvey's viewpoint of political and economical independence. Malcolm X was presented as an opposite to Martin Luther King, Jr. because of his rejection of non-violence in their common struggle for justice and civil rights. He believed that the fight should be won "by any means necessary."

Malcolm X was given the responsibility for establishing new mosques in major cities, and was the creator of the Nation of Islam newspaper, *"Muhammad Speaks"* in 1957. In July of 1959, the Nation of Islam took center stage when Malcolm X appeared in a television documentary called, *"The Hate That Hate Produced,"* causing the group's membership to double to 60,000 within weeks after the broadcast. Malcolm X became one of the most sought-after speakers on college campuses and participated in a number of television debates on race relations in the United States.

Civil Rights Movement

http://peacemakervoices.wordpress.com/2010/02/23/black-civil-rights-america-in-the-1950s

The successful litigations of Thurgood Marshall and the NAACP were steadily chipping away at the wall of segregation, but mass-actions protests that instigated an immediate reaction were becoming the preferred mode of remonstration. Direct-action campaigns multiplied in size and number. In 1952, the Regional Council of Negro Leadership (RCNL), under the direction of Theodore Howard and Medgar Evers, organized a successful boycott of service stations in Mississippi that refused permission for blacks to use the restrooms. The RCNL distributed close to 20,000 bumper stickers that read, "Don't Buy Gas Where You Can't Use the Restroom."

In 1953, the RCNL organization demanded the integration of Mississippi schools while Howard led additional campaigns to expose the brutality of the Mississippi state highway patrol against blacks, and also encouraged blacks to make deposits in the black-owned Tri-State Bank to counteract the credit squeeze by the White Citizens' Council. Annual meetings organized by the RCNL between 1952 and 1955 in Mound Bayou drew crowds larger than 10,000, guest speakers included Thurgood Marshall, Rep. William L. Dawson of Chicago, Rep. Charles Diggs of Michigan, and Alderman Archibald J. Carey, Jr.

The Baton Rouge Bus Boycott of 1953 had somewhat of a spontaneous beginning. Martha White, on her way to work, sat in the only seat available in the "white only" section, the police were called, but Rev. T.J. Jemison was able to keep Ms. White from being arrested. Rev. Willis Reed along with Rev. Jemison led the boycott that began on

A Reflection

June 20, 1953. The ridership on the buses in the city was 80 percent black, large enough to make a significant economic impact, thus raising the confidence of Reed in the success of the mission. Mass meeting were held at Rev. Jemison's church during the boycott. The boycott of the Baton Rouge bus system ended segregated seating after one week with Ordinance Number 251. The compromise reserved the two front rows for whites and the two rear rows for blacks. Some wanted to continue the protest, but Jemison felt the goal had been achieved. This boycott would serve as the inspiration for the Montgomery, Alabama Bus Boycott a few years later.

The 1955 Montgomery Bus Boycott was strategically orchestrated by Edgar Nixon who was then the local president of the NAACP. Nixon had been planning a challenge to the segregation of public buses in Montgomery for some time, but was waiting for a suitable candidate to be arrested. That person was found in Rosa Parks who refused to give up her seat in the "white" section of a public bus on December 1, 1955. Nixon solicited the aid of black ministers in the community to support the bus boycott, and on December 5, 1955 the Montgomery Improvement Association (MIA) was formed.

Martin Luther King, Jr. was selected to lead the boycott. More than 95 percent of blacks refused to ride the buses. King and 156 protesters were taken into custody for "hindering" a bus, and King spent two weeks in jail. Violence escalated during the boycott, King and Ralph Abernathy's houses were firebombed along with four black Baptist churches. The Montgomery bus boycott lasted 381 days focusing national attention on southern segregation and establishing Martin Luther King as the leader of the Civil Rights Movement. On November 13, 1956 the Supreme Court ordered the integration of buses in Montgomery. This victory united the country in the movement rather than just the struggle of individual cities or states. This mass direct-action protest led to the formation of the Southern Christian Leadership Conference in January 1957 to broaden the movement.

Six months after the success of the Montgomery Bus Boycott, a Tallahassee, Florida bus boycott was initiated by students at Florida A.M. University in 1956. The boycott was taken up by Rev. C.K. Steele, president of the Tallahassee chapter of the NAACP. The boycott of the city bus system lasted from May to December, but total integration of the buses in Tallahassee was not achieved until 1958.

In reaction to the successes of the Civil Rights Movement, southern whites in power started to attack the NAACP with intentions to destroy the organization and halt the fight against discrimination and equal rights. Law suits were filed and injunctions prevented the NAACP from operating in some states. During this time, 246 branches were shut down in an orchestrated effort to sidetrack the organization through litigation and deplete its operating funds. In 1957, the NAACP spun off the Legal Defense and Educational fund after much harassment by the Internal Revenue Service and the U.S. Department of Treasury. The Legal Defense and Educational Fund would continue to fight racial discrimination in court, while the NAACP would utilize more nonviolent confrontations and sit-ins.

The Black Church

"But a religion true to its nature must also be concerned about man's social condition....Any religion that professes to be concerned with the souls of men and is not concerned with the slums that damn them, the economic conditions that strangle them, and the social conditions that cripple them is a dry-as-dust religion."
Martin Luther *King Jr.*

The Southern Christian Leadership Conference (SCLC) was formed to organize antisegregation protest movements in other communities in the South. It was perceived that a church-related organization would be more palatable. The NAACP was comprised of lawyers who preferred to operate in the courts; whereas the SCLC would be comprised of ministers leading local movements. Nine experienced men emerged as leaders, Reverend Martin Luther King, Jr., leader of the Montgomery bus boycott, president; Reverend C.K. Steele, leader of the Tallahassee bus boycott, first vice president; Reverend A.L. Davis, leader in the bus protest of New Orleans, second vice president; Reverend Samuel Williams, leader in efforts to desegregate Atlanta buses, third vice president; Reverend T.J. Jemison, leader of first mass bus boycott in Baton rouge in 1953, secretary; Reverend Fred Shuttlesworth, leader of the mass direct action movement in Birmingham, corresponding secretary; Reverend Ralph Abernathy, a leader in the Montgomery bus boycott and confidant of Dr. King, treasurer; Reverend Kelly Miller Smith, local NAACP President and activist of Nashville, and Lawrence Reddick, a scholar at Alabama State College, and an activist of the Montgomery bus boycott. All of these leaders were black educated southerners and clergymen, with the exception of one.

Churches played a more dominant role in the Civil Rights Movement during the late 1950s, they disseminated information, raised capital to support the movement, publicized

A Reflection

meetings and agendas, encouraged their members to join the NAACP and SCLC, and to register to vote. Activist clergymen tended to be more educated ministers who encouraged political participation for their members. Congregational services and mass meetings galvanized members to join in the struggle for social justice.

In M.L. King's first speech before the Montgomery bus boycott mass meeting he laid the moral foundation for the movement; *"We are not wrong in what we are doing. If we are wrong, then the Supreme Court of this nation is wrong. If we are wrong, the Constitution of the United States is wrong. If we are wrong, God Almighty is wrong ..."* Yet some churches were still reluctant to be directly involved in demonstrations fearing retaliation, but opened their doors as a refuge for meetings. Church bombings during the 1950s had become regular occurrences in cities of the Deep South, and in Birmingham they were epidemic. Rev. Fred Shuttlesworth, leader of the Civil Rights actions in Birmingham, later affirmed the mission at a Civil Rights meeting in 1958: *"This is a religious crusade, a fight between light and darkness, right and wrong, good and evil, fair play and tyranny. We are assured of victory because we are using weapons of spiritual warfare."*

Near the end of the 1950s, black ministers known as the "Philadelphia Four Hundred" reprised the "Don't Buy Where You Can't Work" tenet of the 1930s in their offensive against rampant unemployment in the city. Members of their congregations were advised to avoid doing business with establishments that discriminated in hiring. The church took further responsibility in preparing black constituents for job placement with education and skill training opportunities. Of the more than 10 million blacks in the country, seven million attended church, with the economic value of the churches being over $250 million. The black church and religion became a force and influence in every aspect of our lives.

The Nation of Islam experienced a rebirth after the war. Elijah Muhammad, who had served time in prison for resisting the draft, focused his recruitment on those who were dejected or immersed in criminal activity. His desire was to transform black people who had been oppressed and rejected. Elijah Muhammad taught a combination of basic fundamentals of Islam mixed with Black Nationalism. By the end of 1959, the Nation's membership had grown near to 100,000 in the United States. Members gave 25 to 33 percent of their income to the Nation for businesses ventures and the construction of schools and temples. The teachings promoted self-respect, a strict moral character, and racial unity. The Nation of Islam supported a program that promoted economic self-sufficiency for African Americans through the ownership of their own black businesses.

The Black Press

The black press, as well as the mainstream press, was operating under precarious conditions during the 1950s. The anti-communist atmosphere amid the McCarthy accusations led black newspapers to temper their radical stance to placate their conservative advertisers. Charlotta Bass, publisher and editor of the California Eagle, a suspected member of the communist party, was a target of FBI investigations. Readers who feared guilt by association read the less militant Los Angeles Sentinel, driving the Eagle close to ruin, and prompting Bass to sell the paper in 1951.

The black press was understandably subjective in instances relative to racial equality and the end of Jim Crow. Ethel L. Payne, called "the first lady of the black press," was known for asking the tough questions. Working as a White house correspondent for the Chicago Defender, Payne questioned President Eisenhower about his plan to enforce the decision by the Commerce Commission to end segregation in interstate travel. His irate response made national headlines.

Black newspapers and publications played a more influential role in the struggle for civil rights than even the black church. They exposed the injustice of segregation and reported it nationwide complete with all its abominable details. The black press exposed the lynching and growing reprisals against the black community by racist white organizations hoping to stifle the significant steps forward after the Brown v. Topeka Board of Education decision. The black newspapers provided visibility and commentary that mobilized the black community in the protests of the Civil Rights Movement. Black newspapers emphasized the strength of the ballot and motivated blacks to register and then vote.

At the beginning of the 1950s, most news stories pertaining to African-Americans were still not covered in the mainstream news. The *Amsterdam News* was the first newspaper to focus on Malcolm X, publishing his column, "God's Angry Man." Black press coverage of the Emmett Till's murder in 1955 and the subsequent trial changed that circumstance with many unanticipated results. *The Chicago Defender* along with *The Amsterdam News and The Pittsburgh Courier* covered the heinous crime against Till extensively until the dramatic story was picked up by the mainstream press. Black publications stirred ire and emotion with the pictures shown of the heartache and grief of a mother whose child was murdered. The mutilated body was front page material and the injuries were described in graphic detail, giving black people across the nation an "up close and personal" account of Emmett Till's lynching. The press coverage was

A Reflection

instrumental in galvanizing huge numbers of black people, mass meetings of 25,000 in New York, 20,000 in Detroit, and 15,000 in Cleveland were held in outrage over the murder and acquittal.

The Civil Rights Movement had become big news, black reporters participated in sit-ins and other direct-action protests to give a full account of the experience, and they covered the Montgomery boycott, the marches, the speeches, and the riots. The mainstream press could not continue to overlook the national news stories and began regular coverage for white dailies to attract black readers.

Black newspapers had been traditionally weekly publications, but *The Chicago Defender* became *The Chicago Daily Defender* on February 6, 1956. White-owned newspapers began to integrate their reporting staff enticing black journalist with increased pay and exposure. Increased competition and the introduction of news divisions in radio and television contributed to the decline in circulation of black newspapers.

Daisy Bates and her husband L.C. Bates published a local black newspaper in Little Rock, AR called the *Arkansas State Press*. The Bates, with a substantial readership, used their paper as a voice for civil rights, publishing violations of the U.S. Supreme Court decisions. Their paper consistently ran articles that condemned the police brutality against black residents and reported on the harassment and murder of black veterans returning home from service to their country. A series of editorials about the death of a black soldier by a white police officer bothered white locals, and white businesses owners who regularly purchased advertising in their paper boycotted them threatening the survival of the newspaper. Nevertheless it was Daisy Bates' involvement with the lawsuit against the Little Rock public school system, and her support of the "Little Rock Nine" and their families that resulted in the total loss of advertising revenue that forced them to close the *Arkansas State Press* in 1959.

In 1950, John H. Johnson, publisher of Ebony magazine, discontinued the Negro Digest and launched *Tan*, an advice magazine. In 1951, Johnson founded the successful *Jet* magazine, a weekly publication that reported the achievements of blacks in a number of fields including, politics, entertainment, and sports. The magazine gave profiles of African-American leaders, covered major civil rights events, and offered frequent editorials on race relations in the nation. The Jet magazine was well-known for its coverage of the Emmett Till murder, Martin Luther King, Jr., and the Montgomery Bus Boycott.

1959

Black Businesses and Professionals

Black businesses of the 1950s encompassed a complete separate black economy that provided a valuable measure of financial security for the African-American community. These businesses ran the gamut from drug stores, grocery stores, auto repair shops, tailor and dress makers, beauty and barber shops, to restaurants, movie theaters, and funeral homes. However, many of these black businesses that experienced the prosperity of the previous decade encountered setbacks as integration spread in more areas and white-owned business realized the profitability within the African-American market. As the doors of more white establishments were opened, black businesses suffered the loss in clientele, and began to close more of their doors. A number of businesses attempted to relocate to other cities to survive; leaving poorer black neighborhoods without the convenience of a host of services within their community.

There were some phenomenal entrepreneurs that created hugely successful businesses and turned them into their own empires in this decade. Lawrence Cormier along with his wife Helen Cecelia established the first African-America oil company in America, Ebony Oil Corporation, in addition to other military technology and food service enterprises in Jamaica-Queens, New York. Eugene V. Roundtree founded All-Stainless Inc. in 1952, which became the nation's largest distributor of stainless steel parts for industry. Henry Henderson started H.F. Industries out of his basement as a subcontractor for the production and marketing of instrumentation and control panels. In 1955, John Barfield and his wife Betty Jane Barfield parlayed part-time cleaning of newly constructed homes into a contract cleaning group of 200 employees, called the Barfield Cleaning Company of Ypsilanti, Michigan. Barfield wrote the *Barfield Method of Building Maintenance* later that year setting the standard for the commercial building maintenance industry.

George E. Johnson founded Johnson products with his wife in 1954. Johnson borrowed a total of $500 to bankroll his new business venture, his first product was a hair relaxer for men called Ultra Wave, and he followed it with Ultra Sheen in 1957, a home hair straightener for women. Willie Stennis and his wife Zelma started their chain of fried chicken restaurants in Los Angeles, California in 1957. In January of 1959, Berry Gordy started Tamla Records, with an $800 loan from his family, and founded his second label, Motown Records, in September 1959. Herman Russell took over his father's plastering business and graduated to larger projects of home building and real estate investment. By the end of the decade, Russell had expanded to general contracting through H. J. Russell Construction Company and the formation of a residential and commercial property

A Reflection

management company called Paradise Management, Inc starting with 18 apartment units.

Samuel B. Fuller was in a class by himself as a businessman. In the 1950s, Fuller was the richest African-American in the United States. Fuller's purchase of Boyer International Laboratories, a white cosmetics company with Jean Nadal as a subsidiary, took his company to another stratosphere with $18 million in sales and a sales force of five thousand. His employees, one-third of them white, called themselves "Fullerites." During the 1950s, he further expanded his empire with Fuller Guaranty Corporation and Fuller-Philco Home Appliance Center. Diversifying his holdings, Fuller became a major shareholder in the Pittsburgh Courier Publishing Company, bought the Chicago Regal Theater, purchased a real estate trust in New York City, owned the buildings that housed most of his branches of business in different cities, and invested in farming and cattle. Towards the end of the decade the White Citizens Council learned of his ownership and organized a boycott of Fuller's Nadal products line.

The Nation of Islam was identified as one of the largest Black Businesses in America during the 1950s, but it was considered a threat to the internal security of the United States. The Nation of Islam has always had a creed of self-sufficiency which motivated them to develop a network of small African-American businesses in a number of large American cities. Their chief long-range economic goal was the creation of a geographically isolated, agricultural-based nation in the American South, where industrial facilities would emerge from the profits from sales of agricultural products to local consumers within and outside of the nation, and to Muslim stores in urban cities.

Extraordinary African-American

Dr. Percy Lavon Julian was a vanguard synthetic chemist, an inventor, an industrial research director, and a wealthy businessman. Julian was the grandson of a slave, born to James and Elizabeth Julian on April 11, 1899 in Montgomery, Alabama. Although Julian was a gifted student, the city lacked a public high school for black students, and he entered Indiana's DePauw University as a "sub-freshman" in 1916 majoring in chemistry. Working as a janitor and waiter in return for room and board in a fraternity house, unable to live in the dorms, Julian graduated valedictorian and Phi Beta Kappa in 1920. Julian relocated to Nashville, TN to teach chemistry at Fisk University. Awarded an Austin Fellowship in Chemistry, Julian went to Harvard University where he completed his master's degrees at the top of his class in 1923. Harvard, wary of the reaction of white students being taught by a black man withdrew his teaching assistantship, leaving Julian unable to complete his doctorate.

Providentially, Julian received a Rockefeller Foundation Fellowship in 1929 to continue his graduate studies at the University of Vienna, where in 1931; he was the third African-American to earn his Ph.D. in chemistry. On his return from Vienna, Julian was barred from professorships at major universities because of his race. He accepted a teaching position at Howard University and in 1932 was offered a position to teach organic chemistry at DePauw University. In 1935, Julian and Josef Pikl, a fellow student he brought from the University of Vienna, synthesized physostigmine, a drug used to treat glaucoma. The drug also showed promise in the treatment of Alzheimers and in limiting the effects of chemical weapons. He received international scientific acclaim, but no faculty position at DePauw, prompting Julian to make the decision to leave the world of academia.

W.J. O'Brien, vice president at Glidden contacted Julian after he requested a 5-gallon sample of soybean oil from the Glidden Company to use as raw material for the synthesis of human steroidal sex hormones. O'Brien offered Julian the director of research position at Glidden's Soya Products Division in Chicago. Julian arrived at Glidden in 1936, where he designed and supervised the construction of the first facility for the production of industrial-grade soy protein, replacing the costly milk casein in several industrial applications. A sample of the soy protein was sent to the National Foam System Inc. where it was used to develop foam that could put out oil and gas fires. During World War II, the foam was used by the military to smother oil and gas fires aboard ships and aircraft carriers.

In 1940, Julian took his research in a new direction when he began work on synthesizing progesterone, testosterone, and estrogen from plant sterols isolated from soybean oil. There were clinical uses for these hormones, but only miniscule amounts could be extracted from a mountain of spinal cords. Julian could produce 100 pounds of mixed sterols daily, valued at $10,000 in sex hormones. His research made it possible to produce hormones in mass quantities. Progesterone was sold on the American market for the first time, reducing the cost of treating hormonal deficiencies.

In April of 1949, Philip Hench, a rheumatologist at the Mayo Clinic, announced the effectiveness of cortisone in the treatment of rheumatoid arthritis and other inflammatory diseases. By October 1949, Julian and his team had synthesized a cortisone substitute, drastically less expensive but equally as effective. Natural cortisone was extracted from the adrenal glands of oxen and cost hundreds of dollars per drop; Julian's synthetic

A Reflection

cortisone cost only pennies per ounce. In 1950, he synthesized pregnenolone. The ability to create ample amounts of essential medical products at less cost drives research and the accumulation of knowledge. His products led to the development of chemical birth control, medicines to prevent miscarriages, drugs to fight cancer, and medicines to suppress the immune system, crucial for maintaining organ transplants.

In December of 1953, after winning a contract to provide Upjohn with $2 million worth of progesterone, Julian left Glidden to form his own research company, Julian Laboratories, Inc. with its headquarters in Franklin Park, Illinois and branches in Mexico and Guatemala. Dr. Julian held more than 130 chemical patents, published vast number of papers, and received a host of awards and honorary degrees. He was the first African-American chemist to be inducted into the National Academy of Sciences, and only the second from any field. Julian sold the U.S and Mexico plants to SmithKline and the Guatemala branch to UpJohn in 1961 for a total of $2 million. He formed the Julian Research Institute in 1964 working on research until his death in 1975.

Employment

There was an accumulation of unfavorable conditions that negatively impacted the employment picture for African-Americans in the 1950s. In the South, agricultural surpluses lessened the demand for farm laborers, while in the North and Midwest, industrial automation and outsourcing to subcontractors eliminated jobs and entry-level positions. In the earlier years of the 1950s, blacks were still migrating out of the South to high-unemployment labor markets of the North. Major industries continued their move out of the cities into the suburbs and rural communities. Whites were able to relocate to the outskirts of the city much easier than black workers. However, the wage differential from the North to the South was sufficient incentive for blacks to pick up stakes despite the increased likelihood of unemployment.

During these years, 80 percent of black men and 47 percent of black women were in the labor force, compared to 85.6 of white men and 36 percent of white women, with the unemployment rate at 10.7 percent for black men versus 4.8 percent for white men, and 9.5 percent for black women versus 5.3 percent of white women. The labor market was much worse for young blacks with 25 percent of them unemployed overall, with an even higher 47 percent in the South where large numbers had worked as farm labor.

Black workers were disproportionately affected by job losses because of their lack of skills and concentration in high-unemployment occupations, with the largest levels of joblessness seen in the Northern states. Additionally the wage gap between blacks and whites, which had narrowed some during the previous decade, had become static as the pay gains for less-educated workers stopped.

Black workers were indeed industrialized, 80 percent of employed black men were in non-agricultural employment. According to U.S. Census data, African-Americans were largely employed in service jobs but were entering new industries and occupations that had previously been closed to them. Black males worked in manufacturing, as mechanics, bus drivers, and policemen. Black male workers in white-collar positions had grown to 7.2 percent, employed as managers, accountants, and salesmen, and the number of craftsmen had grown close to 29 percent. Black women were making gains in employment as well, many were employed in factories, some as clerical or sales workers, and the proportion of black women working as servants or domestics had gone down to 35 percent.

The American Federation of Labor (AFL) and the Congress of Industrial Organizations (CIO) merged in 1955 with a constitutional commitment *"to encourage all workers without regard to race, creed, color, national origin or ancestry to share equally in the benefits of the organization."* The new labor alliance elected two African-Americans as vice presidents; A. Philip Randolph of the Brotherhood of the Sleeping Car Porters and Willard S. Townsend of the United Transport Service Employees. A civil rights department was instated to enforce the non-bias policy along with the Southern Advisory Committee on Civil Rights. Larger numbers of black workers were unionized, comprising 17 percent of meatpacking workers, over 9 percent of coalminers, and 68 percent of tobacco workers. Access to labor unions proved to be a godsend for African-American workers, raising both their status and their wages levels, affording them job security and benefits, but black workers were still discriminated against in local unions. In 1959, Randolph formed the Negro-American Labor Council to secure equal treatment for blacks in labor unions.

Education

Education was the vehicle for black people in the pursuit for equal opportunity and the achievement of the "American dream," but institutional racism was restraining our transformation as a people by limiting our education. By the 1950s, more than 95 percent of African-Americans were enrolling in elementary education, but our education attainment levels in high school were a hindrance to forward movement. According to U.S. Census data, only 12 percent of black males graduated from high school, and of those 85 percent lived in urban areas, while only 6.3 percent in rural farm regions received a high school

A Reflection

education. For black females, 15.5 percent graduated from high school and the numbers also declined for blacks living in rural nonfarm and rural farm areas. For black males the median grade completed was 8.8 years in urban areas, 6.9 in rural nonfarm, and 6.0 rural farm populations. For black females the median years completed were 9.4 in urban, 7.7 in rural nonfarm, and 7.4 in rural farm regions.

The 1950s were breakthrough years in education as victories were won in the fierce battle for access to an equal education. The NAACP had challenged the legitimacy of "separate but equal" education in the courts and the Brown v. Board of Education of Topeka ruling in 1954 stated that segregation in the schools was inherently unequal. Desegregation was ordered with "all deliberate speed" but it was met with vehement opposition particularly in the South. The Ku Klux Klan and the White Citizens Council organized protests in Mississippi and Missouri against the court-ordered desegregation. By 1955, state officials in Ohio, Oklahoma, Tennessee, and Kentucky had taken the lead in initiating the desegregation process, but 99 percent of black students in southern states attended all-black schools.

The greatest resistance by state officials to desegregation was seen in Arkansas when Governor Faubus called out the National Guard to block the desegregation of Central High School. In 1957, President Eisenhower sent in paratroopers to escort the nine black students who would integrate the Little Rock high schools. Governor Faubus went as far as closing Little Rock public schools, issuing vouchers to parents to attend white private schools, and leasing public school facilities to private entities to open private schools in order to prevent further desegregation. These attempts were deemed unconstitutional by the Supreme Court, and the Little Rock public schools reopened and desegregated in 1959.

Massive resistance was also seen in Virginia where public schools were closed to prevent desegregation. Governor Lindsay affected 13,000 students when he shut down schools in Norfolk, Virginia in 1958. The Virginia Supreme Court ordered the reopening and desegregation of the schools in 1959, and "the Norfolk 17" and other black students throughout the state entered once all-white schools. However by the end of 1959, five states, Maryland, South Carolina, Georgia, Alabama, and Louisiana had not been desegregated.

The desegregation of public schools was not the ideal solution for everyone in the black community; among those in disagreement were black teachers. In spite of their inferiority to white schools, a survey taken in 1953 determined that 75 percent of black teachers expressed a preference to teach in segregated schools. As a result of the Brown decision, hundreds of black teachers lost jobs and their opportunities for teaching were greatly reduced.

African-Americans were extremely underrepresented in higher education. According to U.S. Census data, just two percent of black males and less than three percent of black females graduated from college. Racial separation and discrimination in state colleges had been banned by the Supreme Court in the Sweatt v. Painter and McLaurin v. Oklahoma State Regents rulings years before the Brown decision, nevertheless, in 1954, black students made up a mere one percent of freshman enrolled at predominately white colleges and universities. Struggles to increase the levels of education attainment for African-Americans were met with tremendous antagonism maintaining the disparity between blacks and whites and limiting their socioeconomic growth.

Issue of Crime

The first glance at the volume of crime during the fifties shows a 69 percent increase in criminal activity, but a closer look at Uniform Crime Reports shows that of the total 2,612,704 criminal offenses reported in 1959, 39 percent of the arrests were for drunkenness, and 74 percent of those arrested for this offense were white. In 1950, black arrests were 25 percent of the total and 30 percent of the total arrests in 1959. By the middle of the decade there were 98,000 black men and women serving time in prisons or jails throughout the United States. Based on the data, African-Americans were committing a disproportionate number of crimes based on their percentage in the population, but the indisputable fact of the era was that blacks were most likely to be arrested by the police, most likely to be convicted, and most likely to receive a longer sentence than any other race for a similar crime committed.

Blacks were more likely to commit the more violent crimes of homicide and assault, crimes that are more often intra-racial, and the least likely to commit sex offenses or offenses against family and children. There was actually a decrease in the number of homicides form the previous decade. From 1950 to 1959 there was 35 percent drop in the number of homicides committed by African-Americans, down from 2889 to 1891. However, there were 61,700 assault arrests in 1959, more than double the number of assaults in 1950. There was also a two-fold increase in the number of burglary and larceny arrests, rising well above the rate of population gains. Although there was no apparent explanation there was a seven-fold increase in the number of gambling arrests in 1959.

The 1950s exhibited the highest levels of juvenile delinquency ever seen, the arrests and court cases doubled over the last decade. Studies of juvenile delinquency have concluded that delinquency is more prominent in overcrowded poverty-stricken communities among under-privileged youth. Youth gangs multiplied during these years along with the migrant populations in urban areas. Black gangs fought each other, but the majority of conflicts were with white gangs on the boundaries of neighborhoods. Violence erupted over gang turf, particularly in cities with large numbers of migrants like Chicago, New York, and Los Angeles. Curfews were activated to limit criminal activity, and record numbers of arrests were made by police. The greater numbers of black youths incarcerated led to gangs forming within the prison system.

Health Issues

Desegregation in the health-care system was slowly gaining ground in the 1950s. National, state, and local county medical associations and societies were gradually accepting black memberships as racial restrictive membership barriers were removed, but many hospitals still refused black patients and barred black physicians from using hospital facilities. Progress in the integration of white medical schools was slow, at the beginning of the decade five medical schools in the South opened their doors to black applicants. However, by 1957, only fourteen out of twenty-six medical schools in the South admitted black students. The number of black medical students enrolled in predominately white schools rose 31 percent, but the burden of educating black doctors was divided heavily between Howard University and Meharry Medical College, with 69 percent of 761 black students in the 1955-56 class.

The population growth among blacks had far exceeded the number of black doctors. The population had grown nearly 48 percent, while the number of black doctors rose by only 10.5 percent to 4,200. By the end of the decade there was still only one doctor for every 4,500 blacks throughout the country. In the South the ratio was much worse with one doctor to 6,203 blacks, and in Mississippi, 1 to 18,000. Black women were making some advances in the field of healthcare with many being accepted for nurse's training, only to be hired as nurse's aides and paid lower salaries.

A number of health issues were common among poor blacks living in urban towns as well as those settled in overcrowded urban slums. Limited access and the lack of money left minor health conditions like rotten teeth, rat bites, and poor hearing or eyesight untreated. In 1959, the lack of good nutrition and prenatal care kept black infant mortality twice that of white babies, and maternal death rates were four times those of white mothers.

Children suffered with illnesses associated with a poor diet that affected their development. Communicable childhood diseases raised the mortality rate of black children as they suffered with whooping cough, measles, meningitis, and diphtheria at higher levels than white children. Vaccines for whooping cough, polio, and diphtheria were introduced in the 1950s, but vaccines were administered in white schools where black children were not allowed.

Death rates from tuberculosis for African-Americans in New York State still remained four times the rate of whites in 1959. Syphilis was another malady affecting the health of African-Americans with incidences of the disease at 10 times that of whites infected, and four times the death rate.

African-Americans suffered higher death rates from cardiovascular disease, particularly black women. It was speculated that the increased burden of maintaining the family and in many cases being the principal breadwinner created more stress and made them more susceptible to heart disease. Blacks were disproportionately affected by hypertension with mortality three times that of whites.

African-Americans were smoking in larger numbers during the 1950s; the number of black males who smoked cigarettes surpassed the number of white males for the first time. Higher incidences of mental illness were seen among African-Americans, consistent with studies conducted in New York City and New Haven that found a correlation between poverty and mental disorders, as blacks were disproportionately economically depressed.

Despite the disparities in mortality and morbidity between whites and blacks during the 1950s there were significant improvements in the health of African-American, the difference in life expectancy had narrowed to seven years. Many of the diseases that contributed to high mortality and morbidity rates for black people were preventable and treatable, and communicable diseases could have been greatly reduced with improved housing standards and adequate healthcare. As with all the issues that African-Americans struggle against, progress in ending discrimination in medical care would be slow.

Housing

Conflicts and disputes related to housing continued to be at the root of increased racial tensions during the 1950s. Segregation in residential areas became even more delineated as "white flight" out of the inner cities to the suburbs concentrated black migrants into ghettos and slums. The overall black homeownership was 39 percent, with generally high homeownership in the rural south, and comparatively low homeownership in the urban areas of the South and the Northeast where migrants were not likely to be homeowners. The government agencies of FHA, HUD, and the VA reinforced residential segregation

A Reflection

through their refusal of mortgage insurance to blacks in neighborhoods that were not segregated. Towards the end of the decade, only two percent of homes built with FHA funding were occupied by black families.

Great efforts were made to maintain segregation in overcrowded cities as "black belts" were expanded with the increased number of migrants. In Detroit, a six foot high, one foot wide wall was constructed along Eight Mile Road to separate whites from black neighborhoods. In Los Angeles, freeways were built to support segregation lines, and in Chicago a new expressway and 18 tower housing projects were built to divide black and white neighborhoods. White residents participated in ruthless campaigns to prevent the integration of public housing located in white communities.

Black ghettos were filled overcapacity and contributed to dangerous living conditions and substandard housing. The *U.S. News* gave perspective to the crisis in housing stating, "The density of 75,000 persons per square mile in Chicago's 'black belt' is equal to the slums of Calcutta, India." The Housing Act of 1954 was designed to prevent and eradicate slums and urban blight, thus eliminating substandard living conditions for blacks in inner cities. These federally subsidized urban renewal projects were to provide solutions to housing shortages, but African-Americans comprised over 60 percent of those displaced after the demolitions of housing units in urban areas.

Public housing was the government's answer to the lack of affordable housing. Large hi-rise buildings, situated in groups, were the government's model in the 1950s for low-income housing. These public housing projects were being built in the North, Midwest, and the West coast, but were largely situated in black communities perpetuating racial segregation. New York's urban renewal plan demolished more tenement neighborhoods than any other city in the country during the decade. Large-scale high-rise housing projects during this time were constructed solely in black areas to house those displaced. These complexes were commonly referred to as "the projects." Watts was the subject of a housing experiment in 1953, three large housing projects were erected, Jordon Downs, William Nicheron Jr. Gardens, and Imperial Court, that would house 10,000 people. By 1959, one-third of the residents of Watts were housed in "projects." Housing projects served only to concentrate the poverty and the ills that come with it.

With the advent of housing projects, African-Americans who could afford better wanted the nice homes and spacious neighborhoods that whites had in the suburbs, and began their trek out of the ghettos. By 1959, most of the black middle-class has already left Harlem, taking with them the social organization and stability of the community. An article in the *Pittsburgh Courier* (Dec. 7, 1957) noted, "*Loss of middle-class population and business following suburban migration, and deterioration of overcrowded residential areas are causing a decline of urban facilities and seriously endanger economic health of cities.*"

In a number of cities, blacks purchased suburban land to build their own homes, developing suburban black communities. Nevertheless with each measure of progress there was always another obstacle to overcome. Discrimination in local governments halted their endeavors with the extension of land-use regulations to areas that had not been previously regulated, and barred African-American home builders from construction in the suburbs. Urban renewal projects were also used to isolate or drive out these new neighborhoods for blacks, and arson was always a method to contest the movement of black families into white areas.

Building restrictions in zoning and codes raised the cost of homes on the fringes of the inner city and suburbs, eliminating low-income buyers. Regulations wiped out housing developments of blacks, enforcing the racist application of sanitary rules that called for the demolition of existing black homes and restricted new construction.

Violence against blacks who had the gumption to cross the boundaries of segregation reached a high point in the 1950s. Working-class and middle-class blacks who dared to move into white communities were welcomed with physical threats, cross-burnings, and bombings. However, discrimination in housing affected every class of African-Americans, Jackie Robinson and his wife found they were unable to buy a home in the suburbs of Brooklyn even after leading the Dodgers to the World Championship in 1956. Percy Julian bought a home in Oak Park, Illinois in 1951 and became the first African-American family to own property there, his home was fire-bombed on Thanksgiving day before he moved in, and six months after they moved in it was attacked with dynamite. Other prominent black people who had their homes bombed after moving into white communities were Samuel Fuller and Nat King Cole.

Elimination of housing discrimination was a focus of civil rights groups and leaders for many years, but restrictive covenants still operate unofficially across the country in spite of the ban by the Supreme Court. In 1959, fair housing laws were finally being implemented in states to limit discriminatory actions by lenders, builders, real estate agents, sellers, and renters.

A Reflection

Family Structure

Black families experienced significant changes in the 1950, alterations that triggered structural and economical ramifications that impact the majority of African-Americans even today. Most noteworthy was the marriage rate among blacks which peaked during this decade. For the first time in the last fifty years whites were marrying at a higher proportion than blacks. According to U.S. Census data, 70 percent of black men were married. Surprisingly the higher proportions of males married was in urban regions at 72 percent, 64 percent in rural nonfarm regions, and 62 percent in rural areas. Overall, 53.5 percent of black males reported the spouse present in the home. For black women, 78 percent were married overall, with nearly 80 percent of black females married in urban populations, 75 percent in rural nonfarm regions, and 70 percent in rural farm areas. Sixty-one percent of married black females reported their spouse living in the home, an increase over the last decade. Blacks were marrying at an older age, there were more divorces, and men living longer reduced the number of widows.

Black families experienced the baby boom of the 1950s seen throughout the United States. The average size of the black family was 3.82, with 3.61 in urban regions, 4.30 in rural nonfarm, and 5.32 in rural farm regions. The number of legitimate births, or children born to married parents peaked in the latter 1950s and the number of illegitimate births or babies born to single mothers began to increase. While 72 percent of black children lived in a household of both parents, by the end of the decade, 25 percent of black babies were born out of wedlock and 21 percent of black families were headed by a female.

Statistics from the Bureau of Census, Current Population Survey Reports showed less racial differences in premarital conception, except premarital pregnancies among black women were less likely to lead to marriage; between 1950 and 1959 only 19 percent of pregnant unwed black women were married within seven months compared to 60 percent for whites. This decade marks the trend away from black family stability.

The precarious employment situation of African-American men has been the decisive factor in their ability to be the principal provider for a wife and family. The labor-force participation for black women, particularly those in southern states, was increasing while the labor markets for black men were deteriorating. Black men without jobs or in economically insecure positions were less likely to marry or stay with their families. The negative consequences of the decrease in marriage among blacks and the increase in black families headed by a female were higher numbers of black children growing up in poverty, decreased educational attainment, and increased juvenile delinquency. However, during these years only seven percent of black families were receiving Aid to Families with Dependent Children (AFDC), notwithstanding the fact that the monthly AFDC payment was greater than the expected earnings of a full-time employed black male.

The total income earned by black families was $125.8 billion in 1959, disproportionately divided, 20 percent of black families earned half of the income, with the other half split up among the remaining 80 percent. Although the number of blacks living below the poverty level had declined from the previous decade, among 40 to 50 percent still lived below poverty level. Fortunately in the face of economic challenges more black families were able to prosper in the 1950s and the black middle-class population continued to expand. Economic status differences between black families caused a rift in black communities as the more prosperous blacks sought to distance themselves from the dilapidated ghettos and slums.

In 1957, E. Franklin Frazier published a socioeconomic study of class among African-Americans called *Black Bourgeoisie.* His book received critical acclaim in the midst of much disapproval because of his criticism of blacks who integrated with whites as having been "*seduced by dreams of final assimilation*." Frazier's book was an attack on middle- and upper-class blacks, blaming them for exacerbating the social and economic ills of their "underclass" brethren in their "black-flight" from urban cities and black communities in rural southern towns. Frazier characterized the burgeoning middle-class as "an anomalous bourgeois class with no identity, built on self-sustaining myths of black business and society, silently undermined by a collective, debilitating inferiority complex." His opinions were one-dimensional and only served to compound the resentment of poor working-class black families who were essentially trapped in dismal circumstances.

Black Athletes and Sports

African-American athletes were crossing the barrier of segregation in competitive sports one player at a time. Baseball continued its reign as the nation's preferred pastime, and following Jackie Robinson, black ball players were recruited to attract black fans to the gate. Several black stars shined on the baseball diamond during this decade, premiere players included Willie Mays, Larry Doby, Roy Campanella, Don Newcombe, Elston Howard, Ernie Banks, and Henry Aaron.

The 1950s also saw premiere players of the Negro Baseball league like Leroy "Satchel" Paige finally enter into the major leagues. For most like Josh Gibson, the "Babe Ruth of Negro Baseball," the doors opened too late. Satchel Paige, considered by many as the

A Reflection

greatest pitcher in baseball history, was already over forty years old when he joined the Cleveland Indians. During the 1950s, in the twilight of his career, he pitched for the St. Louis Browns mesmerizing the fans with his loaded arsenal of pitches.

Roy Campanella joined Jackie Robinson with the Brooklyn Dodgers, followed later by Don Newcombe as teammates for a few years. Newcombe set records as a pitcher as well as a hitter, and was a National League MVP winner. Campanella was a catcher with a powerful swing, a three-time winner of most valuable player award in the National League, and a large contributor to the winning of five pennants for the Brooklyn Dodgers.

Willie Mays, playing for the New York Giants and later San Francisco Giants, brought unmatched excitement to center field. Mays' legendary catches and home runs earned him the National League MVP award in 1954 as well as the pennant and a sweep of the Cleveland Indians in the World Series. Ernie Banks, playing for the Chicago Cubs, was the hardest-hitting shortstop to ever play in the major leagues. He hit 248 home runs from 1955 to 1960, more than any other player including Mickey Mantle and Willie Mays, and became the first player to win the National League MVP award two years in a row.

Hank Aaron, playing for the Braves, first in Milwaukee and then in Atlanta, was an all around baseball player whose game was subtle but highly effective. Aaron was consistent in his delivery of home runs winning more games than any other player on the field. In 1957, he won the MVP award with 44 home runs, 132 runs batted-in, with a .322 batting average.

***

Professional football was challenging baseball for the top sport position in the nation during the 1950s. Black athletes had distinguished themselves in college football, and in 1952, every team in the NFL had signed a black player with the exception of the Washington Redskins. By the end of the 1950s, African-Americans represented 12 percent of the players in the National Football League.

Joe Perry came into the NFL with the San Francisco 49ers in 1950 and became one of the first African-American star players, increasing the level of excitement in the game with his thrilling runs. Perry, also known as "the jet," for his dominating strength and world class speed, became the first runner to achieve 1,000 yard rushing seasons in 1953 and 1954, and held the rushing record for five years. In 1954, he was the first African-American to be named the most valuable player in the National Football League, and later inducted into the Pro Football Hall of Fame. Perry's teammate, John Henry Johnson, a member of the "Million Dollar Backfield," moved to the Detroit Lions in 1957 where he led them to the NFL Championship. During these years, black players were constrained in speed and brawn positions rather than brain, however in 1953, Willie Thrower of the Chicago Bears became the first African-American football player to play quarterback in the NFL, even if it was only for one game.

Jim Brown exploded into the NFL drafted in the first round by the Cleveland Browns in 1957, and was considered by many as the greatest professional football player of all-time. More impressive were his exceptional accomplishments as a multi-sport athlete. In addition to his long list of football records, he was a stand out in basketball, track, and as a lacrosse player while at Syracuse. During his sophomore year, he averaged 15 points per game and earned a letter on the track team. In his junior year, Brown was named a second-team All-American in lacrosse and first team All-American in lacrosse in his senior year. Brown was also the only rusher in NFL history to average over 100 yards per game in his career. Catching 262 passes for 2,499 yards and 20 touchdowns, Brown was also a superlative receiver out of the backfield. He was voted most valuable player in 1957 and 1958, selected for All-Pro in 1957 and 1958, and voted into the Pro Bowl every season during his career.

The quick game of basketball was slow to bring African-American players into the National Basketball Association. In 1950, three African-American athletes integrated the NBA. Nathaniel "Sweetwater" Clifton, a Harlem Globetrotter, became the first black player to sign a contract with the NBA, playing for the New York Knicks. Chuck Cooper had the distinction of being the first black player to be drafted by a team in the NBA. Earl Lloyd signed with the Washington Bullets that year and was the first black to actually play in a game. Lloyd was also the first black player to make the NBA All-Star Game in 1953.

The black domination of the game of basketball began with Bill Russell. Having led the University of San Francisco's basketball team to perfect records and NCAA Championships two consecutive years, Russell followed this feat by leading the U.S. Olympic basketball team to the gold medal at the 1956 games in Australia. Russell brought his unparalleled game and leadership skills to the Boston Celtics in 1956 and led them to their first NBA title.

The crumble of the color barrier in professional basketball during the 1950s was a major drawback for Abe Saperstein, the owner and promoter of the Harlem Globetrotters, who yielded a great deal of control over black basketball. The Trotters had been one of the top sports attractions in the country, but integration of the NBA gave the most talented black ball players more opportunities to play professionally. Left without competition,

A Reflection

the Globetrotters shifted to entertaining exclusively, traveling the world drawing record crowds with their extraordinary athletic ability and razzle-dazzle performances.

African-Americans had never been formally barred from entering the boxing ring. This was the only sport that had always offered black athletes a chance to compete. A number of great fighters rose to prominence during the 1950s in all weight divisions. Sandy Saddler was the undisputed featherweight champion for most of the decade with 144 wins in 162 bouts. Sugar Ray Robinson dominated the middleweights winning seven title fights for the champion crown.

The heavyweight division, considered the glamour division of boxing, was filled with top contenders after Joe Louis retired. There was Ezzard Charles, Jersey Joe Walcott, Tommy "Hurricane" Jackson, and Archie Moore, but Floyd Patterson, the "Gentleman of boxing," took the center ring in the 1950s as the undisputed Heavyweight Champion of the World. Winner of a gold medal in the 1952 Olympic Games in Helsinki, Patterson returned home to achieve greater conquests in his professional career. Patterson was victorious in twelve straight bouts over the next two years. In 1956, Patterson knocked out Archie Moore in the 5th round and became the youngest fighter to become heavyweight champion of the world at 21, and later the first fighter to regain the heavyweight championship after losing.

Golf and tennis were considered to be sports of the rich during the 1950s and unlike a number of other professional sports clung to their segregated status. African-American golf players were only permitted to play in Chicago, Los Angeles, or in Canada. In 1952, Bill Spiller, Eural Clark, and Joe Louis pressured the PGA with challenges to their exclusion from the San Diego Open golf tournament. It wasn't until 1959 that the Professional Golfers of America offered limited participation to Charlie Sifford, six time winner of the Negro National Open and winner of the 1957 Long Beach Open, as an "approved tournament player." In 1950, Ann Gregory won six out of the seven golf championships including the National UGA Tournament in Washington, and in 1956, she became the first African-American woman to play in the U.S. Amateur Championship in Indianapolis, Indiana.

African-American female athletes were limited to amateur sports with only a few exceptions. In 1951, Betty Chapman became the first black woman to play professional softball in the National Girls Baseball League in Chicago with the Admiral Music Maids. For 1956, 1957, and 1958, Althea Gibson was the top-ranked woman tennis player in the nation, winning the French women's singles championship, and becoming the first black woman to compete in the U.S. National Championships in 1956. In 1957, Gibson became the first African-American to win Wimbledon and repeated the feat in 1958.

There wasn't much open bias among athletes competing in the International Olympic Games, and African-Americans consistently dominated the contenders in the world of track and field. In the 1950s, African-American women comprised over two-thirds of the American women chosen to compete in the Olympics and other major international meets. In the 1952 Olympics, Mal Whitfield repeated his spectacular performance, winning his second gold medal in the 800 meter race. Harrison Dillard, also a previous Olympic gold medal winner, continued his winning streak and brought home more gold in the high hurdles. In the 1956 Olympic Games in Australia, Milt Campbell captured the gold medal in the decathlon after winning the silver in 1952. Rafer Johnson, considered by many to be the greatest athlete in the U.S. at this time, and the favored one to win, secured the silver medal.

The Tennessee State Tigerbelles dominated women's track and field during the 1950s. Mae Faggs Starr became the first woman from the United States to participate in three separate Olympics, 1948, 1952, and 1956. In 1952, Starr won the gold in the 4 x 100-meter relay and a bronze in the 1956 Games. Also a member on the AAU All-American Women's Track and Field team, she won the AAU 200-meter race in 1954, 1955, and 1956, and won the indoor 100-meter race in 1952. Barbara Jones Slater was the youngest woman to win a gold medal in track and field in the Olympic Games at age 15. In 1952, Slater and her teammates won the gold in the 4 x 100-meter relay, and she captured the gold again in the 1955 Pan American Games.

Black Literature

The literature of the day frames the times and experiences of the people. African-American readers and the like related to the works of several black authors during the 1950s that depicted the racism and classism black people endured, as in the autobiographical inspired works of Gwendolyn Brooks' *"Maud Martha"* in 1953 and her book of poetry, *"Annie Allen,"* for which she became the first African-American to win the Pulitzer prize in 1950, James Baldwin's *"Go Tell it on the Mountain"* in 1953, and Richard Wright's continuing saga of *"the Outsider"* in 1953. Chester Himes wrote *"Cast the First Stone"* in 1952, where he graphically relayed the sufferings of life in prison, and was also one of the most popular authors publishing in *Esquire* magazine until 1959. Paule Marshall's book *"Brown Girl, Brown Stones"* was published at the close of decade, giving an account of the lives of black immigrants in New York during the harsh years of the Depression and World War II.

One of the most notable books of this decade was Ralph Ellison's *"Invisible Man"*

A Reflection

published in its entirety in 1952. Through his writings Ellison was able to embody the reality of life as a black person in America. He was able to communicate how black people are seen mainly on the surface, not as individuals, but misunderstood with the depth of our humanity unacknowledged. He was able to blend the undertone of chaos that we live within with the often futility of our struggle, and mesh it with the aspect of lost identity. The common thread running through the works of the 1950s was the awakening or revelation of the despair, poverty, and injustices suffered by black people in American and the need for them to elevate above the subservient role thrust upon them by white society.

African-American Art

African-American art was dominated by abstract expressionism and realism in the 1950s. Charles Alston, James Wells, and Romare Bearden best exemplified the style. Coincidentally Charles Alston and Romare Bearden grew up on the same street and were cousins by marriage, leading to a lifelong friendship. Alston created portraits interpreting the music that was enveloping Harlem over the decades following the Renaissance. In 1953, he got his first solo exhibition at the John Heller Gallery in New York, and became the first African-American instructor at the Museum of Modern Art in 1956.

Bearden's art style evolved throughout the years with his life experiences and historical events. His study of philosophy that began in the 1950's transitioned his work into abstract presentations. James Lesesne Wells put forth a great body of work during the 1950s influenced by his commitment to the Civil Rights Movement. A master printer, his engravings and paintings reflected religious images in expressionism. In 1951, Wells received honorable mention at the Corcoran Gallery of Art's regional show, and in 1958 he received the George F. Muth engraving prize of the Washington Water Color Club.

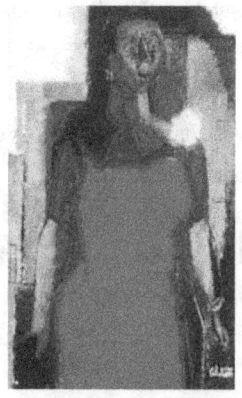  

Blues Singer #4, Alston (1955)   Girl in red, Robert Blackburn (1950)   Looking Back, Wells (1952)

1959

During the 1950s, art galleries were closed to unknown African-American artists hoping to sell their work. Undaunted, a group of 26 African-American youths from Fort Pierce, Florida, who were self-taught landscape artists, now referred to as the Highwaymen, decided they could make a lot money painting large quantities of works using inexpensive Upson board, a roof sheeting product, and framing them with crown molding. Gathering together for all night painting marathons, most would paint ten to twenty paintings in an evening. Not giving the oils much time to dry, the group sold their paintings out of the trunk of their cars throughout the cities of Florida and along the roadsides on the east coast of the state to hotels, businesses, and tourists. The painting were inexpensive, about $25 each, it's estimated that the Highwaymen a produced more than 200,000 paintings.

Black Entertainment

The 1950s saw more African-American actors performing in productions written by African-American playwrights for African-American audiences. The dramatic focus had shifted away from the protest genre to centering on social issues; the perspective of lower-class blacks, an honest view of the North, and the importance of education. Black playwrights were ushering in a more realistic representation of black people in their roles on Broadway with Louis Peterson's *"Take a Giant Step"* (1953), Charles Sebree's *"Mrs. Patterson"* (1954), and Langston Hughes' *"Simply Heaven"* (1957).

Lorraine Hansberry's *A Raisin in the Sun* (1959) ruled the Broadway stage, the most successful African-American play, a phenomenal box office hit with 530 performances, and the first play written by an African-American woman to make it to Broadway. Lansberry's play was a dramatization based on her family's legal battle against segregated housing in the Washington Park Subdivision on the South Side of Chicago. Memorable off-Broadway plays by African-Americans were William Branch's "In Splendid Error" (1954), Alice Childress' "Trouble in Mind" (1955), and A. Clifton Lamb's "Roughshod up the Mountain" (1956).

The end of segregation in the 1950s brought an end to Black cinema as black theaters were put out of business, eliminating the venue for race movies, and consequently their production. The wide array of roles for blacks seen in race films diminished as blacks were offered stereotypical roles in the mainstream movies delivered out of Hollywood. A number of black stars rose during the 1950s with bright talent that could not be dimmed by the quality or quantity of roles. Classic movies from this era were *Carmen Jones, St. Louis Blues,* and *Porgy & Bess.*

A Reflection

The top black female actresses in Hollywood during this decade were Dorothy Dandridge, with her roles in *Carmen Jones* (1954) and *Porgy & Bess* in (1959), Pearl Bailey and her role in *St. Louis Blues* (1958), Ethel Waters in *The Member of the Wedding* (1952), Juanita Moore as Annie in *Imitation of Life* (1959), and Ruby Dee in eight movie roles including *The Jackie Robinson Story* (1950), *No Way Out* (1950), *St. Louis Blues* (1958), and *Take a Giant Step* (1959). Dorothy Dandridge brought her simmering sexuality to the screen in the all-black production of Carmen Jones in 1954 for which she was received an Oscar nomination and a Golden Globe nomination, firsts for an African-American in the Best-Actress or Best-Actor category.

The top black male actors of the day were undoubtedly Sidney Poitier and Harry Belafonte. Poitier was particularly unique, the quiet strength and dignity he brought to the screen resisted boundaries and typecasting. The bevy of roles offered to him propelled his flight to superstardom with leading roles in *No way Out* (1950), *Cry, The Beloved Country* (1952), *The Blackboard Jungle* (1955), and *the Defiant Ones* (1958), for which he became the first African-American male to receive an Oscar nomination for a leading role. Poitier was instrumental in changing attitudes and the stereotyped perceptions of black men.

The 1950s were considered by many as the Golden Age of Television, but for a medium run by corporate sponsors, opportunities for African-American entertainers were nil to almost none. In 1950, *The Hazel Scott Show* debuted; the first TV show hosted by an African-American woman, but was later canceled, unable to draw guest stars or advertising sponsors. As in the early days of radio and film, whites wanted to see blacks as caricatures in stereotypical personas as in Amos 'N' Andy, which was rated 13th in the Nielson rating in 1951 and won an Emmy award in 1952. The NAACP launched an effective boycott against Blatz beer, its sponsor of the show, with CBS announcing "The network has bowed to the change in national thinking." Unfortunately not much had changed when the *Nat King Cole Variety Show* was introduced in 1956, southern stations threaten to boycott, and the show lasted only 13 months unable to attract a national sponsor.

The popularity of jazz and bebop had begun to ebb in the 1950s as rhythm and blues took over as the "urban music." Jazz bands had fewer members and the sound continued to evolve to a slower tempo called cool jazz led by Miles Davis. Rhythm and blues on the other hand was hot, Chess Records in Chicago was dropping hit after hit from blues artists fresh out of the Mississippi Delta. Artists on the Chess label included Muddy Waters, Little Walter Jacobs, Howlin' Wolf, Jimmy Rogers, Chuck Berry, Bo Didley, and Etta James. There was John Lee Hooker and the "King of Blues" B.B. King recording blues hits on other labels, and then there was Ray Charles who created a mix of R & B, gospel, and blues that got him the most lucrative recording contract of the time with ABC-Paramount records. The decade ended with the birth of Motown records in 1959, Berry Gordy established "Hitsville USA" which would later change the face of black music and take it to heights never seen before.

Memorable Moments

Ralph Bunche received the Nobel Peace Prize for his accomplishments as United Nations mediator in the Arab-Israeli conflict in Palestine in 1950.

1950 - Althea Gibson becomes the first African-American to play in a major United States Lawn Tennis Association (USLTA) event. In 1951, she was the first black player to compete at Wimbledon.

In 1950, Gwendolyn Brooks became the first African-American to receive the Pulitzer Prize for poetry for "Annie Allen."

Betty Chapman becomes the first black American professional softball player as an outfielder on the Admiral Music Maids of the National Girls Baseball League out of Chicago in 1951.

In 1952, Charlotte Bass, former owner and publisher of the California Eagle newspaper, was the first black woman to run for a national office, as the Progressive Party's candidate for Vice President.

The Unites States Supreme Court ruled unanimously that racial segregation in public schools was a violation of the Fourteenth Amendment on May 17, 1954.

In the 1954 baseball World Series, Willie Mays of the N.Y. Giants makes "the catch" against the Cleveland Indians.

Louis R. Lautier of the *Atlantic Daily World* became the first black member of the National Press Club in February 1955.

In 1956, Althea Gibson becomes the first black to win a Grand Slam singles title when she wins the French championships. The next year, she makes more history by winning Wimbledon and the U.S. Nationals, the first black to win either.

Martin Luther King Jr. and Jackie Robinson were both awarded honorary Doctor of Laws degrees from Howard University in 1957.

Althea Gibson is named the Associated Press Female Athlete of the Year for tennis in 1957, a feat she repeats in 1958. She is named athlete of the year and first on the cover of Sports Illustrated.

A Reflection

Ella Fitzgerald and Count Basie are the first African Americans to win Grammy awards in 1958.

The play *"Raisin in the Sun"* opens on Broadway starring Sidney Poitier on March 11, 1959.

Billie Holiday dies from a drug overdose on July 17, 1959.

Reflection on a Decade

The decade ending in 1959 requires a penetrating look not merely as the midpoint of the reflection but as the transformative period for African-Americans at the peak of the Civil Rights Movement. As in the journey of the Israelites out of Egypt where the exact destination was somewhat vague, as times goes on there is the recurring feeling that the road traveled is so familiar that possibly we have been here before, simply, we have just gone around in a circle. For the many who continued the exodus out of the South in search of the "promised land" with the optimism that nothing could be worse than their present circumstances, arrived just in time to see a host of jobs and their expectations for employment moving in the opposite direction. Whites in cities favored by black migrants conceded to the expanding girth of the black belts in the inner cities and ran for the suburbs quickening the rate of deindustrialization of urban areas.

The catalyst for change in the 1950s was the Brown v. Board of Education of Topeka Supreme Court decision. The ruling deemed that "separate but equal" was in fact unequal, striking down the legal precedent for segregation. Consequences from this landmark decision were intended and unintended, and both beneficial and detrimental. Jim Crow had finally been put to death. "White only" signs came down and the doors of possibility were gradually opened. The legal victories changed the laws, but without changes in the minds, what was the actual net gain? The mass action protests of African-Americans throughout the country in the 1950s were very effective when they impacted the financial bottom line of major businesses. Black people could sit where they wanted on the bus, eat in fine restaurants, watch movies in any theatre, and entertain themselves wherever their money could afford, but on the other hand black businesses, professionals, and educators suffered as integration spread and the options for black clientele widened.

Most progress frontward results in the proverbial two steps forward and one step back, and so was the advancement in the struggle for equality. African-Americans had made great strides economically over the past twenty years, but were still caught in the cycle of poverty. Limited education kept most in unskilled or low-skilled positions that earned low wages, which trapped them in poor neighborhoods and ghettos with low quality schools that were inadequately financed, where their children were under educated and left unskilled, and a new generation of poverty begins the cycle. Occupational and racial barriers prevented upward mobility on the job. Improved housing eliminated some of the diseases from unsanitary living conditions, but health issues related to stress were on the rise.

The success of the long fight for entry into white establishments didn't come close to filling the void between second-class citizenship and liberty and justice for all. Substantial development for African-Americans needed a strong foundation based on economic and political growth. Black leaders hailed from political offices and the black church espoused the right of black Americans to vote. Out of the ten million potential voters, approximately 5 million were registered. Fear and intimidation kept blacks from the polls in the South, apathy was the culprit in the North, many were not registered, and less than 37 percent voted. Were we losing our resolve or had the splintering of black society into different socioeconomic classes created resentment between us that threatened to breakdown our united front?

Reflection on Fifty Years

Despite the fact that African-Americans were behind in every facet of American society, they were evolving and had journeyed a long way. The growth and progress of an oppressed race of people in these fifty years was miraculous. Black people had taken the best shots that racism could bolster and were still standing. The NAACP had celebrated its 50th anniversary. There was much to look back on and commemorate. The key was not to become satisfied with these accomplishments and advance forward in the journey. Over this first half of a century more than a third of blacks living in the South had migrated north, Midwest, or to the Pacific coast to urban regions in search of better jobs and a higher quality of life.

The political environment for blacks had begun to recover; the democratic stance of the United States in the world required them to practice what they preached. African-Americans were regaining some political power with blacks serving in elected offices, swaying elections, and increasing their numbers at the polls. Nonetheless, it was surprising to discover that with limited privileges, drowning in injustice, lacking representation in government, that a number of blacks did not treasure the opportunity to vote, but it seems not much has changed in that respect.

A Reflection

The black church had solidified their role in the black community facilitating the Civil Rights Movement. The black press which had proved itself invaluable in the struggle for equality but was beginning to be overrun by the white press and television which provided immediate coverage to the rapidly changing events of the 1950s. Blacks were no longer concentrated in the South picking cotton or other forms of agriculture. Blacks were industrialized working in factories. Education attainment had been on an upward chart while illiteracy had dropped from 70 percent to 10 percent. School attendance increased from 50 percent to over 90 percent.

The issue of crime in the African-American community was and still remains a quandary in its causes and solutions. Limiting the scope to this country, America has always been a violent society answering her problems with aggression. Blacks have been on the receiving end of a great deal of this violence and physical attacks, and as a result indoctrinated to a certain extent to confront our personal issues and frustrations with a violent response. Unfortunately with a disproportionate amount of problems to address just in basic living, along with the additional complexities in urban life, amid a dearth of opportunities, should it be surprising that black men were or may appear to be disproportionately violent or use violence as a solution to problems.

A number of health issues related to poor diets and unsanitary living conditions had been dealt with, and the life expectancy for African-Americans had doubled over the last 50 years. The number one health problem for blacks for the better part of these fifty years, tuberculosis, had finally been contained. Improved housing in black communities contributed to improved health, albeit housing projects. Shifts in the family structure were seen with a decline in marriage coupled with more black women having children out of wedlock, contributing to a swell of single-parent households. Were these changes related to economic deficiencies with larger numbers of black men unable to financially support a family or was it more systemic? Were we losing ourselves and whatever identity we may have gained in the aftermath of slavery trying to chase an unknown ideal? What was the goal, was it individual, to work for a living and raise our children, or was it for the uplift of a race of people.

Reflecting on these fifty years, the question that begs an answer is why would the citizens of a country which was founded on freedom, which proclaims all men are created equal, believes in unalienable rights; have to endure great tribulations and monumental resistance in their quest for life, liberty, and the pursuit of happiness. However in our desperation we began reaching for this dream without a real strategy. Was assimilation into white society the best decision or was it our only option?

1969

Image © Getty Images

"A Change Gon' Come" echoed from the voice of Sam Cooke, but it wasn't always the outcome that had been envisioned. Integration was expanding throughout the South, but it wasn't the panacea to all that ailed black folks in America. What good was a front seat on the bus with no job to go to? Who needed to be welcomed into a restaurant if you couldn't pay for the meal? Black people needed employment, and on August 28, 1963, the monumental March on Washington, D.C. united civil rights groups and supporters from across the nation in a demonstration for jobs and freedom.

The march was the brainchild of A. Philip Randolph, reminiscent of his 1941 threatened march purposed to encourage federal job creation for African-Americans, and proficiently organized by Bayard Rustin. Randolph had been the most effective in uniting and organizing black people in mass for more than 30 years, and over 250,000 answered the call. Martin Luther King, Jr. delivered his legendary "I Have a Dream" speech.

A Reflection

The decade of the 1960s gave birth to the "Negro Revolution" with a surge of protests and demonstrations demanding social justice. However, segregation and prejudice would not "go gentle into that good night" as written in the poem by Dylan Thomas, but continued to "rage and rage against the dying of the light." Southern states were obstinate in their refusal to accept blacks and whites together. Governor George Wallace in his inaugural address in 1963 affirmed: *"I draw the line in the dust and toss the gauntlet before the feet of tyranny, and I say segregation now, segregation tomorrow, segregation forever."* The fortitude and enthusiasm that the Civil Rights Movement brought into the sixties came face to face with a fierce onslaught of brutal violence by angry white supremacist groups, prejudiced police officers, and bigoted individuals.

Lead by the militancy of black youths on college campuses, the Movement pressed forward undeterred. The first sit-in of the decade began February 1, 1960 in Greensboro, North Carolina at a Woolworth's lunch counter, but in a matter of days sit-ins had spread like wildfire to black college campuses in fifteen southern cities. Boycotts, pickets, and mass demonstrations were gaining positive results in Texas, North Carolina, Tennessee, Virginia, and Florida, although states in the Deep South harbored racial hatred that wouldn't relent. Turmoil and brutality hounded the organizers of civil rights activities. Steps taken towards integration were met with vicious acts of violence by the Ku Klux Klan, with none more cruel and devastating than the bombing of the 16th Street Baptist Church in Birmingham, Alabama. Four young black girls were killed. The explosive attack galvanized the Civil Rights Movement and intensified political support for the passage of the Civil Rights Act of 1964.

Demographics

The life expectancy for Black Americans had extended slightly to 64 years. Not only living longer, the baby boom was also a major contributor to the nearly 20 percent boost in the African-American population from the previous decade. Nevertheless, the gender imbalance was basically unchanged with 97 black men for every 100 black women.

African-Americans then made up 12.5 percent of the U.S. population, with numbers around 22,581,000. By 1969, approximated 5 million black Americans had made the trek out of the South; only 53 percent out of over 90 percent some fifty years earlier were living in southern states. Black populations had increased by over 43 percent in the Northeast, 33 percent in North Central, and 56 percent in the West regions of the country. Blacks continued exiting rural areas in the South and North Central regions of the country in the 1960s, causing an 18 percent growth over the last ten years in the African-American population concentrated in urban areas. Mississippi and South Carolina were once majority black populated, but by the end of the 1960s, their black populations were diminished down to 37 percent and 30 percent respectively, while Washington, DC still attracting migrants was then 71 percent black.

The black populations of the 34 largest cities in the country had grown by nearly 3 million while the white population was reduced by 2 million. The total suburban populations increased by over 12.5 million with "white flight" from the inner cities, but racial discrimination limited the black movement to the suburbs. However, midway through the decade, the rate of migration for blacks was falling and a reverse migration was beginning as job opportunities in the South were improving. The annual income for a Black male was $5341.64 compared to $8443.70 for a white male, and the annual incomes for black and white females were $3205.12 and $3786.45 respectively. The start of the 1960s found 57 percent of blacks below the national poverty line, even worse in Mississippi, the poorest state in the union, 68 percent were below the poverty line; however by 1969 the number was down to 33 percent.

Mood of the Black Community

"We want freedom by any means necessary. We want justice by any means necessary. We want equality by any means necessary."
Malcolm X, June 28, 1964, Organization of Afro-American Unity founding rally, New York City. (Malcolm X 1992: 47)

Tensions were close to a breaking point in the black community. Blacks living in the North and South were suffering with job discrimination, redlining in housing, and frequent indignities on a daily basis. Forces of oppression had kept African-Americans with their backs against the ropes economically, socially, and educationally, they had no choice but to come out fighting. They had waited long enough for their rightful place in the country built from the sweat of their brow, the nation they had defended with their lives, and were ready to make the final push to full equality. Martin Luther King, Jr. said, *"We're through with tokenism and gradualism and see-how-far-you've-comeism. We're through with we've-done-more-for-your-people-than-anyone-elseism. We can't wait any longer. Now is the time."*

A Reflection

The frustration from the lack of jobs, inferior schools, and police brutality in the black community was boiling over. Ready to take matters into their own hands, weary of the tiresome legal processes that brought change only on paper, black students on college campuses began organizing their own protest campaigns. Emboldened by each successful demonstration they advanced forward into the adversary's domain through sit-ins and freedom rides. As the Civil Rights Movement grew more aggressive in its confrontations so did the level of violence and retaliation they encountered in the Deep South, from Georgia to Mississippi and all through Alabama. Black leaders struggled to keep the masses calm and the movement nonviolent as volcanoes of anger rumbled below the surface in black communities.

As the decade progressed and battles became fierce, a more militant atmosphere was evolving. Disillusioned with the outcomes from the nonviolent direct-action campaigns favored by SCLC and CORE and the murderous attacks on black churches and neighborhoods, SNCC and even more revolutionary groups that espoused self-defense in the fight for civil rights emerged. The Deacons for Defense and Justice group was organized with the realization that racist law enforcement agencies would not protect the lives and property of black people, they had to arm themselves in self-defense against hate groups like the Ku Klux Klan. During the March Against Fear in the summer of 1966, after being arrested, Stokely Carmichael of SNCC declared, *"This is the twenty-seventh time I have been arrested and I ain't going to jail no more! The only way we gonna stop them white men from whuppin' us is to take over. What we gonna start sayin' now is Black Power!"*

Civil Rights Movement

1969

Direct –action campaigns regained center stage during the 1960s in a decade filled with national demonstrations and mass mobilizations. The student-led sit-ins were the driving force behind the momentum that propelled the Movement forward in 1960. Beginning in February, sit-ins expanded from lunch counters to libraries and then to movie theaters, hotels, and other segregated public facilities, even "wade-ins at white-only beaches and swimming pools.

In April of 1960, a conference was organized at Shaw University in Raleigh, North Carolina for student activists by Ella Baker, the director of the SCLC. The purpose was to coordinate future activities and share experiences, and out of the meetings the Student Nonviolent Coordinating Committee (SNCC) was created. By the end of the year, 70,000 people in more than 100 cities across 20 states had participated in sit-ins. More than 3,600 protesters were arrested and 187 students were expelled from colleges, except the sit-ins were working, lunch counters and restaurants had been integrated in 112 cities, but in Alabama, Mississippi, and South Carolina, segregation was entrenched and it would take greater efforts to transform these states.

The first desegregation campaign in a small southern town was initiated by my father, Reverend Cordell Sloan, in Lebanon, Tennessee in 1960. Rev. Sloan was a young educated Presbyterian minister sent to Lebanon to establish a church but was unable to ignore the injustices that flooded the small community. He was the catalyst for school desegregation in Lebanon as he attempted to enroll his two sons in McClain Elementary in March 1961.

Although he was unsuccessful, the black youths from the local high school were inspired and joined him as activists in a number of protest pickets, sit-ins and stare-ins through their community. Many black adults were reluctant based on their fear of retaliation and loss of work.

At the start of the new school year, Rev. Sloan and his students attempted to enroll in McClain Elementary and Lebanon High School and were yet again unsuccessful, but the incident ignited strong support within and outside of the small town. Black farmers put up their land as collateral to finance the lawsuit filed by Avon Williams and Z. Alexander Looby against the Wilson County School System. In September 1961, they finally won their battle against segregation with the court ruling in their favor. Sloan responded in a an interview for Jet Magazine in April of 1962 saying, *"They want me to knock on doors and talk about milk and honey, but my people need equality – a place where they can peacefully drink the milk and eat the honey."*

A Reflection

In 1960, the Supreme Court decision in Boynton v. Virginia ended the segregation of bus terminal facilities and passengers traveling on interstate buses. Besides another legal victory, CORE organized the "Freedom Rides" to bring the ruling into actuality. On May 4, 1961, joined by SNCC members, the freedom riders boarded a Trailways bus and a Greyhound bus in Washington, DC bound for New Orleans. They traveled without incident in the Upper South, but in the Deep South they crossed into a war zone. One bus was bombed and the riders fled for their lives, while the riders on the other were brutally beaten. Joined by more freedom riders from other organizations, the new riders boarded in Birmingham but over 300 were arrested in Jackson, Mississippi.

Inside jail the freedom riders were subjected to inhumane conditions to break their willpower, but they remained determined. Prompted by concerns for their safety, President Kennedy sent the National Guard to escort the freedom riders, and later pressured by Martin Luther King, Jr. and public sentiment for freedom riders, Kennedy ordered the Interstate Commerce Commission (ICC) to issue a new desegregation order, and "white" and "colored" signs were removed from the terminals.

Voter registration campaigns were next on the agenda for SNCC. Following the Freedom Rides, local leaders in Mississippi including Medgar Evers petitioned SNCC to assist them in registering black voters in the state. The extreme resistance to blacks registering to vote in Mississippi required a unified and coordinated effort of every civil rights organization to have any impact. The Council of Federated Organizations (COFO) was formed in February of 1962 with representatives from CORE, the NAACP, SNCC, and later SCLC. Voter registration in the Mississippi Delta was an uphill battle against intimidation, literacy tests, arrests, physical attacks, and even murder. Blacks who dared to register were fired from their jobs and evicted from their houses. Undaunted, voter registration campaigns expanded throughout the state and to neighboring states; Alabama, Louisiana, Georgia, and South Carolina.

In 1963, Fred Shuttlesworth, cofounder of the SCLC, invited Martin Luther King, Jr. and the SCLC to Alabama, feeling it was time to tackle segregation in Birmingham. Unequal treatment and unemployment for blacks that was more than double that for whites spurred the movement. Shuttlesworth's "Birmingham Campaign" was to push for equal job opportunities for blacks and to end the segregation in restaurants, stores, and public facilities. "Project C," the name given to the plan stood for confrontation, the strategy was to confront segregation using nonviolent direct action through boycotts, rallies, and peaceful demonstrations that would provoke mass arrests. Shuttlesworth, familiar with the temperament of Police Commissioner Bull Connor, anticipated that Connor would respond violently attracting national attention that would expose the injustices of segregation.

The campaign began on April 3, 1963 with boycotts of downtown stores, sit-ins at lunch counters, and a march on City Hall, with protesters being arrested daily. Disobeying a court order to end protests, King was arrested on April 10th; it was there he wrote his "Letter from Birmingham Jail," he was released on the 20th of April. James Bevel proposed that children be allowed to demonstrate, and on May 2, over 1000 black students marched in downtown Birmingham. The police arrested hundreds, and when more returned the following day, Connor ordered the police and fire departments to forcibly end the protests. Children were attacked by police dogs and sprayed with high-pressure fire hoses. The blatant display of violence and cruelty on television and in newspapers shocked the nation and caused international outrage.

On May 10, 1963, "The Birmingham Truce Agreement" was reached between black leaders and the Birmingham Chamber of Commerce. Public facilities would be integrated, "Whites Only" and "Blacks Only" signs would be removed, blacks would be hired in businesses within two months, and the protesters would be released from jail without bail. Bull Connor lost his position as police commissioner, and King was credited with a victory. There would be no time to revel in the success of the campaign, white racists groups began vicious attacks with the bombing of the Gaston Motel room where King and the members of the SCLC had stayed, and the firebombing of the home

A Reflection

of Alfred King, M.L. King's brother. Shootings, violent attacks, racial conflicts, and general mayhem spread through southern cities, prompting President Kennedy to send 3,000 federal troops to Birmingham to federalize the Alabama National Guard.

Fanatical groups like the Ku Klux Klan and the White Citizens Council, driven by an irrational deep-rooted hatred, were desperate to prevent blacks from gaining any racial equality, and continued to resort to terrorist attacks on the black community. In June, Medgar Evers was assassinated, shot in the back in front of his home in Mississippi. In September, Klan members bombed the Sixteenth Street Baptist Church in Birmingham, killing four black girls and injuring more than a dozen others, and on the same day two black teen-age boys were shot, one by police, the other while riding his bike. The toll of the racial unrest in Birmingham was 10 people killed, 35 black homes and churches bombed, and 20,000 arrested in civil rights demonstrations.

The idea of the 1963 March on Washington was originated by A. Philip Randolph marking the 100th anniversary of the Abraham Lincoln's Emancipation Proclamation, and it was controversial from the start. A number of civil rights leaders were skeptical about the march, concerned that if there was violence it would be damaging for the movement. Others disagreed on the focus and objectives for the march. Randolph and King with the SCLC wanted to use the march to bring national attention to the economic concern of unemployment and civil rights struggles of African-Americans, the NAACP and Urban League wanted the march to support President Kennedy's civil rights bill, and SNCC and CORE wanted to show dissatisfaction towards the Kennedy administration for their lack of support in the Civil Rights Movement. Malcolm X condemned the march, calling it the "farce on Washington."

In 1964, the campaign to register African-American voters in Mississippi was renewed with "Freedom Summer." Armed with a new strategy designed to suppress the violence experienced in the previous drive, 1000 out-of-state volunteers that were 90 percent white, came to Mississippi to help register blacks to vote. The project organized by the Council of Federated Organizations established Freedom Schools, a network of around 40 voluntary summer schools held in churches, porches, and under trees. The students ranged from young children to elderly adults. Unfortunately, the violence of the murderous Klansmen was always lurking in the shadows. On June 21, 1964, James Chaney, Andrew Goodman, and Michael Schwerner were arrested by the sheriff and member of Klan, held in jail until darkness came, then released to an ambush of Klansmen who abducted them and murdered them. Front page news, the nation was again shocked by the heinous acts of hatred in the South.

1969

Resistance to black voter registration drives had reached an impasse in Dallas County, Alabama, as both sides of the issue dug in with the determination that "I shall not be moved." The Dallas County Voters League of Selma, Alabama working with SNCC contacted Martin Luther King and the SCLC for help in overcoming the blockade of government officials, White Citizens Council, and the KKK. Subsequently a march from Selma to Montgomery was scheduled on March 7, 1965, now referred to as "Bloody Sunday," to confront Governor George Wallace on the killing of a protestor by a state trooper and the violation of their right to register to vote. The group of 600 marchers was attacked near the Edmund Pettus Bridge by a gang of state troopers with billy clubs and tear gas.

Martin Luther King, Jr., joined by 2500 marchers, walked to the Bridge two days later in a "ceremonial" march on March 9; unable to remove the injunction against the march, they turned back in obedience to the court order. The third and historic 'Selma to Montgomery March' began on March 21, with nearly 8000 marchers and spiritual leaders from various religions walking 12 miles a day and sleeping out in fields. The march ended on Thursday, March 25, as the enlarged crowd of 25,000 participants approached the capitol building where King gave his confident "How Long, Not Long" speech.

In June of 1966, James Meredith, the first African-American student to integrate the University of Mississippi, started his "March Against Fear" from Memphis, Tennessee to Jackson, Mississippi to protest racism and encourage blacks not to give in to fears of violence. During the march, Meredith was shot and injured. Martin Luther King (SCLC) and Stokely Carmichael (SNCC) along with other civil rights organizations continued the march in his name. Midway through the march the tone had shifted from SCLC's "Freedom Now" to SNCC's "Black Power."

The second phase of the Civil Rights Movement began in 1967 with plans for the Poor People's Campaign. Moving forward from segregation as the focus, the campaign was to commence the war on poverty and heighten the economic concerns and housing issues for the poor of all races in America. A march was planned for the spring of 1968, where the poor from all over the United States would canvass federal agencies throughout the capitol to persuade Congress to pass meaningful anti-poverty legislation. Regrettably, Martin Luther King, Jr. was assassinated on April 4, 1968 and the campaign lost its fervent leader. Demonstrators were disheartened and grew weary of the protest.

A Reflection

Political Climate

The decade began with the Civil Rights Act of 1960 which established the federal inspection of local registration polls and provided penalties for whoever, by threats or force, willfully prevents, obstructs, or interferes with another's attempt to register to vote or actually vote. The bill was signed into law by Eisenhower on May 6, but proved to be ineffective, having added a mere three percent in additional black voters to the electoral roll. Nevertheless, the 1960 presidential election victory went to John F. Kennedy in a narrow margin over Richard Nixon, with over 70 percent of African-Americans voting for Kennedy. Expectations for civil rights legislation were high based on the rhetoric heard in his campaign speeches to court black voters. However, as president, Kennedy was reluctant to risk losing his southern support by focusing on civil rights; he opted to appease black leadership with 40 appointments of African-Americans to federal government posts, and in 1962 signed executive order 11063 banning racial discrimination in federal supported housing and facilities.

The White House administration preferred to "keep the president out of this civil rights mess," but the volatility of the 1960s with its racial skirmishes taking place in the South forced Kennedy to move from the fence and take a stand. He first had to intervene with protection for the Freedom Riders and then in Alabama when Governor Wallace blocked the doorway to prevent the integration of the University of Alabama. Kennedy addressed the nation on June 11, 1963 to state his initiative for civil rights legislation stating:

> "Now the time has come for this Nation to fulfill its promise ... The fires of frustration and discord are burning in every city, North and South, where legal remedies are not at hand ... A great change is at hand, and our task, our obligation, is to make that revolution, that change, peaceful and constructive for all ... Next week I shall ask the Congress of the United States to act, to make a commitment it has not fully made in this century to the proposition that race has no place in American life or law."

Among a number of other related objectives, the March on Washington scheduled for August 28, 1963 was purported to be in support of the passage of the civil rights legislation proposed by Kennedy although he declined the invitation to speak. The civil rights bill was moving through Congress and had won the endorsement of Republican House and Senate leaders, but Kennedy would not live to see its passage, he was assassinated on November 22, 1963 while on a political trip in Dallas, Texas. Vice President Lyndon B. Johnson was sworn in hours later.

President Johnson was able to push the Civil Rights Act of 1964 through Congress using the public sentiment for Kennedy as the impetus to honor his bill on July 2, 1964. The bill outlawed discrimination in voting, outlawed segregation in public accommodations, enforced desegregation in public schools, prohibited federal funding of programs that discriminated, and prohibited legal discrimination on the basis of race or sex, and created the Equal Opportunity Employment Commission to monitor and enforce the law. Johnson became an invaluable advocate for the Civil Rights Movement during his presidency, and was re-elected as president in 1964 with 95 percent of the African-American vote. He entered into his second term unabashedly supporting the struggle of African-Americans in his special message to Congress after the attack of state troopers on demonstrators in the March from Selma to Montgomery:

> "Even if we pass this bill, the battle will not be over. What happened in Selma is part of a far larger movement which reaches into every section and state of America. It is the effort of American Negroes to secure for themselves the full blessings of American life. Their cause must be our cause, too, because it is not just Negroes but really it is all of us who must overcome the crippling legacy of bigotry and injustice. And we shall overcome."

Johnson began his second term with the introduction of more civil rights legislation through the Voting Rights Act that would eliminate illegal restrictions, including literacy and knowledge tests to keep blacks from voting, assuring their right to vote in all elections, local, state, and federal. The bill was signed on August 6, 1965. Federal examiners were sent to seven southern states to assist in the registration of black voters, the number of African-American voters rose by 450,000 within one year, and as a result more blacks were elected to public offices. Conversely, with each step of progress during the 1960s there was always a violent white backlash from racists groups. When Viola Liuzzo, a civil rights worker was murdered, Johnson denounced the Ku Klux Klan as a "hooded society of bigots" and was the first president to arrest and prosecute members in nearly 100 years.

During Johnson's term in office he also issued Executive order 11246 in 1965 to "correct the effects of past and present discrimination" with affirmative action. The order prohibited federal contractors from discriminating against any applicant or

A Reflection

employee based on race, religion, or national origin. The order required that contractors take affirmative action to ensure equal opportunity for those who previously suffered discrimination. Johnson explained:

> "You do not take a person who, for years, has been hobbled by chains and liberate him, bring him up to the starting line of a race and then say, 'you are free to compete with all the others,' and still justly believe that you have been completely fair...This is the next and the more profound stage of the battle for civil rights. We seek not just freedom but opportunity."

Lyndon Johnson had truly been a champion for civil rights during his presidency, in 1967, he nominated Thurgood Marshall, noted civil rights attorney, to the United States Supreme Court, where he became the first African-American to serve as an Associate Justice. Johnson ended the decade with the Fair Housing Act of 1968, which stated: the Civil Rights Act of 1968 prohibits discrimination in the sale, rental, and financing of dwellings, and in other housing-related transactions, based on race, color, national origin, religion, sex, familial status and handicap...

At the end of the 1969, 66 percent of blacks eligible to vote in the South were registered, Carl Stokes in Cleveland, Ohio and Richard Hatcher in Gary, Indiana were elected as the first black mayors, and there were ten African-American members serving in Congress including one woman, Shirley Chisholm and Senator Edward Brooks. However, 75 percent of whites resented the speed of progress for blacks during the decade and took it to the polls, Republicans gained 47 seats in House and three senate seats in the midterm election of 1966, and Nixon beat Hubert Humphrey in 1968.

African-Americans and Vietnam War

An estimated 275,000 African-Americans served in the Vietnam War. The military conflict began in November of 1955, but U.S. involvement didn't escalate until the early 1960s, which progressed into a torrent of bombing campaigns called *Operation Rolling Thunder* in 1965, and later included large numbers of combat troops deployed for a ground offensive. The draft was instituted to maintain a steady supply of soldiers to fight. The majorities of draftees were poor, unemployed, uneducated, and disproportionately black, while college students, essential civilian workers, and middle- to upper-class whites were offered deferments or served in the National Guard. With little or no representation on state draft boards, African-American were unduly drafted and more likely to see combat in Vietnam.

1969

Project 100,000 was launched in 1966 to remedy troop shortages. Military requirements were relaxed to allow larger numbers of youths from poor urban cities to enlist and advance in the military. Forty-one percent of the 350,000 inductees were black and 40 percent of these soldiers received combat assignments and had casualty rates double those of any other enlisted men. Between 1965 and 1967, black men constituted less than 10 percent of the soldiers but accounted for 22 percent of the combat-related deaths in Vietnam. In 1965, one out of four soldiers killed in action were black. In 1967, 64 percent of eligible black men were drafted in comparison to 31 percent of eligible white men. Intense criticism by black leadership over the high number of blacks losing their lives prompted the Army and Marine senior officers to lessen the number of black soldiers on the frontlines to reduce African-American casualties. For the remainder of the war black casualties were more in line at 13 percent.

The shortage of jobs and opportunities for African-Americans in civilian life motivated many to volunteer for military service and to re-enlist at higher rates than whites, although less than four percent advanced as officers. Interviews of black enlisted men revealed that 60 percent agreed that black people should not fight in Vietnam because of the racial problems they had in the United States. Impatience with the never-ending conflict and mounting casualties of young black men, and the simultaneous stateside battles for equal rights, strengthened the opposition from the black community. In 1967, Martin Luther King, Jr. spoke out against the "cruel irony" of blacks fighting for a nation that treats them as second-class citizens, denying them the liberties and justice deserved.

> "We were taking the black young men who had been crippled by our society and sending them eight thousand miles away to guarantee liberties in Southeast Asia which they had not found in southwest Georgia and East Harlem. And so we have been repeatedly faced with the cruel irony of watching Negro and white boys on TV screens as they kill and die together for a nation that has been unable to seat them together in the same schools. And so we watch them in brutal solidarity burning the huts of a poor village, but we realize that they would hardly live on the same block in Chicago. I could not be silent in the face of such cruel manipulation of the poor."

In 1968, black soldiers were just about 13 percent of the Army and Marines, yet they made up half the men in front-line combat units. Though, the number of battlefield losses of black soldiers was brought down as the war dragged on.

A Reflection

Black Riots Reign

Peace Be Still
Master, the tempest is raging.
The billows are tossing high.
The sky is o'er shadowed with blackness,
no shelter or help is nigh.
Carest Thou not that we perish?
How canst Thou lie asleep,
when each moment so madly is threatning,
a grave in the angry deep?
--Mary Baker, 1874

The 1960s were characterized by the frustrations and racial unrest in black ghettos across the nation that exploded in devastating riots. During 1963, the first major riot of the decade took place in Cambridge, Maryland as a demonstration against segregation got heated, black youths threw rocks at white businesses, and a shootout ensued. The governor declared martial law and the National Guard was brought in to quiet the disorder.

The following year ushered in a series of "long hot summers" with violent riots and destruction beginning in Harlem on July 18, 1964. A fifteen year-old was shot by a white off-duty police officer igniting a fierce riot. Around 8,000 blacks reacting to yet another act of police brutality flooded the streets setting fires, breaking windows, and looting businesses. The riot broadened to Bedford-Stuyvesant and went on for six days, in the aftermath there was one fatality, more than 100 injured, and over 450 arrests. Less than a week later in Rochester, New York another riot broke out because of suspected police brutality, protestors burned buildings, destroyed cars, and looted stores for three days. At the end of the turmoil, four were killed, 350 injured, nearly 1000 arrested, and more than $1 million in damages.

The outbreak of rage in black urban cities of the North was contagious. It extended to the ghettos in Paterson and Elizabeth, New Jersey, where bottles and bricks flew through the streets from rooftops and out of windows as pent-up anger and resentment overflowed. Racial tensions between blacks living in slums and the police escalated as black people tired of the disrespect, unprovoked assaults, and shootings and killings by police in their neighborhoods. Incidences in Chicago and later Philadelphia underscored the realization that tolerance had reached its limit. Even rumors of police misconduct inflamed angry mobs to take to the streets wrecking havoc on white-owned businesses and pillaging whatever was in their path. More riots broke out in 35 other cities and towns including Atlanta. Poverty and want within the ghettos would increase the likelihood that food and clothing stores were the chosen targets.

The infamous Watts riots in Los Angeles, California were instigated on August 11, 1965 and stretched into five days. The fuse that ignited the time bomb was a confrontation with police and a black man suspected of drunk-driving and his family. At the scene, a crowd of onlookers grew to well over 1000 with an hour and began to get hostile as the man resisted arrest and the police became more aggressive. Rumors spread in the area bringing the deep-seated anger and irritation of the community to the surface in a wave of lawlessness.

Passing motorists were stopped and attacked, cars were turned over and burned, businesses were vandalized and looted, and protestors attacked policemen while snipers held back firemen as the crowds shouted "burn baby burn." As the days passed the riot with as many as 8,000 participants extended out of Watts and 15,000 National Guards were called in. In the end, 34 people were killed, 1,032 were injured, and 3,438 were arrested. Six hundred buildings were damaged, and of those 200 were completely destroyed. Televised nationwide, the scene in Watts looked like the battlefront of a warzone. All in toll there was $40 million in damages.

The riot in the black ghetto of Hough in Cleveland, Ohio in July of 1966 was set off by racial tensions over a sign that said "No Water for Niggers" placed on the door of a white-owned bar. A group of blacks that congregated outside the establishment chanting "Black Power" grew with each hour until it had extended over 23 blocks. The Cleveland police only aggravated the situation and the National Guard was called in, except that only served to move the riot to other sections of Hough. The melee went on for nearly a week, ending with four deaths, 30 injured, 300 arrested, and 240 fires. The similar root cause for the quick eruption of violence and mayhem of the riots were unemployment and extremely poor housing situations.

In Newark, New Jersey, rumors that a black taxi driver had been killed in police custody triggered six days of rioting in an already disgruntled black community. A crowd gathered in front of the police precinct throwing bricks and bottles until police ordered them to disperse. As the crowd disbanded some began to break into stores taking the

A Reflection

violence with them to their own communities downtown and in the Central Ward. The state police were alerted and two days later still in the midst of unrest the National Guard was called up, conversely, their presence seemed to aggravate the situation. By the time order was restored, 23 people had lost their lives, 725 had been injured, nearly 1500 arrested, and property damage was estimated at $30 million.

The most destructive riot was in Detroit in July of 1967 which began shortly after police burst into a bar where patrons were celebrating the return of two Vietnam veterans. Police proceeded to arrest all 82 of the people attending the gathering. Minutes later eyewitnesses of the incident began breaking windows and looting the stores in the neighborhood. The crowd grew larger as the day progressed until it became a huge mob unmanageable by city police. Many of the rioters were armed and shooting. The fervor of the mob spread to sections of the city, and state police were brought in to gain control.

The mayhem of riot only grew with widespread acts of police brutality accompanied with the violation of rights and regulations, looters as well as innocent bystanders were victimized. Over days the violence and arson escalated, 483 fires were set destroying black businesses along with others. Unable to restore order, President Johnson sent in Federal troops with tanks and machine guns to rein in the chaos, but the riot had expanded to more cities including, Flint, Grand Rapids, and Saginaw. After five days, 43 people, black and white, had been killed, 367 injured, and 7231 arrested. Over 2500 stores had been burned or looted, 412 building destroyed, and 388 people left homeless. The total of damages ranged from $40 to $80 million. As in other cities, the riot was precipitated by police brutality, resentment over poor housing, and the frustration from the loss of jobs in the inner city.

The assassination of Martin Luther King, Jr. on April 4, 1968 unleashed a multitude of riots and civil unrest across the country in more than 100 cities, led to between 45 and 60 deaths, 2,600 injuries, and the arrest of more than 21,000 people. Property damage in cities throughout the nation amounted to $65 million.

Black Leadership

Distinguished as one of the most important African-American leaders of our time, and the most influential woman in the civil rights movement, Ella Jo Baker was also one of the most uncelebrated. A human rights and civil rights activist for more than thirty years prior to 1960s, Baker was the essential ingredient in the three prominent black organizations fighting for racial equality. Ella Baker had served as director of branches in the NAACP, as well as president of the New York branch. She was a key organizer of the SCLC, still, not a man or a minister; she would not have a leadership post. Her greatest influence was evident as the "Godmother of SNCC," which fully embraced her philosophy of group-centered leadership and campaigns on the local level. The "Participators Democracy" that Baker embodied had a foundation of individual involvement and the decentralization of leadership. Always critical of the idea of a charismatic leader at the helm, Baker espoused, *"Strong people don't need strong leaders."* In her opinion, *"the movement made Martin, and not Martin the movement"* and she pushed activists to take control of the movement.

Leadership for African-Americans during the sixties was composed of various committed local leaders and networks dedicated to achieving equal rights within their communities, they on occasion used the influence of national leaders to further their causes. Rev. Fred Shuttlesworth was a lead organizer in the Freedom Rides and "Project C" in Birmingham working with CORE, a group-centered organization and also the SCLC, a leader-center organization, to use mass direct-action and the national exposure to accomplish his objectives. Medgar Evers and the NAACP, a leader-centered organization worked with SNCC in the Freedom Summer to further voter registration campaigns in Mississippi. The complex challenges in progression of the Civil Rights Movement required a combination of leadership styles to support each other.

Martin Luther King, Jr. (SCLC) and Malcolm X (NOI) were both charismatic figures of leader-center organizations during the 1960s. King's efforts in the Civil Rights Movement centered on more than desegregation, and of 'the promised land of integration,' he explained, *"Desegregation simply removes legal and social prohibitions. Integration…is the welcome participation of Negroes in the total range of human activities."* King's philosophy of nonviolence was to expose the moral shame of America through confrontations and to lead his enemies to redemption. He felt activists must have a willingness to suffer for the greater good. The foundation for his beliefs was love, agape love -- the love of God. On the other hand, Malcolm did not believe all men were equal, he felt blacks were superior to whites, and promoted the separation of the races. Malcolm was an advocate for fighting back; he said blacks should defend themselves by any means necessary.

Although there were significant differences in their approach to uplifting Black America, they both evolved personally and philosophically as a result of their roles as leaders. King was changed by his trip to Chicago in 1966 where he was subjected to

A Reflection

more hate and hostility than he had ever experienced in the South. Discouraged he stated, *"The triple evils of racism, militarism, and economic exploitation are incapable of being conquered as long as profit motives and property rights are considered more important than people."* King saw that the civil rights fight needed to shift to economic justice. Malcolm X was transformed by his trip to Mecca; afterwards he disavowed racism, no longer called for the separation of blacks, and became a supporter of the fight for civil rights. These two courageous men lived under constant threats on their lives, and both met their deaths from an assassin's bullet, Malcolm X in 1965 and Martin Luther King, Jr. in 1968.

> Master, with anguish of spirit
> I bow in my grief today.
> The depths of my sad heart are troubled.
> Oh, waken and save, I pray!
> Torrents of sin and of anguish
> sweep o'er my sinking soul,
> And I perish! I perish! dear Master.
> Oh, hasten and take control!
> --Mary Baker, 1874

Stokely Carmichael took over as chairman of SNCC in 1966 replacing John Lewis, and so began the transformation of the organization. Whites were excluded as the group became more radical with "Black Power" as the new slogan and dropped their commitment to nonviolence. A Black Nationalism tone emerged as they shifted the focus. Carmichael insisted, *"Integration is irrelevant, Political power is what black people have to have."* Carmichael resigned in 1967 and was replaced by H. Rap Brown. Leadership changes in CORE with Floyd McKissick replacing James Farmer caused a similar ideology shift during the same period. CORE expelled its white members and supported the concept of Black Power. CORE rejected nonviolence as behind the times, McKissick explained to the press, *"The right of self-defense is a constitutional right, and you can't expect black people to surrender that right while whites maintain it...you can't have white people practice violence and expect black people to remain passive."*

The Black Panther Party

In March of 1966, Stokely Carmichael and SNCC leaders formed an all-black political party in Alabama called the Lowndes County Freedom Organization, using the black panther for its emblem, it was also known as the Black Panther Party. Inspired by the group and Stokely Carmichael's call to form separate black political organizations, Huey Newton and Bobby Seale used the powerful image of the panther for their revolutionary group established in October of 1966, calling it The Black Panther Party for Self-Defense. On the same wave length as the Deacons for Defense in Louisiana, they first organized to protect the Oakland area and local neighborhoods from police brutality. Advocates of Black Power but not anti-white, the Panthers declared:

> "We do not fight racism with racism. We fight racism with solidarity. We do not fight exploitative capitalism with black capitalism. We fight capitalism with basic socialism. And we do not fight imperialism with more imperialism. We fight imperialism with proletarian internationalism."

The Party's newspaper, *The Black Panther*, was edited by Eldridge Cleaver, the eloquent spokesperson for the Party, with a circulation of 250,000. The philosophy for the Party evolved as it grew, but was mixed with socialist and communist ideas, self-determination, and black pride. By 1968, the BPP had grown considerably with branches formed in every major city from coast to coast, and at the end of the decade membership was close to 10,000. More inspired by Malcolm X, believing that the Civil Rights Movement had failed, the BPP issued their platform in a Ten-Point Program in which they demanded freedom for all blacks, full employment, decent housing and education, an end to the murder of blacks by the police, land, and justice and peace.

The original objective of the Black Panther Party was to serve the community and defend the people against their oppressors, but white society was intimidated by the militant disposition of the organization and fearful of members who openly carried weapons. Law enforcement officials on the local, state, and federal levels were determined to discredit and destroy the Black Panther Party. Informers were used to infiltrate the organization, police raids were orchestrated where members were murdered by police. Thirty-nine Black Panthers were shot by the police in their homes or on the streets.

Nation of Islam and Malcolm X

The 1960s saw the popularity of the Nation of Islam increase as the number of black Muslims reached 100,000. Rising racial tensions and disillusionment were being felt by some in the black community towards the progress of the Civil Rights Movement. Malcolm X, the principal spokesperson for the Nation during the early 1960s, and the

A Reflection

most sought after speaker in the country, not only possessed a compelling presence but was a captivating orator who attracted the young and more militant youth of the time.

Malcolm X and the NOI's platform stressed Black Nationalism, pride and self-sufficiency for black people versus seeking to be a part of white society. The common belief between Malcolm X and Martin Luther King, Jr. was African-Americans must overcome racism and oppression, even though they differed in their approach to achieve that goal. The cornerstone of the Civil Rights Movement was nonviolence whereas Malcolm stated blacks must be prepared to defend themselves. Still, many viewed their criticism of the Civil Rights Movement questionably; they talked tough, but did nothing, while nonviolent militant blacks were on the frontline in mass direct-action campaigns.

Nonetheless, in 1963, Malcolm's relationship with Elijah Muhammad and the Nation of Islam had become tenuous to say the least. Amid personal jealousies from other ministers surrounding Malcolm's increasing power and celebrity in addition to scandal with the Nation, Malcolm began to question the moral foundations of those he had held in high esteem. Muhammad had been accused of adultery and fathering five children by three former secretaries, confronted by Malcolm he gave no denial merely biblical reasons, shattering Malcolm's faith in him. The divorce between Malcolm and the Nation of Islam was imminent after he was suspended from his duties by Elijah for 90 days following his "chickens come home to roost" comment to JFK's assassination. The split was permanent, and in March of 1964 Malcolm formed the Muslim Mosque Inc, and thus began the numerous attempts on his life.

In the spring of 1964, Malcolm made a pilgrimage to the holy city, Mecca. Seeing so many Muslims of different nationalities worshipping together he realized that *"My true brotherhood includes people of all races, coming together as one."* Following his return to the states Malcolm accused Elijah of ordering the death of anyone who joined his organization. In February of 1965, his house was fire-bombed, and one week later on February 21, at the Audubon Ballroom in Harlem, Malcolm X was assassinated by three black men while delivering a speech at the age of 39. The Nation of Islam was suspected of the perpetrating the murder since the three men were black Muslims in the NOI, but Elijah Muhammad emphatically denied having any responsibility.

1969

The Black Church

"If the church does not recapture its prophetic zeal it will become little more than an irrelevant social club with a veneer of religiosity. If it does not participate actively in the struggle for economic and racial justice it will forfeit the loyalty of millions and cause men everywhere to say it has atrophied its will."

Martin Luther King, Jr. --- *Chicago Defender*, January 19, 1963.

The black church was at the forefront of the battle for equality and civil rights during the 1960s filling a larger role in the organization and participation of direct-action protests. Clergymen used their leadership positions to further their goals as activists. Churches were active in a number of functions; financial resources were contributed, the facilities were used as meeting halls, and the congregation provided a valuable network and ready source of demonstrators to be mobilized. The campaigns took on the persona of a church revival with prayers, songs, and sermons that stirred members into action and lifted their spirits through the vicious confrontations.

The perception that all black churches supported the Civil Rights Movement is inaccurate; endorsement for the Movement was far from unanimous. The majority of religious leaders objected to church involvement for a variety of reasons. Many clergy in the North, such as Rev. Joseph H. Jackson, pastor of the largest black church in Chicago, Olivet Baptist Church, preferred to see changes made through the legal system and supported the NAACP and Urban League. Ninety percent of pastors in southern states feared retaliation. While some affirmed that the church was obligated to use its moral authority to rally against injustice and oppression, others insisted that it wasn't church business. Differences in opinions split the National Baptist Convention when Martin Luther King, Jr. moved on to form the Progressive Baptist Convention.

Central in the philosophy of the Civil Rights Movement were the Christian principles of turning the other cheek and loving thy enemy. As stated by King, "*I am grateful to God that, through the influence of the Negro church, the way of nonviolence became an integral part of our struggle.*" The Southern Christian Leadership Conference (SCLC) coordinated its largest mass demonstrations in conjunction with local churches in Montgomery, Birmingham, Tallahassee, Baton Rouge, Nashville, and numerous other cities. Black churches worked in cooperation with SNCC and Core to organize sit-ins and provide bail money for student protestors.

A Reflection

Black churches were seen as the focal point and nucleus of the Movement and as such remained targets of retribution by extremist white groups including the Ku Klux Klan. In 1963, the 16th Street Baptist Church in Birmingham, Alabama, a meeting place for civil rights leaders to plan strategies, was bombed killing four young girls. Thirty-six other black churches were also fire-bombed in that year. Throughout the decade a great number of black churches were bombed from Louisiana, Georgia, to Alabama, up to North Carolina and Pennsylvania, New York, and Rhode Island, and clear to the West coast in California.

Along with the fight against bigotry, the urgent needs of the black community were unabated during the 1960s. While the civil rights movement was a priority; there were many pressing problems that could not be solved with a march or a demonstration. There were deplorable housing conditions, unemployment, and inadequate education and training for blacks all over the United States. Black activist ministers took initiatives in their churches to improve the social conditions of the congregation. Rev. William Borders of the Wheat Street Baptist Church in Atlanta realized the direct connection between economic freedom and civil rights and established a credit union, an employment agency, a day care center, and a clinic within the church. In the 1960s, he worked to create the first federally subsidized, church-run rental housing project for low-income residents in the nation.

Rev. Leon Sullivan, pastor of Zion Baptist Church in Philadelphia, recognized that more had to be done to address job discrimination and unemployment in the black community. *"Integration without preparation is frustration."* Feeling it was the churches responsibility to provide job training to the bevy of unskilled black workers in the area, Sullivan founded the Opportunities Industrialization Center (OIC) on January 24, 1964 in North Philadelphia. His efforts were to offer "a whole new dimension to the civil rights picture, placing emphasis on production rather than protest." In the first year, 300 black men and women were enrolled in eight training programs for restaurant work, electronics, drafting, and sewing, and by 1966, over 1500 black workers had been successfully trained and employed.

The Black Press

By 1969, black-owned newspapers had seen their best days. The Civil Rights Movement was now national and international news and mainstream dailies and television broadcasts covered every dramatic moment that took place from the North to the South and from coast to coast. Most African-American newspapers were weeklies and could not compete with the immediate daily coverage. News of the church bombing in Birmingham had been widely covered in the white mainstream media before black weekly papers could get the story out.

Integration so strongly fought for by the black press since its inception was ultimately its undoing. Black newspapers with black reporters more often than not had the inside track on developments relating to planned activities and detailed information from the black communities, but mass media was becoming more integrated and large white media corporations had the revenue to court the top black journalists away from struggling black newspapers with promotion promises and higher salaries.

The Black press had become accustomed to wielding a significant amount of political power and influence, offering a black perspective on the protest confrontations and race riots, but with the passage of civil rights legislation many of their aims had been achieved, bringing their relevance into question. Nevertheless, selling newspapers was a business and dependent upon profits. Much of the basic revenue came from advertisers, and white companies didn't feel the need to advertise in black newspapers. The increased costs of printing and distribution forced many papers to narrow their distribution areas close to their base. Consolidation rescued a few smaller papers, while some of the larger black newspapers were able to weather the storm.

In 1965, there were around 150 African-American newspapers with about three million readers, yet black readers in greater numbers were shifting to reading mainstream papers, and the circulation of black newspapers were down between 50 to 75 percent.

There were two black dailies, *The Defender* and *The Atlanta Daily Word*, and both were experiencing dramatic declines in readership. Halfway through the 1960s, the *Daily Word* saw its circulation drop to 16,000, down from 75,000 at its peak, and by 1969, the *Chicago Defender's* circulation had dropped from 257,000 at its peak to 33,000. *The Pittsburgh Courier* also saw it readership sink to 20,000 from its high of 202,000.

The sixties were revolutionary and the new generations of newspaper readers wanted to hear a more militant voice, unable to sustain their circulation or capture the new audience, quite a few smaller black newspapers faded away. At the start of the decade, the Nation of Islam began publishing *Muhammad Speaks*, a weekly paper sold on street corners and door-to-door by members of the Nation, and soon became the most widely read black newspaper nationally with a circulation of 600,000. In 1965, the *Black Panther* was founded in Oakland, California by the Black Panther Party, and by 1969, boasted of

A Reflection

a national circulation near 100,000. *The Black Scholar*, a journal of African-American studies, political commentary, and a host of critical concerns for the black community, was also founded in 1969 by Nathan Hare.

Monthly magazines that catered specifically to black interests were unaffected by mainstream media. *Ebony* and *Jet* Magazines continued to thrive, in 1964, *Ebony* took in $5.5 million in advertising revenue, and the following year on its 20th Anniversary, *Ebony* celebrated 900,000 copies sold each month. The magazine's coverage of Martin Luther King, Jr.'s assassination included the Pulitzer Prize winning photos of Moneta Sleet. The monumental success of these magazines inspired Edward Lewis and Clarence O. Smith to create *Essence Magazine* in 1969.

Extraordinary African-Americans

Rev. Dr. Martin Luther King, Jr.

Martin Luther King's role in the Civil Rights Movement is perceived in many different lights with varying opinions. To some he was the epitome of Moses, leading African-Americans to the Promised Land, to others he was a symbol or figure head for a Movement that had numerous leaders across the country, and some even say the Movement made King versus King influencing the Movement, but whatever the point of view, he is unanimously acknowledged as an extraordinary African-American. Whether he happened to be at the right place at the right time is irrelevant, whether he was plunged into a role he had not aspired to does not detract from the fact that he made the ultimate sacrifice for his beliefs and the civil rights struggle.

Martin Luther King, Jr. was born on January 15, 1929 in Atlanta, Georgia to educated middle-class parents. A bright student, King attended Booker T. Washington High School where he skipped the ninth and twelfth grade and enrolled in Morehouse College at the age of fifteen as the third generation of King men to study at the school. He received his B.A. degree in 1948 and went on to Crozer Theological Seminary in Pennsylvania where he was awarded his B.D. in 1951. King having won a fellowship at Crozer, started the doctoral program at Boston University and received his Doctor of Philosophy in Theology on June 5, 1955. It was in the Boston that he met his wife, Coretta Scott, and from their marriage four children were born.

In 1954, King became pastor of the historic Dexter Avenue Baptist Church in Montgomery, Alabama. In December of 1955, segregation on the city buses in Montgomery reached an impasse after the arrest of Rosa Parks. A group of ministers and community leaders in the city united and formed the Montgomery Improvement

Association to organize a boycott of the bus system. Martin Luther King, Jr., new in town, was fortuitously elected president and in his own words, "*suddenly catapulted into the leadership*" and thrust onto the national stage.

The Montgomery Bus Boycott captured the attention of mass media and King became the voice of the Civil Rights Movement and founder of its nonviolent protest philosophy. Before the end of the thirteen month boycott, King was arrested and his home was firebombed, but the successful integration propelled his status as an effective leader to great heights for African-Americans who were desperate for change. Known for his ability to inspire the masses, King was a much sought-after speaker to galvanize direct mass-action campaigns.

At the age of 27 in 1956, King was referred to as the militant Baptist minister in newspaper articles. Despite numerous daily calls of death threats he forged ahead organizing the Southern Christian Leadership Conference as a platform for further nonviolent mass movements in the fight for equality and civil rights. For the next few years King authored several books and traveled extensively speaking before crowds of thousands in the fight against injustice. In 1959, he made a trip to India to gain further insight into Gandhi's philosophy of non-violent resistance. Speaking on Indian radio King said,

> "Since being in India, I am more convinced than ever before that the method of nonviolent resistance is the most potent weapon available to oppressed people in their struggle for justice and human dignity. In a real sense, Mahatma Gandhi embodied in his life certain universal principles that are inherent in the moral structure of the universe, and these principles are as inescapable as the law of gravitation."

Nonviolent protests were the centerpiece of demonstrations in the Civil Rights Movement, taken up by students in sit-ins and by the Freedom Riders in their campaign against interstate travel segregation.

Martin Luther King, Jr. became the pastor at his father's church, Ebenezer Baptist Church in 1960, although most of his time and energy focused on the campaigns of the SCLC. The SCLC and King lead a desegregation campaign in Albany, Georgia in 1961 that prepared them for the nonviolent protests to come against segregation by merchants in downtown Birmingham, Alabama in 1963. The Birmingham campaign brought monumental national and international exposure to the Civil Rights Movement with the contrast between the peaceful demonstration lead by King against the vicious dog and

A Reflection

fire hose attacks of Bull Connor on black children. King's subsequent arrest incited a host of detractors and a flood of criticism from fellow clergymen; he answered them in the "Letter from Birmingham Jail" where he eloquently articulated his motivation and commitment as a leader in the struggle for justice. The letter gave additional insight into his feelings about the difficulty of his leadership position:

> I began thinking about the fact that I stand in the middle of two opposing forces in the Negro community. One is a force of complacency, made up in part of Negroes who, as a result of long years of oppression, are so drained of self respect and a sense of "somebodiness" that they have adjusted to segregation; and in part of a few middle-class Negroes who, because of a degree of academic and economic security and because in some ways they profit by segregation, have become insensitive to the problems of the masses. The other force is one of bitterness and hatred, and it comes perilously close to advocating violence.

King and a prominent coalition of black leaders used the momentum from the Birmingham demonstration to organize a massive protest march for jobs and support for Civil Rights legislation on August 28, 1963 in Washington, D.C. The march was incredible, attended by more than 250,000 people, and King delivered his powerful and most memorable "I Have a Dream" speech. At the end of 1963, King was declared "Man of the Year" in *Time* magazine, and in 1964, at the age of 35, he was awarded the Nobel Peace Prize for his nonviolent approach in the Civil Rights Movement. King was requested to lend his experience and influential leadership to the March from Selma to Montgomery in 1965.

Beginning in 1966, Martin Luther King began to widen his focus to address the economic issues of all poor people, acknowledging that integration would end poverty and the wage gap between blacks and whites. In 1967, he became more vocal in his opposition to the Vietnam War stating: *"A nation that continues year after year to spend more money on military defense than on programs of social uplift is approaching spiritual death."* In 1968, King and the SCLS started the "Poor People's Campaign" to shift the Movement to tackle unemployment and economic justice. King traveled to Memphis, Tennessee to lead a march with garbage workers; there he delivered his "I've Been to the Mountaintop" speech. The following day on April 4, 1968, Marin Luther King, Jr. was assassinated while standing on the balcony of the Lorraine Motel.

The extraordinary characteristics of King were his endurance, his courageousness, and his righteousness which overshadowed the human flaws that afflict us all. King admitted in 1968, *"I'm frankly tired of marching. I'm tired of going to jail. Living every day under the threat of death, I feel discouraged every now and then and feel my work's in vain, but then the Holy Spirit revives my soul again."*

Luke 9:62 says: "Any man who puts his shoulder to the plow and takes it away, is not fit for the Kingdom of God." Early in his ministry King realized the mission for his life when he said, *"I have begun the struggle and I can't turn back. I have reached the point of no return."* He could have chosen to cast down his lot and opt for a secure life as pastor of his church, but he kept his nose to the grindstone and pushed forward. Having traveled millions of miles, giving thousands of sermons and speeches, being arrested dozens of times, and physically assaulted several times, receiving numerous accolades, awards, and honorary degrees, King wanted to be remembered in this way:

> I'd like somebody to mention that day that Martin Luther King Jr. tried to give his life serving others. I'd like for somebody to say that day that Martin Luther King Jr. tried to love somebody. I want you to say that day that I tried to be right on the war question. I want you to be able to say that day that I did try to feed the hungry. I want you to be able to say that day that I did try in my life to clothe those who were naked. I want you to say on that day that I did try in my life to visit those who were in prison. And I want you to say that I tried to love and serve humanity. Yes, if you want to say that I was a drum major. Say that I was a drum major for justice. Say that I was a drum major for peace. I was a drum major for righteousness. And all of the other shallow things will not matter.

No leader can be everything to everyone or fulfill the expectations of so many. Martin Luther King, Jr.'s legacy is as profound as his life. We all have much to aspire to in his "Dream."

Berry Gordy, Jr.

An extraordinary African-American is one who positively impacts the lives of many, inspires and encourages many, one who takes their expertise to a greater elevation and changes our world for many generations to come. Berry Gordy, Jr.

A Reflection

fits the description as the founder of the Motown Record Corporation and head of the most successful black-owned music company in history. In 1967, the Interracial Council for Business Opportunities (IBCO) awarded Gordy the business leadership award stating

> "Mr. Gordy has accomplished more than creating a leading recording and entertainment company. Besides fashioning a new dimension in American music with the 'Motown Sound' he has demonstrated the opportunities existing in business today and has inspired other young people to plan business careers."

Berry Gordy, Jr. was born in Detroit, Michigan on November 28, 1929, the seventh of eight children. Raised by parents who were self-employed, Berry inherited their entrepreneurial spirit and desire to control his own destiny. Anxious to make his fortune, Berry dropped out of high school in his junior year to become a boxer. In spite of winning twelve out of fifteen matches, his boxing career ended abruptly when he was drafted into the U.S. Army during the Korean War in 1951.

Berry's first business venture after returning from Korea was a record store, the 3-D Record Mart, specializing in jazz music. Not able to get the store off the ground, Berry began working on the assembly line of an auto plant. Fatefully, through a family friend he was able to meet Jackie Wilson, who then recorded a song Berry co-wrote with his sister Gwen and Billy Davis. *Reet Petite* was a modest hit, but Wilson recorded four additional songs by Gordy including the major hit, *Lonely Teardrops* over the next two years. Berry and Gwen added to their hits with *All I Could Do Was Cry* for Etta James.

Gordy used his songwriting profits to move into producing. After discovering the Miracles in 1957, he quickly recruited a select group of talented artists, borrowed $800 from family members and created Tamla Records and later the Motown record label, which were later merged into Motown Record Corporation on April 14, 1960. Gordy expanded with the addition of the International Talent Management, Inc, and Jobete Music Publishing Company. After several hits songs that had been picked up by other labels, the Miracles hit, *Shop Around*, rose to #1 on the R&B charts at the close of 1960 and #2 on the Billboard chart in 1961. A flood of hits were soon to follow beginning with *Please Mr. Postman* by the Marvelettes and *You Beat Me to the Punch* by Mary Wells. In 1963, Motown was the seventh largest producer of singles in the United States with eighteen hits on major charts, in addition to Jobete receiving five BMI music awards.

Under the direction and guidance of Berry Gordy, Motown expanded and diversified into television and Hollywood acquiring an elite stable of artists that included Martha Reeves and the Vandellas, the Temptations, the 4 Tops, Smokey Robinson and the Miracles, Gladys Knight and the Pips, Tammi Terrell, Marvin Gaye, Stevie Wonder, and the Supremes, who became the most popular female group in history. Berry Gordy became the most powerful single individual in the popular recording industry. In 1964, Motown had 47 songs on recording charts, and in 1968 had three of the top four hits of the year. In 1965, Gordy was named "Small Business Man of the Year" and in 1967, established the Motown scholarship for musical excellence via the United Negro College Fund. Supportive of black initiatives, Gordy donated $25 thousand to the Poor People's Campaign in 1968.

Great success rarely comes without controversy. Discord grew among artists who became disgruntled with contracts and their compensation. Criticism by performers and disagreements with management caused strained relationships among producers and artists resulting in a number of court proceedings and lawsuits. Even a few parted ways seeing Motown as a family-controlled organization with no upward mobility. Money and egos make a volatile mix particularly in the entertainment industry, with vicious competition that employs deceit and trickery to lure artists to switch labels.

Smokey Robinson vouched for Berry Gordy's integrity explaining that in many instances young performers lack knowledge about income taxes, are unfamiliar with the complexity of management, negotiations and promotion, and have the misconception that they made Berry Gordy, and not the reverse. Nevertheless, several facts remain undisputed; Berry Gordy built something of substance and value from an idea or dream, and became a "pacesetter in the world of entertainment."

Black Business and Professionals

By 1969, the typical businesses owned by African-Americans were still Mom-and-Pop establishments with few employees. Traditional businesses were centered on retail or personal services. Most were beauty shops, barber shops, restaurants, cleaners, shoe shine or repair, and funeral homes, all basically protected markets in the 1960s. Gains in desegregation by the Civil Rights Movement served to increase opportunities for white businesses to extract greater profits from black consumers. Earnings shrank quickly from black food stores and restaurants.

The number of black businesses and the number of black professionals in the black community fell into another downward phase during the 1960s for several reasons. The

A Reflection

national economy may have been in expansion, but for black people the lack of gainful employment was causing a contraction, the second reason was increased integration that diluted their share of black consumer market. Lastly, and most devastating was the urban renewal programs that were spreading across the country.

Black-owned businesses under segregation gave the black community a sense of pride and self-sufficiency, but urban renewal programs in the 1960s targeted African-American neighborhoods wiping out prominent black business districts in inner cities. Known as the "Black Wall Street" in Durham, NC, "Paradise Valley" in Detroit, Auburn Avenue in Atlanta, Henry Street in Roanoke, VA, and the "Albina District" in Portland, Oregon, black business havens were being destroyed to make way for public facilities, interstates and freeways, and housing projects.

African-Americans have always been a strong consumer market, and in 1969, black business receipts totaled nearly $4.5 billion. At the end of the decade the number of black-owned or controlled banks had doubled to 22 from 1963. Popular thinking at the time was that business development in the black community would be the answer to the deficient economic conditions of black people through the creation of jobs, and by raising the standard of living in the ghetto. Black businesses tended to hire more black workers than white-owned establishments. Nonetheless, the majority of black businesses were small, service oriented, in a limited number of industries, and unable to pay higher wages. In 1969, there were only 38,304 black businesses in the U.S. with paid employees, the equivalent of around 23 percent. The national market for African-American firms was limited to a mere three industries, insurance, publishing, and health and beauty products.

An exception to the rule was the H.J. Russell Construction Company formed in 1962 in Atlanta, Georgia. Russell had taken over his father's plastering company and had progressed from building duplexes to 400- and 500-unit complexes. In 1963, he contracted the plastering of the Atlanta County Stadium, and later in the decade Russell successfully bid on his first large project as a sub-contractor on one of the tallest building in downtown Atlanta, The Equitable Life Assurance Building. In 1968, H.J. Russell became one of the largest contractors in the Southeast building HUD homes.

Employment

The bulk of the changes experienced by African-Americans in the sixties were contingent on their employment circumstances. Census data reported that by the end of 1969 the proportion of blacks living below poverty level had dropped to 27 percent.

1969

Quality employment was the passport to middle-class status out of the confinements of the black ghetto, but on the other hand, unemployment negatively impacted black family stability, restricted education attainment, and raised the frustration level in urban cities and turned them into incubators for violent rioting.

Black unemployment levels escalated across the country exacerbated by the mechanization of cotton production in the South, a decreasing demand for unskilled labor with urban industrialization in the North, and lay-offs from government jobs due to reductions in nonmilitary spending. Unemployment among blacks ranged between 10-17 percent, always 2-3 times the rate for whites, with over 29 percent of young blacks unable to find work.

The black labor force in the decade was concentrated among workers from 22 to 54 years of age. According to U.S. Census data, the number of professional or technical workers had doubled over the last ten years to 21 percent, blue collar workers in manufacturing and transportation also increased considerably with numbers rising to 60 percent, 18 percent were employed in service industries, and less than one percent worked in private households. The number of black workers employed in agriculture had fallen to less than three percent, and the number of farms operated by blacks in 1969 had dropped to 104,000. Nevertheless, disparities in earnings between black and white workers persisted. Blacks in the work force earned less than two-thirds of what whites earned, and half worked part-time or under 40 hours. Eighty-five percent of those out of work were seeking full-time positions.

The Bureau of Labor Statistics reported that the employment gap between black and white workers increased over the last decade; blacks had less skilled jobs and the lengths of their unemployment was longer than whites. The Johnson administration, proactively involved in the labor market, began pressuring businesses to open positions to African-Americans previously reserved for white men. Successful passage of the 1964 Civil Rights Act and Title VII prohibited discrimination by employers on the basis of race color, religion, sex, or national origin. The Equal Opportunity Commission was created to control discrimination in the workplace; enforcement particularly in the South brought increased job opportunities and higher wages. By the end of the 1960s, black workers had seen gains in comparative pay levels.

The auto industry was the most integrated of all industrial companies in America with African-Americans totaling more than 20 percent of Detroit's auto workers. Functioning as both a blessing and a curse for black workers as they were making inroads in the higher-paying manufacturing jobs, new automated technology eliminated greater numbers of unskilled workers on assembly lines. The Trade Union Leadership Council pressured the big three auto makers,

A Reflection

Chrysler, Ford, and General Motors to enlarge the number of blacks in skilled positions and as foremen, but minimal openings were seen and next to none were employed in white-collar jobs.

Black workers responded to the mood of black militancy and calls for black power by organizing the Revolution Union Movement (RUM), the Dodge Revolutionary Union Movement (DRUM), and several other movements that united into the League of Revolutionary Black Workers. As fate would have it, the recession beginning in 1969 trimmed thousands of black militants from the industrial work force. The fortunate ones who held onto their jobs prospered and moved forward in the hunt for the American dream.

Education

> "The youngsters of today must direct their attention not only to the matter of racial identity and racial realization through African Studies, but they must make certain they are not left behind in the scientific and technological revolution, because if they are, they will be in a hopeless force. If the young Negro cannot become a part of this advancing technology, his whole revolution will have been in vain."
> --A. Philip Randolph, EBONY Magazine May 1969

The educational attainment level for blacks continued to rise during the 1960s. Enrollment rates for blacks in elementary school was over 90 percent by 1969, and the number of persons classified as illiterate was less than four percent. The median number of years completed by black males in the range of 25 to 29 years of age had extended to 12.2 from 10.5 in the previous decade. The overall graduation rate in the United States peaked at 77 percent in 1969. For African-Americans, the decade closed with 31 percent of blacks over the age of 25 having graduated from high school, for those in the age range of 20 to 24 years, the graduation rate had doubled to 62 percent. In post-secondary education four percent of black students completed four or more years of college, compared to 11 percent of white students.

The Brown v. Board of Education desegregation order was certainly moving at a deliberate speed, albeit as slow as possible. At the beginning of the sixties, only 49 southern school districts in the South had been desegregated, and a mere 1.2 percent of black students in 11 southern states were attending integrated schools. By 1969, close to 78 percent of black students in the South attended schools that were 90 to

100 percent segregated.

The White Citizens Council sponsored 150 all white schools or "segregation academies" in the South with enrollment around 300,000 in elementary and secondary schools. In Prince Edward County, VA, segregationists in government closed all public schools for five years as the alternative to integration. The Supreme Court ordered the schools reopened in 1964, although white students stayed enrolled in private schools delaying the desegregation order for several more years.

The Supreme Court decision to provide an equal education to all students had more impact on faculty and administrators. The desegregation in the South was actually seen as "disintegration" as black educators and black authorities were eliminated or displaced in public education systems in the South. The National Educators Association released a task force study in 1965 that concluded 93 percent of African-Americans educators interviewed had been "displaced or downgraded" as a result of desegregation. The lack of safeguards for black educators and administrators contributed to hundreds of dismissals of black teachers and principals in the South, particularly in Missouri, Oklahoma, Texas, and West Virginia. By the end of 1969, the number of black teachers had dropped substantially while the number of white teachers increased.

The Johnson Administration introduced a number of social programs to improve the educational opportunities for minorities and the poor as part of the "War on Poverty" in efforts to counteract the realization that "poor children do poorly in school." Head Start was designed to offset the disadvantages of underprivileged preschool children; Project Follow Through was an extension of the Head Start to maintain the gains through primary grades. Community Education provided tutors and recreational activities, the Upward Bound program was a pre-college preparation program, and Job Corps provided training for careers in various areas.

Black students were attending predominately white colleges and universities at a higher rate in the 1960s than their enrollment at Historically Black Colleges and Universities (HBCU's). Many were opting for the superior resources and funding even though studies had shown that black students performed better at black institutions. The greater injustice was that during the 1960s, uneducated blacks were able to find employment easier than those who were educated, limiting the upward mobility that was to be gained from achieving a college education.

Increased educational attainment and greater knowledge among black students planted seeds of self-confidence and discontent, a combination that turned many into student

A Reflection

activists as leaders and protestors. The upheaval seen throughout the 1960s attracted them to organizations within the Civil Rights Movement even as others identified with Black Nationalism. These intellectual activists which included Amiri Baraka (Leroi Jones) and Angela Davis pushed the ideology of "Black Power" and the development of political power to uplift the black community.

The Issue of Crime

The 1960s were full of violence and criminal activity of every category. Consequently, before looking at the crime statistics for African-Americans during this decade we must be careful to distinguish crime from riots and nonviolent demonstrators. The major source of arrests during the decade was civil rights protestors. The focus of crime in this reflection is on index crimes, which are split into two categories, violent and property. Violent index crimes are committed against an individual, such as homicide, assault of rape, property index crimes are burglary, theft, and arson. The percentage of blacks arrested for index crimes had gone down to 44.7 percent halfway through the 1960s.

Insofar as the wide held belief that blacks are genetically inclined to commit crimes, it should be re-stated that the proclivity to participate in criminal activity is related to poverty, family stability, and residence in inner ghettos and not race or ethnicity. The greater proportion of criminal activity among blacks can be attributed to the disproportionate numbers that are classified as poor, disadvantaged, and unemployed.

Males make up half of the population, but encompass 90 percent of the persons arrested for crimes. In addition, the males between the ages of 11 to 25 make up less than 25 percent of the population, but represent 75 percent of those arrested for serious crimes, and then blacks, while less than 11 percent of the population in this decade, comprised 30 percent of those arrested for serious crimes. The tendency for blacks to commit more crimes of homicide and assaults seemed to continue through the 1960s as well. Rates of assault/battery and homicide have been consistently higher in southern states among both blacks and whites. In 1967, 80 percent of the estimated 300,000 persons incarcerated in the United States were people of color; however, there is the element of racial discrimination in law enforcement and the criminal justice system that inflates the number of black arrests and convictions. During the 1960s, the Legal Defense Fund moved into the forefront as the strongest advocate for transforming the criminal justice system.

The criminal activity in the black community was reaching a perilous point in the late 1960s, and the number of robberies had risen by 119 percent. The African-American crime rate increased with the growth of the black population; however, the proportion of blacks arrested for all offenses did not keep up with the population rate. Despite the atmosphere of militancy in the black community the proportion of blacks arrested for index crimes actually went down. Nevertheless, illegal drugs were becoming a critical problem in poor black areas. The number of arrests due to narcotics had doubled from 1966 to 1967. The growing availability and use of drugs and narcotics were related to other crimes like burglary, robbery, prostitution and even more serious acts of violence with addicts driven to commit crimes to support their habit.

Between 1960 and 1967 juvenile arrests involving illegal drugs surged close to 800 percent. The number of juvenile delinquency cases had increased in nine consecutive years as neighborhood gangs swelled in numbers. Beginning in the mid-1960s, black juveniles from the "baby boom" were arrested for violent crimes at five times the rate for young whites. Black communities on the defensive became more assertive in the fight to curb the growing gang activity through "Citizen Cooperation" and crime reporting campaigns.

Finishing out the decade, the *Pittsburgh Courier* published an article on the findings of an analysis on the unfairness of the criminal justice system against blacks. The National Commission of the Causes and Prevention of Violence dispelled many of the myths relating to African-Americans and crime. The report stated that men and women are most likely to be victimized by a person from their own race; more blacks are attacked and assaulted by whites than blacks attack and assault whites; blacks are more likely to be the victims of serious violent crime; black women are at a larger risk than white women of being attacked; black men are the most likely victims of robbery and assaults with a deadly weapon; black women are the most likely victims of forcible rape and assaults, economic and income levels are greater factors than race in the commission of a crime; and blacks are treated more harshly than whites in court.

Health Issues

"Of all the forms of inequality, injustice in healthcare is the most shocking and the most inhumane." Martin Luther King JR., 2nd Annual Convention of the Medical committee for Human Rights, March 25, 1966.

There was significant improvement in healthcare for blacks in the 1960s, but there were still insufficient hospital facilities available for blacks living in the South. In Atlanta,

A Reflection

Georgia where blacks made up 50 percent of the population, they only had use of 630 of the 4,500 hospital beds. Similarly in Birmingham, Alabama where blacks constituted 40 percent of the population, just 574 of the 1,762 hospital beds were set aside for blacks. Healthcare and hospitalization for blacks in Northern cities wasn't much better with access to hospitals limited by the lack of admitting privileges of black physicians particularly in private hospitals. Most black patients were admitted to general hospitals, county hospitals, or public facilities. Although these municipal hospitals have improved over time, the level of care was second-rate due to inadequate funds and less qualified personnel. Integrating hospitals was a necessity in order to provide any measure of equality in healthcare.

The number of black physicians in the United States was estimated to be around six thousand or two percent of all physicians in 1968. In Mississippi during this time there were a mere 47 black doctors for nearly one million black people, no training facilities for black doctors or nurses, and no municipal hospitals. Black medical schools started recruitment programs to address the dearth of African-American healthcare professionals, and private white medical school doors were opened, but because of the inferior elementary and secondary education received by black students, few were able to meet entrance requirements. In 1968, less than 800 medical students were black out of approximately 33,000 students.

The 1964 Civil Rights Act prohibited discrimination on the basis of race by federally funded programs and institutions. The Department of Health, Education, and Welfare had the task of enforcing the law, but still subtle and overt forms of racial prejudice were seen by black physicians in healthcare facilities. Congress followed this legislation with the Medicare Program, which provided insurance coverage for most individuals over 65 years. Practically all hospitals received federal funding, requiring them to adhere to all the provisions of the Civil Rights Act prohibiting racial discrimination. African-Americans were then supposed to have greater access to healthcare through the Medicare and Medicaid programs, and by law, hospitals and the staffs were forced to integrate. However, closing the disparities in health between blacks and whites would not be resolved through legislation. In order to bypass rules against discrimination, hospitals and healthcare facilities left predominately black communities, limiting their access to medical care. The Legal Defense Fund and the NAACP filed numerous complaints against hospitals in eight southern states for discrimination against black patients, employees, doctors, and nurses.

The mortality rate for infants was used as a determinant of the health of the population. At the end of the 1960s, the mortality rate of black infants had declined to 30 per 1,000 live births, joining the lower mortality rate seen among white infants. Recognition for these changes could be given to the 1964 Food Stamp Act that distributed $300 million to provide better nutrition for the disadvantaged. By 1969, additional gains were seen in maternal mortality, tuberculosis, and pneumonia, the causes of morbidity for blacks became more aligned with whites, shifting to heart disease and cancer, albeit at 1.5 times the rate. Hypertension was a critical health concern for blacks, along with notable increases in cirrhosis of the liver and homicide. Drug abuse and addiction to narcotics was a growing problem for urban ghettos, 80 percent of drug addicts lived in New York, Detroit, Chicago, and Los Angeles, and 75 percent were blacks or Hispanics.

Major health issues in the black community were greater than basic medical care and treatment of diseases, there were social health problems, environmental health problems, the lack of adequate medical services, and the inadequate use of medical facilities offered. Large numbers of blacks did not take advantage of the polio vaccine causing a rise in its occurrence. Illnesses common to the poor in urban slums were rotten teeth, impaired vision left untreated, rat bites, and sicknesses related to malnutrition or a poor diet. Incidences of syphilis had increased 300 percent from the last decade, with unreasonably high levels among blacks and teenagers. The lack of education on health facilities and services that were available and distrust towards doctors were also contributors to the disparity in healthcare. African-Americans were also the victims of mal-practice due to bigotry with the involuntary sterilization of countless poor blacks in the 1960s, some without knowledge and some coerced.

Housing

The housing issues for African-Americans in the 1950s only became more divisive during the 1960s as the Civil Rights Movement pushed for racial equality. In Thomas Pettigrew's analysis of racial discrimination he stated, *"Residential segregation has proven to be the most resistant to change of all realms - perhaps because it is so critical to racial change in general."* The overcrowded slums designated for blacks in the central cities of states in the North and South continued to deteriorate, "white flight" to suburbia continued, de-industrialization and job losses continued, and the poverty and degradation of urban life became more entrenched.

A Civil Rights Commission Report stated that 57 percent of black housing was substandard and unacceptable. Most structures had inadequate bathroom facilities,

A Reflection

were without running water and plumbing, and lacked central heating. Trash and garbage fed the infestation of rats while the poor and uneducated residents were trapped without sufficient income to move. According to U.S. Census data, in 1969, African-Americans had the highest median of monthly mortgages or rent and utilities than all races with payments at $95. Many black families paid unreasonable rents for bad housing, much more than amounts paid by whites in better homes. In Harlem, 20 percent of black households were paying more than $80 per month to reside in deplorable living conditions. Corrupt real estate agents added to the fray by preventing blacks from buying or renting in better neighborhoods or in the suburbs.

The urban renewal begun in the previous decade declared more victims as African-Americans living in slums were marked for displacement and relocation. The complaints of "urban renewal means Negro removal" resounded in inner-cities from Atlanta to Birmingham and in Chicago to New York. Beautification initiatives were seen as efforts to supply white suburbanites with interstate highways to commute to work in the city without having to see or travel through ghetto communities. Housing shortages were exacerbated as dilapidated neighborhoods filled with poor and working class blacks were demolished without increasing the supply of affordable homes. Blacks on average paid 35 percent of their household income trying to keep a roof overhead.

Frustrations and disillusionment reached a peak in the mid-to-late-1960s spreading across the country in outbreaks of rioting. The common denominator in the urban cities overrun with chaos was a combination of inferior education, unemployment, and slum housing. In 1966, Atty. General Kalzenbach announced that a study by the Department of Justice concluded that *"the wretchedness of ghetto life, agitated by disease and despair, joblessness and hopelessness, rat-infested housing and long impacted cynicism"* were to blame for the violence and riots of the 1960s. The Demonstration Cities and Metropolitan Development Act of 1966 gave the Department of Housing and Urban Development the authority to put into action the "Model Cities" program. Selected cities would receive aid for implementing social, economical, and physical improvements in blighted neighborhoods with high levels of unemployment, crime delinquency, and disease. HUD received applications from 193 cities.

Middle-class blacks, business owners, and professionals left the ghettos for better housing in safe and economically secure areas at every opportunity, and at the beginning of the 1960s, 39 percent of African-Americans owned their own homes. However, the homes they were able to buy due to redlining and the steering of black families away from white neighborhoods tended to be older with less amenities and modern appliances, although they cost more than comparable homes purchased by whites. Blockbusting was commonly practiced by the most underhanded of real estate brokers. White homeowners would be advised to quickly sell their homes at below-market prices before values fell lower because of blacks coming into the neighborhood, they would then sell the homes to black families at above-market prices doubling their profits. Title VIII of the Civil Rights Act of 1968, called the Fair Housing Act of 1968, prohibited any discrimination concerning the purchase, rental, and financing of housing based on race, religion, or national origin. The Fair housing Act also established federal penalties for blockbusting.

Family Structure

Changes in the black family structure were becoming more visible throughout the 1960s, changes that would jeopardize the stability of the African-American family and result in greater numbers of blacks ensconced in the cycle of poverty. According to the Census Population Report, 64 percent of black men were currently married and 77 percent of black women were currently married, these proportions were lower than any previously recorded data. In 1969, 69 percent of black families were in the husband-wife category with 74 percent of black men heading the husband-wife primary family. Twenty-five percent of black families were headed by women in comparison to only 10 percent of white families being headed by women early in the 1960s, but by the end of the decade the number of black female headed households had grown close to 29 percent. Even with the decline in the number of black traditional families, the majority of black adults were married with their spouse within the home.

In 1960, 67 percent of black children were born to married couples and lived in a home with both parents, but by the end of the decade the number had gone down to 60 percent. Additionally, the number of illegitimate births of black babies had escalated over the past decade to 31 percent in conjunction with a lower proportion of children who resided with both parents. The two major changes affecting the black family during this decade were the decline in the marriage rate and increased unemployment among black men.

The controversial 1965 Moynihan Report claimed that the decline in black family stability was the root cause of blacks achieving limited socioeconomic gains during the 1960s. Moynihan's views were an extension of E. Franklin Frazier's perception that "deviant" family behaviors were manifest from a southern plantation culture which persisted for many generations after emancipation. Moynihan referred to black families

A Reflection

as a "tangle of pathology" resulting from a "legacy of slavery," he stated: *"In essence, the Negro community has been forced into a matriarchal structure which, because it is so out of line with the rest of society, seriously retards the progress of the group as a whole. He has no values and culture to protect."* Nonetheless, U.S. Census data collected over the past sixty years have refuted the theory that rural southern blacks who migrated to urban cities were responsible for the changes in black family structure in the North and West.

Additional research studies have proposed that the rise in the employment rate and income level of black women were the cause for the regression in the rate of marriages, stating, as more black women became self-sufficient they were less likely to marry. The educational attainment of black women also had a negative impact on the rate of marriage, educated women tend to have fewer children than those less educated. Economic factors identified by researchers Ellwood and Crane that impacted the structure of black families were welfare benefits and job earnings. Studies conducted in the slums of Chicago and in the ghetto neighborhoods of Washington D.C. reported that broken marriages and children born out-of-wedlock were frequent occurrences.

Prior to the 1960s, a number of states had used several discretionary rules to disqualify black mothers who needed assistance. The Civil Rights Movement won Supreme Court decisions that removed state mandates barring them from receiving benefits. Consequently, welfare rules were blamed for the absence of black men heading their families by deeming the children ineligible for benefits if the father was present in the home. Popular belief asserted that Aid to Families with Dependent Children (AFDC) encouraged child bearing without the benefit of marriage and increased the number of black women heading households and acted as a discouragement for women to work. During the 1960s, approximately 14 percent of black children received AFDC assistance. Although the majority of welfare recipients have always been white, welfare was credited with the reduction of the black poverty rate from 55 to 32 percent by 1969. Welfare dependency has also been blamed for the rise in teenage mothers, increased crime, and the breakdown of the black family.

Black Athletes and Sports

The world of sports in America continued to evolve during the 1960s as the Civil Rights Movement spread integration in colleges and universities and created more opportunities for black athletes to showcase their talents in sports arenas. Professional sports were less segregated as higher numbers of black athletes signed contracts

1969

with teams who wanted to stay competitive and increase their fan base. By the end of the decade, 36 percent of players in professional baseball were black, 34 percent of players in the NFL-AFL were black, and black players dominated professional basketball representing 56 percent of the players. Despite the advances of black athletes desegregating sports teams across the nation, the black athlete was still miles away from being an equal and achieving the American dream. Superstar athletes were still second-class citizens in the South and segregation in the stands was nonetheless a reality.

By the beginning of the 1960s, Negro Leagues were a thing of the past. Major baseball leagues were expanding to twenty teams and opening 100 roster spots for ball players. Plenty black players had endured year after year in the minor leagues but only 13 out of 100 spots were given to black players. Some cities in the South were resisting the steady onslaught of integration and that included America's favorite pastime, a number of southern ball clubs snubbed teams with black players refusing to play them. The National League, the first to integrate, had 64 African-American ball players, 50 percent more black players than the American League.

Great players of the decade included Bob Gibson, Willie Mays, Dick "Richie" Allen, Maury Willis, and Frank Robinson. The best all-around player during the 1960s was Frank Robinson, playing for the Baltimore Orioles, winning the MVP award in 1961 and 1962. Robinson reached his pinnacle in 1966, winning the Triple Crown, batting .316, 49 homeruns, and 122 runs-batted-in, taking MVP, and topping it off with the World Series.

Maury Willis, player for the Los Angeles Dodgers, proved that speed does kill even in the game of baseball, stealing 104 bases in 1962. His incomparable speed demonstrated that not only heavy hitters can win games. Willis led the league in stolen bases for six consecutive years, exciting the fans and frustrating his opponents. Richard "Dick" Allen, player for the Philadelphia Phillies, debuted in 1964 with one of the greatest rookie season on record. Allen led the league with 125 runs, 13 triples, 80 extra base hits, and 352 total bases. Allen made the All-Star team three years in row beginning in 1965, and finished his career with a .318 batting average 201 hits and 38 doubles.

Without a doubt, Bob "Hoot" Gibson with the St. Louis Cardinals was the star player on the diamond in the 1960s. A two sport athlete, and former player with the Harlem Globetrotters, Gibson was called "the hottest hand in pro baseball." Described as brilliant, magnificent, and superb, Gibson put his fierce determination behind every pitch. In the 1962, season he made the National League All-Star team, pitching 22 scoreless innings. He was selected eight more times to play on the National League All-Star team.

A Reflection

Gibson threw 3117 strikeouts, carried the Cardinals to two World Series in 1964 and 1967, was named MVP in 1968, and won two National League Cy Young awards in his baseball career.

Willie Mays, named player of the decade, two-time MVP winner, playing for the San Francisco Giants, continued to dazzle and amaze fans with his spectacular catches in center field winning his eleventh straight Gold Glove awards in the majors in 1968. At the end of the decade, Mays had 577 career home runs, second only to Babe Ruth, with Hank Aaron following close behind with 537 runs. Reggie Jackson, dubbed "Mr. October," was drafted by the Kansas City A's in 1966 thrilling the fans with his flash and consistent play in the field and at bat.

Integration, proving to be a two-edged sword, was opening doors for black players at white colleges across the country to the detriment of black college football programs. Talented black athletes were heavily recruited by white schools and HBCU programs were forever weakened. Black players were now the shining stars on white college teams, providing a taste of defeat to segregated southern programs. Ernie Davis was to be the next superstar, following in the footsteps of Jim Brown. Davis was the top-rated player on the top-rated team of Syracuse. Winner of the Heisman Trophy in 1961 and drafted by the Cleveland Browns, he would never play one minute of professional football. Struck by leukemia, he died at only 23 years of age. Orenthal James "O.J." Simpson, running back for USC, led the nation in rushing in 1967 and 1968, won the Maxwell Award, the Walter Camp Award, UPI player of the year, and was the winner of the Heisman Trophy in 1968. Simpson was drafted by the AFL Buffalo Bills in 1969.

Professional football was challenging professional baseball as the premiere sport in the country, and African-American players were taking the lead on the field. The new American Football League was creating more opportunities for black athletes to play pro football, averaging 17 percent more black players than the NFL. Gale Sayers, playing for the Chicago Bears, was "Rookie of the Year" in 1965, leading the league with 22 touchdowns and 132 scored points and an offensive record of 2,240 yards in his 2nd year, second only to Jim Brown. Jim Brown, star of the previous decade, was still the supreme runner in the history of football, carrying the ball for 12,312 yards, scoring 129 touchdowns, setting eleven NFL records, and earning MVP in 1964, before his retirement in 1966. Leroy Kelly effectively filled the void left by Jim Brown, leading the NFL in rushing yards (1205 yards) in 1967.

Black players were intimidating on the defensive teams in professional football. In 1963, the Los Angeles Rams assembled David "Deacon" Jones, Roosevelt Grier, and

Lamar Lundy, all six foot five inches or taller and each over 255 pounds, to form three-quarters of the "Fearsome Foursome," called "the most dominant line in football history" by Dick Butkus.

African-American athletes raised the level of excitement in the game of basketball in college and in the professional leagues. The unstoppable Lew Alcindor, later known as Kareem Abdul Jabbar, at seven foot one inches, scored points at will while playing at UCLA. The team was undefeated until Alcindor was injured in his junior year. During the 1967-1968 season, the NCAA passed a no-dunk rule to limit the offensive game of black players. Elvin Hayes, playing at the University of Houston, was considered to be the top college player in the country. UCLA and Houston, both undefeated were scheduled for a showdown where Alcindor and Hayes would matchup on January 20, 1968, in what was dubbed the "Game of the Century" in college basketball. Alcindor played poorly with an injured eye and the Houston Cougars won a close victory.

In professional basketball, Wilt Chamberlain, at seven foot two inches, was the greatest offensive player in the history of basketball, averaging 50.4 points per game and scoring 100 points in one game during the 1961-1962 season. Unparalleled in speed and coordination Chamberlain was approached by pro football scouts and boxing trainers and promoters. Although Chamberlain was the leading scorer in the NBA for six consecutive seasons and leading rebounder for four seasons, he had never led his team in college or as a professional to a championship until the 1966-1967 season with the Philadelphia 76ers.

In 1966, Bill Russell was the ultimate defensive player in the NBA. His exceptional leaping ability demonstrated in blocked shots and pulled rebounds were the foundation of the Boston Celtics winning line of attack. In the competitive rivalry between Russell and Chamberlain, the edge went to Russell who outplayed Chamberlain by shutting down his offensive game and picking up his rebounds. In the 1966-1967 season, Bill Russell became coach for the Celtics as well as player.

Other fantastic players of the decade included Nate Thurmon, Walt Bellamy, Hal Greer, and Oscar Robertson. There was also Dave Bing who won 1966-1967 Rookie of the Year playing for the Detroit Pistons, and Earl "the Pearl" Monroe who was Rookie of the Year in 1967-1968 with the Baltimore Bullets averaging 24.3 points per game. Monroe was "the consummate showman," dribbling and passing the ball behind his back with finesse. Elgin Baylor led the Los Angeles Lakers to the NBA Championship in 1968, and in 1969, Bill Russell took the Celtics to victory in the NBA Championship before retiring as coach and player.

A Reflection

***

"I am the Greatest." Muhammad Ali, born Cassius Marcellus Clay, Jr. was an intriguing sports figure from the start. Winner of six National Golden Gloves and the National Amateur Athletic Union boxing tournaments in the light heavyweight category, Clay qualified for the 1960 Olympic team, brought home the light heavyweight gold medal, and then turned pro. Fighting as a heavyweight with a record of 19 victories, boasting "float like a butterfly, sting like a bee," Clay defeated Sonny Liston and became the heavyweight champion on February 25, 1964. After the fight Clay announced his conversion to the Muslim religion, his joining the Nation of Islam, and his name change to Muhammad Ali. In 1967, the U.S. Army called for Ali's induction into military service, but he refused citing his religious beliefs and stated "*I ain't got no quarrel with them Viet Cong... No Vietcong ever called me nigger.*" Ali was consequently arrested, stripped of his title, his boxing license was suspended, and he was convicted of draft evasion. Muhammad Ali appealed his conviction and by the end of the decade the case was still before the U.S. Supreme Court.

In 1967, the World Boxing Association staged an elimination tournament among the top heavyweight contenders to determine the winner of the vacant WBA Championship. On April 27, 1968, Jimmy Ellis defeated Jerry Quarry in a split decision and won the heavyweight championship, which he held for the rest of the decade. Joe Frazier had an amateur record that laid claim to wins in three Middle Atlantic Golden Gloves heavyweight championships in 1962, 1963, and 1964, and the 1964 Olympic boxing gold medal. By 1967, Frazier had won 14 bouts, all by knockouts and was the #1 contender for the vacant heavyweight crown. Declining to participate in the elimination bouts, Frazier fought Buster Mathis for the also vacant New York State Athletic Commission World Heavyweight Championship and won.

During the intense civil rights struggles of the 1960s, black athletes were being approached and asked to boycott the Olympic Games to protest their second-class citizenship and not represent America in international competition. However, with the Olympics being one of the venues where black athletes had historically competed freely support was strong among athletes who had trained all their lives for this moment. Wilma Rudolph, the "Black Gazelle," was the Queen of the Track in the 1960 Olympics in Rome, audiences were captivated by her "combination of grace, beauty, and speed." Rudolph was clearly the fastest woman in the world and the first American woman to win three gold medals, winning the 100m, 200m, and the 400m relay. In 1960 and 1961, she was named the Associated Press Female Athlete of the Year. Rafer Lewis Johnson won the Olympic gold in 1960 in the decathlon.

The 1964 Olympic Games in Tokyo showcased the fastest man and woman in the world, Wyomia Tyus and Bob Hayes, both winning gold medals in the 100m sprint. Nonetheless, it was the controversy of the 1968 Olympic Games in Mexico that is indelibly marked in our memories. The threat of boycotts of the track and field events filled the air but they never materialized. Jim Hines and Charles Green won the gold and silver medals in the 100m race, and Tommie Smith and John Carlos won the gold and bronze medals in the 200 meter race, but it was during the awards ceremony when the America flag was raised and the anthem was played that Smith and Carlos lowered their heads and raised their black-gloved fists defiantly into the air in a gesture of protest that spoke volumes to the injustices suffered by black Americans. Before the day was over the two athletes had been stripped of their medals, expelled out of the Olympic village, and banned from any future Olympic competitions.

Tennis and golf were two sports where few African-Americans could break the color barrier. Charlie Sifford finally became a member of the PGA tour in 1961, and won the Greater Hartford Open invitational in 1967 and the Los Angeles Open in 1969. In tennis, Arthur Ashe won the NCAA singles title in 1965, and in 1968 Ashe won the United States Amateur Championship and the first US Open, becoming the only player to win both in the same year.

Literature

James Baldwin continued his writing in the sixties publishing *Another Country, The Fire Next Time, Tell Me How Long the Trains Been Gone*, and the *Blues for Mr. Charlie*, but his mentee, Maya Angelou, who called him her brother, wrote the bestseller in African-American literature during the 1960s, "*I Know Why the Caged Bird Sings.*" Inspired by her mentor James Baldwin after the assassination of Martin Luther King, Jr. on her birthday, April 4th, Maya poured out her grief while writing *I Know Why the Caged Bird Sings*, published in 1969. The book, which covered her first seventeen years, was the first in a series of six autobiographical works, was the first non-fiction book by an African-American woman to reach the best-seller list, and was nominated for a National Book Award. Having had more occupations and careers than ten individuals put together, as a cook, waitress, a madam, a singer, a dancer, a civil rights activist, a poet, a novelist, a professor, an actor, and a director, Maya Angelou gained international fame with her first

A Reflection

autobiographical novel.

African-American Art

African-American artists were very much a part of the protests of the 1960s; they began to protest their exclusion from major exhibitions and influential art galleries. Speaking from the canvas or from a variety of mediums including collages, sculptures in wood, stone, and plaster, they visually presented the struggle of black people in America. In abstract or the social realist style, their displays shouted "Black is Beautiful." Yet no matter the level of talent, many black artists were unable to make a living through their art lacking the opportunities and connections of white artists.

Prominent artists of the decade included Jacob Lawrence, who by this time was referred to as "great," Romare Bearden and his collages, and Sam Gilliam whose geometric figures, bold colors, and unsupported draped canvases followed the trend of modern art. Charles White, a native of Chicago, embodied the mood of the 1960s with his social realist style portraying black men and women and expressing their strength and determination, and pride. White received newfound attention to his art in the Black Conscious movement of the 1960s. On his use of symbolic characters, White explained:

> "I use Negro Subject matter because Negroes are closest to me. But I am trying to express a universal feeling through them, a meaning for all men… This does not mean I am a man without anger—I've had my work in museums where I wasn't allowed to see it. But what I pour into my work is the challenge of how beautiful life can be."

"Awaken from the Unknowing" – Charles White (1961)

1969

Two Brothers Have I had on Earth – One of Spirit, One of God– Charles White (1965)
Courtesy of Heritage Gallery, Los Angeles, CA, Charlotte Sherman

Entertainment

The explosion of protests in the Civil Rights Movement of the 1960s created a new and even more militant generation of protest plays in Black theatre. LeRoi Jones, the prolific writer of the 1960s, later known as Amiri Baraka, contributed to the protest plays with *The Dutchman* (1964), for which he won an Obie Award, about a sadistic encounter between a white woman and a black man on a New York subway. *The Slave* (1965) and *The Toilet* (1965) further emphasized the depth and effects of race issues in America. Fellow protest writer, James Baldwin's *Blues for Mister Blues for Mister* (1964) was based on the murder of Emmett Till and questioned the value of non-violent protest amid incessant violence and killings.

The Black Arts Movement (BAM) breathed new life in black community theatre groups. As part of the BAM, the Black Arts Repertory Theatre was established by Baraka in 1965 to offer cultural poetry, music, and art to the streets in black neighborhoods. Black theaters sprung up in urban cities across the country, the New Lafayette Theatre in New York, the Free Southern Theatre in New Orleans, the Concept East Theatre in Detroit, and several theaters in Chicago. Through these theaters came black playwrights, directors, and managers. Black acting ensembles were also established in urban cities throughout the country, The Negro Ensemble sponsored plays written by black authors

A Reflection

for black actors, of which several had successful runs on Broadway like Ossie Davis' *Purlie Victorious* (1961).

All-black casts were seen in long running plays during the decade with Langston Hughes' *Black Nativity* which opened on Broadway on December 11, 1961 and became a Christmas classic, and *The Blacks: A Clown Show*, written by Jean Genet, which ran for 1,408 performances making it the longest running off-Broadway non-musical production of the decade. Notable cast members of *The Blacks* were James Earl Jones, Roscoe Lee Brown, Cicely Tyson, Louis Gossett, Jr., Godfrey Cambridge, Charles Gordone, and Maya Angelou.

As the decade moved forward, productions like Martin Duberman's *"In White America"* (1964), a stage documentary of blacks in the United States, *The Owl and the Pussycat* (1964) and *Hallelujah, Baby!* (1967) were evidence that plays on and off Broadway were becoming more integrated in their productions. Clifford Odet's *Golden Boy* was updated and adapted especially for Sammy Davis Jr. to play the lead character, and black actors were playing roles that had been written specifically for whites. *No Strings* (1967), starring Diahann Carroll, was bold enough to even portray an interracial romance.

Changes were seen in Hollywood during the 1960s as more dramatic roles were seen for blacks outside of the preferred genre of musicals for black productions. Black actors of darker complexions were expanding out of stereotypical roles. Sidney Poitier already a superstar grew into the megastar of the 1960s as a top box office draw. He exploded on the screen in the movie feature of *Raisin in the Sun* in 1961, and followed with the sophisticated *Paris Blues* (1961), also starring Diahann Carroll, and in 1963 became the first African-American to win the Best Actor Academy Award for his performance in *Lillies of the Field*. In 1967, Poitier was the highest grossing actor on the silver screen with three megahits, *To Sir, with Love, In the Heat of the Night,* and *Guess Who's Coming to Dinner?* Abbey Lincoln received a Golden Globe nomination in 1969 for her performance in *For the Love of Ivy* opposite Poitier.

Diahann Carroll was the most successful black actress during the 1960s; she starred on stage, the big screen, and on the little screen, and maintained a successful singing career as well. Diahann won a Tony Award for her role of Barbara Woodruff in the musical *No Strings*. In between acting roles Diahann Carroll stayed busy with her nightclub act. In 1968, she starred in the television series *Julia*, portraying a nurse and widow raising her son, becoming the first African-American woman starring in a television series in a non-stereotypical role. Carroll won the Golden Globe award for Best Actress in a Television Series and was nominated for an Emmy for her leading role in 1968.

Although blacks were making some progress in roles in front of the camera, positions behind the camera were off limits with few exceptions. One of the rare occasions was financing of *The Learning Tree*. The movie was the first Hollywood film written, directed, produced, and composed by an African-American. All tasks were filled by Gordon Parks, a successful photographer and journalist for *Life* Magazine. Based on his semi-autobiographical novel, *The Learning Tree* was made into a feature film released in 1969. This classic and poignant film touched the full range of our emotions while representing a more realistic view of life as a black person growing up in the racist society of America.

Television as a medium had taken over as the most influential entity over thoughts and actions. Fred MacDonald described it in his book, "Blacks and White TV," as *"the most powerful communicator ever known."* In the early 1960s, blacks were making guest appearances on variety shows and occasionally were seen in episodes of series where roles were written for a black actor, but most shows were void of any black actors. In 1963, the NAACP and CORE were demanding equity in employment for blacks in every phase of the entertainment industry, and campaigns spilled into protests for equal time and programming on television. By the second half of the 1960s, TV executives were becoming more sensitive to the Civil Rights Movement and the $30 billion black market, and consequently so began what MacDonald (2009) called "The Golden Age of Blacks in Television."

By the end of the 1960s, there were over 25 television shows with blacks as the leading character or in a supporting role appearing regularly. In 1965, Bill Cosby starred in "I Spy," the first Africa-American to star in a weekly dramatic series. The series ran for three years and Cosby won three Emmy Awards for the three seasons as the best actor in a continuing dramatic series. Sammy Davis, Jr. And Lesley Uggams were featured in their own variety shows, even though both were short-lived. Then again, there were many successful series that emerged in the decade that featured black actors, Denise Nicholas and Lloyd Haynes in *Room 222*, Gregg Morris in *Mission Impossible, Julia, Mannix*, and *Mod Squad* to name a few.

***

Black music and musicians ran the gamut during the 1960s, from opera, to gospel, popular music, and rhythm and blues, black voices rang out from coast to coast. Black

A Reflection

divas were present in every genre, Leontyne Price reigned supreme in opera appearing with the Metropolitan Opera, Mahalia Jackson was the "Queen of Gospel" singing at the March on Washington and Martin Luther King's funeral, Dionne Warrick ruled the top of the charts in popular music, and Aretha Franklin was the "Queen of Soul." For the early years in the decade Sam Cooke, the "King of Soul" had the ears of the country with hits songs like *You Send Me*, *A Change Is Gonna Come*, *Chain Gang*, *Bring it on Home to me*, *Cupid*, *Wonderful World*, and *Twisting the Night Away*.

James Brown, also known as the "Godfather of Soul," was probably more accurately the Father of Funk. Brown's funk sound evolved during the 1960s as he began to emphasize the downbeat in songs *"Out of Sight"* and *"Papa's Got a Brand New Bag* in 1965. The funk music style underscored the 'on the one,' the first beat of each measure, heard in *"Cold Sweat"* (1967) and *"Mother Popcorn."* Reluctant to take a stand in the Civil Rights Movement, Brown released *"Say It Loud, I'm Black and I'm Proud "* after Martin Luther King's assassination in 1968, and *"I Don't Want Nobody to Give Me Nothing, Open Up the Door, I'll Get It Myself"* in 1969.

There was also the Rock and Roll of Little Richard, the guitar brilliance of Jimi Hendrix, along with the energy of Ike and Tina Turner, but needless to say, the music that most characterized the 1960s was the Motown sound. The timeless music of artists and groups like the Temptations, the Marvelettes, Four Tops, Marvin Gaye and Tammi Terrell, Supremes, Stevie Wonder, Gladys Knight and the Pips, and Smokey Robinson and the Miracles, the Spinners, and the Jackson 5, broke down racial barriers and became the "sound of young America" with 110 top-10 hit songs.

Memorable Moments

Wilma Rudolph became the first American woman to win three gold medals at the 1960 Olympic Games in Rome as the fastest woman on the earth.

Muhammad Ali won the National Golden Gloves and went on to win the Gold Medal in the 1960 Olympics.

W.E.B. Du Bois died on August 27, 1963 at the age of 95.

On August 28, 1963, the largest demonstration of the civil rights movement, organized by A. Philip Randolph drew a crowd over 250,000, and featured speaker Martin Luther King, Jr. and his "I Have a Dream" speech.

Sam Cooke was shot and killed under suspicious circumstances on December, 11, 1963 at the age of 33.

1969

In the 1964 Tokyo Olympics Games, Bob Hayes won the 100m in a record 9.1 seconds.
In 1964, Althea Gibson became the first black woman to earn her LPGA player's card.
Beginning in 1965, blacks were drafted into the Vietnam War, 9.5 percent of troops and 13.5 percent of fatalities.
Malcolm X was assassinated on February 21, 1965 in Manhattan, New York by three members of the Nation of Islam.
The Selma to Montgomery March for voter rights was March 7, 1965, "Bloody Sunday," where 600 civil rights demonstrators were attacked by police with nightsticks and tear gas.
Satchel Paige, at 59 years old, pitched his last game with the Kansas City Athletics in September of 1965, the oldest player to pitch in the league.
Langston Hughes died on May 22, 1967 at the age of 65.
Martin Luther King, Jr. was assassinated on April 4, 1968 in Memphis, Tennessee.
At the 1968 Olympic Games in Mexico, Tommie Smith and John Carlos raised their black gloved fists as a symbol of black pride, explained by Smith, "The totality of our effort was the regaining of black dignity."
The first black studies program was coordinated by Nathan Hare at San Francisco University in 1968.
Arthur Ashe was the first African-American man to win the U.S. Open in 1968.
Jimmy Hendrix plays at Woodstock, giving an electrifying and unforgettable performance of "The Star Spangled Banner" in 1969.
Leontyne Price ended an eight-year run at the New York Met in 1969 after 118 performances.
H. Rap Brown published his controversial autobiography, "Die Nigger Die!" in 1969.
James Earl Jones won the Tony Award for best actor for his portrayal of Jack Johnson in the play *"The Great White Hope"* on Broadway in 1969.
Moneta Sleet, Jr. became the African-American to win the Pulitzer Prize for Feature Photography for his photograph of Coretta Scott King at the funeral services for her husband Martin Luther King, Jr.
The #1 hit song of 1969 was Aquarius/Let the Sun Shine In" by the Fifth Dimension.
The Dance Theater of Harlem was established by Arthur Mitchell in 1969.
Ruth White became the first black woman named national fencing champion and the youngest to win a major U.S. fencing title at age 17 in 1969.

A Reflection

Reflection on a Decade

A panoramic view of the 1960s corroborates the widespread opinion that these were indeed "turbulent" years, absolutely a decade of churning and agitation. Our world was tossed and stirred and mixed in attempts to integrate and bring together diverse people, ideas, politics, philosophies, and socioeconomics statuses. The opposing pulls between the old traditional and segregated American with those who resisted change, and those who yearned for monumental changes in search of a better America, one true to her creed, had become more emboldened and powerful. The tension between these forces had risen to a fever pitch during these years and urgency was felt on both sides of the struggle. The confrontations and returned hostilities that characterized the Civil Rights Movement had grown in frequency and magnitude as the demands for change grew louder. The retaliation through physical attacks on protestors, the firebombing of churches and homes, and the brutal attacks on innocent children were cataclysmic for blacks in America.

At the close of 1969, there were significant changes seen from the previous decade. For one change we were Black people, the term Negro was now socially unacceptable. The catalysts for change were the accelerated protests from the black community in the Civil Rights Movement, the accommodating political climate set forth by President Lyndon B. Johnson, and the widespread media coverage of the debauchery that was segregation that led America to examine her conscience. The passage of the Civil Rights Acts of 1960 and 1964, the Voting Rights Act of 1965, and the implementation of affirmative action were instrumental in more blacks gaining the right to vote in southern states, more blacks gaining employment in federal jobs, and more blacks being elected to political offices on every level of government.

Few economic changes were evident in the black community over the last decade; the employment gap had not wavered and black leaders had turned their focus toward increasing job opportunities and economic independence. Educational attainment continued to rise, but black-on-black crime remained a serious problem in urban areas. The overall health of African-Americans had improved despite the limited access to healthcare. Urban renewal intent on removing slums, built new housing that poor blacks could not afford, exacerbating the inner-city housing crisis. Moreover there was a disturbing and detrimental trend in the foundation of the black family, the decline in the marriage rate and the growth in the number of women raising children as single-parents.

Much had been ventured, but what had been gained. Integration turned out not to be the panacea to the problems of black people; poverty was still the indomitable opponent.

1969

Running as fast as you can and still losing was disheartening. There hadn't been a road map or a big picture, the Civil Rights Movement had no master plan, charts, or bench marks. What was the ultimate goal, not just desegregation? Doubts about large numbers of black achieving high levels of education began to swell, and for those with more education, discrimination kept them from advancing forward. Northern blacks were discouraged, their problems were not solved by desegregation or legislation, poverty, unemployment, and indecent housing were ever present.

Black Child's Pledge

I pledge allegiance to my Black People.
I pledge to develop my mind and body to the greatest extent possible.
I will learn all that I can in order to give my best to my People in their struggle for liberation.
I will keep myself physically fit, building a strong body free from drugs and other substances which weaken me and make me less capable of protecting myself, my family and my Black brothers and sisters.
I will unselfishly share my knowledge and understanding with them in order to bring about change more quickly.
I will discipline myself to direct my energies thoughtfully and constructively rather than wasting them in idle hatred.
I will train myself never to hurt or allow others to harm my Black brothers and sisters for I recognize that we need every Black Man, Woman, and Child to be physically, mentally and psychologically strong.
These principles I pledge to practice daily and to teach them to others in order to unite my People.
---The Black Panther, October 26, 1968
by Shirley Williams

A Reflection

1979

The 1970s represented the aftermath, the aftermath of the civil rights struggle, of the riots, of the black power movement, and of the war. Countless lives had been sacrificed and what was there to show for the struggle, what were the successes and the spoils? The country was in the midst of an economic slowdown with massive layoffs in the steel industry, and competition from Japan and Germany challenged American domination of world markets. Inflation in food prices, housing, energy, and medical care costs were devastating and provoked high unemployment while earnings remained relatively stagnate. African-Americans were feeling the brunt of the recession as the numbers living below poverty level accelerated to more than 30 percent.

The determination and hope from the previous decade had given way to fatigue and disillusionment. The unified front had been weakened by divisions in ideology and the loss of leadership, and more devastating was what Marable (1980) described as the class separation between the stable middle-class and the underprivileged lower-class in the black community. Other disturbing trends evident in this decade expressed in the Los

Angeles Sentinel (3/20/86) were the *"increasing breakup of the Black family, the decline in American economic growth, rising black unemployment and a misdirected public debate on race."*

The fight had shifted from civil rights to economic rights, but the momentum had died with Malcolm, Martin, and the Black Panthers. An advisory panel to the U.S. Commission on Civil Rights determined that the most urgent problem affecting the civil rights of minorities in this country and specifically in the South was unemployment. The Urban League Report of the State of Black America relayed that it was in a state of crisis. Many of the hard fought gains were eroding or being reversed. Jim Crow had been beaten, at least in the courts, but new problems rose with continued urban renewal, white-flight, deindustrialization of urban cities, more crime and delinquency, and a building resentment from large numbers in the white community who felt too much had been compromised too quickly.

Things were tough all over, but on the other side of the coin we still had our pride. Jesse Jackson's poem reminded us *"I am Somebody."* The celebration of Kwanza was conceived by Ron Karenga to promote cultural nationalism as African-Americans became aware of their African heritage. We now recognized the rich legacy of our forefathers and Africa as the mother of civilization. "Black is Beautiful." We raised the flag with the *red, black, and green*. We were the descendants of Kings and Queens. We shouted out "I'm Black and I'm Proud," we raised our fists as a show of a power and presence, and we walked with our afros held high knowing "I've got Soul and I'm Super Bad."

Demographics

The life expectancy for Black Americans improved further to 68.5 years, and the median age was 25 years. The ratio of black men to black women varied from urban to rural areas and in different regions of the country, and the gender imbalance had worsened over the last decade. According the U.S. Census data, in urban areas and central cities there were about 12 percent more black females than black males, or 88 males for every 100 females, 11 percent more black females outside of urban areas on the fringes, while in rural areas of the country there were only three percent more black females than black males, or 97 males for every 100 females. Overall, looking at 270 U.S. metropolitan cities, the ratio was about 91 males to every 100 females (Kiecolt & Fossett, 1997).

Blacks now made up 11.7 percent of the population, with numbers around 26,683,000. Larger numbers of blacks were located in urban cities of the Northeast, North Central,

A Reflection

and Western regions of the country, but 26 percent of blacks located in the Southern region lived in rural areas. However, the numbers of African-Americans living in poverty-stricken ghettos swelled by 164 percent in the 1970s. The white populations in the suburbs grew by 12 percent during these years while the black suburban population grew by nearly 43 percent, albeit in segregated outlying communities.

Most notable was the reverse migration trend that began halfway through the 1970s as metropolitan areas continued to de-industrialize and employment opportunities diminished. Population growth among African-Americans in the North and central cities of the United States was flat. By the end of 1979, it was estimated that more than 40 percent of blacks migrating south were returning back home on the same path they had traveled to the North. In the last half of the decade 194,000 blacks had migrated to large southern cities and even some back to small rural communities.

Income levels among African-Americans were falling and the number of black middle-class declined. The annual income for a black male was $11,404.46 compared to $16,703.67 for a white male, and the annual incomes for black and white females were $7810.66 and $7893.76 respectively. The incomes for black women made some progress on closing the gap between white women.

Mood of the Black Community

But these words are tired
and I'm tired
and you're tired
and everybody's goddamn tired
tired
students tired
Black folks tired
Liberals tired
Revolutionaries tired . . .
---June Jordon, 1973

Black people were tired; they had agitated, pushed, prodded, and marched. They had stood up, sat-in, gone to jail, gone to court, gone to school, and even gone to war. They had played all the trump cards for the privilege to eat in white restaurants, shop in white stores, and use public facilities reserved for whites. To say that black Americans were

1979

dissatisfied with the outcome of what many were calling the end of the Civil Rights Movement would be a grave understatement. What had been fought for, migrated in search of, and many had been willing to die for, was the most important and ever elusive economic security found in a steady job with quality wages. Notwithstanding affirmative action policies, job discrimination had yet to be conquered. Most of the faithful warriors were dead, and the young didn't have a taste for the battle, so the struggle laid dormant in the 1970s. Gil Scott-Heron perceived it as the *"Winter in America,"* the title of his 1974 album, he explained:

> "In our hearts we feel that spring is just around the corner: a spring of brotherhood and united spirits among people of color. Everyone is moving, searching. There is a restlessness within our souls that keeps us questioning, discovering and struggling against a system that will not allow us space and time for fresh expression… We approach winter the most depressing period in the history of this industrial empire, with threats of oil shortages and energy crises. But we, as Black people, have been a source of endless energy, endless beauty and endless determination.

No stranger to oppression, hard times, or feeling the blues, black people had a history of finding the proverbial silver lining. We reveled in the knowledge of who we were and where we had come from. African heritage became a part of our culture, feeling intense pride from renewed race-consciousness, we became afrocentric. We wore our hair natural, giant afros and braids, and sported dashikis and caftans. We were soul brothers and soul sisters, "Can you dig it," then "Give me five on the black hand side." After a trip to Africa in 1979, Richard Pryor was transformed by his identity discovery and personal connection to the Motherland; he vowed never to say the word "nigger" again in his stand-up comedy monologue.

The decade of the 1970s were a great time "To Be Young, Gifted, and Black" as first sung by Nina Simone in 1970. The television miniseries phenomenon "Roots" had us fired up. Black superheroes graced the big screens, Curtis Mayfield sang "We're a winner," and Soul Train was hot and we were all on board. We had gone through the pulsations of disco, and were caught up in the beat of the inner-city, break dancing to the beat of the Sugar Hill Gang's first hit, "Rapper's Delight." Being black was hip!

A Reflection

Political Climate

Vernon Jordan referred to the political climate of the 1970s as the "New Negativism, No to effective government; No to full employment; No to affirmative action, No to efforts to revive our failing cities, and No to inclusion of black and brown people into the mainstream." This political conservatism or white backlash with fervent sentiments against any further concessions that would benefit African-Americans and other minorities drowned out the muffled voices of the Civil Rights Movement. President Lyndon Johnson's decision not to seek re-election amidst the chaos and divisions within the nation left the field wide open for presidential candidates.

Increasing numbers of blacks were registering to vote throughout the South. Cognizant of the overwhelming support of the Democratic Party by African-Americans, Nixon relied on "the Southern Strategy" to win over southern states. Nixon pandered to the resentment of southern whites over desegregation and exploited their fears of riots and competition for jobs hoping to motivate southern white Democrats to shift to the Republican Party. The new wave of conservatism gave the push to Richard Nixon as he narrowly defeated democrat Hubert Humphrey for the presidency in 1968 and a landslide victory against McGovern in 1972.

Nixon's policy of "Federalism," which proposed smaller government and the return of power to states and municipalities, specifically on the issue of desegregation of schools, focused on the pullback on the Great Society programs. In 1970, Senator Moynihan advised Nixon to consider a period of "benign neglect" on racial issues. Whites had grown irritated with the protests and demands from blacks and with the recession were anxious about additional competition for jobs. Nixon called for a pause for white America to adjust and accept the changes and upheavals of the previous decade. Nixon's racist tendencies colored his policies during his presidency with a 1972 petition to Congress to pass a constitutional amendment to ban school busing for racial balance. His presidency ended with his resignation on August 8, 1974. His legacy was the appointment of four conservative judges to the U.S. Supreme Court, undoubtedly a setback for African-Americans seeking justice and equality through the courts.

Gerald Ford took office after the Scandal of Watergate in the midst of much racial discord and controversy over busing for school desegregation. Ford was initially reluctant to take a stance on the issue, but later declared his opposition to busing and criticized the courts for forcing local school districts to comply with court ordered desegregation. After his blunder about the Brown Decision he remained silent on discussions of civil rights for the remainder of his presidency. He lost his presidential bid in 1976 to Jimmy Carter who got close to 90 percent of the black vote. Although Carter was also opposed to school busing he did state that "the time for racial discrimination is over." In 1977, Carter signed the Public Works Employment Act in support of affirmative action, which required that a minimum of 10 percent of federal funds in each grant awarded to state or local governments for public works projects by the Department of Commerce must be contracted to minority-owned businesses.

The political power of the black community grew with the number of registered voters. Over the 1970s decade the number of black elected official rose to 4,890 from 1,469 in 1970. The first black mayor of a major southern city was elected, Maynard Jackson, in Atlanta in 1973, Thomas Bradley was elected mayor of Los Angeles in 1973, Coleman Young was elected mayor of Detroit in 1974, and Marion Barry was elected mayor of D.C. in 1979.

Black leadership

There was an absence of unifying leadership among African-Americans during the 1970s. Discord and deaths among leaders of prominent black organizations of the 1960s lead to the decline and splintering of groups that led the Civil Rights Movement, the SCLC and SNCC, and the more militant groups of the Black Panthers and the Nation of Islam. By the mid-1970s, the Black Power Movement that began with SNCC and formed the Black Panthers ceased to exist. The Black Panthers had been reduced to a local organization centered in Oakland, California. The SCLC led by Ralph Abernathy after King's assassination focused on registering voters. Jesse Jackson, another former member of the SCLC formed PUSH, People United to Save Humanity. Unfortunately no black leadership organization of the 1970s had enough mass appeal to garner the support of the black community in significant numbers to be effective.

Grass roots organizations and local black activists in small towns and communities located in the South were satisfied to rely on their own efforts to forge ahead and bring change. Preferring independence from national leaders and nation organizations they sought inclusion and power to change their lives for the better by seeking local political offices. Through much diligence many campaigns were successful and black candidates became aldermen and mayors in a number of southern towns. Still, this newfound political representation failed to make inroads on economic reform and employment for black Americans, which remained the top issue on local and national African-American agendas.

A Reflection

In 1972, nearly 10,000 African-Americans and Black leaders from every affiliation gathered from across the country and met in Gary, Indiana from March 10 through the 12 for the first National Black Political Convention. Three thousand invited delegates that consisted of elected officials, Democrat and Republican, religious leaders, Christian and Muslim, black nationalists and supporters of integration put together a National Black Political Agenda with objectives and goals to improve the plight of blacks in America. As the crowd chanted "It's Nation Time" hope was renewed in the future as attendants coordinated a political strategy to address critical issues for the black community and increase the number of blacks in Congress.

Transformation and revolution through protest had progressed to advancement through political representation. The focus was now electoral participation. Major cities throughout the Unites States were home to large black populations with concentrated support for the Democratic Party, which was becoming recognized as the black party. Whites, largely Democratic in the South were deserting their Party in support of the Republican Party, and votes in major city elections were divided along racial lines. A noteworthy exception was evident in the 1972 election of Andrew Young, a black man from a majority-white district in Georgia, and his re-election in 1974 and 1976. In 1977, Andrew Young was the first African-American appointed as U.S. Ambassador to the United Nations.

Despite the fact that more black candidates were elected to public offices, their impact in making positive changes for black communities was minimal. Young blacks, uneducated on the compromise of politics and the significance of voting, along with poor blacks who had become cynical about the effectiveness of black politicians, were not exercising their right to vote, thus proving that those who need to vote are the least likely to vote. The thirteen black members of Congress at the start of the decade, in efforts to organize and concentrate their legislative powers, established the Congressional Black Caucus to positively affect the concerns related to the black community. Denied audience by President Nixon, the Caucus boycotted his 1971 State of the Union address stating: *"We now refuse to be a part of your audience."* Nixon later agreed to meet with the group giving them national recognition.

The beleaguered NAACP struggled during the 1970s with their relevance in the black community and with lawsuits that threatened to plunge them into bankruptcy. In 1976, two judgments from separate Mississippi lawsuits went against the NAACP, a $240 thousand award to a highway patrolman in a libel suit and a $1.25 million award to white merchants in Port Gibson and Claiborne County for damages they incurred during a boycott. The NAACP appealed the decisions in both cases and in 1977 the libel judgment was reversed and the boycott judgment was also later overturned by the U.S. Supreme Court. The NAACP had begun to lose membership in the advent of the more radical Black Power Movement and the fallout continued even after the militant era ended, with membership numbers down by 60 percent to 200,000 by the end of the 1970s. The board of directors elected the first African-American executive director, Benjamin Hooks, who pledged to grow NAACP membership and restore its treasury.

The Urban League was headed by Vernon Jordan, a young attorney, for ten years beginning in 1971. Under his leadership the League was more aggressive in persuading blacks in political participation through voting. Programs to address the problems of underprivileged blacks were developed by the Urban League. Jordan instituted the Urban League Review which provided an annual report on the status of black Americans.

The Black Church

Church attendance declined in the 1970s in black churches as well as white churches. For some, increased education and income lessened their need for solace from the church. The Black Church in its evolution branched out to accommodate and fulfill the expanding and varying needs of the black community. The role of the black church has always been controversial and hotly debated, with some feeling they have obligations in the political and economical uplift of their congregations, others feeling they should be the principal educator of their members, and the more traditional belief is that they exist simply to save the souls of their flock. Nevertheless, the ever faithful black church, minus the significant power and influence of the 1960s, continued to confront the persistent problems of unemployment, education, crime, and other social issues in the black community.

Despite the fact that most black churches resisted involvement in the Civil Rights Movement and the Black Power Movement, they garnered the reputation of being the black institution on the forefront of social change. Most black churches indirectly supported the struggle for social justice through organizations like the SCLC and the NAACP. While more than a few clergymen turned politician and sought public offices, many like Rev. Charles Riley of the Church of New Life in Philadelphia, thought that religion should be removed from politics. Rev. Riley argued that *"black religions should not be used as a vehicle for social or economical change."* Conversely, Shirley Chisholm stated that the church was not living up to its responsibility to provide education and leadership to the black community.

A Reflection

A number of spiritual leaders of the era sought to strengthen the black church by re-defining its relationship to Christianity. Albert Cleage, a black nationalist, and the originator of the Black Christian National Movement, changed the name of his church in Detroit, Michigan from the Shrine of the Black Madonna to the Pan African Orthodox Christian Church. Cleage was quoted in his biography, "The Prophet of the Black Nation," by Hiley Ward as saying:

> "Jesus was the nonwhite leader of a nonwhite people struggling for national liberation against the rule of a white nation, Rome. Here is the parallel between the life and times of Jesus and the conditions of blacks in America. Jesus was a revolutionary black leader… That white Americans continue to insist upon a white Christ in the face of all historical evidence to the contrary and despite the hundred of shrines to Black Madonnas all over the world, is the crowning Demonstration of their white supremacist conviction that all things good and valuable must be white."

Cleage's motivation was to enlighten the black community with a clearer understanding of African history and the view that Jesus was black and he was the salvation for black people. Through these teaching black people would be empowered to approach their social, economical, and political challenges with greater confidence and independence. Additional shrines were started in Atlanta, Georgia and Houston, Texas.

Similarly, James H. Cone developed the Black Liberation Theology, which related the nature of the gospel of Jesus Christ to the experiences of blacks as an oppressed people. In his book titled, *A Black Theology of Liberation*, Cone explained Christian Theology as being based on Jesus being the liberator of those victimized, whereas black people have been oppressed by white racism. His basic principles for his Black Liberation Theology were:

> "Christianity is essentially a religion of liberation. The function of theology is that of analyzing the meaning of that liberation for the oppressed community so they can know that their struggle for political, social, and economic justice is consistent with the gospel of Jesus Christ. Any message that is not related to the liberation of the poor in the society is not Christ's message. Any theology that is indifferent to the theme of liberation is not Christian theology."

The Nation of Islam went into different directions in the 1970s following the death of

Elijah Muhammad. Succeeded by his son, Wallace Muhammad, the Nation became more aligned with orthodox Islam and minimized the anti-white beliefs that they had been associated with. Wallace Muhammad changed the name of the organization in 1976 to the World Community of Islam in the West. Louis Farrakhan, leader of the New York Mosque, and prominent leader within the Nation left the group in 1977 and started a new group using the original name, "Nation of Islam," structuring it on the old foundations of Wallace Fard Muhammad and Elijah Muhammad.

The Black Press and Media

Black newspapers suffered declines as a result of wider spread integration gained through the Civil Rights Movement. The elimination of black-owned businesses lowered the number of advertisers for black newspapers leaving them starved of the bread and butter key to their survival. A number of black papers folded and others were forced to reduce their staff to stay in business. The black press faced further challenges in the loss of readers to radio and television and the loss of black journalists usurped by white publications and other media. Even so, reports on the death of the Black press have been greatly exaggerated. The role of the black press could not be filled by any other entity. Black newspaper circulation climbed to its highest height during this decade, from, 4.6 million in 1970 to 10 million in 1973, and then to its highest peak of 13 million in 1976 (Owens, 2001). Notably, *Muhammad Speaks* had the largest circulation of black newspapers peaking at 600,000 in the 1970s.

The Negro Digest, the primary facilitator for the Black Arts and Black Consciousness movement changed its name to the Black World in 1970 in the spirit of the times. The scholarly magazine had been the vanguard in enlightening the black community in political, economical, and spiritual concerns as well as offering a venue for cultural expression. Black intellectuals and poets like Amiri Baraka, Nikki Giovanni, Sonia Sanchez, and Dudley Randall were given a national spotlight. Publication of the Black World ended abruptly in 1976 by Johnson Publishing because of the fall in readership, but it was purportedly in reaction to threats of withdrawal of advertising from all Johnson publications due to pro-Palestinian/anti-Israel articles.

The black press had always been on the front line in battling the adversaries of African-Americans covering issues unknown or unimportant to the mainstream press. Vernon Jordon addressed the annual convention of the NNPA in Houston, TX in June of 1973 imploring the publishers of the black press to stay the course in informing and

A Reflection

educating the black community in the shifting struggle for equality and social justice. Jordon cautioned leaders in the black press: *"So the civil rights in the '70s will be less dramatic and less popular. It will be an era of trench warfare, requiring knowledgeable technicians skillfully monitoring and exposing racism in the twilight zone of America's institutional policy-making processes."*

Throughout the 1970s, the role of the black press and media evolved and expanded with an assortment of magazines, radio stations, and television programming to provide the black community with alternatives to white media. The function of the press had moved forward from primarily a combatant role or vehicle of protest to a versatile medium of communication that spoke to the black community and the diversity within it. The black consciousness of the times had African-Americans hungry for positive images of themselves represented in the media. A number of local and regional publications emerged to meet the demand. The most successful publications, Ebony and Jet, had grown to circulations of 1,288,149 and 623,933 respectively. In 1970, two other national black magazines were published; *Essence Magazine* and *Black Enterprise*, founded by Earl G. Graves.

The National Black Network, the first black-owned radio news network in the country, was established in 1972 through the efforts of Eugene Jackson, Sydney Small, and Del Raycee and began broadcasting in New York City to 40 affiliates. In 1975, WGPR-TV in Detroit became the first black-owned commercially licensed television station in the U.S., developed by the WGPR, the Detroit-based International Free and Accepted Modern Masons. In 1978, Max Robinson becomes the first African-American news anchor on national television for ABC-TV.

Black Businesses and Professionals

Black Enterprise's annual list of the top 100 black firms in 1979 stated their total gross receipts at $1.2 billion. The top five companies earned 20 percent of the revenue. Topping the list was Motown Industries with $64 million, (2) Johnson Publishing at $61 million, (3) Fedco Foods at $45 million, (4) H.J. Russell Construction at $41 million, and (5) Johnson Products at $35.5 million. Auto dealers and service stations were the leading sector for black businesses with $1.1 billion in total gross receipts, even though they owned only 80 franchises out of 25,000, followed by food stores with 786 million in gross receipts.

The 1977 national economic survey of the U.S. Census Bureau revealed that African-

1979

American businesses experienced substantial growth in their numbers during the 1970s reaching a sum of 231,203 firms nationwide. Black businesses with paid employees grew 46 percent to 39,968, while companies without employees grew only four percent to 191,235. Nearly 83 percent had single individuals as owners, were started by blue collar workers or marginal white collar workers, were undercapitalized, had no paid employees, were concentrated in service or retail, went bankrupt within three years, and had gross receipts ranging from $3000 to $15,000. Taking into account the total income of $125 billion earned by blacks, the gross receipts for black businesses totaling $8.6 billion were a tiny share of the American market, less than two percent of the $4 trillion generated by American businesses.

Black businesses in American were disadvantaged by race in their drive to be successful and faced tremendous challenges in acquiring capital, gaining access to white markets, and growing competition with white corporations interested in capturing the black consumer market. The majority of black-owned businesses were "Mom and Pop" enterprises that were located in urban areas and poor communities where shoplifting and break-ins were persistent problems. The recession of the mid-1970s and the economic downturn that closed out the decade caused cutbacks in employment and black businesses lost ground in spite of their greater numbers. Most black companies had not been in business long enough to build foundations that could weather the storms of economic recessions and high interest rates.

The biggest increase in black firms was in the finance, insurance, and real estate division, with black bank ownership increased by 54 percent during the 1970s. Black banks were committed to building up the black community for their mutual benefit, but were compromised by their lending to black businesses and entrepreneurs whose ventures failed and as a result loans were not repaid. Dr. Edward Ballard, chairman of the board at the Bank of Finance, stated in the Los Angeles Sentinel (October 25, 1973) that the black community suffers from "economic suffocation" because of our feeling of inferiority. Black professionals deposit their money in white institutions and black shoppers take their money out to white suburban malls, and none of this money is re-used in the black community. "We have got to stop robbing each other," he said. Black businesses that are loyal and locate in black neighborhoods are robbed instead of patronized.

Black businesses were also handicapped by their inability to advertise or promote their firms. Raymond Sommerville spent three years compiling and cataloging black businesses in New York to produce the Black Pages Business and Professional Directory.

A Reflection

The 100 page book of ads and listings of products and services offered by minority-owned businesses was first published in 1971. Sommerville told reporters: *"I feel that it is very important to the black community, particularly to the young people, to have some knowledge of the wide range of skill being performed everyday by the blacks who make a significant contribution to the economic growth of our society."* The Black Pages provided affordable exposure to black-owned businesses and were developed in a number of other urban cities throughout the U.S. In 1978, Ken Reid, former financial analyst on Wall Street, developed the *Black Pages* in Atlanta, GA to showcase its black business owners; his publication is now known as the *"Bible of Black Businesses."*

African-Americans were advancing forward as professionals in the 1970s. The majority of black professionals were still in the teaching field and for the first time the number of doctors and lawyers surpassed the number of clergy. The number of lawyers and judges surged by more than 300 percent rising from 3,728 in 1970 to 15,1333 by the end of the decade. The number of doctors and surgeons increased by more than 100 percent, rising from 6,106 in 1970 to 13,243 by the end of 1979. During this decade the number of teachers rose 35 percent to 362,937 and the number of clergy rose 20 percent to 16,045. Educational institutions accounted for a third of black middle-class employment. Black women lagged behind black men in every profession except for teaching, where they made up about 80 percent of teachers in primary and secondary education. Over the decade they gained ground as physicians (24 percent) and lawyers (31 percent), yet not much in the male dominated profession as clergy, being only 5.9 percent.

Extraordinary African-American
"Failure is a word I don't accept."

John Harold Johnson's words epitomize the extraordinary accomplishments achieved by himself and his wife, Eunice Walker Johnson. This dynamic couple was instrumental is putting forth a positive image for African-Americans that emphasized success, beauty, and individuality in their mission as founders of the Johnson Publishing Company and Fashion Fair Cosmetics. Limited stereotypes were dismantled when blacks were positively represented in all aspects of society; in politics, education, business, sports, and entertainment in their publications. They provided an example of how education and diligence translate into success, and exhibited the power and influence of the black market. Although Johnson Publishing Company and Fashion Fair Cosmetics are still privately owned and operated by the Johnson Family, their business enterprises generated a number of opportunities in publishing and opened doors for African-Americans in advertising, merchandising, photography, and fashion.

John Harold Johnson was born on January 19, 1918 in Arkansas City, Arkansas, raised by his mother and step father. Johnson attended a packed segregated school where he repeated the eighth grade rather than stop going to school. Johnson said, *"My mother was the influence in my life. She was strong; she had great faith in the ultimate triumph of justice and hard work. She believed passionately in education."* Lacking any prospects to improve their lives during the Depression his family migrated to Chicago in 1933 with hopes for better jobs and a high school for John to continue his education.

Johnson enrolled in DuSable High School while his parents looked for work, but jobs were scarce, they survived on welfare for two years until his stepfather found work with the Works Progress Administration. Johnson was ambitious and excelled in high school; he was student council president and editor of the school newspaper and class yearbook. Upon graduation in 1936, he received a scholarship for tuition at the University of Chicago, and was invited to speak at a dinner hosted by the Urban League. After his speech Harry Pace, president of Supreme Life Insurance, was impressed and offered him a job.

Johnson's go-getter attitude helped move him up from office boy to Pace's assistant within two years. In his position he acquired a wealth of knowledge of how to run a business and how to organize reading material while preparing a monthly digest of newspaper articles. He thought that a magazine similar to the *Reader's Digest* geared to African-Americans would be a "black gold mine." Johnson's mother helped him finance his dream with a $500 loan where she used her furniture as collateral; he also mailed out offers for discount charter subscriptions to Supreme Life policyholders and raised $6000 to publish the first edition of *Negro Digest* in 1942. The journal was filled with news, history, literature, art, and culture for African-Americans. The circulation reached 50,000 within six months, and 100,000 at its height.

John H. Johnson's significant other, his wife and business partner, Eunice Walker Johnson was born an April 2, 1916 in Selma, Alabama. A graduate of Talladega College with a degree in sociology in 1938, and of Loyola University Chicago with her master's degree, Eunice shared her husband's passion for education. Together, John and Eunice worked to produce the top black owned publishing and black owned cosmetics conglomerates in the world. Following the accomplishment of the *Negro Digest*, their next venture *Ebony* Magazine, patterned after *Life* and *Look* magazines, was an even greater triumph selling out its first run of 25,000 copies in 1945. The publication focused

A Reflection

on the achievements of talented blacks, race relations, current civil rights events, and the black struggle in America. Their next project was in 1950, *Tan*, an advice magazine, and their next great sensation was *Jet*, a pocket-sized weekly news magazine released in 1951. Johnson's controversial decision to display the body of Emmett Till on its cover was pivotal in arousing the ire of the black community and strengthened the resolve of the Civil Rights Movement.

Eunice was the creator and director of the Ebony Fashion Fair. Initially begun in 1958 as a sponsored fashion show for a women's auxiliary fundraiser to benefit a hospital in New Orleans, the production was a bona fide success. The Johnsons took the fashion show on the road to support a number of other charities with more than half of the proceeds going to scholarships. The tour featured black models of all shapes and sizes, promoting black designers, and launched a mail-order catalog in 1959. The tour became an annual event, visiting 200 cities in the United States, Canada, and across the Caribbean, putting on 5,000 shows exhibiting high fashion for African-American women, and raising over $50 million for charities during its fifty years. Mrs. Johnson traveled to fashion capitals all over the world to bring her audiences "the most lavish styles."

The success of Ebony Fashion Fair and Mrs. Johnson frustration in finding suitable make-up for her models led to the creation of Fashion Fair Cosmetics in 1973, a line of skin-care and make-up products specifically designed for black women. Fashion Fair was marketed to high-end department stores throughout the country, and expanded to include fragrance and hair products that answered the needs of African-American women and became the number one make-up and skin care company in the world for women of color.

The Johnson's expanded their empire with additional publications including *Ebony Jr.*, started a book publishing division, became major investors in *Essence Magazine*, formed Supreme Beauty with hair products for men and women, purchased several radio stations, and started a television production company. Johnson's business savvy, with circulations of 900,000 for *Jet*, and 2,300,000 for *Ebony*, developed Johnson Publishing to a huge conglomerate with close to 3000 employees and sales topping $388 million, placing Johnson, the first African-American on Forbes' list of the 400 wealthiest Americans. Johnson Publishing was also named the number one black business by *Black Enterprise* four times.

Johnson served on the board of directors for a number of major corporations and philanthropic organizations including Chrysler, Zenith Radio, and Dial Corporation.

1979

John H. Johnson received numerous awards and accolades for his endeavors over the years. In 1972, he was named publisher of the year by his publishing peers in the United States. Johnson was given the Horatio Alger Award and the Wall Street Journal Dow Jones Entrepreneurial Excellence Award. He also received over thirty honorary doctoral degrees from colleges and universities throughout the U.S. In 1996, President Clinton awarded Johnson with the nation's highest civilian honor, the Presidential Medal of Freedom.

John H. Johnson reflected:

> "There is no secret to success. You have to have a bit of luck, and you have to be at the right place at the right time. I was fortunate enough to have a mother who taught me very fundamental things about success. She taught be that you have to earn success, which means you have to prepare yourself, you have to work hard, you have to have faith. You have to believe that things are possible."

Employment

The decade of the 1970s began with black unemployment at a six year high of nine percent, although it was commonly believed that the rate was much higher than the official statistic given. Fifteen percent of the auto workers on strike during this time and ineligible for unemployment benefits were African-American. The earning gap between blacks and whites, which had been narrowing, stabilized as more black males struggled to find full-time employment. Whitney Young, executive director of the National Urban League, stated that the economic outlook for blacks was *"more desperate than any time since the Depression, and absolutely tragic in its consequence for millions of black Americans."*

De-industrialization of urban cities continued into the 1970s and was exacerbated by the outsourcing of American manufacturing jobs; more than a million jobs were shifted to foreign soil. Corporations wanted cheap labor and less interference from unions. Trade and industry hubs had moved to outlying areas with 60 percent of retail businesses located in the suburbs. According to HUD, employment in ten major cities had fallen from 50.8 percent in 1970 to 41.6 percent in 1976. Metropolitan areas with concentrated populations of blacks were being economically drained as industrial employers followed the tax breaks to the suburbs, to the South, and even out of the country. High interest rates had pressed the nation into recession and black unemployment surged higher.

A Reflection

According to U.S. Census data, the unemployment rate among African-Americans had nearly doubled during the 1970s from five percent to nearly 10 percent, twice the rate of white unemployment.

For blacks in America, the financial reprieve had been short-lived and hard times abounded yet again. In the midst of the recession, the role of affirmative action was being diminished; cuts were seen in welfare, food stamps and public housing. Of those blacks who had jobs, many were in low-paying or part-time positions. For companies reducing their workforce blacks workers were disproportionately laid off, as the last-hired they were the first-fired. The U.S. Commission on Civil Rights determined that during the 1970s recession, African-American workers accounted for 60 to 70 percent of laid-off workers despite being only 10 to 12 percent of the workforce. Another major contributing factor was the decrease in demand for unskilled workers. According to U.S. Census data, 53 percent of blacks were in unskilled positions at the end of 1979.

While urban areas suffered from plant closing, suburban areas were experiencing job growth. Private companies and the federal government moved jobs to outlining areas taking half of the jobs of the inner cities with them. An article published by Louis Martin in the *Chicago Defender* (9/19/70) reported that jobs within St. Louis declined nine percent while jobs in the St. Louis suburbs rose 144 percent. Similarly in Baltimore and D.C., jobs rose six and 38 percent, while the number of jobs in the suburbs of these cities jumped 161 and 322 percent respectively. However, the majority of blacks were disadvantaged geographically in applying and acquiring employment in the suburbs because of basic discrimination in hiring, a lack of public transportation, and no access to affordable housing. The recession became a common excuse for blacks not being hired.

The worst of the unemployment for African-Americans was evident among black youths with their actual unemployment exceeding 60 percent. On July 8, 1975, the *Daily Defender* reported on the testimony of William Lucy, president of the Coalition of Black Trade Unionists, before a Congressional economic subcommittee about the bleak job situation for young blacks, "if the nation accepts the president's plan, half a generation of black youth will reach their mid-20s without ever having held a secure and productive job."

At the end of 1979, changes in the level of black unemployment were negligible from the end of the recession in 1975. Black unemployment was 2.4 times that of white unemployment and even three times the level in some states. The nation was indifferent to high numbers of black people without jobs, blaming them for their lack of marketable skills while maintaining inferior education in black inner city schools and fighting busing. Vernon

Jordon warned in the Urban League's 1979 State of Black American report amidst predictions of another recession, *"the condition of black Americans verges on the brink of disaster."*

Education

Education attainment became more important for African-Americans in the 1970s as the demand for skilled workers increased and wages for those without high school diplomas declined. Around the beginning of the 1970s, school enrollment had risen close to 90 percent for blacks and whites across the country. The median years of school completed were 12.0 for black males and females, a marked increase from 9.8 years over the precious decade. The achievement gap between blacks and whites was reduced but not eliminated during these years as reading scores of black students improved.

Blame for the persistent achievement gap between black and white students was being tossed about from inadequate funding to inner city schools, to lackadaisical teachers, and also to uninvolved parents. A report in Chicago showed black students on the South side failing at rates 15 to 20 times higher than white students attending schools on the North side. A black teacher complained of the lack of accountability by the city's public schools that resulted in higher rates of failure in predominately black schools.

Desegregation was the court-ordered solution to raise the quality of education for black children. Amid schools located in segregated neighborhoods, busing was the main vehicle for integration. Controversy over "forced busing" preoccupied the subject in education during the 1970s. Most blacks and whites alike were against it and court cases challenging the legality of busing flooded the courts. In the 1971, the Supreme Court landmark case, Swann v. Charlotte Mecklenberg Board of Education, ruled that it was lawful to require student busing out of their neighborhoods to achieve desegregation. However, in 1974, the Supreme Court Milliken v. Bradley decision limited forced busing across district lines.

In time, southern schools became much more integrated than schools in the North, but the percentage of blacks attending majority black schools remained relatively unchanged during the 1970s at about 63 percent. Furthermore in 1978, a study of 100 cases of busing in northern urban cities by Nancy St. John found no evidence of significant academic improvement for black students.

Estimates for the graduation rate among minorities vary along a wide range from 50 to 85 percent, depending on whether GED or certificates of attendance are excluded in the statistics. According to national U.S. Census data, at the end of the 1970s, graduation rates among blacks averaged 51 percent, ranging from 45 percent in the South to 69 percent out west. These rates were much improved over the 31.4 percent average over the last decade, with less than 25 percent in the South and 49 percent in the West. High school graduation rates among all students peaked by the early 1970s and then began to decline, however the decline was basically concentrated among young men. An independent study by Heckman and La Fontaine (2007) using Census IPUMS data to analyze graduation rates determined that 61 percent of black males and 72 percent of black females graduated from high school or received a GED in 1979.

The decline in high school graduates explained the slowdown in college enrollment and the number of educated workers in the work force. The black gender gap or the differential growth of black women pursuing higher education is attributed to their higher numbers graduating from high school. At the start of the decade only 16 percent of black high school graduates went on to attend college, but by 1979, 28 percent of black women and 31 percent of black men were enrolled in two- or four-year colleges. According to Census Bureau data, the number of black college students had grown from seven percent in 1970 to 11 percent in 1977, with numbers around 1.1 million. The number of black college graduates at the end of 1979 was around eight percent compared to 17 percent for whites.

Desegregation in higher education created unintended consequences for historically black colleges and universities that proved detrimental to their long term survival. Predominately white institutions (PWI) began aggressively recruiting talented black students and enrollment at HBCU's started a downhill course. Nevertheless, with the increased visibility of African-American students on PWU campuses white students who had been denied admission complained of reverse discrimination through affirmative action policies. In 1978, a lawsuit challenging affirmative action, Regents of University of California v. Bakke, was brought by a white student who had been denied admission into the medical school, claiming he had been discriminated against in favor of less qualified blacks being admitted. The U.S. Supreme Court ruled against quotas but allowed race to be used as a factor in university admissions.

The court's decision to limit affirmative action undermined efforts to provide equal access to higher education, which was the basis for affirmative action policies. During the 1970s, more blacks were enrolled in PWI than in black schools even though black students had more success attending black schools and higher graduation rates. Over 35 percent of all Bachelor degrees awarded to black students were from HBCU's. However, much of the growth seen in blacks enrolling in higher education institutions was disproportionately seen in community colleges or other schools that didn't offer B.S. or B.A. degrees.

The Issue of Crime

Shortfalls in education and employment translated into increased levels of crime committed by African-Americans in the 1970s. The old English proverb that says "idle hands are the devil's workshop" still holds true, black on black crime was rising with the unemployment rate. Congressman Augustus Hawkins of California avowed: *"We have more crime because we live in a society whose socioeconomic conditions are so wretched that they are conducive to criminal behavior."* Crime in the black community had become epidemic. Harlem which once held the hopes and dreams of African-Americans *"has become one of the most dangerous places in the world,"* said Orde Coombs in an Article published in *New York Magazine*. In the first six months of 1979, there had been 8600 robberies, 9000 burglaries, 3300 acts of criminal assault, and 200 homicides.

The crime rate among blacks continued to climb throughout the decade of the 1970s giving it the largest 10-year increase in homicides. Southern cities with higher percentages of blacks in the population had higher murder rates. Black homicide rates ranged from six to nine times that of whites. In 1975, 51 percent of murder victims were black. Black people were four times more likely to be robbed, assaulted, and raped than whites. Black men and women were more likely to be victims of violent crime, and more likely to be arrested for violent crimes. The basis for the rise in criminal activity in the black community had not changed from previous decades; poverty, unemployment, and racial prejudice, and the rising crime levels fanned the flames of racial hostilities. Ramsey Clark's book "Crime in America" affirmed that:

> "Crime usually exists in those parts of our cities with the highest rates of disease, the poorest housing, the most under-employment, the least adequate transportation, the fewest recreation facilities, the most exploitive merchants, the lowest life expectancy, and generally the least healthy places to live."

The Department of Justice's Bureau of Justice Statistics released a profile of persons admitted into prison in 1979. The data showed that most had no high school diploma, most had never married, very few had served in the military, but most were employed. One-third had a family member who had been incarcerated, one-third was under the influence of drugs, and about half were drinking at the time of the offense.

A Reflection

The major problems for law enforcement agencies were narcotics and juvenile offenses. Black residents in high crime areas were forming vigilante groups to protect themselves and their property against criminal activity. The 1970's witnessed the escalation of gang activity in large major cities across the country, which were becoming more dangerous with greater access to lethal weapons. Gang violence, robberies and beatings, and gang related homicides were becoming common. In 1975, the New York Police Department reported 275 gangs that included the Savage Skulls and the Black Assassins. In Los Angeles there were over 60 gangs, the two largest being the Crips and Bloods. Gang membership expanded throughout the Midwest, from Chicago to Ohio with many being recruited while in prison.

By the end of 1979, there were nearly 500,000 inmates in America's prison system, of these inmates disproportionate numbers were black males, constituting more than half of the prisoner population. The reform of the penal system had been deemed a failure with problems ranging from law enforcement to inequities in criminal justice. Prisons were grossly overcrowded and had a 60 percent repeater rate among prisoners. The objective of these so-called correctional centers to rehabilitate only served to punish. Black juveniles were taught to be better criminals while in prison. Granted there is discrimination in arrests, prosecution, sentencing, and in granting of parole, but the first point of action should be in lowering the crime rate.

During the 1970s, Atlanta, Georgia refused to relinquish its spot in the top three for violent crimes among blacks. In the summer of 1979, four children disappeared and were later found murdered. These crimes would later become a part of a series of killings called the "Atlanta Child Murders." These crimes continued for two years with 28 black victims. A 23 year old native of Atlanta, a black man named Wayne Williams, was arrested, charged, and convicted of two of the murders.

While there is a certain degree of understanding of the root of crime, that doesn't remove the responsibility from the perpetrator. There is sympathy for the plight of life in the ghetto, the frustration is understood, but the criminal actions cannot be condoned. Our humanity and morality mustn't be sacrificed in answer to injustice, for that only shifts us from being the oppressed to the oppressor of ourselves.

Health Issues for African Americans

The United States Census Bureau reported gains for African-Americans in health during the decade of the 1970s, but the nation was in the midst of a healthcare crisis, in desperate need of medical treatment and prevention for the underprivileged. Half of the blacks living in America didn't have hospital insurance. Proposals of a national health plan were emerging from black members of Congress including Julian Bond, Senator Edward Kennedy, and from the Urban League to address the nation's health problems and provide medical services on an equal basis to all segments of society, particularly in rural and impoverished areas.

The major health problem and number one killer of black Americans was high blood pressure. Thirty percent of the black population suffered from high blood pressure. Factors that increase blood pressure are stress, cigarette smoking, excessive alcohol, and an unhealthy diet. Hypertension led to high death rates from heart disease, kidney failure, and stroke. The rate of hypertension diagnosed in black males between the ages of 25 to 44 was 15 times that of white males and the rate for black females was 17 times that for white females. Hypertension or symptoms of high blood pressure were found in 48 percent of black women taking birth control pills at an average age of 23. Unfortunately, other illnesses were pervasive among African-Americans, they were four times more likely to die of kidney disease, twice as likely to die of cirrhosis of the liver, twice as likely to die of diabetes, five times as likely to die from tuberculosis, and five times more likely to die of childbirth complications.

Black cancer rates were also higher and had risen 32 percent over the last three decades. A study by the American Cancer Society showed that not only were cancer rates for blacks higher than those of whites, but their mortality rates had increased 36 percent. Death from cancer of the prostate climbed 137 percent among blacks while rising a much lesser 39 percent among whites, followed by lung and colon cancer. The result of their study concurred with scientists at Howard University that cited environmental and social factors contribute to the differences in rates. Blacks were exposed to industrial carcinogens and cancer-causing agents, while having limited education relating to early detection. In 1973, HEW issued a report that smoking was a major health problem with cigarettes relating to lung cancer and other cardiovascular diseases, and causing low birth weights and unfavorable outcomes of pregnancy.

Blacks were more likely to suffer chronic illnesses, but were less likely to visit a physician. Black people visit the doctor less than whites do, although visits did increase with age. Black women were more likely to visit the doctor than black men. The lack of preventative healthcare can be attributed to the high cost of medical care and limited medical facilities available. Blacks had not made much progress with insufficient physicians, constituting only two percent of medical doctors. Towards the end of the

A Reflection

decade there were still 133 counties nationwide with a half of a million people without one doctor. In a report by the Southern Regional Council, the South is still lagging behind the rest of the nation in healthcare. There were 47 counties in 11 southern states that didn't have one doctor practicing. Of these counties, 23 were in Texas, 14 in Georgia, four in Florida, two in Virginia and Tennessee, one in Mississippi, and one in Alabama.

The health of black children was a serious concern during this decade. The life expectancy of a black child was six years less than a white child. For children in rural areas impure water leading to dysentery was a problem, in urban areas lead poisoning from paint chips was a problem, but the issue of greatest concern was infant mortality. Chicago had the highest infant mortality rates in the nation in 1974. The rise in the number of teen mothers and their lack of prenatal care were factors with 61.5 percent of births being illegitimate, 15 percent being premature, and 20 percent were to adolescent mothers.

Dr. Robert Adair, District Health Officer for Harlem, spoke on the health crisis in New York. In an article in the New York Amsterdam News (3/6/71), Adair stated that Harlem had an infant mortality rate twice that of the rest of the city at 42.6 deaths in 10,000 live births, venereal diseases were twice that of the rest of New York, and alcoholism was a growing problem. Deaths relating to diabetes, influenza, and pneumonia were rising, but the number one health problem in Harlem was drug addiction with the number of addicts close to 50,000. Similar medical situations were seen in large urban like Chicago, Detroit, and Los Angeles.

Even with prenatal care and screening for venereal diseases and cervical cancer, many blacks don't seek healthcare until it is severe. Poor blacks were also the victims of incompetent and dishonest physicians. Two million unnecessary surgeries were performed each year and low-income blacks were subjected to more than their share. Low-income blacks unable to afford consultations or the benefit of a second opinion were subjected to unnecessary surgeries.

Housing

In the economic downturn of the 1970s, housing suffered the heaviest blow with a slowdown in construction, inflationary pricing of new homes and exorbitant interest rates. Restrictive zoning codes kept blacks from living in specific areas reserved for whites. Problems related to the concentration of poor blacks in central cities and the white middle-class in the suburbs aggravated racial tensions. Plans for federally integrated housing projects in Michigan and Missouri by HUD were blocked through the rezoning of vacant land. The Model Cities program which had been developed to raise the quality of life in urban cities was a victim of budget cuts by President Nixon at the start of the decade. Nixon furthered his attack on housing for African-Americans when he banned "forced integration" in residential neighborhoods stating, *"I believe that forced integration of the suburbs is not in the public interest."*

Housing shortages continued to plague the black community and the numbers of blacks living in poor ghettos grew as incomes began to shrink. According to HUD, employment in 10 major cities dropped from 50.8 percent in 1970 to 41.6 percent in 1976, and the bulk of retail was now located in the suburbs. Most blue collar jobs had shifted to the suburbs leaving the labor force in the central city. Samuel Jackson, assistant secretary for Metropolitan Planning and Development in the Department of Housing and Urban Development explained the dilemma for black laborers: *"Where you live often determines where you work – and if you work. They cannot get housing in the suburbs, and inadequate mass transportation prevents them from busing there. Consequently many of the city's unskilled laborers are cut off from job opportunities."*

In 1973, the federal government placed a freeze on operating subsidies to local housing authorities pushing several to the point of bankruptcy. Landlords began to deny housing to welfare recipients. In New York, across the five boroughs, thousands of families who had been evicted from usable housing for a variety of reasons were relocated to temporary housing in rundown and crime-ridden hotels, commonly referred to as welfare hotels. Social services subsidized the housing and paid excessive rents to these overcrowded profiteering hotels, in some cases five to ten times the original amount paid by the tenant in their previous home. Elderly blacks suffered most from the effects of inflation, trying to survive on fixed incomes. Seventy-five percent were living in substandard housing and only 30 percent owned their homes.

Efforts to eliminate housing discrimination in Chicago were met with formidable opposition when the Chicago Housing Authority was ordered to immediately choose low-income public housing sites, with specifications that for every one unit built in a predominately black neighborhood, three dwelling units of public housing were to be built in a white neighborhood. Delays in the construction of these scattered-site housing units and the fight to address deteriorating living conditions in Chicago spread to other cities and resulted in the passage of the Community Reinvestment Act of 1977. The CRA was designed to reduce discriminatory credit practices against low-income neighborhoods. Black buyers were steered to predominately or

A Reflection

exclusively black neighborhoods or were mislead on the availability of units.

An article published in Black Enterprise reviewed black home ownership in the 1970s using data from the 1980 Census. African-Americans lived in 10.7 percent or 8.6 million of the dwelling units in the United States with a market value of $129 billion. Within this number, 3.8 million were owned and 4.8 million were rented. The growth in home ownership for blacks slowed during this decade as mortgage interest rates skyrocketed, between 1970 and 1975 home owner growth was 5.2 percent and from 1975 to the end of the decade growth had declined to 2.7 percent. In 1979, close to 44 percent of black households were homeowners, of these 49 percent were located in central cities. The number of blacks buying homes in the suburbs rose at an annual rate of 5.5 percent compared to 3.4 percent in central cities. However, some were low-income suburban neighborhoods on the periphery of the center city, some were in all-black towns, and 40 percent were in white neighborhoods. The median value of homes owned by blacks tripled from $10,700 in 1970 to $33,500 by the end of the decade.

The decline in home ownership for black Americans beginning in the 1970s had lasting repercussions that cannot be recompensed. In America, home equity comprises 60 percent of the total wealth of the middle-class. In essence, the accumulation of wealth through property that could have been passed through generations was halted.

Black Family Structure

The money crunch and high oil prices of the 1970s wrecked havoc on African-American families, from the dirt poor to the middle-class; there was a definite challenge in making ends meet. From newlywed couples to senior citizens who had married during the depression, inflation and falling incomes strained the fibers that held families together. As previously stated, the total black income earned in 1979 was $125 billion, but half of the income was earned by less than 20 percent of the families. According to the U.S. Census Bureau, the median black family income was $13,615 in 1979. The lowest incomes for black families were seen in the Southern states averaging $11,595, with the highest seen in north central states at $14, 692.

Black Enterprise showed the median black husband-wife income where the wife is employed at $15,700, 60 percent above the median income where the husband was the sole bread winner.

Unemployment was the catalyst for change in the black family structure. Joblessness weakens the marital stability of any family, but the disproportionately high unemployment among African-American males impacted far greater numbers of black families. Marriage rates for black women over the age of 15 continued to fall throughout the 1970s while the marriage age rose. According to the Census data, 44 percent of black women were married, 34 percent were single, 12.7 percent were widowed, and nearly 18 percent were separated or divorced. The ratio of black men to black women shown in Census data was 88 to 100 or a 2,000,000 shortfall in the supply of black men. Speculation on the reasons for the decline in marriage for African-Americans ranged from the supposed black matriarchy, to the lower number of available black men, and to the lack of income sufficient enough to provide for a family. By the end of the decade, 40 percent of all black families were headed by a female with a median income ranging from $5900 to $7810 depending on where you get the statistics. Divorce rates were climbing steadily, and two-thirds of elderly black women were widows, however, only 20 percent of the black women in female-headed families had ever been married.

In 1976, the number of black babies born to unmarried women exceeded 50 percent of all black births. Teenage mothers accounted for half of these babies born out of wedlock. Less than half of black children lived in a home with two parents, around 40 percent in urban cities and over 61 percent on rural farms. Forty-four percent of black children lived in female-headed single-parent families, compared to 12 percent of white children. The economic strain of being a single-parent perpetuated the cycle of poverty, one-third of black children received AFDC benefits. Dr. Phyllis Wallase, PhD in economics stated that *"the earnings of black women are the crucial determinant of the black family's standard of living...and black women are the most economically deprived people in the country."* As a result, 70 percent of the children living below the poverty level were in families headed by women. Amid the economic hardship the bonds within black families were strong and they were more likely to have other members under the age of 18 from extended family in their households. Half of the families headed by elderly black women had other related children living under their roof.

The size of families was getting smaller, possibly due to more difficult economic times. Declines were marked in the number of births among two-parent black middle-class families and college educated black females. Conversely, female-headed families on average were having more children than husband-wife families. Debates on whether welfare benefits influenced decisions of black women to have children out of wedlock were common among policymakers; some felt that AFDC payments induced black women to have more children without the help of a husband. Understanding why black

A Reflection

women who were dependent on AFDC payments would have additional children is complicated, but the belief that it was to receive the paltry AFDC benefits that aren't adequate to care for a family is definitely unfounded.

Black Athletes and Sports

Sports were seen as a quick path out of the ghetto for African-American athletes, even if it was a myth without substance. At the end of the decade, only 900 blacks in the United States earned a living as professional athletes. Estimates by Harry Edwards of young blacks who stated that professional athletics was their first or second career choice topped three million in 1979. Educators complained that sports were overemphasized in the black community. On the other hand, integration of college athletic programs across the country gave black athletes the opportunity to compete on a national level at top universities, albeit at the expense of athletic programs at historically black colleges and universities. One of the last greats to come out of a HBCU was Doug Williams, a quarterback at Grambling University, who broke nearly all passing records in 1977, the first black from a HBCU to make the major All American teams.

By the late 1970s, the ACC and the SEC were integrated and male black athletes dominated college athletic sports, particularly in football and basketball. The lack of money, training, and role models for black females limited their participation in college sports. Title IX was supposed to expand opportunities and provide more equitable funding for women's athletics, but it was ineffective in producing the desired result, sports dominated by men brought the profits.

During the 1970s, racial stereotypes and numerous theories were back in conversations to justify why blacks excelled in sports including the notion that black people were "athletically superior and intellectually inferior." Martin Kane wrote a controversial article published in the January issue of Sports Illustrated in 1971 titled "An assessment of 'Black is Best.'" The article explored and expounded on the scientific research that suggests that racial distinctions and physical differences *"enhanced the athletic potential of the Negro..."* Harry Edwards, a sociology professor, took issue with the Kane article stating that the research did not use a random sample from the black population, *"data came from black athletes of proven excellence...To generalize these findings to the whole black population is scientifically dubious."*

Nevertheless, the article reported on the proliferation of black athletes in profession sports,
> "Today there are 150 blacks out of 600 players in major league baseball, 330 out of 1,040 in football and 153 out of 280 in basketball.

1979

Of the players on the professional leagues' 1969-70 all-star teams, 36 percent in baseball were black, 44 percent in football and 63 percent in basketball."

More African-American players were leaving their marks on the professional football field in the 1970s. Growing numbers of black players were changing the NFL with world class speed and explosive power while spicing up the game with their personalities and culture. The burgeoning excitement black players brought to the game boosted their following of American sports fans to 70 percent, overtaking baseball as the number one sport in the nation. No player brought more flash to the game than O. J. Simpson, named NFL Player in the Year in 1973 after being the first professional football player to rush for more than 2,000 yards in a single season. Elmo Wright of the Kansas City Chiefs brought some ethnic flavor to the game when he performed the first touchdown celebration dance in the end zone on November 18, 1973.

In 1972, Joe Gilliam, a two-time All-American from Tennessee State University (HBCU), was drafted by the Pittsburgh Steelers and in 1974 became the first black starting quarterback in the NFL. The Pittsburgh Steelers dominated the NFL in the 1970s with players like "Mean Joe" Green, considered by many to be the "one of the greatest linemen ever." Mean Joe, a defensive tackle, was the strength of the legendary "Steel Curtain" defense that powered the Steelers to three Super Bowl Championships before the end of the decade. Green's commercial for Coca-Cola in 1979 is still considered to be one of the best Super Bowl commercials of all-time.

Walter Payton, otherwise known as "Sweetness," was drafted by the Chicago Bears in 1975 and answered their prayer for a player to replace Gale Sayers. In 1977, Payton broke O.J. Simpson's rushing record with 275 yards against the Minnesota Vikings and was later selected for the Pro Bowl and was chosen as the game MVP. In the following season he was the league's leading scorer with six touchdowns and was named America's Most Valuable Player by the pro Football Writers and the Associated Press.

During the 1970s, fewer black athletes were choosing to play baseball as scholarships for football and basketball became more plentiful. Professional baseball was also loosing the popularity contest with sports fans as their following dropped to 54 percent, taking the backseat to pro football and basketball as black athletes preferred the more direct path to bigger contracts skipping the minor leagues. Some athletes like Moses Malone and Darryl Dawkins entered professional sports fresh out of high school.

The world of professional sports was changed during this decade with the concept

A Reflection

of free agency. Previously players were owned indefinitely limiting competition and salaries. Curt Flood, baseball player for the St. Louis Cardinals, filed a $1 million lawsuit alleging violation of antitrust laws in 1970 after being traded without permission or proper notification. The case went to the Supreme Court although the ruling favored Major League Baseball. However, in 1976, after similar grievances and arbitration the courts upheld the Sietz decision and the MLB and the Player's Association signed an agreement allowing players to become free agents after six years.

Black stars shining on the baseball diamond throughout the 1970s included Reggie "Mr. October" Jackson playing for the Oakland A's until 1975 and finishing out the decade with the New York Yankees. Jackson was selected for the All-Star team eight times, a five time winner of the World Series, and a two time winner of World Series MVP during this decade. Hank Aaron hammered in his 715th homerun on April 8, 1974 breaking Babe Ruth's record. Vida Blue, a teammate of Jackson with Oakland before playing with the San Francisco Giants, was selected six times as an All-Star player and a three time World Series Champion. Willie Stargell had a banner year with the Pittsburgh Pirates in 1979, winning the Babe Ruth Award, the National League MVP, his second World Series Championship, Worlds Series MVP, and the National League Championship Series MVP, the only player to receive all three trophies in the same year.

Professional sports fans gravitated to the spectacular style of play of the American Basketball Association (ABA). The image most evoked in the mind from the ABA would be that of Julius "Dr. J." Erving. As a rookie in 1971, Erving scored 27 points a game with the Virginia Squires using his flair for playing "above the rim." In 1973, Erving signed with the New York Nets and led them to the ABA Championships in 1974 and 1976 as ABA MVP and ABA Playoffs MVP. Dr. J. was a five time ABA All Star, well known for his signature slam dunk from the free throw line in Slam Dunk Contests. At the end of 1979, the Philadelphia 76ers bought his contract.

After several years of discussion, and in the face of opposition from the players, the NBA and the ABA merged in 1976. The ABA revolutionized the NBA with its wealth of talent, infusing it with the flamboyant style of its players bringing the three-point shot and the slam dunk contest. ABA players like Artis Gilmore, Earl "the Pearl" Monroe, George "Iceman" Gervin, and Julius "Dr. J" Erving, thrilled fans with their defiance of gravity and magic finger rolls. Still, the NBA had Kareem Abdul-Jabbar who towered above the able competition in the 1970s winning the NBA MVP five times. Kareem started the decade as Rookie of the Year and MVP of the Finals and went on to be an All Star player nine times.

1979

***

The professional sport of boxing reached a crescendo in the 1970s with historical battles between heavyweight warriors masterfully promoted by the infamous Don King. Joe Frazier started the decade out as heavyweight champion but the coveted title belt would be worn by many. Anticipation around the return of Muhammad Ali was put to rest in 1970 with his victory over Jerry Quarry in the preview to the "Fight of the Century" in 1971 against heavyweight champion Joe Frazier at Madison Square Garden. In their first match-up Frazier took the victory, but later lost the heavyweight title in 1973 to George Foreman in the second round of a bout in Kingston, Jamaica. Ali, on his own mission struggled and received a broken jaw and his second career defeat from Ken Norton in March of 1973. Six months later Ali avenged his loss to Norton in a tune-up to his second fight against Joe Frazier billed as *The Rumble in the Jungle* on October 30, 1974 in Zaire. Ali won a unanimous decision after 12 rounds and regained the Heavyweight Championship of the world.

Muhammad Ali and Joe Frazier went to war again on October 1, 1975 in a fight promoted as the "Thrilla in Manila," but it turned out to be the actual fight of the century. Meeting for the third time with one win each, and some degree of bad blood boiling between them, this bout would reveal the true undisputed heavyweight champion. Ali taunted Frazier in the press saying *"It's gonna be a thrilla, and a chilla, and a killa, when I get the Gorillas in Manila,"* but his insults meant to intimidate, served only to strengthen Frazier's resolve to win. The Thrilla had all the excitement of a rollercoaster ride as both fighters took turns on the offense, boxing and brawling, giving as much as they got, receiving devastating punishment to their bodies from their opponent as well as the heat. Muhammad Ali got the victory even though they were both beaten past the point of recognition, with Ali saying the fight was stopped just before he was about to quit. Ali said of Frazier, *"He is the greatest fighter of all times, next to me."*

On February 15, 1978, Leon Spinks, fresh from the Olympics with only seven professional bouts, defeated Muhammad Ali in a fifteen round split decision in Las Vegas winning the undisputed World Heavyweight Championship. Forfeiting his World Boxing Council belt, Spinks agreed to a rematch with Ali rather than fight the #1 contender Ken Norton. On September 15, 1978 in New Orleans, Muhammad Ali defeated Spinks and made history as the first boxer to win the World Heavyweight Championship for the third time. The WBC named Ken Norton as their champion and the belt was taken by Larry Holmes on June 9, 1978.

A Reflection

The great moments in sports during the 1970s would have to include Arthur Ashe winning his second Australian Grand Open in 1970 and his triumph at Wimbledon in 1975, making him the first and the only black man to win the singles title. Also memorable, the 1976 United States Olympic boxing "Dream Team" with Howard Davis, Leo Randolph, brothers Leon and Michael Spinks, and "Sugar" Ray Leonard was considered to be the best in Olympic history, dominating their bouts, bringing home five gold medals, and foreshadowing the future champions of prizefighting in the United States.

Lest we forget, Edwin Moses and his trademark 13 steps in the 400m hurdles were legendary. Moses captured a gold medal in the 1976 Olympics setting a world record of 47.63 seconds. In September of 1977, he commenced his winning streak of 122 races that included another Olympic gold medal, two World Championships, and three World Cups. Moses' consecutive victories would last nine years, nine months, and nine days.

Black Culture and Entertainment
"An artist paints his own reality."

Sugar Shack (1976) --Ernie Barnes

The artist who best depicted and embodied the 1970s was Ernie Barnes. A modern day renaissance man who first excelled in athletics as a professional football player for six years, then evolved into a brilliant painter, a writer, and an actor on the big screen and television. Barnes is considered to be the founder of neo-Mannerism with a technique similar to Michelangelo and Raphael that emphasized elongated limbs and dramatic poses of bodies in motion. Barnes' work propelled black art into the mainstream during this decade with his *The Beauty of the Ghetto* exhibition, a collection of 35 paintings, touring major cities across the country from 1972 to 1979.

Barnes stated his inspiration as, *"I am providing a pictorial background for an understanding into the aesthetics of black America. It is not a plea to people to continue to live there (in the ghetto) but for those who feel trapped, it is...a challenge of how beautiful life can be."* Barnes received international exposure after his celebrated painting *Sugar Shack* appeared on the hit television series *Good Times* as well as a variation on the album cover of Marvin Gaye's "I Want You" in 1976. Barnes also painted works featured on a number of album covers and painted pieces for the character JJ Evans on *Good Times* while the series ran.

"Late Night DJ"--Ernie Barnes

Literature

More African-American authors found themselves on the coveted bestsellers lists in the 1970s. Toni Morrison published her first novel, *The Bluest Eye,* as did Alice Walker with *The Third Life of Grange Copeland* in 1970. Ernest Gaines' novel, *The Autobiography of*

A Reflection

Miss Jane Pittman, published in 1971, broke new ground when the book was made into a television movie in 1974. The made-for-TV film was one of the first to honestly portray black characters with dignity, depth, and understanding.

The blockbuster of the decade was *Roots: The Saga of an American Family*, written by Alex Haley and published in 1976, for which he won a Pulitzer Prize, and became the best-selling African-American author in history. On a personal note to state the significance of Roots at this time, every graduating senior at my high school in 1978 was given a copy of Roots as a gift from the school. The common thread among many of the books of the 1970s was the experience of generations of black people in America, the struggles, the triumphs, achievements and failures, and most important their humanity.

Entertainment

The 1970s was the decade of black expression. The Watts 103rd Street Rhythm Band's hit song "Express Yourself" in 1971 urged us that *"whatever you do, do it good."* Not only were black actors and entertainers doing it good, but they were finally getting the recognition that had for so long been denied. The audience for contemporary black theatre and entertainment was growing, and the black theatre ensembles basked in the resurgence of their popularity. The African-American stage was transformed during this decade, moving away from protest plays towards works that provided a deeper insight to the black experience. Black playwrights and all-black casts boldly stepped into the spotlight with a variety of productions that conveyed the essence of black culture in all its joys and sorrows.

The 1970s were witness to the revival of the all-black musical productions of earlier decades. Classic stage dramas like *Purlie* (1970) and *Raisin in the Sun* (1973) were adapted into musicals that won critical acclaim as well as commercial success and Broadway rolled out the red carpet for more African-American productions. Melvin van Peebles, true to form, contributed his controversial *"Ain't supposed to Die a Natural Death"* in 1971 and was followed by Vinette Carroll's *"Don't Bother Me I Can't Cope"* in 1972. The decade was peppered with a number of magical productions, most notable, "The Wiz," which opened on Broadway at the start of 1975, winning seven Tony Awards, including Best Musical, with a run of 1672 performances in more than four years. *"Bubbling Brown Sugar,"* which featured the music of the Harlem Renaissance, opened in 1976 and packed the house for nearly two years with 766 performances.

African-Americans found a voice through Ntozake Shange with her play *"for colored girls who have considered suicide/ when the rainbow is enuf,"* which opened on Broadway in 1976. Described as a "choreopoem by Shange, the play was composed of twenty poems that presented a sample of the multifaceted realities of life for black women in America. The cast of seven covered a full range of emotions expressed in poetry, music, and dance. The drama won an OBIE Award as an off-Broadway play, and was nominated for a Tony Award in 1977.

The money to be made from the African-American market had been discovered and big business was ready to capitalize. Hollywood was anxious to get in on the action and started the decade with a steady flow of black formulaic movies commonly referred to as blaxploitation films. By 1975, there had been nearly 200 low-budget action made-for blacks movies with more than half of them released in 1973. The box office successes of Cotton Comes to Harlem (1970), Shaft (1971), and Sweet Sweetback's Baadasssss Song (1971) were followed by *Superfly, Blackula, Black Caesar, Foxy Brown, Cleopatra Jones, Mandingo,* and *Blackenstein.* The superstars of the genre included Richard Roundtree, Pam Grier, Tamara Dobson, and Fred Williamson. A number of quality black films like *Sounder, The Great White Hope, Cooley High, Lady Sings the Blues,* and *Buck and the Preacher* punctuated the era of black exploitation with top-rated performances by Cicely Tyson, James Earl Jones, Sidney Poitier, and Bill Cosby.

Midway through the 1970s, blaxploitation films were near the end of their profitable run and work for the actors starring in these movies was drying up. Few survivors were able to transition to others genres with the exception of Richard Pryor. The consummate entertainer, Pryor played drums in a night club before making his mark as a stand-up comedian. Throughout the decade he made 12 comedic album recordings that included "That Nigger's Crazy (1974)," "...Is it Something I Said? (1975)," and "Wanted: Live in Concert (1978)."

Pryor was one of the most prolific actors on film during these years appearing in 22 movies, starring in *Silver Streak, Which Way is Up?, Greased Lightning, The Wiz,* and *Richard Pryor: Live in Concert.* Incredibly, Pryor found time to write for hit TV shows: *The Flip Wilson Show* and *Sanford and Son,* as well as his own show that premiered in 1977, which was canceled after four episodes by network censors. Richard Pryor pulled no punches in his comedic delivery using profanity, racial epithets, and whatever colorful vulgarities he deemed appropriate, although, after a momentous trip to Africa he vowed never to use the word "nigger" in his act again.

African-Americans still had a ways to go on the small screen under the weight of

A Reflection

commercial sponsors or the lack thereof. Racial bias in television was challenged in the 1970s by the NAACP citing the lack of blacks in front and behind the camera. A lawsuit won against Cox Enterprises did result in more blacks seen on television and in jobs behind the scenes. During the 1970s, black actors had roles on 19 primetime network series; however, most of these television dramas and similarly in daytime soap operas acquiesced with the one token-black as seen in shows like *Mission Impossible, Mod Squad, Ironside,* and *Mannix.* Nevertheless, African-Americans made major breakthroughs as the main characters in situation comedies or sitcoms during this time with shows that included *Good Times, Sanford and Son, That's My Mama, What's Happenin?,* and *The Jeffersons.*

Quality television featuring African-Americans in a positive and realistic light were seen in the made-for-televisions movies based on black history or the autobiographies of prominent black figures. Cicely Tyson starred in a number of these programs, beginning with her most celebrated role, the *Autobiography of Miss Jane Pittman,* followed by her portrayal of Wilma Rudolph in *Wilma,* Coretta Scott King in *King,* and of Harriet Tubman in *A Woman Called Moses.* Tyson also starred in the phenomenal television mini-series *Roots: The Saga of an American Family* based on Alex Haley's book in 1977, which had unparalleled Nielsen ratings, and won nine Emmy Awards and a Golden Globe. The monumental success of the show was followed with a sequel broadcast in 1979, *Roots: The Next Generations.*

In a class by itself was *Soul Train,* "the hippest trip in America," was a 'must watch' for young blacks on Saturday mornings. Music had always been a fundamental part of black culture and *Soul Train* took us away as we immersed ourselves in the live performances of the latest music by the hottest artists of the day on television. Interactive TV at its best, we danced with the dancers, discussed their outfits, and imitated the different hairstyles. It was part of our sustenance; we were nourished by it, grew up on it, and still dance down the Soul Train line.

The African-American music scene exploded like fireworks in the sky during the 1970s. Bright stars rose to the top and stretched out to find their place to shine. Rhythm and Blues was the staple, but there was the jazz of Miles Davis, then there was the funk of Parliament and Sly and the Family Stone, the disco of Donna Summer, the reggae of Bob Marley, and the hip hop rap of the Sugar Hill Gang. Motown was not the dominant sound of the 70s but was still a force to be reckoned with. We couldn't get enough of The Jackson 5 and their youthful energy as they pumped out the hits with Michael's boyish voice singing like he'd been here before. Innovative arrangements characterized the Philadelphia Sound and it spread across the country with the Delphonics, Manhattans, Blue Magic, and the Stylistics.

Our social consciousness was raised by the musical geniuses of Marvin Gaye, Stevie Wonder, and Curtis Mayfield who wrote and sang the music that epitomized the times. Opening with Marvin Gaye's *"What's Going On?"* in 1971, moving to Curtis Mayfield's soundtrack for the movie of the same name *"Superfly"* in 1972, and then Stevie Wonder's *"Innervisions"* in 1973, these artists put the struggles of the black community to music. The lyrics sang about racial injustice, war, life in the ghettos, poverty, drug abuse, crime, pollution, hopelessness and hopefulness, they touched our emotions and made us think.

The 1970s were also distinguished musically by the dance rhythms of tight bands with blaring horn sections, booming basses, and monster beats on the drums. Each band had their own unique flavor and we had to have every one, essential to any collection, was Earth Wind and Fire, the Ohio Players, the Isley Brothers, Rufus and Chaka Khan, LTD, and the Commodores. Sly and the Family Stone and these bands took us higher, but it wasn't enough. We wanted the funk of George Clinton's Parliament and Funkadelic and the harmonies of the Ojays. We needed to hear the soul from our "Black Moses," Isaac Hayes and our "Queen of Soul," Aretha Franklin, had to have the sexy bass of Barry White and the angelic range of Minnie Riperton, required the spark of Al Green and the chic style of Natalie Cole, we craved the freakiness of Rick James and the mellow sound of Roberta Flack, and lived for the smoothness of Peabo Bryson and the sassiness of Chaka Khan. We wanted it all and the music of the 1970s gave it to us.

Memorable Moments

On September 18, 1970, Jimi Hendrix died of a drug overdose at the age of 27.
In 1971, Althea Gibson was inducted in the International Tennis Hall of Fame.
The prison riot in Attica began on September 9, 1971.
Mahalia Jackson, the "Queen of Gospel," died on January 27, 1972.
Shirley Chisholm became the first black woman candidate for President at the 1972 Democratic Convention.
Billboard magazine awarded Marvin Gaye the *Trendsetter of the Year* award.
On April 8, 1974, Hank Aaron broke Babe Ruth's World Record of 714 homeruns and finished his career with 755 homeruns.
Martin Luther King, Jr.'s mother, Alberta King, was shot and killed on June 30, 1974 by a

crazed gunman as she sat at the organ of the Ebenezer Baptist Church.

In 1974, Carole Simpson became the first African-American woman to anchor a major network newscast on NBC News.

In 1976, Barbara Jordan was the first African-American and woman to give the keynote address at the National Convention of the Democratic Party.

Alex Haley's Roots miniseries began airing on January 23, 1977 for eight nights with the finale recorded as the third-highest rated U.S. television program ever.

Max Robinson became the first African-American broadcast network news anchor in the United States on *ABC World News Tonight* in 1978.

On November 18, 1978, there was a mass suicide of 909 members of the primarily black following of the Jim Jones Temple in Jonestown Guyana.

Hazel W. Johnson became the first black woman to be promoted to the rank of General in the U.S. Army in 1979.

Willie Mays was inducted in the Baseball Hall of Fame in 1979.

Reflection on a Decade
"we have become as quiet as the bricks of
the building and as quiet as the grass growing beside
the buildings
and we have become the silence that kills the struggle…
and what will survive what we have become…"
-- June Jordan 1973 (Black World/Negro Digest)

The vision of the decade ending in 1979 was looked upon with a degree of trepidation as to whether this was a turning point in the evolution of African-Americans. Was this a pause in the action between the rounds of a hard-fought matchup or had we given up on the dream too tired and too discouraged to continue? Gone were the mass action campaigns and protests without charismatic leaders to motivate us, we had lost our voice and the power that flowed within our unity. The African-American community was deteriorating on so many levels, economically, socially, and educationally, and we were immobilized without a strategy to halt or reverse the damage. The lack of employment opportunities and jobs with meager wages served as inhibitors to positive change, but they did act as catalyst for increases in crime and gang activity.

The political favor had turned towards corporations as jobs were exported out of the

1979

country worsening the economic recession. The toll from the loss of manufacturing jobs in the inner cities for the predominately unskilled population of black people had been devastating and demoralizing, a half million more blacks drifted below the poverty level. Income, which was the basis for acquiring education, housing, medical care, and family stability was absent or either inadequate. The faith that right would conquer wrong had been shaken, church attendance was down, and high school graduation rates had peaked and were moving down. The number of black couples making the commitment to marriage was down, and divorce numbers were up, and the number of babies born to single mothers multiplied. Black families were trapped in overcrowded housing projects and the rate of crime in the ghettos was exploding with the number of black men being locked in prisons rising.

The circumstances were starting to sound like a never-ending story; discrimination, no jobs, low pay, inadequate training and education, and glass ceilings. The obstacles that kept us from moving forward as a people were relentless. What was the purpose of integration if it didn't provide a clearer path to a better standard of living except for a select few? The class divisions further separated blacks and the challenges among the different social and economic levels began to change. Divisions between black men and women became apparent although not understood, but contributed to the breakdown of the black family. Could this be where the train pulled into the station and the journey was suspended? Is this the time when everyone got off and went in varying directions, as said in mantra of the 70s to "Do your thing."

A Reflection

1989

citydata.com

The stark picture of the decade that ended in 1989 was overrun with images of cold harsh realities that characterized this decade. For black Americans, things were tough all over again, and they were bearing the brunt of yet another recession and skyrocketing inflation. Joblessness, the same old song, was playing at a higher volume with the unemployment rate at the highest level since the Depression, and twice that of the 1970s. Numbers hovered around 10.8 percent across the nation and were at an all-time high for African-Americans at close to 21 percent. The inner cities were flooded with out of work black people who couldn't pay rent or mortgages and lines lengthened in front of homeless shelters. Social programs were being slashed at the worst possible time and the government offered cheese and butter as a pacifier. New words to express the changes were added to our vocabulary, Reaganomics, homelessness, drive-bys, and crack.

The boundaries of the ghettos in metropolitan areas expanded as the number of blacks crossing the line into poverty escalated. Survival in the ghetto was troublesome, dealing with innumerable problems and a limited amount of hope for things to get better was hard enough, and then came the invasion of crack. A cheap highly addictive derivative of cocaine, first seen on the West coast in 1984 before its proliferation in urban cities in the mid-West and East coast, crack decimated poor black neighborhoods with rising levels of criminal activity. A sub-culture of hustling to get by was born within the slums of the inner city leaving many poor blacks detached from a normal existence without recourse for escape. Gang violence, drug addicts, robberies, and prostitution were reaching epidemic proportions and the prison population tripled.

The underground culture of hip hop and rap that had developed in the late 1970s moved to the forefront and spread from coast to coast during the 1980s. Young blacks vented their frustrations and protests over the semblance of being disregarded and ignored by mainstream society and lost themselves in the hip hop culture. Self-expression was at the heart of hip hop, DJs emceeing and scratching on turntables, rappers going head to head, b-boys and b-girls break dancing to the beats, and graffiti artists displaying their unique style. Hip hop culture was a declaration on the relevance of urban life in the "hood."

Efforts to close the ever growing divide between lower-class poor blacks, middle- and upper-class blacks, and to counteract the negative conditions that were swelling internally and externally revitalized the philosophy of Afrocentrism. Africa was acknowledged as the "homeland" and through the perspective of Afrocentrism, black people could see themselves in a positive light no longer defined by European and Western terms. They could dispel the notion that they originated from an inferior race and consequently gained self-respect and pride in their heritage. Defined by Cain Hope Felder as a means of "reestablishing Africa and its descendants as centers of value," Afrocentrism viewed Africa as the creator of the arts and sciences and the foundation of modern civilization.

Demographics

Black Americans were the second largest group in the population in America in this decade, making up 12.3 percent of the population, with numbers around 30,511,000. According to Census data from *We the Americans: Blacks*, the African-American population grew 13 percent over the last decade; the median age was 27.5 years with one-third of the black population under the age of eighteen. In 1989, the life expectancy for Black Americans increased to 68.8 years, still six years less than that of whites, and 62 percent of the blacks over the age of 65 were women. Black women continued to outnumber black men with 53 percent of the black population female and 47 percent male. Around the middle of the 1980s, black Americans were referred to as Afro-Americans or African-Americans as a response to the atmosphere of Afrocentrism,

A Reflection

even so, there were many blacks who resented the new euphemisms, those who saw themselves as Americans without any further classification needed.

The majority of the black population was concentrated in the Southern region at 53 percent. The reverse migration that began in the previous decade continued as blacks moved out of the North and migrated back into the South and out to the West. The percentage of blacks living in the South was increasing for the first time in the century. Eight-four percent of blacks resided in metropolitan areas across the nation. The top five cities with the largest black population were New York City with over 2 million, followed by Chicago, Detroit, Philadelphia, and Los Angeles. "Black flight," which was the growing numbers of blacks moving out of inner cities to suburbs, was on the rise, although the trend was at a much slower pace than white flight and central cities were more apt to be largely black populated. Blacks made up more than half the population in Detroit, Washington, DC, New Orleans, Baltimore, and Memphis.

By the end of the 1980s, there were more black women than black men in the labor force. The annual income for a Black male was $19,417.03 compared to $28,894.69 for a white male, and the annual incomes for black and white females were $15,319.29 and $16,135.65 respectively. The income earned by black married-couple families was 83 percent of that earned by white families. Disparities in income between blacks and whites contributed to 31.8 percent of blacks living below the poverty level.

Mood of the Black Community
Don't push me cause I'm close to the edge
I'm trying not to lose my head
It's like a jungle sometimes it makes me wonder
How I keep from going under
--- The Message by Grand Master Flash and the Furious Five

Black people were under pressure, being pushed from all sides, unemployment, homelessness, hunger, gang activity, crime, drugs, AIDS, and survival was becoming a preoccupation. It seemed like they couldn't catch a break. The hard times of the 1970s only seemed to get worse as the period of "benign neglect" morphed into blatant disregard. Most blacks had no confidence in the political system and felt abandoned by political leaders and rejected by society. Racial intolerance intensified as it always does when there's not enough to go around, not enough jobs, not enough housing, and not

1989

enough hope for the future.

Hard times made us enemies of one another as fear and desperation set in. Those who had found some level of financial security were sick and tired of those who couldn't. Frustration gave rise to blame and criticism of the poor, *"they don't try to help themselves"* and *"they don't have to live like that."* Most of America was feeling selfish with the level of uncertainty about jobs, and opposition to affirmative action was growing. *"I got mine, you get yours."* The black community reeled from the massive cuts of social programs. Blacks were asking each other how bad could it get and what's next? Just when you thought things couldn't get much worse, then there was 'Crack.'

The black community always seemed to be under attack and the latest nemesis was among the most vicious. Crack turned neighbor against neighbor and brother against brother and even child against mother. "Black on black crime," a critical issue in black ghettos skyrocketed with the invasion of crack, killing the addict, the dealer, and the innocent bystander. It was a plague that took victim after victim without discrimination, the young and old, male and female, and the educated and ignorant. Poor black communities became war zones: enter at your own risk. The African-American community bled and became helpless and hopeless. Pleas to the government for help were answered with: "just say no" or we lock you up and throw away the key.

Political Climate

The political climate of the 1980s went from temperate under Jimmy Carter to frigid under the Reagan administration. In a 1989 interview on CBS, Reagan stated, *"One of the great things that I have suffered is this feeling that somehow I'm on the other side"* of the civil rights movement. The review of Reagan's policies before his presidency and afterward seem to further substantiate that impression. Ronald Reagan began his presidential campaign in Philadelphia, Mississippi, the city infamous for the murder of three civil rights by the Ku Klux Klan during "Freedom Summer" in 1964. Moreover, in a press conference following his inauguration Reagan began his attack on affirmative action stating, *"I'm old enough to remember when quotas existed in the United States for purposes of discrimination and I don't want to see that again."* By the end of 1989, three cases challenging affirmative action before Supreme Court had been decided, the rulings voided the use of set-asides where issues of past discrimination had not been proven and limited the use of statistics to prove discrimination.

Reagan moved ahead in his presidency to level attacks against the poor and those he characterized as "welfare queens" through devastating cuts to Medicaid, food stamps, and

A Reflection

child nutrition assistance programs where blacks were over one-third of the beneficiaries. Budgets for public housing and Section 8 rental subsidies were also cut by 50 percent. Huge reductions in the numbers of persons eligible for social programs were instituted including Aid to Families with Dependent Children, unemployment compensation, and federal education programs and student loans were greatly reduced. Insensitive to the issues of the black community, the response to the continuing problem of racial inequality and poverty was to slash programs that assist African-Americans who suffer disproportionately from poverty and unemployment.

A racial bias was prevalent during the Reagan years; credit available to black business was limited and a report by the Civil Rights Commission in 1982 reported that black farmers received only one percent of all farm ownership loans and just 2.5 percent of all farm operating loans, hastening the decline of the black farmer. The USDA Civil Rights Office was shut down later in the same year. Reagan attempted to remove the ban on tax exemptions for private schools that practiced discrimination; and Congress had to override a number of his controversial vetoes which included his veto of the Civil Rights Restoration Act in 1988, and the veto of sanctions on the apartheid regime in South Africa. Reagan was also opposed to the recognition of Dr. Martin Luther King's birthday as a national holiday.

Reaganomics not only eliminated jobs, it took a tough stance against labor unions, and froze the minimum wage at $3.35 an hour. A reverse Robin Hood, he took from the poor and gave to the rich. The top marginal tax bracket was lowered from 70 percent to 28 percent during the Reagan presidency to benefit the wealthy with the idea that their prosperity would "trickle-down" to improve the prospects of the poor and less well-off. In addition to the tax cuts, Reagan commenced the largest peacetime military build-up ever seen in world history taking the country from being the largest lender to the largest debtor. Martin Luther King, Jr. gave a warning in a speech in 1967 where he said, *"A nation that continues year after year to spend more money on military defense than on programs of social uplift is approaching spiritual death."*

Reagan began his "war on drugs" with the Anti-Drug Abuse Act during his second term with a budget of $1.7 billion. The drug enforcement bill instituted a mandatory minimum penalty for drug offenses and even higher sentences for crack cocaine. The Act also eliminated parole in the federal system to ensure that prisoners would serve 85 percent of their sentences. The bill was a costly failure which led to huge numbers of blacks flowing into the prison system without reducing the amount of drugs available on the streets.

1989

Throughout the 1980s, Reagan dismissed or denied the presence or impact of racism in his administration and in the country as a whole even as his policies further divided blacks and whites socially and economically. Reagan even questioned the motives of African-American leaders saying, *"Sometimes I wonder if they really mean what they say, because some of those leaders are doing very well leading organizations based on keeping alive the feelings that they're victims of prejudice."* Even black members of the GOP were disappointed in the number of African-Americans appointed to positions during the Reagan administration. At the end of 1989, black Americans held less than two percent of all the elected offices in the nation.

Black Leadership
If we accept and acquiesce in the face of discrimination, we accept the responsibility ourselves and allow those responsible to salve their conscience by believing that they have our acceptance and concurrence. We should, therefore, protest openly everything... that smacks of discrimination or slander. ~Mary McLeod Bethune

Black leaders during the 1980s faced the same challenges and discrimination that had besieged African-Americans in the fight for civil rights but the political landscape had become exceedingly conservative. Coalitions and power groups were formed between the NAACP, SCLC, the Urban League, and other black organizations to unite their efforts, but the prominence of these black leadership organizations from the civil rights movement seemed to have faded in effectiveness and importance. The latest strategy was to gain increased political power to affect changes that would improve the lives of black people. The limiting factors were the hesitation of blacks to put money into political campaigns, to serve as unpaid volunteers, and the disinterest of eligible black voters in participating in the political process, all the necessities to run a winning campaign. Large numbers of the black population questioned the relevance of black leaders, national and civic, and considered them out of touch with average blacks or incompetent.

Despite the racial tensions that had resurfaced and the conservative atmosphere, the number of blacks candidates elected to public offices grew steadily. For the most part, the black elected officials were educated professionals or successful businesspersons with middle-class backgrounds and were elected from majority black districts. In 1989, there were 7226 black elected officials with 24 elected in the 101st Congress. There were 250 black mayors in cities north and south and from the East Coast to the West Coast,

A Reflection

members of the National Conference of Black Mayors, had combined constituents of more than 20 million. Black mayors recognized as new power in major cities included David Dinkins in New York, Harold Washington in Chicago, Maynard Jackson in Atlanta, and Tom Bradley in Los Angeles.

Despite the fact that African-Americans held less that 1.5 percent of public offices, a few black politicians were able to excel to high level positions in the Democratic Party. The year 1989 was a remarkable year for black politicians; Ronald H. Brown was elected chairman of the Democratic Party, the first black to head a major political party, and Rev. William Gray III, of Pennsylvania was the highest ranking black in Congress as the House Majority Whip. Additionally, Douglas Wilder was elected governor of Virginia and became the first African-American governor in American history. One dilemma for black politicians in this decade was their accountability for the interests of black people versus going mainstream and moving up in political ranks. To win mainstream elections black politicians had to distance themselves from race-based politics, having to run the gauntlet on allegiance to their own to vie for white votes.

Nevertheless, the political inroads of the few black leaders lacked the capacity to alter or change the course of the Republican agenda in the discount of minorities and the poor. A number of black organizations expressed the need for a national leader or a mass action campaign that would let those in power know that they would not be ignored. Efforts to establish an independent black political party at the start of the decade by the National Political Assembly failed in spite of over 2000 delegates attending the founding convention. In 1983, a coalition called the Black Leadership Forum, comprised of the leaders from twenty-five national black organizations in the country, decided they would launch a presidential campaign with a black candidate.

In 1984, Jesse Jackson, of Operation PUSH (People United to Save Humanity) entered the presidential primary race as a Democratic candidate. Jackson received more than 18 percent of the votes, and in 1988, again entered the presidency race. Jackson doubled his previous support and received around 7 million votes and 25 percents of the delegates at the Democratic Convention. Jesse Jackson was a polarizing force in the world of politics. Black Democrats were divided in their support for his candidacy as president; many didn't see him as a viable candidate. The differences in opinion resulted in some blacks calling others "Oreos." The GOP used this discord in their campaigns to attract black voters to the Republican Party.

1989

An article written by Dr. Marable in the Pittsburgh Courier in May of 1989 gave an assessment of the African-American Summit whose goal was to develop a political strategy to address the problems plaguing the black community. In his view the summit was unsuccessful in putting together a coherent or complete approach to Black Empowerment. Marable noted that a number of speeches were made that outlined the issues and concerns but no clear solutions came out of the meeting. Harold Cruse (1987) surmised the underlying principle contributing to the lack of direction in moving forward saying, *"The truth is, however, there exists in Black America no such organized black leadership consensus that is either willing or able to replace, oppose or simply ignore and bypass the organized remains of the old, civil rights-welfare leadership."*

The Black Church

The oldest black church in the United States, First Bryan Baptist Church, celebrated its 200th year in 1988, a testament to the strength and resiliency of the black church. As the oldest African-American institution the black church has the mission to address the social, economical, and political crises that affect the black community. From their unique position, the black church is the only true support that can directly intervene and nurture the ills suffered by African-Americans. Yet, for the last two decades the church has withdrawn from the leadership post in the struggle for black empowerment, and many have begun to question whether the contemporary black church is addressing the needs of its community.

The African-American Pentecostal Church grew exponentially during the 1980s while the other protestant denominations lost members. There was also resurgence in the number of storefront churches in urban areas. These ministries filled the needs of those members who wanted the security found in small congregations with fewer restrictions. Members wanted to be among people they could identify with and where they felt the atmosphere was more genuine. In smaller congregations the pastor knows his members and their problems and there is a sense of togetherness. Most pastors of storefront churches were not formerly educated, were born in the South, and raised in rural communities. Among those that attended these new churches, most felt that the older and larger churches had lost their mission and morals in attempts to change with the times and increase their memberships.

The leadership within the black church still wields significant power politically through the support of their congregations, particularly in local elections. Notwithstanding the

A Reflection

fact that the bonds between the black church and secular organizations like the NAACP and Urban League have weakened as their significance in the black community waned during this decade, the black church has stepped up and given its support to the political campaigns of a number of black politicians. Black clergy mobilized African-American voters for black candidates in mayoral races throughout the country, including Harold Washington in Chicago. They also assisted Jesse Jackson in his mass voter registration drives for his presidential campaigns.

A growing consensus says that the black church is responsible not only for the spiritual needs of the black community but for the physical needs as well. For the black church to survive and continue as the "guiding force" it must be concerned about the economical needs of its members.

In the midst of the discussion, the black community remains starved for leadership and solutions making it susceptible to new and different philosophies and approaches. The new voices of black clergy range from the very staunch traditional to the hip hop gospel, and although the black church is still dominated by male pastors, there has been a dramatic rise in the number of women enrolling in seminary during the 1980s and growing numbers of couples partnering as clergy.

Looking at the different approaches among the new generation of black church leaders some used the ample resources of their large congregations to build up their community and some used the funds for their own gain. Rev. Floyd Flake, pastor of Allen A.M.E. in Queens, New York, with 4,000 members, invested their resources in the community; they built an $11 million senior citizen complex with 300 apartments and founded the Allen Home Care Agency that provided meals and home care for the sick and elderly. They also established the Allen Christian School which has 480 students enrolled and managed the South Jamaica Multi-Service Center providing clinical services and nutrition programs to the community. Additionally, the Allen church purchased and reconstructed a ten store block-front on a commercial strip in Jamaica. In 1985, the market value of the accumulated assets of Allen A.M.E. was approximately $18 million (1984-1985 Annual Financial Report, Allen A.M.E. Church) (Wilson, 1988).

Another pastor who went further than just pouring their resources in a bigger church was Rev. Charles Adams who established a free health clinic to provide healthcare for those without insurance during the economic downturn. The Hartford Memorial Baptist church leaders wanted to reconstruct their northwest Detroit neighborhood to foster economic growth and generate jobs for the community. In 1985, the church began building an 80,000 square foot shopping center with a grocery store, drug store, and restaurant at a cost of $17 million. Rev. Adams explained, *"The church finds itself in a situation where it is the best continuing, organized entity in the black community for the acquisition and redevelopment of land, the building of business enterprises and the employment of people."*

A different approach was seen on the West coast from Frederick K.C. Price, pastor of the Crenshaw Christian Center, who used the abundant resources to enlarge his ministry. A mega-church by any definition, the Crenshaw Christian Center had 13,000 members, an annual income of $10 million, and a television ministry called "Ever Increasing Faith" that aired on 100 television and radio stations. Price's church is non-denominational but has a Pentecostal-style of worship that attracts large numbers of people with the practice of "faith healing." Price preaches a prosperity message that says "giving money to God will bring the money to the giver." Referring to his church members as "customers" and selling 40,000 tapes of his church services each month, Price believes that "big business does not pollute the purity of religious faith."

Overall, the problems of the black community are many and the individual efforts of some black churches are insufficient to make significant improvements on a broad scale, but the churches do have considerable power and influence with the millions that are invested in financial institutions and should insist that these banks reinvest in the black community. Rev. Franklyn Richardson, pastor of Grace Baptist Church in Mt. Vernon, New York and General Secretary of the National Baptist Convention, USA, stated *that "Given our tremendous economic resources, it is possible for the church to create projects that will revitalize our communities, empower our people and revive their spirits."*

Black Press and Media

In 1989, there are about 185 black newspapers published in roughly 150 cities across the Unites States. Over this decade, black newspapers experienced sharp declines in their readership as black media outlets expanded. In 1980, *The New York Amsterdam News* had a circulation of 81,200 but by the end of the eighties their circulation had dropped to 31,584. Black newspapers are historically weekly publications with few exceptions; limited operating revenue from advertisers prevented them from expanding to daily papers. White-owned businesses and corporations were still reluctant to advertise in black newspapers, feeling it unnecessary, that blacks saw their ads in mainstream

A Reflection

papers. In 1984, the *Advocate* in Mississippi published the names of white businesses that did not advertise in their paper in a successful campaign to raise the number of white establishments who purchased advertising.

Black newspapers have been tenacious in their mission to fight for the economic and social equality for African-Americans. In the eighties the strategy shifted, black editors were committed to helping black Americans gain political power to accomplish their objectives. There were black newspaper columnists on both sides of the aisle concerning Jesse Jackson's run for the presidency in 1984. Some saw it as only a symbolic campaign without any chance of victory. Others saw his candidacy as an educational process that emphasized black voter participation and political awareness and therefore it was a success.

The National Newspaper Association (NNPA) started a campaign in the 1980s to liberate Nelson Mandela and end apartheid for South African blacks with a barrage of articles and editorials that revealed the injustices and devastation of the system of apartheid. On the other hand, the black press was also criticized for "dumbing down" on the content and news features. In an article published in the Los Angeles Sentinel, Earl Ofari asked, *"Why are black publications so obsessed with sports and entertainment?"* It may be that editors are under pressure to sell papers and America's fascination with celebrities sells papers. Black magazines are especially guilty, using athletes and entertainers on the cover to attract readers. Black newspapers did make some attempts to balance their news with feature stories, but they suffered lower readerships than the colorful magazines. Consequently, black youths are exposed to a minimum of positive role model types and become overly fixated on celebrities.

A few black journalists were breaking through the glass ceiling and making inroads in the mainstream press. In 1981, Pamela McAllister Johnson became the first African-American woman to head a non-black daily newspaper when she was named publisher of the *Ithaca (NY) Journal*. Robert C. Maynard became the first African-American publisher of a major metropolitan daily newspaper when he purchased the *Oakland Tribune* in 1983.

The overwhelming success of black magazines paved the way for more. In 1985, Johnson Publishing Company added *EM* or *Ebony Man* to its line-up of magazines. Albert Fornay, Jr., editor of *EM* said, *"The goal of EM is to enhance the lifestyle of black men and inform them how best to live that style."* In 1989, Wilmer Ames, in conjunction with Time Warner's magazine division launched *Emerge* as "Black America's

Newsmagazine." *Emerge* tackled the controversial subjects of civil rights, affirmative action, religion, economic empowerment, education, the criminal justice system, sexism, as well as black culture. *Upscale Magazine* was also launched in 1989 by Bernard Bronner of the black hair care Bronner Brothers Corporation.

African-Americans were running head first against a brick wall trying to expand ownership in electronic media. Blacks felt excluded in the competition for radio and television station licenses and were at a disadvantage in acquiring frequencies on AM and FM radio bands. Eugene D. Jackson, president of the National Black Network, speaking to an audience at Howard University in 1980 said, *"Black America cannot hope to fully realize its economic and social goals without gaining a measure of ownership of the nation's communication apparatus."* During the eighties there were about 140 black-owned radio stations across the country. For every new station started, another failed and was sold, a casualty of limited advertising support.

In 1980, Robert L. Johnson launched Black Entertainment Television, the first black-owned and operated national cable television station in the United States. Based in Washington, D.C., the network was started with an initial investment of only $15,000, but by then end of 1989, BET had 22 million subscribers and estimated revenues over $23 million. In 1988, W. Don Cornwell and Stuart Beck launched Granite Broadcasting Corp, the first African-American broadcast holding company, operating 14 television stations in six states.

Black Businesses and Professionals

There were approximately 340,000 black-owned businesses in the United States in 1989 with the majority concentrated in personal services and retail trade industries. The bottom line of many of these black businesses suffered during this decade undermined by the Reagan Administration and its cuts to federally-funded grant and loan programs that supported small and minority businesses. Affirmative action programs were being relaxed and set-asides eliminated, and the recessions of the 1980s, along with increased competition only exacerbated the situation. Historically, black businesses focused on the black market and their earnings fluctuated with the quantity and quality of the employment of black workers. During the eighties black businesses and professionals enlarged their market to include the mainstream economy and began acquiring existing businesses versus starting their own from scratch.

In 1989, growth was stagnating among the top 100 black-owned businesses in the nation and sharp declines were seen in their employment levels. Total revenues for the

A Reflection

100 largest black-owned companies in the nation were $6.81 billion. Beginning in 1988, there were two lists in the Black Enterprise annual top 100 black-owned businesses, the industrial and service 100 and the Auto 100. Sales for the top 100 industrial and service companies were $4.28 billion and sales for the top 100 auto dealers were about $2.5 billion. The black auto dealers were the hardest hit by the slowdown in the economy and the shift of buyers away from American-made to foreign made cars. Earl G. Graves, publisher and editor of Black Enterprise magazine said, *"Black-owned businesses are part of the mainstream, and they mirror what happens in the economy."*

In 1989, TLC Beatrice International Holding Inc. topped the Black Enterprise 100 list of black-owned businesses for the third year in a row with reported sales above $1.95 billion, the first black-owned company to cross the billion dollar mark. Based in New York, TLC Beatrice International is a food manufacturing company that operates on four continents with 11,000 employees. The number two company was Johnson Publishing with $216.5 million in earnings and third was the Philadelphia Bottling Company with $200 million in gross receipts. North Carolina Mutual is the nation's oldest and largest black financial institution and stands at the top of Black Enterprise insurance companies. The company began selling life insurance close to 100 years ago and now has $215.7 million in assets.

Also in 1989, Softsheen, a black hair products firm, and number six in the BE 100, was selected as company of the year by Black Enterprise. The company was created in 1964 by Edward and Bettiann Gardner in the basement of their home on the South side of Chicago. The Gardners saw a void in the market in the supply of hair products formulated for black hair and worked to fill it. They developed several successful products and the company was growing, albeit slowly, until 1979 when they introduced a product that reduced the time it took to get the tremendously popular Jheri Curl. Care Free Curl was the product, the rocket that would take Softsheen to top of black hair care businesses. Capitalizing on its success, a complete line of Care Free Hair products was launched and in three years company earning went from $500,000 to $55 million in 1982. The phenomenal growth of the company had leveled off by 1989 with sales of $87.2 million as hair styles changed and the Jheri curl was no longer in vogue.

African-American businesses and professionals need the support of the black community for continued success, but the community doesn't always know who and where the black businesses and professional are in order to do business with them. In 1989, Millicent Redway and Lynrod Douglas, a married couple in New York, put together the Black Pages Network to support their black business community. Their hope was to economically empower the area with the theme "Recycling dollars in the community." C. Diane Howell, producer of the Oakland Black Expo, had the same sentiment of increasing the exposure for black businesses. In 1989, she put together the first edition of the Black Business Listings paper to promote black businesses and professionals.

Black Employment

After four years of Ronald Reagan and his trickle-down economics the country was headed into another recession and the unemployment rate for black Americans was 15.2 percent, having been as high as 21 percent in 1983. According to the Bureau of Labor Statistics, the jobless rate of African-Americans was twice the rate of the overall jobless rate, and 42 percent of blacks between 16 and 19 were without jobs. Black males suffered the worse joblessness with unemployment in ghettos as high as 80 percent. These figures discount the number of blacks that were under-employed and those that had given up looking, discouraged from a lack of job opportunities and no hiring. Reagan also ended quotas for Japanese auto companies, a move devastating for American car manufacturers. The UAW predicted 200,000 jobs would be lost in the auto industry, of which 80,000 of those were held by black employees. Competition for jobs grew as more countries around the world became industrialized. Additional manufacturing jobs dropped off as America continued to de-industrialize throughout the eighties.

Halfway through the decade, the black civilian labor force had grown to 12.3 million, more black women were entering the workforce and the gap between black men and women had closed with 4.99 million black men and 4.98 black women employed. The majority of black workers were still disproportionately found in lower-wage occupations and part-time positions. The quality and quantity of jobs available to workers with limited education and training was rapidly declining as manufacturing jobs were outsourced leaving mostly service-related jobs with menial pay. Jobs that were created during the 1980s were within the service sector and paid minimum wage. Nearly one in four black workers was employed in a service job.

Fewer blacks were pursuing managerial or skilled labor professions. By 1985, professional black women outnumbered professional black men, 109,203 to 79,361 in corporate America. However, due to corporate downsizing, black managers were usually the first to be eliminated.

Statistics compiled by the U.S. Census in 1989 illustrated the representation of African-Americans in various occupations. The data revealed that blacks made up 36.5 percent of

A Reflection

cleaners and servants, 38.1 percent of those employed in garbage removal, 26.7 percent of the domestic servants, and 22.6 percent of the countries bus drivers. Occupations that had the least number of blacks included a mere 0.2 percent of pilots, 1.3 percent of farmers, 2.1 percent of architects, and only three percent of the lawyers.

The minimum wage was frozen at $3.35 during the eighties and the income growth among African-Americans was halted and wages were stagnant throughout the decade. The gap between whites and blacks in employment rates and earning rates was expanding, with blacks even suffering income declines. In 1986, John Jacob, president of the National Urban League, commented on the disparities between blacks and whites and the exclusion of blacks in the economic booms and recoveries saying, *"The blunt fact is that Blacks never make up for the ground they lose in recessions...If whites had such a high unemployment rate it would be called a Depression."* The gap between low-income and higher-income blacks was also widening with the loss of better paying unskilled jobs. For those less educated blacks there was even a decline in income levels when compared to those with college degrees.

Blue collar workers were the hardest hit during this decade and over 27 percent of blacks in the labor force were blue collar union workers. By 1989, according to the U.S. Department of Labor's Bureau of Labor Statistics, the unemployment rate for African-Americans had improved, but was still around 10 percent. The CEOs and heads of manufacturing companies that were eliminating jobs inferred that it was the greed of the labor unions and workers who demanded higher wages that put themselves out of work, but more correctly it was the greed of employers for higher profits that displaced workers in search of cheap labor. By 1989, the manufacturing output from the East and North Central regions had been reduced close to 50 percent, while the output in the South and West increased by 29 percent and 18 percent respectively.

Education

My son said, Daddy, I don't wanna go to school
'cuz the teacher's a jerk, he must think I'm a fool
And all the kids smoke reefer, I think it'd be cheaper
if I just got a job, learned to be a street sweeper
Or dance to the beat, shuffle my feet
Wear a shirt and tie and run with the creeps
'cuz it's all about money, ain't a damn thing funny
You got to have a con in this land of milk and honey

1989

Educational attainment for African-Americans has progressed significantly over the decades. Illiteracy was no longer a concern, and with compulsory education, over 95 percent of all students are enrolled in school beginning with kindergarten. According to U.S. Census data, the median year of education for the black population is 12.3 years. However, there is no shortage on inconsistencies in the determination of graduation rates in this country. Some of the contradictions can be attributed to how the numbers for those who have gotten their GED are counted. Government statistics show 63 percent of blacks are graduating from high school trailing white graduation rates of 78 percent. Although educational attainment has not varied much over the last decade, data from the National Center for Education Statistics show that the completion rate for those aged 18 to 19 showed a slight decline in 1989 to 71.6 percent.

One aspect of the educational gap between blacks and whites is lower scores on vocabulary, reading and math tests, including the SAT. This gap appears before kindergarten and carries on into adulthood. Even though the achievement gap had begun to narrow by the end of the 1980s, a study of the 1989 applicants to five highly-selective universities found that the combined SAT score for white students was 186 points higher than the corresponding SAT average for black students. Additional studies have shown that family income differences alone have almost no effect on children's test scores. Low-expectations from teachers and parents can affect testing levels. Higher test scores are associated with access to books, parents reading to the child, and exposing the child to educational exhibits and experiences. Closing the educational achievement gap is important to closing the economical gap, students who score higher are more successful.

The primary educational issues for black Americans are the level of high school completion, subsequent enrollment in postsecondary education and training programs, the college graduation rate, and the persistent gap between white students. There is also a marked difference in the graduation rates of students attending school in urban areas versus students in rural areas. At the end of 1989, the number of black students that did not graduate from high school was 20.6 percent in urban areas and 29.4 percent in rural areas while the numbers for white students were 11.2 in central cities and 16.2 percent in rural areas. In 1986, only 47 percent of black high school graduates attended college. While there have been increasing numbers of black high school graduates, it has not converted to an increase in college enrollment. In 1989, only 11.9 percent of the black population over age 25 graduated from college, half the level of whites.

A Reflection

Reasons for the low number of blacks enrolling in higher education have run the gamut, from lack of preparation, lack of motivation, and the lack of ability, but more accurately the basis is more financial. The Reagan administration decreased the amount of grants and the number of guaranteed student loans at black colleges in addition to shifting the lion's share of aid from grants to loans during a period of economic strain for minorities. The total financial aid packages declined three percent while the tuition costs rose higher. Enrollments at Historically Black Colleges and Universities (HBCU's) declined during the first half of the eighties and the number of black students attending predominately whites schools in the South rose to 43.5 percent in 1988. Escalating education costs contributed to 51 percent of blacks and Hispanic students enrolling in post-secondary education to opt for less expensive community colleges.

Dr. Luther Williams, president of Atlanta University, stated that the educational standards and educational achievement at all levels for all students has declined over the last two decades. "Blacks were more likely to be in education or the social sciences than in mathematics, engineering, or the sciences." The number of degrees awarded to African-Americans was falling in the 1980s as blacks were dropping out in higher numbers. Much of this decline was among black males as black women were earning the bulk of African-American college degrees. In 1989, the graduation rate for black men was 35 percent and 43 percent for black women. Nationwide, only 37 percent of black freshman who entered college in 1989 earned their degree in six years; conversely, 59 percent of white freshman earned their degree in the same period.

The Issue of Crime

But then you wind up droppin' outta high school
Now you're unemployed, all non-void
Walkin' round like you're Pretty Boy Floyd
Turned stick-up kid, but look what you done did
Got sent up for a eight-year bid

Crack

During the early 1980s, there was a glut of cocaine on the illegal drug market. Ever resourceful drug dealers decided to convert the powder to a smokeable form of cocaine that would be profitable and easy to produce. Crack first appeared in Los Angeles, San Diego, and Houston, and in 1982, the first "crack house" was discovered in Miami.

Crack crossed racial lines, social barriers, and economic levels. It was a hot commodity in the suburbs as well as the ghetto. At the end of 1984, the first "crack babies" were being born in Los Angeles. As the use of the drug rose among women, mothers who used crack were having low birth-weight babies and fetal death rates increased. By 1985, the crack epidemic in the United States was raging, drug dealing gangs were fighting over territory, crack users had no limits to what they would do to get the drug, and the rest of the community was caught in the crosshairs.

In 1986, crack was available in 28 states and Washington, D.C., and by 1987, you could buy crack in all but four states. The fast money was as intoxicating for the dealer as the drug was for the user. With high unemployment among young blacks between the ages of 16 to 19 nearly 40 percent, here was the opportunity to make more money than they had ever seen in their lives. Even young black children could earn $100 to $200 a day as couriers. Violence was an integral part of the drug trade; drive-by killings became common occurrences and crack-related murders skyrocketed in urban cities. After crack came on the scene, the homicide rate for black males between 14 and 17 years of age doubled and the rate for black males between 18 and 24 years of age was rising almost as fast. In 1988, a study done by the Bureau of Justice Statistics reported that crack use was tied to 32 percent of all homicides and 60 percent of drug-related homicides in New York City.

Black on Black Crime

The 1980s were characterized by an explosion of Black on Black crime. The crack epidemic and drugs were the catalysts for much of the criminal activity and were viewed as the most serious criminal problem for black communities. Jim Cleaver wrote in the Los Angeles Sentinel (10/30/75) about the drug plague, "*It has become the scourge of the black community and until it is removed, there will be no peace for any of us who dwell within the ghetto walls.*" The high levels of unemployment for blacks, particularly young black males, funding cuts in job training and social programs, less money spent on education, and the rising poverty level created a perfect storm leaving the black community vulnerable to the highs and lows of illegal drugs and quick money. According to the Bureau of Justice statistics, 29 percent of black households were touched by crime in 1989.

Street gang recruitment spiked during the eighties as did violent crimes. Armed gangs like the Crips and Bloods were drawn to the fast profits of crack cocaine and turf wars intensified raising the levels of violence in urban black communities. The most common

A Reflection

crimes for which blacks were arrested in 1989 were drug possession or abuse, theft, and simple assault, but the gun violence by young blacks and juveniles in the 1980s caused a dramatic rise in the number of homicides. African-Americans had the highest murder rate among victims and offenders. Black males had a 1 in 30 chance of being a murder victim and 94 percent of black murder victims were killed by another black. Homicide was the leading cause of death for black men between the ages of 15 and 44. At the start of the 1980s, the homicide arrest rate for blacks was four times the white rate, by the end of the decade; the black murder rate had doubled to eight times the white rate.

The number of African-American men locked in the prison system has grown continually since the 1920s. At the start of the 1980s, less than one percent of black men were incarcerated, but by 1989, the number of black men in jail surpassed that of white men. The national jail population was 42 percent black, and over 41 percent of juveniles in correction facilities were black. In 1989, a black male born in that year had a 29 percent chance of being imprisoned at some point in his life. In 1986, Congress passed The Anti-Drug Abuse Act of 1986 which established federal mandatory minimum sentencing guidelines. Judges were required to give minimum sentences based on the type and the amount of the drug. More African-Americans were being sent to prison for disproportional amounts of time. Convictions for possession of two ounces of cocaine or marijuana received the same sentence as second-degree murder: fifteen years to life.

The media attention that followed the 1987 cocaine overdose of basketball Len Bias provoked a political response to bolster the "War on Drugs." The federal government increased the number of tasks forces and built more prisons, more money was being spent on incarceration than education. States and local police bombarded the black ghettos to reduce gang and criminal activity. Aside from filling up jails and prisons, no solutions to the over abundance of crime in the black community had been found. Consequently, 13 percent of black adult males have lost the right to vote as convicted criminals; in some states 40 percent of African-American men are permanently disenfranchised.

Health Issues

New challenges to the health of Black Americans surfaced in the 1980s and probably contributed to a slight decline in the life expectancy to 69.4 in 1989 for black men and women. The U.S. Department of Health and Human Services reported that the major reason for the 5.6 years difference between black and white life expectancy was drug dependency or alcohol abuse. The growing health disaster for the black community in the 1980s was two-fold. Before the scourge of crack use could be contained the even more serious threat of Acquired Immune Deficiency syndrome (AIDS) was spreading across the nation and throughout the black community. AIDS is caused by the human immunodeficiency virus (HIV) and is transmitted by sexual intercourse with an infected person or from sharing needles with an infected intravenous drug user, or from an infected mother to her child during pregnancy or birth.

Blacks were at a higher risk for contracting AIDS and accounted for 22 percent of the AIDS related deaths. By 1987, black people accounted for 25 percent of Americans with AIDS even though they comprised just 12 percent of the population. AIDS was initially perceived as a gay man's disease, except 11 percent of cases were caused by heterosexual contact with drug abusers or men who had served time in prison. In New York City, 31 percent of the AIDS cases were black and it had become come the city's third leading cause of death for black men after homicide and hypertension. Additionally, 51 percent of all the American women with AIDS were black and 55 percent of the children infected were black. The rise of the spread of HIV and AIDS in the black community was attributed to sexual promiscuity and prostitution that was linked to crack use.

The U.S. Department of Health and Human Services reports heart disease as the leading cause of disability and death for African-Americans in the 1980s with a 50 percent higher mortality rate than whites. Risk factors for heart disease were hypertension, cigarette smoking, high cholesterol, diabetes, and obesity. Hypertension was also the chief cause of kidney failure and strokes. Blacks suffered from high blood pressure or hypertension at twice the rate of whites, and according to the Task Force on Black and Minority Health, 50 percent of blacks suffered from the disease. The African-American diet of "soul food," which is considered to be somewhat unhealthy, was a contributor to the increased cases of hypertension among blacks.

The second leading cause of death among African-Americans was cancer; blacks have higher incidences of cancer with higher mortality rates. Breast cancer rates for black women increased rapidly during the 1980s and black males had twice the risk of developing prostate cancer than white males. Lung cancer was the most lethal, and blacks are more likely to develop the disease than other races. Over 80 percent of the cause of lung cancer is related to smoking. Cigarettes are linked to various health problems, yet 34 percent of blacks still smoke.

The third leading cause of death for blacks in the 1980s was diabetes and blacks were more likely to suffer from the disease, particularly black women. One in four black

A Reflection

women over the age of 55 has diabetes. The top risk factor for type II diabetes is obesity and rapid rises were seen in the levels of obesity in the United States. In 1989, over 50 percent of black women were obese. Heredity does play a role in a person's health status, but nutrition, smoking, alcohol and drug abuse, as well as the environment can affect one's general health condition.

A positive in the health conditions of blacks was the decline in infant mortality rates. Even with this improvement, the disparity persists, the black infant mortality rate is double that of white infants. Around 11 percent of black mothers don't receive any prenatal care. Premature births with low-birth weights, poor nutrition, drug abuse, and sexually transmitted diseases were the leading causes for black infant mortality. Black babies are twice as likely to die before their first birthday as white babies.

Overall, blacks have a poorer quality of health than whites in the United States. Poverty has an adverse affect on health conditions more than any other factor. In 1989, according to the National Center for Health Statistics, African-Americans make fewer visits to physicians for annual check-ups than whites and use hospital emergency rooms as their first contact for medical treatment, and one-third of blacks don't have private health insurance. The racial disparities in healthcare treatment are the result of income, education, adequate health insurance, and access to necessary healthcare.

Housing

Broken glass everywhere
People pissin' on the stairs, you know they just don't care
I can't take the smell, can't take the noise
Got no money to move out, I guess I got no choice
Rats in the front room, roaches in the back
Junkies in the alley with a baseball bat
I tried to get away but I couldn't get far
'cuz a man with a tow truck repossessed my car

The condition of housing for African-Americans in the 1980s was varied across a wide spectrum. According to Census data in 1989, 43 percent of African-Americans owned their home or were buying and 56 percent were renters. Also according to the Census, the median value of black-owned homes in the United States was $50,700, 40 percent lower that white owned homes, and black renters paid a median of $329 in rent. Some blacks were concentrated in rundown crime ridden housing projects, others lived in single-family homes in central cities, and growing numbers resided in suburban communities.

The 1980s added a new word to our vocabulary, homeless, as the precarious economic circumstances of the 1980s wrecked havoc on employment for blacks causing shifts in the housing situations for each group. In the early eighties, families with children made up 36 percent of the homeless and were the fastest growing segment of the homeless population, most from the loss of a job. African-Americans were disproportionately represented in the homeless numbers across the nation comprising over 38 percent of the people out on the streets with some surveys suggesting that their fraction may be closer to 50 percent. These estimates excluded those doubling and tripling up with relatives and friends. In New York, over 200,000 were doubled up in overcrowded housing.

An article in the *New York Amsterdam* declared homelessness as the No.2 problem in the United States during the 1980s, second only to AIDS, with the number of homeless being about 600,000 on any given night. The number of families without shelter escalated so quickly that the country was ill-prepared to handle the problem. Nonprofit shelters and welfare hotels opened to house homeless from one end of the country to the other. The environment of many of the shelters and hotels was demoralizing amidst danger and unsanitary conditions. The major cause for the homeless epidemic was the lack of affordable housing, which was exacerbated by urban renewal, unemployment, and drastic cuts to housing by the Reagan administration. Federal monies for housing subsidies for the poor were severely reduced during the eighties. Halfway through the decade, the number of low-cost rentals had gone down to 5.6 million, while the total of low-income renters had risen to 8.9 million.

In the 1980s, 48 percent of residents housed in public housing were black. Public housing projects had become places of last resort for the poorest of individuals and families, and over the years they had become overrun with crime, drugs, and violence. Safety within the community became a big issue as response times to emergency calls were significantly longer. Mobility programs were developed in the late eighties to help working minorities transition into affordable housing. Section 8 vouchers and housing transfers were used to help low-income blacks move into integrated neighborhoods. Middle-class blacks desperate to live in a better environment tried to move as far away from the urban ghettos as they could, but unable to move into expensive suburbs, they usually relocated in predominately black neighborhoods.

According to Census data, in 1989, 30 percent of African-Americans lived in neighborhoods that were 90 percent black or greater. Contrary to the belief that blacks

A Reflection

wanted to live in all-black areas, a research study found that 82 percent of blacks surveyed preferred a racially mixed community that is approximately half black. Around 90 percent felt that they would be unwelcomed in mostly white neighborhoods. In 1987, HUD received 800 complaints of housing discrimination. A 1989 study for HUD showed that discrimination in housing was still a problem for minorities and limited their options in buying a home. Racial discrimination by banks, real estate agents, and landlords went unmonitored by the Reagan administration during the 1980s. Even though community organizations uncovered blatant redlining by banks using Federal Home Mortgage Disclosure Act information, HUD and justice departments failed to take legal action or sanction banks that violated the Community Reinvestment Act, which barred racial discrimination in lending.

Family Structure

The evolution of the black family was continual, but was it in the direction that we want to go? By 1989, there were over 5 million African-American families in the United States. According to Census data at the end of the decade, 39 percent of the black families were two-parent families and 61 percent were headed by a single-parent. Single-mother families accounted for 56.2 percent of all black households and 4.3 percent were headed by single-fathers. During the eighties, black women were marrying at older ages, the number of black women in their thirties that had been married dropped to 61 percent. In 1989, according to Census data the number of African-American women who were married declined to 43 percent, compared to 79 percent of non-Hispanic whites. The decline in marriage among African-Americans is joined with an increase of single mothers. This decline in the number of marriages among black Americans is the main contributor to the destabilization of the black family.

In 1989, more than 65 percent of African-American babies were born to unmarried mothers, more than 56 percent had incomes below the poverty line, and 50 percent were on welfare. The changing structure of the black family with growing numbers of single-parents was increasing the level of poverty for black people; almost 32 percent of black families were living below the poverty threshold, and more than half of black children under the age of three were in poor households. The high levels of joblessness and incarceration among black males were blamed as the reasons for the break-down of the black family, but the trend away from marriage toward single-parenting extends across all economic classes. Black women had higher unwed-birth rates, higher separation rates, and higher divorce rates than women of other races.

1989

The birthrate among teens continued to decline during the 1980s, albeit those who were having babies were less likely to be married. Black women were having babies at a younger age than white women and were having larger families. There has been wide speculation that Aid to Families with Dependent Children (AFDC) or welfare payments were responsible for the growth of black single-parent families, except research has shown there is no relationship between the changes in the structure of black families and welfare. The rise in the number of unmarried women having babies is the result of culture and value changes along with limited numbers of "marriageable" black men. In 1988, there were only 89 black males for every 100 black females.

A plethora of research on the growing reluctance of black men toward marriage shows that a large part of the hesitancy on the part of black men to marry is related to their employment and income and the ability to provide for a family. However, even though more black men and women were choosing not marry during the 1980s, unprecedented numbers of black children were being born without the benefits of a stable family. Black single-mothers with lower earnings have become the sole supporters of the majority of black households with meager child support payments and welfare assistance.

According to U.S. Department of Commerce, the median income for black families at the end of the 1980s was $21,420, 58 percent of the median income for white families. The median weekly earnings were $472 in 1989 compared to $680 for white families. Black married-couples fared better with median incomes of $33,780, 84 percent of white families. The median income for black married-couples where only the husband worked was $30,780, when both the husband and wife worked the median income rose to $47,250. The number of black married-couple families where both the husband and wife were earners expanded to 66 percent during this decade, and the proportion of black families with median incomes over $50 thousand grew to 14 percent by 1989. The median income of black families headed by women was $12,130.

Black families experienced both social and economical setbacks during the 1980s. High levels of joblessness, increased poverty, declines in marriage, illegitimate births, drug use, gang violence, and inadequate healthcare, all served to jeopardize the future of the black family. The elimination of social programs funded by federal and state governments were sabotaging the progress of black people, however, the changing attitudes about what behavior is acceptable and what is wrong was also having a negative effect on black families.

A Reflection

Sports and Black Athletes

African-American athletes were dominating the world of sports in the 1980s, specifically in the popular sports of football, basketball, and track and field. Many were motivated by an aspect of black culture that promotes athletics above academics and the possibility of being one of the fortunate few who sign a multimillion-dollar contract. Even though African-Americans made up only 12 percent of the total population in 1989, black athletes constituted 73 percent of the NBA, 57 percent of the NFL, and 21 percent of the MLB. Based on numbers from the NCAA, it was a similar situation in college, 60 percent of male Division I basketball players and 51 percent of football players were black. Africa-American women also had a strong presence in college athletics, comprising 35 percent of the female Division I basketball players and 31 percent of the cross-country track and field athletes.

Black athletes with superior physical size, agility, and speed were rising quickly to the top in amateur and professional sports. Researchers were continuing the discussion of whether the athletic skills were genetically based, comparing the physiques of black and white athletes. Speculation as to what this ability could be attributed to became a frequent source of sports conversations. Jimmy "The Greek" Snyder, a sportscaster on the NFL Today Show, was fired after an interview in January of 1988 where he said, *"The black is the better athlete...and he practices to be the better athlete, he's bred to be the better athlete because this goes way back to the slave period."* The stereotypical idea that blacks are superior physically but inferior intellectually is common place in the sports world and is used as an excuse to keep blacks on the field and out of the front offices.

Al Campanis, general manager of the Los Angeles Dodgers, and close teammate of Jackie Robinson, appeared on ABC's Nightline in 1987 in an interview with Ted Koppel to celebrate Robinson's entrance into the Major Baseball League. Campanis responded to the question of why so few blacks were in management positions in baseball by saying, *"I truly believe they may not have some of the necessities to be a field manager or perhaps a general manager...They are gifted with great musculature and various other things. They're fleet of foot...Now as far as having the background to be club presidents, or presidents of a bank, I don't know."* In his defense, Frank Robinson, the first black manager of baseball, stated that Campanis was a decent man who was just expressing the popular thoughts of many in baseball.

Despite the fact that the winningest coach in the game of football, Eddie Robinson of Grambling State University, was black, professional football teams claimed that they couldn't find black coaches with expertise and experience. Civil Rights Organizations like the SCLC were becoming more vocal in their concerns about the lack of African-Americans coaching in professional sports and absence of a black head coach or offensive or defensive coordinator in the NFL. Finally in 1989, Art Shell was hired by the Los Angeles Raiders, becoming the first black head coach in the NFL and the second in professional football history. One year earlier, John Grier, became the first black referee in the NFL, promoted from field judge after seven seasons.

The 1980s was also the decade for the black quarterback; more black players were leading on the field from high school football teams to predominately white college teams and HBCUs. Black quarterbacks were already playing in the Canadian Football League (CFL) and in the United States Football League (USFL). By the late 1980s, three black quarterbacks in the NFL, Warren Moon with the Houston Oilers, Randall Cunningham with the Philadelphia Eagles, and Doug Williams with the Washington Redskins had led their teams to the playoffs. In 1988, Doug Williams was the first black quarterback to start in a Super Bowl game, win the Super Bowl Championship, and be named the Super Bowl MVP.

Genetically or environmentally, these athletes were built for speed and were the premiere running blacks of the 1980s. The elite list of players who rushed and crushed game and season running records throughout the decade included Marcus Allen, Earl Campbell, Eric Dickerson, Tony Dorsett, Walter Payton, all in the NFL, and Hershel Walker in the USFL. Walter "Sweetness" Payton was undoubtedly the best of the best, breaking Jim Brown's career rushing record of 12,312 in 1984 and taking the title of the football's all-time rusher.

The popularity of professional basketball went through a lull during the end of the 1970s; some reasoned because there were too many blacks in the league, there was even talk of reducing the number of teams in the league down to twelve from twenty-three and lowering the number of games played by ten. Three out of four of the professional teams were burning cash and not making money. Providentially, the thrills and excitement returned for fans with the arrival of Earvin "Magic" Johnson at the start of the decade. NBA attendance rebounded quickly, setting new crowd turnout records across the country. Magic Johnson and his on the court rivalry with Larry Bird captivated fans with awesome passes and breathtaking shots that lifted the league out of its doldrums.

The Los Angeles Lakers may have dominated in NBA Championships during the 1980s under the leadership of Kareem Abdul Jabbar and Magic Johnson, but there was definitely no shortage of superstars in league. As the eighties progressed, new energy from talented

A Reflection

athletes like Isaiah Thomas, Dominique Wilkins, Hakeem Olajuwon, and Patrick Ewing elevated the game to next level. Just when we thought it couldn't get any better, Michael Jordan joined the Chicago Bulls, and the discussion of who is "the greatest basketball player of all-time" reached a fever pitch.

By 1989, there were five African-American coaches in the NBA, but there were new challenges in the league to conquer. The drug use epidemic that was pervasive throughout the black community had spread into the world of professional sports. The use of cocaine and free-basing was taking growing numbers of players out of the game. Coaches and executives in the NBA estimated that more than half of all basketball players used cocaine or free-based.

The number of African-Americans playing professional baseball was dwindling as more black athletes preferred the fast money associated with football and basketball. One exception was Dave Winfield, the highest-paid baseball player at the start of the decade after signing a $23 million contract with the New York Yankees. Still, black ball players were being relegated to positions in the outfield or at first base. Two incredible black players rose above the rest, one at bat and the other on the pitcher's mound. These exceptional players, Darryl Strawberry and Dwight Gooden, were teammates with the New York Mets. Darryl Strawberry was one of the fiercest sluggers in baseball during the eighties. He entered the major leagues playing for the New York Mets in 1983 at 21 years old, standing 6-foot-6, Strawberry ruled over home plate with his powerful long left-handed swing. He played 122 games, hitting for a .257 average with 26 homeruns, 7 triples and 74 RBIs, and was voted the National League's Rookie of the year. Strawberry was voted to the All-Star game every year for the rest of the 1980s and helped lead the New York Mets to the World Series Championship in 1986.

When Dwight Eugene Gooden, dubbed "Doc Gooden" or "Dr. K," stood on the pitcher's mound the baseball clinic was open. Moving up to the majors in April of 1984 with the New York Mets, Gooden was only 19 years old but he was armed with a 98 MPH fastball and devastating curve ball. He ended the season with 17 wins and was the youngest player to appear in the All-Star Game. Gooden led the league and broke the rookie record with 276 strikeouts and was voted "Rookie of Year" in 1984. In 1985, Gooden played the most pitch perfect season in baseball history, 24 wins, 268 strikeouts, earning the major league's Triple Crown in pitching. He also became the youngest player to win the National League Cy Young Award. The Mets won the World Series in 1986, unfortunately, it was also the year that Gooden's drug problems came to

1989

the forefront, he tested positive for cocaine in 1987 and entered a rehabilitation center.

Vincent Edward "Bo" Jackson was an outstanding two-sport athlete and All-American in both football and baseball. In his senior year at Auburn University, his batting average was .401 with 17 homeruns and 43 RBIs, a running back on the football field he rushed for 1786 yards with 17 touchdowns and was the 1986 Heisman Trophy winner. Bo Jackson was the No.1 draft pick in the NFL selected by Tampa Bay even though he was committed to baseball and signed with the Kansas City Royals in June of 1986. In his rookie season, Jackson led the Kansas City Royals with 22 home runs, a .258 hitting average, 45 RBIs, and 10 stolen bases, and that didn't discourage the Oakland Raiders from selecting him in the 1987 NFL Draft.

Bo stated that baseball was his No. 1 priority and football would be his "hobby" between seasons. In the fifth game of his football rookie season he ran for a Raiders record of 221 yards in one game, scored three touchdowns, including a magnificent 91-yard touchdown run, moreover, he ended the season with 554 yards in 81 rushes. When Jackson returned to baseball in the spring of 1988 he got the starting job in leftfield. In 1989, Bo Jackson led the American League with 21 homeruns, started for the American League All-Star team, and was voted MVP of the All-Star game.

***

African-Americans have always reigned supreme in the sport of prize fighting, however, the 1980s signaled a changing of the guard in the boxing ring. Not only had Joe Louis died, but in the same year Muhammad Ali, well past his prime at 38 years of age, stepped into the ring for the last time and faced the obvious, boxing was truly a young man's game. Larry Holmes ruled as the heavyweight champion in the first half of the decade, in spite of that, the celebrated division lacked the talent and drama that sparked the rivalries of the 1970s.

The boxing fervor of the early 1980s belonged to lower weight classes. There was the unforgettable electric excitement generated by Aaron Pryor in the welterweight division. Pryor successfully defended his title ten times during the decade, defeating the formidable Alexis Arguello twice to retain his WBA World Jr. Welterweight title. Yet, it was the middleweight fights that knocked out boxing enthusiasts. There were five unique fighters, all world champions that brought courage, machismo, competitiveness, dedication, and glamour to the fight game with an intensity that nearly brought their fans to blows. The dramatic matchups up between rivals Wilfred Benitez, Roberto Duran, Marvin Hagler, Tommy Hearns, and Sugar Ray Leonard created thrilling performances that even Hollywood couldn't have scripted better.

A Reflection

The battles began with the two legendary matchups between Roberto Duran and Sugar Ray Leonard (1980), one win each, then Leonard beat Hearns (1981), then Benitez beat Duran (1982), Hearns beat Benitez (1982), Hagler beat Duran (1983), Hearns beat Duran (1984), and then in the fight dubbed "The War," Hagler beat Hearns (1985). This set up the ultimate matchup, a fight between Sugar Ray Leonard and Marvin Hagler. Leonard had once said, "The fight would be terrific, the greatest fight that boxing had ever seen, the biggest moneymaker so far, but it'll never happen." Needless to say, the fight did happen, but it was an anti-climatic finish with Leonard winning on points, and some even thought Hagler was the victor. The rivals ended the decade with Leonard defeating Duran and a draw between Hearns and Leonard (1989).

Yet again, there was no need for disappointment among boxing fans; the crescendo building inside the ring, was none other than "Iron Mike" Tyson, and he would take the fight game to more exhilarating heights. Mike Tyson was incredibly powerful with awesome speed to match, winning his first fight at 18 years of age by a first round knockout. In his 28th fight, Tyson won the WBC Heavyweight Championship title at the age of 20 in a match against Trevor Berbeck in 1986. Intimidating and tremendously effective, Tyson unified the heavyweight titles of the WBC, WBF, and the IBF, and became the undisputed champion; he triumphantly defended his titles five times before the end of the decade.

***

The 1980s were groundbreaking years for black women in basketball. In 1981, Lynette Woodard scored the most career points in the history of women's college basketball and won the Wade trophy. Cheryl Miller, star on the Riverside Polytechnic High School, scored 105 points in one basketball game, before becoming a standout at the University of Southern California. These two women led the U.S. women's basketball team to their first gold medal in the 1984 Olympics. Lynette Woodard also became the first women to play for the Harlem Globetrotters in 1985.

African-Americans excelled in amateur or more appropriately non-professional athletics during the 1980s competition in the International Olympic Games. The U.S. boycotted the 1980 Games, but in 1984 black athletes returned to claim the gold. Carl Lewis repeated Jesse Owen's amazing feat, winning four gold medals in the 100m, 200m, the 4 x100m relay, and the long jump, and then won the 100m and long jump gold medals again in 1988. Valerie Briscoe-Hooks delivered an equally impressive performance in the 1984 Olympics, winning three gold medals in the 200m, 400m, and the 4x400 relay in record breaking fashion. Evelyn Ashford set an Olympic record in the 100m, Edwin Moses continued his winning streak and took the gold medal in the 400m hurdles, and Bobby Weaver grabbed a gold medal in freestyle wrestling.

Black women athletes had a higher profile during the 1980s with stellar performances in the 1984 and 1988 Olympics. Zina Garrison was ranked No. 4 in the world of tennis, and won a gold medal in the women's double and the bronze in singles at the 1988 Olympic Games. Debi Thomas, winner of the U.S. Figure Skating championship in 1986 was expected to take the gold in the 1988 Olympics, but with an ill-fated misstep, she became the first African-American to medal in the Winter Olympic Games with a bronze.

Jackie Joyner-Kersee and her sister-in-law Florence Griffith-Joyner graced the world with spectacular performances in track and field. Jackie Joyner-Kersee proved herself to be the "world's greatest woman athlete," winning the Olympic Silver for the heptathlon in 1984 and capturing the gold medal at the Olympics in Seoul, Korea in 1988 for the long jump and the heptathlon breaking the 7,000 point mark. Florence Griffith-Joyner, christened Flo-Jo, was mesmerizing as she set an Olympic record in the 100m and the 200m, anchored the team in the 4x100m relay, and ran in the 4x400m relay, winning three gold medals and one silver as the "fastest woman in the world." Flo-Jo surpassed Wilma Rudolph's Olympic record and became the first woman in forty years to win four medals in a single Olympic game.

Black Literature

The second Renaissance in African-American literature began in the 1980s, as a new generation of black writers emerged. The difference in this re-birth is that it was the voices of black women that resonated in higher volumes during this decade. Of even greater significance in this rise of black writers was that mainstream publishers now recognized the talent and popularity, and specifically the profitability in African-American books. Black people were hungry for stories that they could identify with, words of the same struggles and pains, expressions of similar dreams and desires, and black writers were anxious to be heard.

Toni Morrison added to her repertoire with *Tar Baby* and *Dreaming Emmett*, but it was her *Beloved* that took readers on a supernatural voyage through her mind's eye. Even though the book was based on a true story of a runaway slave who would rather kill her children than let them be returned to live the life of a slave, Morrison took the facts and weaved them with her imagination and created a masterpiece for which she won the Pulitzer Prize in 1988.

A Reflection

Gloria Naylor hit a homerun out of the stadium with her first book *The Women of Brewster Place* (1982) which told the stories of seven very different black women. The Kansas City Star reviewed it best saying, *"Without out telling us what to feel, she makes us feel by baring the emotions of her characters, real women aching with life."* The novel was the winner of the National Book Award in 1983. Naylor followed her triumph with novels, *Linden Hill* (1985) and *Mama Day* (1988) where she cracked the door for readers to look into the secret societies among black that are unknown to most.

J. California Cooper mastered the art of the short story. A successful playwright, she wrote her first collection of short stories, A Piece of Mind, in 1984. Reading a story written by Cooper is like a mellow Saturday sitting on your Granny's back porch as she snaps green beans, listening to her recount an old story, comfortable, familiar, patient, with never a wasted word, and a lesson to take with you. Her next collection, *Homemade Love* (1986) won an American Book Award, and the third book of the decade was *Some Soul to Keep* (1987).

Alice Walker's *The Color Purple* (1982) was an epic book in the black community; we were all lost in the story and the characters, Miss Celie, Mister, Shug Avery, Sofia, and Harpo. The story was honest and unapologetic, showing the strengths and weakness of black people, laying out various truths that we have all seen or experienced, but never spoke of, and many of us want to deny or forget. *The Color Purple* received the Pulitzer Prize for Fiction and the National Book Award for Fiction in 1983, and was adapted to a movie for the big screen in 1985. Walker published another book before the end of the decade, *Temple of My Familiar* (1989).

Terry McMillan whets our appetites for more with her novels Mama (1987) and Disappearing Acts (1989) during the 1980s. Women readers were attracted by her no-nonsense writing style and totally related to the subject matter of both books. McMillan tells stories from the heart and strikes every emotion with no shame in her game, it is what it is. The common thread among these writers was their ability to introduce you to characters, where you knew them personally, you never wanted the story to end, you were attached, and you needed to keep reading.

Artists of the Decade

By 1989, African-American artists had their work exhibited in major galleries, prominent museums, and municipal art centers all over the world. Most of the black artists who are represented in museums at this time were traditional artists, in the sense that their pieces were considered to be fine art by the art world. However, nearly all the art that was created in this decade is contemporary art, no matter whether the style was abstract, realism, or impressionism. Artists could freely express themselves without trying to fit into any particularly genre or trend.

One of the artists to move into the forefront during the 1980s was Martin Puryear, an abstract sculptor whose work was exhibited in The Museum of Modern Art. A minimalist, working with wood, stone, wire, or steel, Puryear created simple but very sophisticated shapes and forms that visually stirred both an intellectual and emotional reaction. In 1989, Martin Puryear was the first African-American artist to represent the United States in an international art exhibition; he won the grand prize with his exhibit of nine sculptures at the 20th Bienal de Sao Paulo.

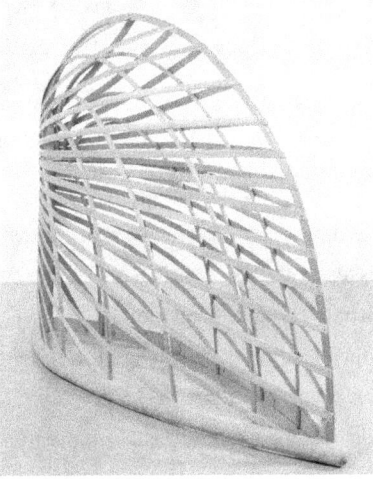

Martin Puryear, Courtesy Matthews Marks Gallery

Robert Colescott studied with French painter, Fernand Leger in the early 1950s, and he may have been influenced by him to depict the common man is his work. Colescott's painting style was characterized as neo-expressionism, which displays the human body or familiar in a rough manner using vivid colors. Colescott boldly approached the line between fascination and fear with his paintings, a political satirist who spoke through his canvass, his works were filled with blatant overtones of racism, poverty, murder, and sexism. Colescott said his painting *Emergency Room* was *"a vivid allegory for the whole country."* Colescott was the first black artist to represent the United States in a solo exhibition at the Venice Biennale.

A Reflection

Robert Colescott Emergency Room (1989)

Entertainment

The 1980s was an award winning decade for African-Americans in stage and theater. The past commercial successes of the black musicals of the 1979s paved the way for all-black casts on and off Broadway, and stage enthusiasts were not disappointed. The plays and performances of the eighties started on a high note and resonated there with *Sophisticated Ladies*, *Lena Horne: The Lady and Her Music*, and *Dream Girls*, opening on Broadway in 1981. *Sophisticated Ladies*, based on the music of Duke Ellington ran for two years with 767 performances, Lena Horne delivered 333 awesome performances from May 12, 1981 to June 30, 1982, but *Dream Girls* was a mega-hit, starring Jennifer Holiday, Sheryl Lee Ralph, and Loretta Devine, the musical ran on Broadway for almost four years and over 1500 performances. A definite dream come true, the play won six Tony Awards and five Drama Desk Awards, and a Grammy.

The decade was not short on drama; in 1981, the Negro Ensemble Company at the Theatre Four staged *A Soldier's Play*, a play written by Charles Fuller about a murder mystery on a segregated military base in Louisiana in 1944. The play explored the depth of anger and resentment that some blacks have towards each other as a result of racial experiences. The original cast included Adolph Caesar, Denzel Washington, Larry B. Riley, and Samuel L. Jackson. The play ran for 468 performances and won the Obie

Award for Distinguished Ensemble Performance, the 1981 Drama Critics' Circle Award Best American Play, the 1982 Outer Critics Circle Award Best Off-Broadway Play, and the 1982 Pulitzer Prize for Drama.

August Wilson, a veteran of the Black Arts movement of the sixties, staked his claim on the theater world in the 1980s beginning with *Ma Rainey's Black Bottom* in 1982, which moved on to Broadway in 1984, and was nominated for the Tony Award for Best Play. *Jitney* premiered in 1982, *Joe Turners' Come and Gone* premiered in 1984, but it was *Fences*, which starred James Earl Jones, that was his tour de force. Premiering on Broadway in 1987, *Fences* ran for 525 performances and set a nonmusical Broadway production record when it grossed $11 million in one year. In 1987, the play won the Drama Desk Award for Outstanding Play, the Tony Award for Best Play, and the Pulitzer Prize for Drama.

Besides these black Broadway productions, Whoopi Goldberg's one-woman show in 1984 and the musical revue *Black and Blue* in 1989, there was another world of black theater. What's more, the largest black theater audience is the one that has never seen a Broadway production. In the 1980s, after the success of *Mama I Want to Sing*, a gospel musical that ran for eight years in Harlem grossing over $25 million in the first five years, there was *Beauty Shop* in 1987 that grossed $33 million. These productions went on the road, the "urban circuit" or dubbed the "chitlin' circuit by Henry Louis Gates, Jr., taking their plays to black people across the country. A new genre developed as these inexpensive but highly profitable productions were imitated by a number of producers using similar formats and characters.

Movies

The result of the end of the blaxploitation era of the 1970s was the exclusion of black actors in Hollywood. In 1981, out of the 200 movies made that year, there were only 12 parts for black males and only a single part for a black female. The NAACP was close to calling a boycott of the motion picture industry unless more roles were designated for African-American actors. The explanation for the lack of blacks in movies was that they were not box office attractions, yet Richard Pryor was box office gold in the early eighties starring in *Stir Crazy*, *The Toy*, *Brewster's Millions* and *Bustin Loose*. Eddie Murphy followed closely in his footsteps, blowing up box offices in *48 Hours*, *Beverly Hills Cop*, *Trading Places*, *The Golden Child*, and his basically black movies, *Coming to America*, *Harlem Nights*, and his stand-up comedy, *Raw*.

A Reflection

The black movie high points were definitely in 1984 and 1985 with the releases of *A Soldier's Story* and *The Color Purple*. Both films had been very successful stage plays that had appeared on Broadway earlier in the decade, and both had stellar cast members. Adolph Caesar, Denzel Washington, and William Young reprised their original roles from the play in *A Soldier's Story*. Similarly, both films were nominated for several academy awards, three for *A Soldier's Story* and eleven for *The Color Purple*, nevertheless neither of the films won. Both films were extolled by critics, except *The Color Purple* made the big bucks, grossing $142 million worldwide.

There was a handful of black actors who had supporting roles in the blockbusters of the 1980s, Howard Rollins in *Ragtime*, Lou Gossett in *An Officer and a Gentleman*, Morgan Freeman in *Lean on Me* and *Driving Miss Daisy*, Gregory Hines in *Cotton Club*, Danny Glover in the *Lethal Weapon* movies and *Places in the Heart*. Despite the fact that blacks spent $700 million a year on movies, we had no clout in Hollywood, if we wanted acting parts; we needed to make the movies. Prince Nelson Rogers stepped up to the plate with his independent film *Purple Rain* in 1984, which needless to say, was a smash hit, making more than $80 million and winning an Academy award for Best Original Song. Prince followed up with *Under the Cherry Moon* (1986) and *Sign O' the Times*.

Spike Lee, next up at bat, hit a home run with *She's Gotta Have It* in 1986, a movie about an attractive, independent black woman juggling three men. The film was shot in less than two weeks on a $175,000 budget and grossed over $7 million. Lee followed with his musical-drama *School Daze* in 1988, and blew audiences away with his controversial hit *Do the Right Thing* in 1989. Robert Townsend contributed *Hollywood Shuffle* in 1987, a spoof on the treatment of blacks in Hollywood, and Keenan Ivory Wayans put out his hilarious *I'm Gonna Git You Sucka* in 1989, which was a spoof on the black action or exploitation films.

African-Americans were continuing to break new ground on the small screen during the 1980s. Still, the cold hard fact remained that television programming is largely based on ratings and the sponsorship of individual shows. Black people made up only about 12 percent of the U.S. population in this decade, meaning any successful black television show would have to appeal to a significant number of the white audience in order to survive. Based on the track record of past shows with black characters, white viewers have demonstrated that they prefer to watch blacks in comedic roles versus serious or dramatic roles. As a result television networks were more likely to pick up the black shows that were situation comedies or sitcoms.

1989

There were 18 black shows that made it to the TV screen in the 1980s, although most didn't make past their pilot season. However, there were several successful shows that ran for several seasons. In the early eighties networks were using the tried and true comedy genius of Redd Foxx in *Sanford* and *The Redd Foxx Show*, and Sherman Hemsley as Deacon Ernest Frye in *Amen*, a character reminiscent of George Jefferson. Broadcast networks were unable to resist the old formula of the smart talking housekeeper in *Gimme a Break!*, starring Nell Carter, and the cliche of the smart talking kid in *Different Strokes*, starring Gary Coleman and Todd Bridges, and in *Webster*, starring Emmanuel Lewis.

By the mid-1980s, black actors and black audiences wanted to move away from the stereotypical representations of blacks and wanted a more realistic and balanced view of black life. Sitcoms developed by Bill Cosby and Tim Reid were determined to provide a different perspective in their portrayal of black characters in *The Cosby Show*, *A Different World* and *Frank's Place*. *The Cosby Show*, by far the most successful show to air during the 1980s, was representative of a well-to do black family living in Brooklyn, New York, a doctor, his attorney wife, and five children. Racial issues were not the focus of the show; Cosby's intention was to educate the audience on basic issues common to everyday life. The spin-off, *A Different World* gave a glimpse into college life for black students at HBCUs. Tim Reid's show, *Frank's Place*, in which he and he wife Daphne Reid starred, was an intelligent and classy show that was not as fortunate in gaining the white audience, and ran for only one season.

In 1988, the *Eyes On The Prize* documentary covering the Civil Rights Movement in American from 1954 through 1985 was run on PBS. Produced by Henry Hampton and narrated by Julian Bond, the program was divided into two parts, America's Civil Rights Years and America at the Crossroads. The documentary was broadcast in a series of 14 one hour segments and was *"the most critically acclaimed documentary on civil rights in America."* There were several notable made-for-TV movies shown in this decade, *The Marva Collins Story* (1981), *The Medgar Ever's Story* (1983), and *The Women of Brewster Place* (1989).

Music

Black music or R&B of the 1980s can't be defined or classified in any specific category; the music ran the gamut of funk bands, soul, pop, jazz, gospel, and hip-hop. There were girl groups, guy groups, duos, and individual singers that expressed all the many moods and emotions of the times. It didn't matter if you were old school or fresh, whether you were feeling radical, romantic, or reflective, the music of the eighties had

A Reflection

it covered; musically there was something for everybody. The birth of the music video brought us the performances of our favorite singers and musicians up close and personal in the comforts of our living rooms.

The path to becoming a black superstar in the music industry involves crossing over to pop music charts. Michael Jackson, Prince, Whitney Houston, and even Tina Turner made the trip and had officially arrived in the land of Superstardom in the 1980s. Michael Jackson went one step further and became the "King of Pop" and "The Artist of the Decade" with his 1982 *Thriller* album selling 110 million copies worldwide. Number one hits, *Beat It*, *Billie Jean*, and *Thriller* made the record the best selling album of all time. Jackson won four Grammys in 1983, and eight in 1984. His release of *Bad* in 1987 dominated the charts with a record of seven hit singles.

Prince Rogers Nelson was an absolute powerhouse in the 1980s, composing, producing, singing, and playing practically all the instruments on his album. In addition to producing four albums for The Time, Prince released nine albums of his own in the decade. *Purple Rain* was his biggest hit of the decade selling over 13 million copies in the U.S. with *"When Doves Cry"* and *Let's Go Crazy* reaching No. 1 on the Billboard. Prince earned the unique status of having a number one single, album, and movie all at the same time.

Whitney Houston's voice took the world by storm with the release of her first album *Whitney Houston* in 1985, with three #1 singles and selling 25 million copies. Her second album *"Whitney"* had four #1 singles and sold 20 million copies. Houston's first albums were filled with songs chosen to appeal to pop audiences and Houston was accused of selling out, but good music and financial success couldn't be wrong. Tina Turner also appealed to a broader pop or even rock audience with her glorious comeback in the 1980s with her 1984 album, *Private Dancer,* selling 20 million copies. Turner earned her first #1 hit single for *What's Love Got To Do With It*, for which she won four Grammy awards.

There were several other black artists who were able to climb the pop charts as well as appeal to R&B audiences in the 1980s, the list included Janet Jackson, Lionel Richie, Patti LaBelle, Anita Baker, and Deniece Williams. In 1986, black recording stars grossed $2 billion. Generally, black music fans may not understand the financial gains for musicians that crossover but they know what they like, a strong vocal performance, a beat we can dance to, and lyrics that touch the soul. Ageless artists like Stevie Wonder, Marvin Gaye, Smokey Robinson, and Aretha Franklin were still doing their thing, as well as Earth, Wind & Fire, The Isley Brothers, Maze, The Whispers, and

Rick James. New rising stars included Evelyn "Champagne" King, Sade, Stephanie Mills, and Angela Winbush.

The soul artistry of black male singers was at a premium in the 1980s, there was the sexy Teddy Pendergrass, the classic Peabo Bryson, the arousing Freddie Jackson, the sensuous Will Downing, and the ultimate in Luther Vandross. When you wanted to dance, you had to have The SOS Band, The Dazz Band, The Gap Band, Atlantic Star and Midnight Star. If you wanted to party and tear the roof off, you needed Zapp, Lakeside, Brass Construction, and ConFunKshun.

Teddy Riley, producer and member of the group Guy, is credited with the merging of R&B and hip hop to create "new jack swing." New Jack artists included Keith Sweat, Jodeci, Bobby Brown, and Bell Biv DeVoe. Hip Hop and rap music grew even bigger during the 1980s, becoming a cultural phenomenon. Among the many rappers, there was Grandmaster Flash and The Furious Five, Run-DMC, Public Enemy, Big Daddy Kane, NWA, and LL Cool J. The beatboxers were Doug E. Fresh, Biz Markie, and the Fat Boys. Salt-N-Pepa was one of the first all-female rap groups and the first to have an album reach gold or platinum status with "Push It."

Memorable Moments

On June 1, 1980, Vernon Jordan survived an assassination attempt by white supremacist Joseph Franklin.
On May 16, 1983, Michael Jackson amazed viewers with the "moonwalk" in his performance of "Billie Jean" on the Motown 25: Yesterday, Today, Forever television special.
Guion Stewart Bluford, Jr was the African-American to go into space as a member of the 1983 space shuttle Challenger crew.
In 1984, Ernie Barnes was appointed as the Official Sports Artist for the XXIII Olympic Games.
In 1984, Vanessa Williams was the first African-American woman to be crowned Miss America.
January 20, 1986 was the first observance of Martin Luther King, Jr. Day as federal holiday.
Rita Dove was the first black woman to win the Pulitzer Prize for Poetry in 1986.
In 1987, Jackie Joyner-Kersee was voted the Associated Press Female Athlete of the Year for track.
In 1988, Florence Griffith Joyner was named the Associated Press Female Athlete of the Year.
Rev. Barbara Harris was the first woman elected as Episcopal Bishop in the history of the

A Reflection

Anglican Church on February 12, 1989, the first woman after the death of Jesus Christ to achieve this standing.

In 1989, Bertram Lee and Peter Bynoe became the first African-Americans owners of a major league Sports franchise when they bought the Denver Nuggets for $65 million.

Reflection on a Decade

The overwhelming scene of the decade ending in 1989 encompassed vivid images of a devastating battle with multitudes of casualties in its aftermath. The dictionary defines war as a prolonged conflict between states, nations, or other parties typified by extreme aggression, social disruption, and usually high mortality. So by definition, black people had definitely been in a war and had suffered great losses during the 1980s. Ambushed from all sides, African-Americans sustained a direct hit from unemployment near Depression levels and were blind-sided with Reagan budget cuts that knocked down funding for job training, welfare and food stamps, housing subsidies, and educational grants. Crack was ruthless and took no prisoners in the black community, AIDS definitely didn't discriminate, and gang warfare and its senseless killings were at an all-time high. The ghetto or the "hood" was unmistakably an urban battlefield.

African-Americans suffered more setbacks in the 1980s as affirmative action policies and social programs that had offered a leg up were weakened or eliminated. The locomotive to progress had run into some roadblocks, more aptly the brakes were put on the train and at some points even shifted in reverse. Few economic changes were seen during the decade as income growth was frozen along with the minimum wage and the economic gap between blacks and whites was widening again. Racism and violence accompanied the lean years of the recession, hate bombs were sent through the mail to the NAACP, a black federal judge was killed, along with a black city alderman in Savannah, and young blacks walking through all-white neighborhoods were routinely attacked. The lack of moral tone and outrage coming from the Reagan White House only served to increase racial discord.

The catalysts for change in the 1980s were a conservative political climate, additional losses in manufacturing jobs, and rising levels of unemployment. Regrettably, most of the changes were not beneficial for the black community. Crime rates rose dramatically as increasing numbers of black males abandoned the educational path for the quick money of the streets in gang activity and selling drugs, and newly built prisons were being filled to capacity with young black men. Urban blight and the displacement of low-income blacks was a critical issue as the numbers of homeless families escalated. The traditional black family structure continued to breakdown as 61 percent of black families were a headed by a single-parent. Patrick Moynihan wrote, *"A community that allows a large number of young men to grow up in broken families, dominated by women, never acquiring any stable relationship to male authority, never acquiring any set of rational expectations about the future – that community asks for chaos."*

The breaks in the black community were becoming more apparent as the economic gap between poorer blacks and middle-class blacks expanded and the groups moved in different directions. Those who had acquired sufficient resources, education and training, and above average employment were ready to chart their own course. Increasingly, blacks were retreating back to the South in search of stability and jobs frustrated by the limited opportunities in large metropolitan cities. An atmosphere of complacency with the way things were was spreading; those who had found some measure of success had become weary of the fight for social justice, while those less fortunate didn't see the point and gave up.

A Reflection

1999

The Million Man March

Million Man March Poem
The night has been long,
The wound has been deep,
The pit has been dark,
And the walls have been steep...
---Maya Angelou

Surveying the landscape of the decade ending in 1999 gives the impression that the break in progress might have ended and the journey may get back on track. The economy was in recovery and prospects for African-Americans had begun to look brighter. A surge in job creation promoted the spirit of optimism. Unemployment for blacks was at a historic low at 7.2 percent although it was still double the rate for whites. The decade ushered in a period of introspection among black people and a renewed determination to improve the lives of the poor and disadvantaged. It was a time of reorganization and focus, a period to take our problems and concerns back to the White House while there was an ear that would listen.

1999

The Million Man March took place on October 16, 1995 and was the largest demonstration seen in Washington, DC history. Attended by 500,000 to 800,000 black men, participation was 2-3 times the number that attended the March on Washington in 1963. The march was organized by the Louis Farrakhan and The National African American Leadership Summit under the leadership of Dr. Benjamin Chavis in alliance with local chapters of the NAACP to encourage black men to take responsibility for themselves, their families, and the black community. Mobilizing the black community was the underlying focus with emphasis on voter registration and the restoration of black concerns on the national political agenda.

The boom in the economy during the 1990s offered a reprieve to African-Americans as doors were opened for black urban professionals referred to as "Buppies" to get a taste of the American dream. Increased employment opportunities added to the numbers of black middle-class as their number surpassed half of the black population. Conversely, as well as this segment of black people may have been doing, there were still a third of blacks that fell below the poverty line, and for this segment the problems were chronic and a viable solution remained elusive.

Racial tensions that simmered below the surface in America bubbled over the top during the 1990s. This racial divide between blacks and whites was broadened during this decade with the inflammatory verdicts from two high-profile court cases, the acquittal of four police officers charged with the brutal beating of Rodney King on April 29, 1992 and the acquittal of O.J. Simpson for the murder of his ex-wife Nicole Simpson and Ronald Goldman on October 3, 1995. The explosive reactions to the judgments on these verdicts were split along racial lines with the opposing sides viewing them as grave miscarriages of justice. Violent riots broke out in Los Angeles neighborhoods after the Rodney King verdict releasing pent-up rage and disappointment which lasted for five days with casualties of 54 killed, hundreds injured, more than 7000 arrested, and over $1 billion in property damages.

Demographics

Blacks still made up 12.9 percent of the U.S. population, with numbers around 36,419,434. The black population increased 21.5 percent over the last decade. At the close of 1999, 54.8 percent of African-Americans lived in the Southern region of the country, 18 percent lived in the Northeast, 19 percent lived in the Midwest, and 10 percent lived in the West with California having the fifth largest black population. The median age

A Reflection

for black people had risen to 30 years but was still 5 years younger than the median for the total U.S. population, and 32 percent of blacks were under 18 years of age. The life expectancy for black Americans had increased to 71.4 years as blacks were living longer than previous generations, although only eight percent of the black population was over 65 years of age. The sex ratio of African-Americans was the lowest of all races with 90 males per 100 females.

According to Census data, close to 58 percent of blacks live in the inner cities of metropolitan areas. New York, Texas, Georgia, and Florida, and California were the states with the largest African-American populations. New York City still had the largest black population, 2 million persons, making up 28 percent of the total population. Chicago had the second largest with 1.6 million black residents. There were ten states that were home to 60 percent of the black population in America: New York, California, Texas, Florida, Georgia, Illinois, North Carolina, Maryland, Michigan, and Louisiana. The reverse migration of blacks that had gained steam in the 1980s was extending from the West coast. The sinking economy of California in the early 1990s rushed 103,000 blacks back to their roots in the South, but by the end of the decade an additional 221,000 were traveling out of the West.

The unemployment rate for black Americans had fallen to a thirty year low during the 1990s to less than eight percent and the number of blacks living under the poverty level declined to 23 percent. There was a decline in the number of black males in the labor force, from 75 percent to 70.5 percent while the number for black females in the labor force remained virtually unchanged. In 1999, the median earnings for African-American households was $30,134 compared to $51,244 for white families. The median income of African American men was $21,343 compared to $29,797 for white men, and the median income for African American women was $15,581, compared to $16,079 for white women.

Mood of the Black Community

"Cause they say 2000 zero zero party over, oops! Out of Time!
So tonight I'm gonna party like it's 1999!"
-- Prince

The economic boom of the 1990s spurred by advances in science and new technologies, specifically the World Wide Web, provided some much needed relief for the African-American community with more job opportunities and higher wages. *"In the land of milk and honey you've got to have money,"* and in the 1990s we were determined to get our hands on some. Luther Vandross' 1994 remake of *"Ain't No Stoppin Us Now"* embodied the mood of blacks in these years. Black people wanted to finally get ahead and live a better life one way or another. Nonetheless, this wave of prosperity created deeper rifts in the black community, divisions between generations and division between economic classes. Black people were moving into separate worlds, the philosophy of one: How high can you go? The other: How low can you go, and both were approached with similar enthusiasm.

The 1990s was a decade of pushing the envelope. Everything was done to excess. Black people pushed past the limits or boundaries that had been holding them back. We had jobs. We made some money and we got credit. We bought houses we couldn't afford and spent more than we made. But these were some good times. The more fortunate middle-class appeased their taste for the finer things in life, went out to restaurants, concerts, and plays, and were patrons of the arts. They dressed well and smelled good, drove good, and took expensive vacations with their families.

The under-class of blacks became more isolated and the young created their own society within hip-hop culture. The common thread was the obsession with the accoutrements of what we believed represented success, and it was done to excess. The culture was influenced by rap music and developed new attitudes and fashion. The initial message of protest and empowerment degraded into sexism and gangsta rap. Misogynistic behavior and the disrespect of black women by black men were in excess. The glorification of the hustle and the romanticizing of crime and violence were in excess. It was all about game, and the winner was the one who held the cash.

Political Climate
Inaugural Poem for Bill Clinton

Here on the pulse of this new day
You may have the grace to look up and out
And into your sister's eyes, into
Your brother's face, your country
And say simply
Very simply
With hope
Good morning.
---Maya Angelou 1993

A Reflection

The political climate for African-Americans during the Clinton presidency was definitely the calm after the storm. The change in tone was due to Bill Clinton's genuine care and concern for black people. His southern background and childhood experiences that kept him in close contact with blacks provided him with a comfort level around black people that previous presidents did not possess. Clinton had a clear understanding of the black experience and the disadvantages that accompanied that reality. Because of this knowledge he was a proponent and defender of affirmative action stating,

> "Affirmative action was intended to give everybody a fair chance, but it hasn't always worked smoothly & fairly. Today there are those who are determined to put an end to affirmative action, as if the purposes for which it was created have been achieved. They have not. Until they are, we need to mend affirmative action, most certainly, but not end it."

In the 1995 Adarand v. Pena case, the Supreme Court in a landmark decision ruled against government racial preferences, stating that race is not a sufficient condition for a presumption of disadvantage and the award of favored treatment, all race-based classifications must be judged under the strict scrutiny standard. Clinton believing that affirmative action was necessary used an executive order to continue the use of race in the allocation of government funds. As President, he approved a new program that would assist minority-owned businesses in competition for government contracts, specifically those in industries where discrimination was still a factor.

The most significant aspect for African-Americans during the Clinton years in the 1990s was the strong economic growth. Withstanding over two decades of devastating unemployment, drastic shrinking of social programs and the severe reductions in education aid and opportunities, the black community could now reap some benefits from the longest economic expansion in the history of the country. The creation of over 22 million jobs under the Clinton administration were crucial in cutting the unemployment of black American in half, from 14 percent at the start of the Clinton years to 7.3 percent at the end of 1999. As a result the poverty rates for blacks in the nation dropped to lowest level ever.

Nevertheless, the political transformations of the era wielded a double-edged sword as welfare reform moved to the top of the agenda. Clinton, at ease with black people enough to discuss the need for welfare reform on their own territory, addressed the congregation at the Memphis Church of Christ. Clinton mused that if Martin Luther King were to reappear at his side today that he would say:

"I fought for freedom" he would say, "but not for the freedom of people to kill each other with reckless abandon, not for the freedom of children to have children, and the fathers of the children to walk away and abandon them as if they don't amount to anything. I fought for people to have the right to work but not to have whole communities and people abandoned. That is not what I lived and died for."

Clinton explained his intentions avowing, "*I promised to 'end welfare as we know it', to make welfare a second chance, not a way of life, exactly the change most welfare recipients wanted it to be.*" Additional efforts by the president doubled the earned-income tax credit in 1993, provided $3 billion in new resources to move welfare recipients and non custodial fathers into jobs, increased the minimum wage by 90 cents, created the Access to Jobs initiative to help provide transportation services, and provided tax incentives to encourage businesses to hire welfare recipients and low-income workers.

Bill Clinton wanted to promote diversity in government and appointed the most diverse cabinet and administration in history with African-Americans comprising 13 percent of administration appointees and 16 percent of the federal bench nominations. His cabinet included a number of African-Americans in key positions, Clifton Wharton, Jr., as Deputy Secretary of State, Ron Brown served as Secretary of Commerce, Mike Espy as Secretary of Agriculture, and Jesse Brown as Secretary of Veterans' Affairs.

The Clinton administration was at odds with a Republican Congress yet he tried to sustain a political environment that attempted to right the wrongs of the nation. Martin Luther King, Jr. said, "The time is always right to do what is right." In 1997, Clinton gave a formal apology to the 400 victims of the Tuskegee Experiment acknowledging responsibility publicly:

"The United States did something that was wrong, deeply, profoundly, morally wrong. It was an outrage to our commitment to integrity and equality for all our citizens. We can end the silence. We can stop turning our heads away. We can look you in the eye and finally say on behalf of the American people what the United States Government did was shameful, and I am sorry.

A Reflection

Black Leadership

At the end of 1999, there were 8,936 African-Americans holding political offices in the United States, a record of 41 blacks serving in Congress and 484 black mayors, with the majority of black political officials being at the local level. In spite of the fact that blacks in the South were the least likely to vote than those in other regions of the country, most of the blacks who held elected offices were in Southern states. The leadership for the black community was generally spread between state and local black elected officials, the Congressional Black Caucus, the black church, and national civil rights organizations. On the other hand, the divide between black politicians and civil rights leaders continued to grow as the years post-civil rights movement stretched out. Murmurs of criticism towards black politicians were being amplified as the black community became disenchanted with the lack of changes that would benefit the black people as a whole. Black mayors were faulted for having no "black agenda" and catering to the business community.

African-American women were gaining more political clout during this decade occupying 35 percent of elected offices held by blacks. In 1992, Carol Mosely-Braun was elected to the U.S. Senate for Illinois, the first black woman to hold this office. Most of the new black leadership wanted to use a "color-blind" approach to politics that would appeal to non-Black voters. Ron Brown explained the position of black politicians, *"We have to understand what it takes to play in the big leagues. While you understand you never forget your roots, you also understand that you have a broader responsibility."* All the same, the black voter participation was declining with the exception of national elections. With more than 22 million eligible black voters at this time, only 37 percent of them voted in the 1994 Congressional election.

Black politicians also had to withstand the heat from both sides, finding themselves the object of numerous investigations and accusations of impropriety by Republicans and others hoping to put the brakes on blacks entering the political arena and arresting the power of those already in office. Marion Barry was one who found himself on the hot seat. After a six year investigation by the FBI, a sting operation videotaped Barry smoking crack cocaine in a hotel room with a former girlfriend on January 18, 1990. Convicted for possession with the jury hung on a list of other charges, Barry served six months in a federal prison. Refusing to accept this as the end of his political career, Barry made a bid for city council in 1992 and was elected, and in May of 1994 entered the mayoral race and won, serving as the mayor of D.C. until 1999.

1999

Rev. Al Sharpton, a civil rights activist and voice of the black community in New York, raised his political profile in the 1990s beginning with a run for U.S Senate in 1992. Undeterred by his unsuccessful campaign he ran again in 1994 and loss. Sharpton also tried a run for mayor of New York in 1997, another contest he did not win. Despite his inability to win public support in elections Sharpton played a large role in protesting several incidents in New York during the decade that were controversial with racial connotations.

In the early 1990s a few blacks were appointed to higher leadership positions under the Republican Administration. After Thurgood Marshall's retirement from the Supreme Court, Clarence Thomas was nominated to fill his vacancy by President Bush. The nomination was contentious because of Thomas's experience and his criticism of affirmative action. The hearings revealed accusations of sexual harassment by law professor Anita Hill against Thomas. Despite the sensational television airings of the hearing and sexual harassment charges and objections of fitness to serve, Thomas was confirmed as associate justice. Colin Powell was also selected by George H. Bush to serve as Chairman of the Joint Chiefs of Staff, the highest military position in the Department of Defense and the first African-American to hold this office.

Minister Louis Farrakhan moved to the forefront of black leaders in the mid-1990s with a call for a million man march. Farrakhan urged "a million sober, disciplined, committed, dedicated, inspired black men to meet in Washington for a day of atonement." Although the Million Man March was organized by civil rights leaders, many felt that the tone should be of protest for the conditions of black America instead of atonement. Farrakhan wanted to show the world that their perception of black men was false, "the *image you have of black men is not the image of who and what we really are.*" While most black political and church leaders did not share the philosophy of Minister Farrakhan on a host of issues they did support the goal of the march and attended for the sake of unity. Farrakhan, the keynote speaker among other renowned speakers called for black men to step up and take responsibility for the troubles within the black community and renew their commitments to their families and neighborhoods.

An article published in the June 1995 edition of Black Enterprise called for black business leaders to step up. In an era where the national agenda is focused on economics, and race consciousness has been replaced with class-consciousness, "it's time for business leaders to step up and take the lead." While paying tribute to black community activists, church leaders, and politicians for their many accomplishments toward the true

A Reflection

freedom for African-Americans, the article stressed that "there can be no lasting social, legal or political justice without economic empowerment."

> We will not stand idly by while policies and programs necessary for black business development, and therefore, economic opportunity for all African-Americans, are destroyed. On the contrary, we must--and will--do everything in our power to ensure that African-Americans are full and equal partners in the American economy.

Extraordinary African-American

C. Delores Tucker

C. Delores Tucker was a civil rights activist, politician, and a staunch defender of women and children. Tucker stands out as an extraordinary African-American in the 1990s because of her courage and commitment to black people and her willingness to stand up proudly for her beliefs even when faced with rising opposition and threats to her own safety. C. Delores Tucker is recognized for having the nerve to initiate the much needed conversation on the pros and cons of gangsta rap music. Certainly it has been an effective vehicle for many young men to earn a living, but at what cost to the black community?

In the early 1990s, Tucker became aware of the controversial images and lyrics that were characteristic of gangsta rap music. Immediately she launched a campaign against the violent, derogatory, and misogynistic lyrics by picketing record stores that sold the records. Tucker was highly critical of the lyrics of two of the most popular rappers of time, Tupac Shakur and Snoop Dogg, which provoked a war of words between supporters and detractors of both Tucker and the rappers and their lyrics. Tucker received support from Billboard Magazine editors in a December 1993 editorial:

> "No form of popular music is important enough to justify or excuse racism, sexual bigotry and the endorsement of sociopathic violence… It is an antisocial exercise in self-delusion, and … leads to the death of conscience, the corruption of the spirit, and ultimately the destruction of the individual and community."

Still, there was much criticism that accused Tucker of being narrow-minded and cited the freedom of speech, and some felt her attacks were a form of class warfare against music that was just a symptom of the problems that run rampant in ghettos across the country. Kevin Gray responded in Emerge,

"When Tucker attacks rappers for racial and sexual violence and the denigration of women, she misses the point and the opportunity to do something about that violence. But rather than listen to the conditions described in gangsta rap and work to change them, Tucker is attacking the expression of those feelings."

Born Cynthia Delores Nottage on October 4, 1927 in Philadelphia, Pennsylvania, the tenth of eleven children, to Reverend Whitfield Nottage and Captilda Gardner Nottage, Tucker was a lover of music; she played the piano and saxophone and directed the church choir. She attended college at Temple University and the University of Pennsylvania's Wharton School of Business. She married William Tucker, a construction company owner, in 1951 and they both sold real estate in Philadelphia. In 1955, Tucker became the first female member of the Philadelphia Zoning Board. Tucker was also very active in the Civil Rights Movement raising funds for the NAACP, marched alongside Martin Luther King, Jr. in the 1965 Selma marches in Alabama, and participated in the 1965 White House Conference on Civil Rights with Dr. Martin Luther King. She also founded the Martin Luther King Jr. Association for Non-Violence after his assassination. Known as a master fundraiser, she worked hard on the campaigns of a number of black candidates including Jesse Jackson.

In 1971, Mrs. Tucker was named Secretary of the Commonwealth of Pennsylvania, the first African-American to hold that office, making her the highest ranking black woman in the Pennsylvania state government. Tucker also was responsible for more women judges and African-Americans being appointed to boards and commissions by the Governor. She was also instrumental in implementing an affirmative action program in the state, and as Chief of Elections of Pennsylvania she helped institute voter registration by mail and the reduction of the voting age from 21 to 18.

Although unsuccessful in her own campaigns for political office, Tucker headed the minority caucus of the Democratic National Committee, was a founding member of the National Women's Caucus, chaired the Black Caucus of the Democratic National Committee for 11 years, was a speaker at five Democratic conventions, and even served as vice-president of the Pennsylvania NAACP. Mrs. Tucker's greatest legacy is The National Political Congress of Black Women (NPCBW) which she co-founded in 1984. Tucker was also the founder and president of the Bethune-DuBois Institute, Inc., established in 1991 to promote the cultural development of black youths through scholarships and educational programs.

A Reflection

In 1992, Tucker became the national chair of NPCBW with the reform of the music industry on its agenda. Tucker said she was a witness to the negative effects that gangsta rap had on some of her nieces and nephews stating, *"You can't listen to all that language and filth without it affecting you."* She became a stockholder in Sony and Time Warner so she could protest the recordings of gangsta rap music at shareholders meetings. In 1994, Tucker enlisted the FBI to investigate the sale of the explicit music to minors and her efforts to protest offensive rap was supported by the NAACP and the Congressional Black Caucus held hearings on the subject. In 1994, Tucker protested the nomination of Tupac Shakur for a NAACP Image Award.

In 1995, at a Time Warner shareholders meeting, Tucker asked executives to read aloud the lyrics from some music in which the company reaped profits asking, *"How long will Time Warner continue to put profit before principle?"* Tucker saw the gangsta raps as violent and misogynistic, threats to the moral foundation of the black community, and contributors to black-on-black violence. Tucker explained her motives saying, "I am only trying to save our young brothers rather than hurt them." Unfortunately, many rappers didn't see it that way and retaliated against her, referring to her in disparaging and disrespectful lyrics in several songs.

Mr. Tucker said his wife was *"one of the most fearless individuals that I have ever known. She will take on anyone, anything, if that is what she thinks is right...I tell her there are times you have to compromise, but she is not one who will readily entertain the idea of compromise about anything."* In 1996, C. Delores Tucker was selected by People Magazine as one of the *"25 Most Intriguing People in the World."* None of us can deny the power and influence that music has in our lives. It can set the tone for the era, as the seventies music did for that decade. That is why we must be very careful in the messages that are conveyed.

The Black Church

Most notable when looking at the black church in the 1990s was the boundless racial hatred that inspired the burning of black churches. The black church has always been a fortress for the black community, standing as a symbol of strength and support throughout the tribulations that have befallen African-Americans since days of the Civil War. As the most steadfast institution for black people the church also represents the most significant target for racial attack, and in the 1990s, black churches in the South were once again the victims of arson.

According to data from the Center of Democratic Renewal, there were 80 incidents of African-American church burnings from January 1990 through July of 1996, with more than 30 black church arsons in 1996 alone. The majority of the churches burned were in the rural areas of nine Southern states: Georgia, Alabama, Tennessee, Arkansas, South Carolina, North Carolina, Mississippi, Louisiana and Virginia. In June of 1995, the Christian Knights, members of the Ku Klux Klan burned the Macedonia Baptist Church in South Carolina. Rev. Jonathan Mouzon, pastor of the Macedonia Church, convinced his congregation to file a lawsuit against the KKK in civil court and in July of 1998 the jury awarded them $37.8 million in damages, the largest ever against a hate group. The judgment forced the Klan to sell its land and property.

In 1988, the Jeremiah Project Report, written by Jon J. DiIulio, Jr., gave the eight major denominations of historically black Christian churches: the African Methodist Episcopal, African Methodist Episcopal Zion, Christian Methodist Episcopal, Church of God in Christ, National Baptist Convention of America, National Baptist Convention, USA, National Missionary Baptist Convention, and the Progressive National Baptist Convention. These black denominations have approximately 20 million members in about 65,000 churches. The Church of God in Christ, the Pentecostal denomination, was still the fastest growing denomination in the United States in the 1990s with the main expansion being in poor urban areas. Typically black people were loyal to the denomination affiliation that they were raised in, but church labels were becoming less important as new generations not fully aware of their meanings began "Church hopping" or the changing of churches to whatever or whoever was popular at the time.

Alternatively, there were a growing number of churchgoers who were choosing to attend nondenominational mega-churches where the worship was a major production versus the traditional church service of mainline black denominations. The memberships of the black mega-churches grew to the point where the churches had to be run as businesses. While the large followings have the potential to generate great amounts of money, they also consume greater amount of resources in order to operate. Tithing becomes central and members are taught that those who tithe will be rewarded financially. This prosperity gospel is the message that soothes the souls of frustrated blacks who can't get ahead without a miracle from God. The black church once a haven for poor and oppressed Black people, and an ever-present help for those in need, now serves more as a gathering place for social functions and networking, with status coming from the particular church that you belong.

A Reflection

Larger numbers of black churches were developing community outreach programs to serve the needs of their communities during the 1990s. A National Black Politics Survey done in 1992 found that 86 percent of black churches sponsored some form of community outreach. In 1996, the Welfare Reform legislation "Charitable Choice" provision included churches in the non-profit organizations that could receive contracts to provide social services. This option eliminated the 'separation between church and state' and resulted in more partnerships between the black churches and state and local governments. African-American churches were among the recipients of grant funding to distribute food, assist in housing, provide back to work training, operate Head Start day care centers, and run summer youth programs for the underprivileged. Several of the big churches like Hartford Memorial Baptist Church in Detroit, Allen Temple A.M.E., and the Abyssinian Baptist Church of Harlem were combining the government-funded social service programs with their own economic development projects (Harris).

Black Press and Media

The black magazine market was soft during the 1990s, though black magazines still trumped black newspapers in readership. *Ebony* and *Essence* led in the number of subscriptions followed by *Jet* and *Black Enterprise*. There was also a new generation of magazines born in the nineties to capture the black up and coming audience of readers that included *Emerge, Heart & Soul* and *YSB* (Young Sisters & Brothers). The printed news industry was transformed during the nineties with the explosion of the internet and declines in advertising revenues.

In 1999, there were approximately 400 African-American newspapers in the United States; the National Newspaper Association (NNPA) represented 230 of these black newspapers, an increase over the last decade, with roughly 15 million readers. In 1996, the *St. Louis American* was selected as America's best black newspaper. Competition from mainstream dailies, radio, and the internet hurt the readership of black newspapers in the nineties although it recovered some at the end of the decade. Mainstream newspapers hired black reporters and editors to cover African-American communities, but they cannot substitute the role of black newspapers. George McElroy, editor of *The Informer* and *Texas Freeman*, said, "We cover issues that the major dailies don't see or fail to see. We're closer to problems and concerns in our community. We see them first." John Smith, publisher of the Atlanta Inquirer said, "The Black press is the only source of Black perspective."

A Gallop poll done in 1994 showed that 48 percent of African-Americans were not satisfied with the coverage of black people in their local newspapers, saying that they don't print stories that reflect the lives of most African-Americans. Sidney Morse wrote in the *Pittsburgh Courier* that the mainstream media features on black people are about "*urban crime, entertainment, or sports. The positive stories are frequently about 'drug addiction recovery' or those that depict how a welfare recipient has overcome great odds to enter into the mainstream.*" Blacks feel there is slant against African-Americans in their local papers, while the black press gives another perception or portrayal of African-Americans and a more positive image.

An article written by Stephen Balkaran in the Yale Political Quarterly stated; "*As a result of the overwhelming media focus on crime, drug use, gang violence, and other forms of anti-social behavior among African-Americans, the media have fostered a distorted and pernicious public perception of African-Americans.*" Differences between the black press and the mainstream media during the 1990s in the coverage of the O.J. Simpson trial, the Rodney King police brutality trial and the subsequent riots were blatant. The mainstream press presumed Simpson's guilt and showed bias in their presentation of the facts; printed pictures were darkened to make Simpson appear more frightening. Black newspapers reported the story as "the struggle of a black man searching for justice in a white judicial system" and served as a watchdog with critiques of the mainstream media's mishandling of the story. The riots after the Rodney King verdict were portrayed by the mass media as the black community being lawless and out of control, but reports showed that only 36 percent of those arrested were black with 60 percent being Hispanics and whites; however these facts were not reported.

Black radio stations always have their finger on the pulse of the black community and served as a lifeline during times of crisis. KJLH proved to be an invaluable conduit for the black community during the Los Angeles riots in 1992. For three days the station shut down its regular music format and gave their listeners access to the air waves. Some called in for counseling and others to vent their frustrations. Nonetheless, despite the vital link between black radio stations and their listeners, a number of small independent stations went bankrupt and others were struggling to survive. Radio advertising revenues dropped industry wide making it even tougher on black stations to sell advertisements and compete with white stations that played black music formats.

It was in 1999 that Cathy L Hughes, founder of Radio One Inc., took her company public adding another to the few black-owned companies trading on the NASDAQ. After buying her first radio station in the early eighties, Hughes acquired more

A Reflection

than 70 radio stations. Hughes became the first African-American woman to head a publicly traded company.

Black Business and Professionals

The number of African-American owned businesses continued to rise over the 1990s. According to the U.S. Census Commerce Department, there were 906,500 black-owned businesses in the United States in 1997, totaling around four percent of the more than 20 million businesses in the country. These black-owned businesses employed 713,000 people and generated $71.2 billion in gross sales. Over 41 percent of the black-owned businesses were in five states: New York, California, Texas, Florida, and Georgia. Washington, D.C had the highest percentage of black firms, with 24 percent of its businesses being African-American-owned. Atlanta, called the Harlem of the 90s, had the highest percentage of black-owned businesses relative to the black population with one business for every 7.7 adults.

Generally, about half of black-owned companies adding up to about 405,200, are owned by black women. Sixty-one percent of businesses owned by black women were in the service industry, 17 percent in retail, and 6 percent in real estate, finance or insurance. These black women-owned firms accounted for 261,000 jobs, employing over 28 percent of the black business workforce and generated $25 billion in sales, over 24 percent of the gross receipts for all black-owned businesses.

One theme emphasized by the Million Man March in 1995 was the strengthening of the economy in black communities by patronizing black-owned business. African-Americans earned upwards of $400 billion each year, but the vast majority of the money left the black community. Campaigns like "Black Dollar Days" and "Talk is Cheap, Buy from Black Businesses" encouraged black people to spend their money with the black businesses in their community. At the start of 1996, Muhammad A. Nassardeen, head of Recycling Black Dollars, an organization of 2,000 black business owners in Inglewood, California, initiated the "Change Bank Day" campaign in Los Angeles. The campaign effort accounted for $7 million in new deposits in three black banks and a black credit union in the area. A similar campaign was successful conducted in Atlanta.

More than 90 percent of black businesses were sole proprietorships or owned by individuals, and more than half were in the service industry. Around 49 percent of black-owned businesses earned less than $10,000, 23 percent earned between $10,000 and $25,000, and around one percent had revenues of $1 million or more. Total sales for the

100 largest black-owned companies in the nation listed in Black Enterprise were $14.02 billion. Only 11 percent of African-American-owned businesses had paid employees, but the sales and employment numbers of the largest black-owned companies soared higher as the national economy improved over the decade. Akinola Olajuwon, CEO of Olajuwon Holdings with 73 Denny's restaurants, and brother of pro-basketball's Hakeem, was the third largest employer of black-owned businesses, with 3000 employees and $85 million in revenues.

During the 1990s, African-American-owned businesses shifted away from the expansion and acquisitions of the 1980s. Philadelphia Coca Cola was now the biggest black-owned company in the United States in 1999. TLC Beatrice International Holdings, Inc., having held the largest black-owned business title for ten years consecutive, was broken-up and businesses sold off as it restructured after the death of its founder, Reginald Lewis. Several other large black firms chose to divest in this decade, Radio One went public in March of 1999. A number of black dealers in the auto industry consolidated. Even more than a few black firms that sold black-oriented products were sold to mainstream companies, the list included Johnson Products sold to IVAX, Softsheen sold to L'Oreal, and Russell Simmons sold his remaining interests in Def Jam Records to Seagram. Conversely, Bob Johnson reclaimed BET in 1997 taking it private again.

Black-owned insurance companies were struggling during this decade amid the increased competition in the sector, the number of surviving companies dropped from 31 in 1989 to only 10 in 1999. The resilient North Carolina Mutual Life still topped the list in size and earnings and Atlanta Life Insurance was second. An article published in the Atlanta Daily World stressed the need for blacks to support black businesses in an interview with Charles Cornelius, president of Atlanta Life Insurance. Cornelius, speaking to group of black professionals was quoted, *"As a people we are underinsured, under saved, and underinvested."*

Black Employment

The employment picture for African-Americans was not a pretty one at the start of the decade with the remnants of the 1990 recession and the subsequent layoffs keeping the jobless rate in double digits. Black people suffered disproportionately in the number of layoffs, which has historically been the case in every recession because of the racism that resurfaces whenever times get hard. The Wall Street Journal reported on the uneven layoffs of a significant number of major corporations during

A Reflection

the 1990 recession. Jobs held by blacks were cut at a much higher rate than those held by white workers.

At J.P. Morgan where black employees were 16 percent of the workforce they suffered 30 percent of the job losses when the clerical and data processing operations were relocated to Delaware from New York. Similarly at Coca-Cola where black employees comprised 18 percent of the labor force they received 42 percent of the job cuts when the company decided to downsize. Sears trumped the group with its layoffs, with an African-American workforce of 15.9 percent, Sears reduced its clerical staff and closed the distribution centers that were concentrated in central cities and black employees were hit by 54 percent of the job cuts, three and a half times the rate that whites lost jobs in the company (Taylor, 2003).

Job opportunities in the inner cities were scarce during the 1990 recession as oil prices spiked during the Gulf War; more businesses disappeared from the black community leaving minimum wage service jobs or fast-food restaurants as the few options. In a number of the major cities with larger black populations upwards of 30 percent of the adults were no longer in the paid labor force, some were looking and others had given up on the prospect finding a job. Black people had to become creative to survive and developed their own neighborhood economy as described in the *"Social and Economic Issues of the 1980s and 1990s"*:

> Millions survived in the informal economy, generating a subsistence income through activities as diverse as braiding hair, childcare, collecting and selling recyclable bottles and cans, catering food, auto repair moving, producing and selling crafts, etc. for many who had once held stable blue-collar jobs,.."

Black people had to find alternative ways to earn money, not only because they were more likely to be laid off, but because they also experienced longer periods of unemployment after the loss of a job. A number of studies have shown that applicants with black sounding names receive fewer call backs from potential employers.

The economic expansion of the 1990s dramatically increased the share of blacks in the workforce. According to the Bureau of Labor Statistics, the unemployment for African-Americans peaked at around 14 percent in 1992 and then declined at an average of 0.4 percent each year for the rest of the decade. By 1997 the unemployment rate for blacks had dropped to 10 percent. John E. Jacob, president of the National Urban League argued that African-Americans weren't really participating in the celebrated economic recovery as their rate of employment was still at what was considered Depression-level for whites.

1999

Yet, by September of 1999, the black unemployment rate had fallen to a record low of 7.2 percent. According to the Bureau of Labor Statistics, around 51 percent of black workers were classified as white collar workers, of these, 60 percent were employed in white-collar sales and as clerical workers. These workers were usually non-union, received less than fair pay with limited benefit packages.

A study by Wright and Dwyer on job expansion during the 1990s found that the bulk of the jobs created were on the high end and very bottom of the job structure. Minimal expansion was seen in job creation for the middle distribution. They characterized the 1990s as a time of *"racial polarized job expansion."* The job expansion essentially created "good jobs" and "bad jobs." The lack of increasing numbers of jobs in the middle tier meant there was no upward mobility for those working in low-end jobs. *"Employment for whites expanded sharply among the better jobs in the employment structure, whereas new jobs for blacks and Hispanics were concentrated at the bottom of the employment structure."* The economic gap continued to widen as jobs were racially stratified. More minorities worked full-time jobs that paid wages below the poverty level.

The economic boom that defined the nineties was observed primarily within the high-tech industries, and African-Americans were underrepresented in science and technology occupations. According to the National Science Foundation reports, black women represented a mere 1.1 percent and black men 2.2 percent of all scientists and engineers. Jobs within the science and technology fields typically require a college degree, but blacks were also underrepresented in high-tech jobs that required only a high school diploma. Nevertheless, the lower level of education attainment of African-Americans as compared to other races was a factor that limited their share of high-tech jobs.

Education

African-Americans have made huge strides in educational advancement over the decades, but as long as there is still a racial gap in educational achievement there is still a great amount of progress to be made. A Department of Education study illustrated the magnitude of the achievement gap problem: "In reading and math scores, 17-year-old black students on average performed at about the level of 13-year-old students." The achievement gap is evident at kindergarten, and should be closed at the elementary level or by the secondary levels to prevent the "racially unequal social stratification" that we find prevalent in American society. Once black student are tracked into lower-level classes there is virtually no way of changing their fate.

A Reflection

Integration levels began to diminish during the 1990s as the courts ended the supervision of desegregation program in a number of school districts. Schools across the nation were re-segregating before true integration had even been realized. Close to fifty school districts in various states have abolished their court-ordered desegregation plans. Most schools were basically segregated with a few students of other races attending. The Brown v. Board of Education case proved that a separate education is an unequal education, and after nearly five decades the efforts to provide educational justice for students in poor communities have come full circle. Educational studies have shown that blacks who attend racially mixed schools have a better chance of attending college and black students who attend schools in affluent neighborhoods are more likely to graduate.

The legacy of slavery and discrimination has proved to be devastating for the African-Americans educationally. Prejudices rooted in negative stereotypes, inferior mentality, low morals, emotionally unstable, aggressive, and lazy have proven difficult to overcome, resulting in negative self-recognition that is passed down through generations. Steinberg (1996) contends that the achievement disparities that exist are due to the presumption of many black youths that academic success is incompatible with black identity or "acting white," but school environments can affect achievement. A study done by Claude Steele, a psychology professor at Standard, concluded that "a student who feels he is part of a group that has been negatively stereotyped is likely to perform less well in a situation in which he thinks that people might evaluate him through that stereotype than in a situation in which he feels no such pressure."

The educational firestorm of the decade occurred when the Oakland Unified School District passed a controversial resolution on December 18, 1996 to utilize Ebonics to address the serious educational problems affecting black students in their district. The Oakland School Board's mandate allowed for some instruction in the student's "primary dialect" for "maintaining the legitimacy and richness of such language…and to facilitate their acquisition and mastery of English language skills." Assuming that the school board's heart was in the right place, it's not necessary to legitimize or glorify broken English. Not all black students use the same manner of speaking. Schools across the nation have failed to adequately teach African-American students with traditional methods, but the notion that black children are speaking a separate language that prevents them from learning and Ebonics will improve teaching is beyond preposterous.

For the most part, African-Americans were moving forward in educational attainment. By the end of decade, 72 percent of all African-Americans over the age of 25 were high school graduates according to U.S. Census data. More black people were pursuing higher education than ever, in the fall of 1999, over 30 percent of the black population aged between 18 and 24 enrolled in colleges. The downside of this good report was a growing gender gap between African-American men and women in almost every category of progress in higher education. African-American women were responsible for most of the gains and black men were falling behind in enrollment and graduation. In 1992, there were 537,000 black men attending college compared to 856,000 black women. In 1998, the college graduation for black men dropped to 33 percent while the graduation rate for black women rose to 42 percent.

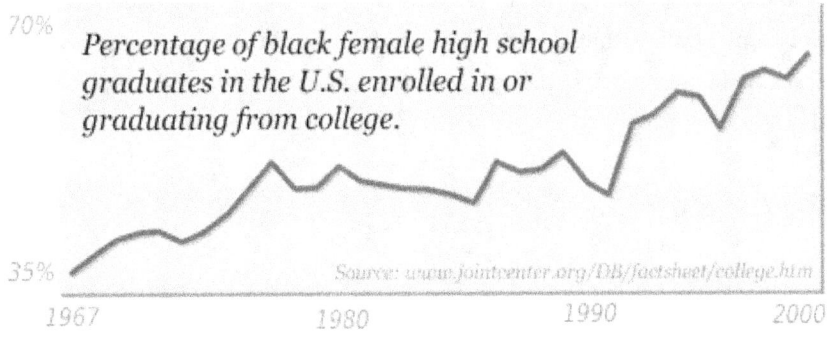

Overall, nearly 2 million blacks in the United States have earned bachelor degrees, over 52,000 have earned doctorates, and in 1996, over 1000 graduated from medical school. Moving forward in the new millennium there has never been a more critical time for African-Americans to push higher in educational attainment. The consequences for the failure to do so will be a handicapped people without the ability to help themselves. Eliminating the education gap is key to closing the economic gap, lowering the level of incarceration, ending health disparities, and stabilizing the structure of the black family.

The Issue of Crime

The 1990s began with the level of violence in the country rising and African-Americans were suffering the bulk of its destruction. The crack epidemic was still wrecking havoc in black communities across the United States and the "war on drugs" seemed to be a losing battle. Sellers, users, and thieves caught up in the turmoil of the drug trade raised the degree of violent crime in the community and the number of blacks victims

A Reflection

multiplied. The magnitude of "black on black" crime during the crack wars turned our neighborhoods into battle zones. Eugene Rivers describes the 'Nightmare' in the Boston Review,

> "Each day, 1118 black teenagers are victims of violent crime; 1,454 black children are arrested; and 907 black teenage girls get pregnant. A generation of black males is drowning in its own blood in the prison camps that we euphemistically call "inner cities." And things are likely to get worse."

The 1980s raised the level of criminal activity among juveniles. In 1999, the Uniform Crime Report stated that 72 percent of juvenile arrests were white and 25 percent were black, starkly, black juveniles were arrested for 54 percent of the homicides committed. Young black men were killing themselves over seven times the rate of white juveniles. The escalation in murder rates among black juveniles started in the mid-1980s and peaked in 1993.

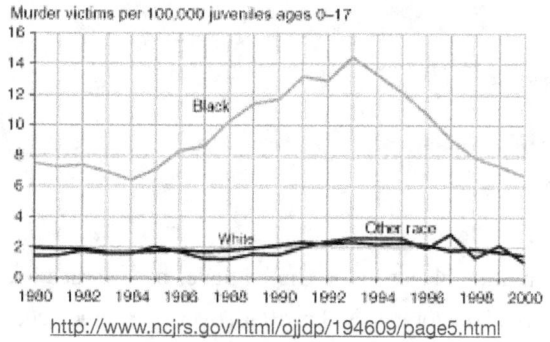

http://www.ncjrs.gov/html/ojjdp/194609/page5.html

There were two dynamics working that were decimating the black males in the large inner cities, the first was the high participation of black males in criminal activity, and the second was the degree of disparate treatment of blacks by the criminal justice system. In 1999, according to Uniform Crime Report (UCR) data, 69 percent of persons arrested throughout the United States were white, 29 percent were black, and the remainder were other races. White arrests accounted for 64 percent of index crime arrests, 66 percent of property crime arrests, and 54 percent of violent crime arrests. Granted, blacks were arrested at disproportionately higher numbers based on their percentage of the population, but were the levels high enough to warrant the face of crime to be a black one. The greatest disparity is seen between the number of arrests and the number of convictions. Blacks were convicted and imprisoned at much higher levels than whites, including black women who were being sent to prison at the same rate of white men. In 1999, African-Americans were being locked in jails at nearly seven times the rate of whites.

At the beginning of the decade homicide rates were at record highs, and blacks were disproportionately observed in arrest rates, school suspensions, and emergency rooms. Data collected by the UCR reported that blacks were arrested for 52 percent of homicides compared to 46 percent for whites. Blacks were also arrested in over 54 percent of robberies and 64 percent of gambling offenses. The total inmates sentenced for drug offenses increased 478 percent over the decade; among African-Americans the levels rose even higher at 707 percent. Blacks were using drugs as a means to earn a living, to buy the cars, clothes, and "bling" that would give them the much sought after social status that eluded most of the poor residents in the 'hood.'

Black offenders were more likely to be sent to prison than placed on parole. During the 1990s, the incarceration rate for black males increased dramatically, rising 63 percent compared to 36 percent for whites and 35 percent for Hispanics. At the start of the decade, close to 10 percent of African-American men were incarcerated compared to two percent of white men, for black male high school dropouts, over 14 percent were incarcerated. By the end of the decade, 25 percent of black male high school dropouts were incarcerated. In 1996, around 60 percent of prisoners in the U.S. had been sentenced for drug offenses, and over half of the inmates were black. Across the United States there were 791,600 black males in jails, more than the 603,032 in college, whereas three decades earlier there were only 133,336 blacks in prison. In 1996, one-third of black men between the ages of 20 and 29 were either in jail or on probation.

The improvement of the economy as the nineties progressed reduced the unemployment rate and poverty level, and the number of crimes committed by blacks dropped 60 percent. The number of arrests among African-Americans for violent crimes dropped 53 percent, and the number of homicides fell 45 percent.

The penalties for being on the wrong side of the law are long-lasting, aside from many losing their right to vote, most employers prefer not to hire convicted felons. Countless numbers of black men with potential have lost the ability to obtain adequate employment to provide for their families. Decisions made in desperation or opting for short cuts most often don't get us to our preferred destination.

Health Issues

The greatest health concern for African-Africans as the new millennium approached

A Reflection

was the health disparities that were pervasive among different ethnic groups in the United States. There are a host of factors that contribute to the racial health disparities, including levels of education, employment, and income, along with preventive healthcare, physical activity, smoking, and alcohol and drug use. A 1999 survey found that 80 percent of blacks feel they don't receive the same medical treatment because of their race. In 1999, the life expectancy for black women was 74.7 years and 67.2 years for black men compared to 77.4 among whites.

As a result of the disproportionate number of blacks suffering from chronic health issues, black churches became more active in health and wellness education through seminars and health fairs that focused on preventive measures. On February 21, 1998, President Clinton set a goal for the nation to improve the health of minorities working with the U.S. Department of Health and Human Services' 'Initiative to Eliminate Racial and Ethnic Disparities in Health by the year 2010.'

The top three leading causes of death for African-Americans have changed over the last decade, stroke has moved up to number three after heart disease and cancer pushing diabetes down to number four. Three of the top ten leading causes of death for blacks are not in the top ten for whites; they are diabetes, AIDS, and homicide. The health disparities are in the incidence, morbidity, and mortality rates, which are generally higher among blacks. According to HHS reports in 1999, deaths from heart disease were 40 percent higher among blacks and deaths from stroke-related illnesses were 80 percent higher.

Hypertension is the most common risk factor for heart disease and stroke and is definitely more prevalent among blacks. A study conducted by John Hopkins University suggested that the additional stresses on blacks, such as living with racial discrimination contributes to the elevated rates of high blood pressure. The incidences of cancer grew by 27 percent among blacks over the decade widening the gap as whites only had a 12 percent increase. Further, the death rate among blacks from cancer was 35 percent higher than that of whites. The DHH reported that black women were having more mammograms in the 1990s, and their rate of breast cancer was higher. Blacks also had a 70 percent higher rate of diabetes than white, they had kidney disease at three times the rate of white, they had pneumonia at 1.5 times the rate of whites, and maternal deaths were 3.4 times that of white mothers with 75 percent preventable, and the overall death rate of blacks between 25 and 44 was 2.5 times that of whites.

The numbers of blacks contracting AIDS increased during the 1990s with blacks accounting for 43 percent of individuals testing positive for HIV or AIDS. Black people were ignoring their increased risk to HIV and weren't taking preventive measure to avoid the disease. In 1999, black males were three times as likely to contract HIV as white males and black females were nine times more likely to contract it than white females. The number of deaths from AIDS increased during the 1990s making it the 8th leading cause of death among black women. In 1999, two percent of blacks were infected with HIV.

Health disparities between black children and other races begin early. Although there were declines in infant mortality during the 1990s, the improvement was much less among black infants, as the black mortality remained twice that of whites. The DHH reported in 1998 that the most educated black women had higher infant mortality rates than the least educated white women. About 13.5 percent of black infants born in the 1990s had a low-birth weight. Over 30 percent of black children were not immunized against DPT. They also contracted childhood tuberculosis at nearly five times the rate of white children. More that 20 percent of black children suffered with childhood anemia, a result of poor nutrition.

Black people must become more committed to improving and maintaining good health. Two of the top ten leading causes of death, homicide and HIV are preventable. The diet is extremely important in maintaining good health. Blacks eat foods that are rich in vitamins and antioxidants, it's the cooking methods that are the culprit, deep frying or seasoning with fat meat and adding gravy made healthy food unhealthy. Higher rates of obesity, diabetes, and heart disease among blacks are associated with an unhealthy diet.

Housing

Queensbridge, the United States' largest public housing development, is located in Queens, New York and has 3,142 apartments. -- Illmatic, en.wikipedia.org

A Reflection

Who would have believed that approaching the new millennium that discrimination in housing would not only be alive and well, but that it would be thriving? Realtors were still discouraging blacks from moving into white neighborhoods, landlords were still refusing to rent to blacks or demanding exorbitant deposits, and banks were still denying blacks mortgages and loans or charging higher interest rates. The further realization was that for blacks to attend better schools, have more access to healthcare, live in safer surroundings with less crime, and have more opportunities for employment they needed to move into white neighborhoods. Residential areas continued to be separate and unequal. Although 23 percent of black families had middle-class incomes, only four percent lived in mostly white or mixed neighborhoods. Most blacks still resided in predominately black areas.

The economic and job growth of the 1990s created a housing boom that opened doors for African-Americans, more blacks owned their homes than at any time in U.S. history. According to the U.S. Census, 46 percent of black households own their home and 53.6 percent were renters at the end of 1999. The Clinton administration reformed the Community Reinvestment Act and enforced the fair housing laws that prohibited discrimination in borrowing, minority access to loans increased, and the number of home mortgages approved to blacks grew by 72 percent. From 1990 through 1999, the number of middle-class blacks living in the suburbs grew to 39 percent.

Housing costs usually represent the largest monthly expense. A Department of Housing and Urban Development study found that 40 percent of renters paid more than they could afford for two-bedroom apartments. Even as the American economy improved during the 1990s, an underclass of the poor and permanently unemployed remained trapped in decrepit housing projects, doubled- and tripled-up with relatives, friends, neighbors, or were homeless as housing prices exceeded their income. Homeless numbers declined during the decade, yet the numbers were still unacceptable and half of the homeless population was black. Congresswoman Maxine Waters explained saying, *"While the rest of the nation is experiencing growing prosperity, low-income families with children are falling deeper into despair."*

By the 1990s, the time had come to admit that public housing projects were not the answer for poor and low-income housing. As these complexes aged, maintenance problems of dilapidated units overwhelmed the resources of the city and high levels of crime and violence amid the drug trade overwhelmed the residents and frustrated law enforcement. Government officials couldn't ignore the predicament or make any more excuses, public housing created more problems than it solved. A change in public housing policy was evident when the $5 billion HOPE VI program was launched in 1992 to address the critical issues of public housing. HUD awarded 446 HOPE VI grants to 166 cities that were used to demolish over 63,000 severely distressed public housing projects and to replace many of them with new mixed-income housing developments. Vouchers were provided to some residents to rent in the private market.

Chicago had the third largest number of public housing units behind New York and Puerto Rico, except its public housing authority was the most mismanaged and its highrises had the most crime and gang activity. Chicago began eradicating its most distressed public housing in 1995. Chicago's most notorious housing project, Cabrini Green, began its first stage of demolition in 1996. The infamous building had once housed more than 15,000 residents. Public housing projects in Baltimore, Philadelphia, and Atlanta were also among those demolished in the 1990s.

Family Structure

According to the U.S. Census Bureau, in 1999 there were 8.4 million black families in the United States. Of these black families, 47 percent were married-couple families, 45 percent were headed by single women, and eight percent were headed by single men. In 1999, just 40 percent of black children lived in two-parent households, more than half of black children lived in single-parent homes as opposed to only 17.2 percent fifty years ago. Black families tended to be larger than non-Hispanic white families, 20 percent of black married-couple families were likely to have five or more members and 14 percent of black families headed by a single woman had more than five members. The number of babies born out of wedlock was growing steadily; the illegitimacy rate among black babies was close to 70 percent in 1999 versus 16.8 percent fifty years ago in 1949.

The economic growth of the nineties decreased the number of blacks living in poverty from 29 percent at the start of the decade to just over 19 percent in 1999. In 1998, the poverty line for a family of four was $16,600. An estimated 9.1 million blacks, around 26 percent of the black population, were living below the poverty line. Less than seven percent of black-married couples were living below the poverty line, but 41 percent of black households headed by single black women and 20 percent of household headed by single black men lived in poverty. Nearly 37 percent of black children were living in poverty, three times the number of white children. In spite of the economic gains for blacks over the decade, one report stated that the average black household had only $200 in financial assets, compared to $18,000 for white households.

A Reflection

Family income for African-American families grew by 29 percent during the 1990s. In 1998 Census survey data, 28 percent of all black families had incomes of $50,000 or higher, compared to 52 percent of white families. The median income for black families was $31,778, compared to $51,244 for white families. For black-married couples, 48 percent had family incomes of $50,000 or higher, 67 percent of single black women households had incomes less than $25,000, and 43 percent of single black men households had incomes of less than $25,000.

The prosperity of the 1990s created the optimal political environment to pursue welfare reform. The goals of welfare reform were set forth in The Personal Responsibility and Work Opportunity Reconciliation Act (PRWORA) of 1996. The three objectives were to reduce dependence on AFDC, to reduce child poverty, and to reduce illegitimacy and strengthen marriage. Opposition to welfare reform was plentiful with Representative Charles Rangel of New York saying, *"Hardest hit would be those areas where teen-age girls have given up on the future so that their only hope is having children -- with or without marriage."* Welfare reform was successful in removing families from welfare rolls, although most were working in low-paying jobs without health benefits that weren't sufficient to cover childcare, food, and rent.

Welfare reform was basically ineffective in strengthening marriage in the black community. At the end of 1999, the marriage rate among blacks was at a record low of 28 percent, but the number of interracial marriages among black men was increasing. In his autobiography, Malcolm X said, *"The black man never will get anybody's respect until he first learns to respect his own women. The black man needs to start today to shelter and protect and respect his black women."* The purpose of the Million Man March of 1995 was to unite black men to atone for their shortcomings as men and to accept their responsibilities as the head of the black family; nevertheless, the glow of the monumental objective seems to have faded.

Sports and Black Athletes

In the approach to the new millennium, African-American athletes expanded their presence and prominence in the world of sports. Success in professional sports garnered notoriety and astronomical amounts of money for those exceptional few black blacks who had the athletic talent to rise above the rest. It seemed like the quickest route of out the ghetto to the life that most could only dream about. Dr. Harry Edwards wrote about the tendency of black parents to push their children in athletics and encourage them to pursue careers in sports. Dr. Edwards explains that black families are four times more like to steer their children towards careers in sports than white families. He refers to the outcome of this propensity as the *Triple Tragedy:*

1. The tragedy of millions of black youths in obsessive pursuit of sports goals that the overwhelming majority of them will never attain.
2. The tragedy of the personal and cultural underdevelopment that afflicts so many successful and unsuccessful black sports hopefuls.
3. The drain in talent potential towards sports and away from much needed areas such as medicine, law, education, economics, politics, and technical fields.

Despite everything, black athletes were dominating the ranks in several professional sports. In 1999, 66 percent of the NFL, 80 percent of the NBA, 64 percent of the WNBA were comprised of black players. The number of black ball players in baseball declined over the decade and by the end of 1999 only 15 percent of the MLB were African-Americans. Despite the high number of black players on the field, African-Americans were still passed over in the front office and coaching positions. In the Northwestern University Center for the Study of Sport in Society 1997 Racial Report Card, there were disparities between the hiring practices in the front offices and of the athletes on the fields in the major professional sports leagues. In the NFL, there were only four black coaches out of 31 teams, the NBA had 5 coaches out of 29 teams, and in the MLB there were three black managers among 30 ball clubs.

Opportunities for African-Americans in the NFL were growing on and off the field. In 1999, Ray Rhodes and his assistants at Green Bay became the first all-Black coaching staff in the NFL. More black quarterbacks were getting their chance to lead on the field following the successful efforts of players like Doug Williams, Randall Cunningham, and Warren Moon. In 1995, Moon currently playing for the Minnesota Viking, became the first quarterback in professional football history to pass for 60,000 yards. Drafted by the Houston Oilers in 1995, Steve McNair became the starting quarterback in 1997, passing for the most yards since Warren Moon. In 1999, McNair led the team, now the Tennessee Titans, to the AFC Championship and the Super Bowl.

There were no positions withheld from African-American athletes in the NBA, black players ruled every section of the basketball court. The NBA had more black coaches than the other major sports leagues, and the Denver Nuggets were partially black-owned. In 1996, Lenny Wilkens, head coach of the Atlanta Hawks, and the "winningest" coach in

A Reflection

NBA history, won his 100th game. The NBA had few dull moments in the 1990s; early in the decade Earvin "Magic" Johnson stunned the world when he announced his retirement after testing positive for HIV. Magic returned to play in the 1992 All-Star Game and won the All-Star MVP Award; he then retired again but returned in 1996 well after the first half of the season, then retired for the final time at the end of the season saying, *"I am going out on my terms."*

Magic Johnson helped revive the popularity of basketball during the 1980s, but the players of the 1990s took the game and its profits into the stratosphere. The 1990s were considered by many to be the greatest decade for professional basketball. The long list of "fantastic" players included Charles Barkley, Clyde Drexler, Tim Duncan, Patrick Ewing, Allen Iverson, Michael Jordan, Karl Malone, Reggie Miller, Alonzo Mourning, Hakeem Olajuwon, Shaquille O'Neal, Scottie Pippen, David Robinson, and Dennis Rodman. Michael Jordan was undoubtedly the superstar of the decade, winning five MVP awards and leading the Chicago Bulls to six NBA Championships in eight years.

The Women's National Basketball Association (WNBA) debuted in 1997, and by the end of the decade had grown to 12 teams. African-American women were the immediate stars of the new league. The first player to sign was Sheryl Swoopes, former basketball star at Texas Tech University. Swoopes, sometimes referred to as the "female Michael Jordan," won the NCAA Championship in 1993, was named National Player of the Year, the AP Female Athlete of the Year, and winner of an Olympic Gold medal on the U.S. Basketball team in 1996. A number of black women have starred in the WNBA including Cynthia Cooper, Lisa Leslie, Tina Thompson, and Lynette Woodard.

The attendance of blacks in baseball stands also fell off over the years. Still, the black players in the majors commanded top dollars. In 1991, Dwight Gooden, became the second-highest paid player in baseball when he signed a three year contract with the New York Mets for $15.4 million, but before the decade was over two second generation ball players, Ken Griffey, Jr. and Barry Bonds would earn more than $7 million a year, with Griffey being the highest paid baseball player in history. These two outstanding athletes were also the subjects of the debate over who was the greatest baseball player of the 1990s.

Ken Griffey, Jr., playing with Seattle Mariners, could hit a baseball, he ranked fifth in most career homeruns, and during the 1990s had 398 homeruns, 1152 RBIs, and 167 stolen bases. Not only did he have a .297 batting average, he was one of the top defensive players, diving and leaping on the field to make the heroic catches that earned him All-Star player and Gold Glove Award winner for ten straight years. Barry Bonds, playing

1999

for the Pittsburgh Pirates and the San Francisco Giants may not have been as popular during the 1990s, but his game was on fire. Bonds was selected National League MVP three times, selected as an All-Star eight times, won the Gold Glove Award eight times, and won the Silver Slugger Award seven times.

***

The decade of the 1990s belonged to heavyweights with more melodrama than a Lifetime TV movie. It began with a heartbreaker for me personally when Mike Tyson lost all of the unified titles, defeated by Buster Douglas by a knockout on February 11, 1990 in Tokyo. Tyson was mentally unprepared and Douglas was inspired by the death of his mother. The fire in the belly of Buster Douglas soon burned out and he lost the heavyweight championship to Evander Holyfield. Holyfield successfully defended his title against George Foreman and Larry Holmes, before losing to Riddick Bowe. Meanwhile, Tyson began his mission to win back all the titles with his win over Donovan Ruddock in 1991. Tyson was taken out of the boxing ring by a series of unfortunate incidents before returning in 1996, when he won the WBC and the WBA titles.

Holyfield and Tyson "Finally" met on November 6, 1996, where Tyson was defeated by Holyfield in the "upset of the year" amid allegations of intentional head butts by Holyfield. Holyfield became the first heavyweight champion since Ali to win the championship belt three times. The heavyweight rematch in 1997 was heart wrenching to watch as Tyson fought in frustration and during the third round bit Holyfield's ear, not once, but again on the other ear before he was disqualified, losing his WBA title. Tyson explained his action saying the bites were in retaliation for Holyfield's intentional head butts.

There were a few superstars rising in the lower weight divisions of boxing in the 1990s, including Roy Jones, Jr., Pernell Whitaker, and Floyd Mayweather, Jr. Roy Jones, Jr., named "Fighter of the Decade" by the Boxing Writers Association of America, won the IBF middle weight championship on his first try in 1993, in the next year he won the IBF super middleweight championship in the "Uncivil War" against James Toney. In 1996, he moved up in weight class and won the WBC light heavyweight title. Jones suffered his first professional loss in his title defense against Montell Griffin, but regained it in the rematch in 1997. In 1999, Jones unified the light heavyweight division becoming the undisputed champion. Floyd Mayweather, Jr. won two super featherweight titles and became the first 1996 U.S Olympian to win a world title.

African-American athletes have always excelled in the Olympic Games and the 1990s were no different. Track and field greats Carl Lewis and Jackie Joyner-Kersee returned for gold.

A Reflection

Carl Lewis won the two gold medals in 1992, in the 4x100 relay and the long jump, and gold for the long jump in 1996. Jackie Joyner Kersee gave an amazing performance to win yet another gold medal in the heptathlon. However, it was Michael Johnson, "the man with the golden shoes," who took the spotlight shattering the world records and winning the Olympic gold in the 200m and the 400 m sprints. Gail Devers, sporting long and flashy fingernails, was the fastest woman in the world, winning the Olympic gold in the 100m in 1992 and 1996. Devers won her second gold medal on the 4x100 relay team with Evelyn Ashford in 1992, where Ashford, at 35 years old won her fourth gold medal, and became the oldest American woman to win an Olympic track and field medal.

Aside from track and field, the U.S. basketball team, "The Dream Team," boasted of players, Charles Barkley, Clyde Drexler, Patrick Ewing, Michael Jordan, Magic Johnson, Karl Malone, Scottie Pippen, and David Robinson, and won the Olympic gold medal in 1992. In 1996, Dominique Dawes, the 1994 U.S. all-around National Champion in gymnastics became the first black woman to win an Olympic gold medal in gymnastics.

Finally, an African-American, Eldrick "Tiger" Woods, would take the predominately white golfing world by storm. In 1996, at the young age of 20, he became the first golfer to win three consecutive U.S. Amateur titles and the NCAA individual golf championship and was named the Sports Illustrated's Sportsman of the Year and PGA Tour Rookie of the Year before turning professional. In 1997, he won the Masters, the youngest to ever win the tournament, and received the #1 ranking in professional golf. Tiger Woods finished out the decade in 1999 with eight championships including the PGA Championship.

Two African-American teenagers, Venus and Serena Williams, left the tennis world in a daze when they exploded onto the court, Venus armed with a 127 mph serve and Serena with a powerful forehand. This dynamic duo was the first sisters to win single titles on the same day in 1999, Venus captured the IGA Superthrift Tennis Classic and Serena got the victory at the Open Gaz de France. In 1998, Venus Williams won the Australian Open and French Open Grand Slam mixed doubles, and in 1999, won the French Open and the U.S. Open Grand Slam doubles. In 1998, Serena Williams won two Grand Slam mixed doubles at Wimbledon and the U.S. Open.

Willy T. Ribbs tried to take the fast track into new territory by becoming the first black to race in the Indianapolis 500. In 1991, Ribbs qualified for the race with speeds over 217 miles per hour. Bill Cosby also made history when he sponsored Ribbs and became the first black to have part ownership of major racing team on the Indy 500 racing circuit. Unfortunately, Ribbs' engine failed and he wasn't able to finish the race, but he did qualify again in 1993. Nonetheless, even with Cosby offering to do free television commercials in exchange for sponsorship, not one corporate sponsor was brave enough to back an African-American driver. In 1994, Ribbs' Indianapolis 500 contract was released.

Black Literature

As we approached the end of the century, mainstream publishers were finally grasping the fact that black people read books. In 1992, Toni Morrison's *Jazz,* Alice Walker's, *Possessing the Secret of Joy*, and Terry McMillan's *Waiting to Exhale* were all on The New York Times Best Sellers' list simultaneously. A Chicago-based market research company reported that African-Americans spent an estimated $296 million on books in 1995. Additionally, a National Educational Longitudinal Study found that 74.3 percent of young blacks read for pleasure at least once a week, compared to 67 percent of young whites. At any rate, the 1990s was an important breakthrough decade in African-American literature, as a number of black contemporary writers with differing subject matter and unique styles "crossed over" gaining larger audiences and commercial success. Black writers were able to command hefty advances for their work as the demand for books continued to grow.

Toni Morrison pressed forward throughout the 1990s not allowing her literary success to slow her down. In 1992, she published two non-fictional works, *Playing in the Dark: Whiteness and the Literary Imagination* and *Race-ing Justice, En-gendering Power: Essays on Anita Hill, Clarence Thomas, and the Construction of Social Reality*, as well as two novels *Jazz* (1992) and *Paradise* (1992). Morrison also was awarded the Nobel Peace Prize for Literature in 1993, the first African-American woman to receive this esteemed honor. Alice Walker, another prolific author, didn't pause after *The Color Purple*, writing more novels, a book of poetry, *Her Blue Body Everything We Know: Earthling Poems* (1991), and non-fictional works that included, *Anything We Love Can Be Saved: A Writer's Activism* (1997) and *Go Girl!: The Black Woman's Book of Travel and Adventure* (1997).

Terry McMillan became a superstar in the 1990s; her books were snatched off the shelves like Earth, Wind, and Fire albums in the 1970s, because you could safely assume it was good. *Waiting to Exhale* (1992) definitely did not disappoint, as most black women at the time had read it and were discussing the finer points in book clubs, over lunch, or on the phone. We could all identify; who wasn't waiting to exhale? *Waiting to Exhale* sold 700,000 hardcover copies and three million in paperback, and was on The New York Times bestseller list for 38 weeks. McMillan's last book of the decade, *How Stella Got Her*

A Reflection

Groove Back (1996), based on her on life, renewed our faith that fantasies can come true.

Gloria Naylor and J. California Cooper were consistently providing great reading material amid a growing talented group of black writers who captured our attention during the 1990s. This group included, Tina McElroy Ansas following up *Baby of the Family* with *Ugly Ways* (1995) and *The Hand I Fan With* (1998), Bebe Moore Campbell contributed two New York Times bestsellers *Brothers and Sisters* (1992) and *Singing in the Comeback Choir* (1998), and Connie Briscoe gave us *Sisters & Lovers* (1994) and *Big Girls Don't Cry* in 1996.

There were four African-American gentlemen in the group who frequented the New York Best Sellers' list with very loyal followings during the 1990s, E. Lynn Harris, Walter Mosely, Eric Jerome Dickey, and Omar Tyree. Whatever these guys wrote, we didn't need to know what is was about or what the critics said, it had to be read. E. Lynn Harris had us hooked to his characters from the beginning, proving it doesn't matter whether the characters are gay or straight, a good story is a good story. Walter Mosely's mystery novel series had us in love with Easy Rawlins even before Denzel brought him to the big screen. Eric Jerome Dickey's *Cheaters* (1999) and Omar Tyree and his *Flyy Girl* (1993) exemplified what was considered urban fiction, where the stories "kept it real" about life in the hood and in the world of Hip-Hop.

Artists of the Decade

The postmodernism philosophy in the 1990s encouraged artistic individuality. It was a time of art for art's sake, whether the approach was avante gard, fine art, folk art, or modern contemporary, self-expression was first and foremost. Painting was the overriding mode of expression during the 1990s. There were new African-American artists emerging, and although they are not listed among the influential artists, they were enormously popular among middle-class blacks who bought millions of their prints each year. The Bill Cosby Show, with black art on the set, inspired even more black families to decorate their homes with African-American art. Popular artists included Annie Lee, Varnette Honeywood, Ernie Barnes, Charles Bibbs, John Holyfield, Leroy Campbell, Paul Goodnight, and James Loveless.

1999

"Reminisce" by John Holyfield

"I Quit" by Annie Lee

"Carefree" by Leroy Campbell

A Reflection

"Lady in Red" by Charles Bibbs

Entertainment

In the 1990s, the Negro Ensemble Company in New York was the only professional equity acting company in the United States. Most black playwrights were missing out on the bulk of money made from theater because there weren't enough resident black theater companies across the nation to stage the plays after they leave Broadway. Even though August Wilson was the most successful and among the most prolific African-American playwrights in our history, most blacks had not seen his plays. Continuing his monumental run on Broadway, Wilson started off the decade with *The Piano Lesson* for which he won his second Pulitzer Prize, followed with *Two Trains Running* in 1990, and Seven Guitars in 1995.

Black musicals were still lighting up the Broadway stages with *Five Guys Named Moe* in 1992, George Wolfe's *Jelly's Last Jam* in 1992, *Bring on da Noise, Bring on da Funk* in 1996, and *The Lion King* in 1997, but it was the play adaptation, "Having Our Say," that fascinated Broadway audiences in 1995. The production was based on the 1993 New York Times best seller book, "Having Our Say: The Delany Sisters' First 100 Years," written by Sarah and Elizabeth Delany. The play gave the oral history of their lives as black women in America and covered more than six generations. Vincent Canby called it *"the most provocative and entertaining family play to reach Broadway in a long time."*

Urban theater grew in popularity over the 1990s as musical plays mixing romance, family conflicts, drug use, with a religious tone hit the stages. The plots may not have been the strongest, some of the characters may have been stereotypical, the comedy may have bordered on slapstick, but the vocal performances were without question magnificent and worth the ticket. Michael Matthews wrote 17 plays beginning in the early 1990 that included *Wicked Ways*, *Mama Don't,* and *I Need a Man*. Matthews's productions further defined the genre and he is considered to be the grandfather of the gospel music stage play. In 1991, David E. Talbert came forward to make his mark in black urban theater with *"Telling It Like It Tiz."* Talbert followed his hit with six more plays in the decade that included *Lawd Ha Mercy* (1993), *What Goes Around Comes Around*, *A Fool and His Money* (1997) and *Mr. Right Now!* (1998-99). Angela Barrow-Dunlap produced *"Why Do Good Girls Like Bad Boyz?"* in 1997, which ran for two and a half years and became the urban theater's top-grossing stage play.

The 1990s were unprecedented in the number and variety of films with African-Americans in starring roles. The decade started off with the wide release of the movie *Glory*, starring Denzel Washington, Morgan Freeman, and Andre Braugher. The film was positively reviewed by critics, but only achieved moderate success at the box office. Denzel was properly recognized for his masterful performance of Trip, winning the Academy Award for Best Supporting Actor, a Golden Globe for Best Supporting Actor, and a NAACP Image Award.

Robert Townsend wrote, directed, and starred in two films in the 1990s, *The Five Heart Beats* (1991) and the *Meteor Man* (1993). *The Five Heart Beats*, co-written with Keenan Ivory Wayans, was loosely based on "guy groups" like the Dells, the Temptations, and the Four Tops. The film covered three decades in the lives of members of the R&B vocal group, *The Five Heartbeats*, portraying the ups and downs of show business amid the personal relationships between the group's members from Townsend's character, Donald "Duck" Matthews point of view.

Spike Lee and John Singleton were triple threats, writers, directors, and producers setting the screens on fire. Spike Lee started of the decade with the very sexy and jazzy *Mo' Better Blues* (1990), the very provocative *Jungle Fever* (1991), the very powerful *Malcolm X* (1992), the very touching *Crooklyn* (1994) and the very poignant *4 Little Girls* (1997). John Singleton exploded on the scene with his debut film, *Boyz n the*

A Reflection

Hood (1991), for which he became the youngest nominee for Best Director in history and the first black nominated for Best director by the Academy. Singleton followed up with *Poetic Justice* (1993), *Higher Learning* (1995), and ended the decade strong with *Rosewood* (1997).

A new genre developed in the 1990s based on the gang life and drug dealers of the 1980s, the first film was *New Jack City* (1991) directed by Mario Van Peebles, then *Juice* (1992), *Menace II Society* (1993), *Above the Rim* and *Sugar Hill* in 1994. There were comedies with black casts that were also big hits, *House Party* (1990) and *House Party II* (1992), *Mo' Money*, *Friday* (1995), *Thin Line Between Love and Hate* (1996) and *Life* (1999). There were some very impressive black action drama films produced in the 1990s that included the western, *Posse* (1993), the sisters were doing it for themselves in *Set it Off* (1994) and the well-written screen plays of *Dead Presidents* and the *Walking Dead* in 1995 were as amazing as their soundtracks.

Lest Hollywood forget that black people fall in love, there was the list of successful black romance movies of the 1990s, *Boomerang* (1992), *Jason's Lyric* (1994), *Waiting to Exhale* (1995), *The Preacher's wife* (1996), *Love Jones* (1997), *How Stella Got Her Groove Back* (1998), and rounded out by the *Best Man* in 1999. There were also the memorable dramas of *What's Love Got to Do with It* (1993), *Amistad* (1997), *Why do Fools Fall in Love* (1998), and *Beloved* (1998). Black actors in demand during the 1990s were Laurence Fishburne, Morgan Freeman, Danny Glover, Denzel Washington, Wesley Snipes, and actresses, Angela Bassett and Whoopi Goldberg.

The Success of the Bill Cosby Show opened the minds of television broadcasters that there was an audience for black shows, and every network wanted one. Black shows were in! By the 1990s, black people were on television morning, noon and night, and late night. There were about fifty six black television shows during the 1990s. In the morning there was the *Montel Williams Show*, *Judge Mathis*, *Judge Joe Brown*, and *Divorce Court* with Judge Mablean Ephraim. There was *The Oprah Winfrey* show in the afternoon, a long list of sitcoms in the evening plus *In Living Color*, and *The Arsenio Hall Show* for late night.

There were plenty of black sitcoms in the 1990s, the most successful shows in alphabetical order were *227*, *A Different World*, *Cosby*, *Cousin Skeeter*, *Family Matters*, *Hangin' with Mr. Cooper*, *In the House*, *Keenan & Kel*, *Living Single*, *Martin*, *Moesha*, *On Our Own*, *Roc*, *Sister,Sister*, *The Fresh Prince of Bel-Air*, *The Jamie Foxx Show*, *The Parkers*, *The PJs*, *The Steve Harvey Show*, *The Wayan Bros.*, and *Thea*. These shows

1999

were positive representations of black people with family, friends, and jobs, being productive persons in society, serving as a counter balance to the hip-hop glorification that was seen in other media. All of the shows on this impressive list have gone into syndication and helped to launch and further propel successful careers for many of the actors who appeared on these shows.

African-American comedy shows were very popular in the 90s. Two highly successful programs premiered in 1992, *ComicView* on BET and *Def Comedy Jam* on HBO produced by Russell Simmons. Both were series that featured new comedians giving them a national spotlight. *ComicView* ran for six seasons and *Def Comedy Jam* for five seasons, and proved to be a valuable spring board for a number of talented comedians that included Martin Lawrence, Chris Tucker, Bernie Mac, Steve Harvey, Cedric the Entertainer, D.L. Hughley, Sommore, Bruce Bruce, Eddie Griffin, Rickey Smiley and Dave Chappelle,

The NAACP was protesting the lack of diversity on TV in the 90s, aside from the "black shows," there was usually just one African-American cast member, "the token black," on the set of most television shows during the nineties. Dramatic shows of every genre, lawyer, cop, or doctor series had one or two black actors or actresses as partner or assistant to add flavor and extra ratings to ensemble pieces. There were a few quality made-for-TV movies during this decade, *Alex Haley's Queen* (1993), *Buffalo Soldiers* (1997), and *Mama Flora's Family* (1998).

***

African-American music went through some significant changes during the 1990s. Studio packaged music and the focus on individual performers had done a horrible thing, they had effectively killed off the tight band groups that jammed the box and entertained black people for over twenty-five years. The electric performances of these funk bands, with the energetic horn sections stepping high and never missing a note, the funky bass, and the monster drummer have been replaced with hip hop dancers. However, there was one constant, one who seemed to get better with time. Michael Jackson grew larger than life as a performer in the 1990s. His string of hit albums was extended, the 1992 Dangerous Tour grossed $100 million, and the HIStory World Tour grossed $165 million, establishing Jackson as an international superstar and a "Legend in His Own Time."

The 1990s was a decade of Divas, and Whitney Houston led the pack. Her splendid performance of the Star Spangled Banner at Super Bowl XXV was released as a single by popular demand and made it to the Top 20 on the US Hot 100. Houston continued to set

A Reflection

records throughout the decade with the single "*I Will Always Love You*" from the soundtrack of *The Bodyguard* movie, selling more than a million copies in one week and becoming the best-selling single by a female artist in history. The soundtrack from the film, *The Preacher's Wife* became the best-selling gospel album in history. Still there was room at the top, as other Divas enjoyed their share of the spotlight during the 1990s; there was the sophisticated and seductive Mariah Carey, the sultry and sensuous Toni Braxton, the sexy and sassy Lauryn Hill, and the sensational and soulful Mary J. Blige.

Girl groups had become popular again; there was En Vogue, SWV, TLC, and Destiny's Child. TLC was without a doubt not just the biggest girl group of the decade, but was the highest-selling female group in history. Group members were Tionne "T-Boz" Watkins, Lisa "Left Eye" Lopes, and Rozonda "Chilli" Thomas. TLC's second album, *CrazySexyCool* was released in 1994 and sold 22 million copies worldwide, with "*Creep*" and "*Waterfalls*" reaching #1 on the Hot 100. The album also won a Grammy for the Best R&B Album in 1996.

The hot guy group of 1990s was Boyz II Men, and was recognized by BillBoard Magazine as the most successful group of the decade. The members of the group were Nathan Morris, Wanya Morris, Michael McCary, and Shawn Stockman and all served as lead singer. Their first album, *Cooleyhighharmony*, was released in 1991 and sold over nine million copies. They had their first #1 single with "*End of the Road*" in 1992, topping charts all over the world for 13 weeks. By the end of the decade, Boyz II Men had won four grammys and sold more records than any R&B group in history with hits like "*I'll Make Love to You*" and "*One Sweet Day*."

The nineties music varied with the different genres, R&B, soul, pop, hip hop, rap, and even gospel merging in an assortment of unique styles. Janet Jackson was one who successful blended R&B and hip hop and was ranked as the second most successful artist of the decade. Babyface, R. Kelly, Aaliyah, Missy Elliot, Jodeci, OutKast, Mary Mary, and Kirk Franklin were other artists who found a niche by fusing different music genres.

What we now know as neo-soul, a mix of jazz soul, and hip hop was developing towards the end of the decade with artists like Erykah Badu, the "First Lady of Neo-Soul." Badu released her first album *Baduizm* in 1998, which went triple platinum and won two Grammys in 1998. Lauryn Hill, a member of the famed group, The Fugees, launched her solo career with the release of "*The Miseducation of Lauryn Hill*" in 1998. The album, a commercial and critical success, won five Grammy Awards including Album of the Year. Maxwell, should have his photo by the word neo-soul in the dictionary, his single *"Fortunate"* was the #1 R&B single of 1999 in Billboard.

Rap music was becoming more popular among young blacks. The rappers of the 1990s included MC Hammer, Salt-n-Pepa, Will Smith a.k.a. the Fresh Prince, Queen Latifah, Heavy D, Tupac "2Pac" Shakur, Snoop Doggy Dogg, Dr. Dre, Notorious B.I.G., Jay-Z, Nas, DMX, and Eve. Nevertheless, great controversy brewed in the world of black music as rap metamorphosed into gangsta rap. The genre had crossed the line in the promotion of violence, the degradation of black women, profanity, drugs, and the thug life. C. Delores Tucker led a group of high profile activists in a fight to boycott gangsta rap artists.

Memorable Moments

On February 11, 1990, Mike Tyson, the undisputed Heavyweight Champion of the World, was knocked out by Buster Douglas in Tokyo.

In 1991, Sharon Pratt Dixon Kelly was the first black woman mayor of a major U.S. city in Washington, DC.

In 1991, President George H. Bush appointed Clarence Thomas to the US Supreme Court to replace Thurgood Marshall becoming the Court's second African American.

In 1992, Carol Mosely-Braun became the first female African-American elected to the U.S. Senate.

In 1992, Mae Carol Jemison, a physician and astronaut, became the African-American woman to travel in space as a member of the space shuttle Endeavor crew.

In 1995, the Mississippi Senate voted to abolish slavery, Mississippi had been the only state that never ratified the 13th Amendment to the Constitution in 1865.

In 1995, Florence Griffith Joyner was inducted into the USA Track and Field Hall of Fame.

In 1996, Special Olympics athlete Loretta Claiborne is honored with ESPN's ESPY Arthur Ashe Award for Courage. Born partially blind, Ms Claiborne ran in 25 marathons, placing twice among the top 100 women in the Boston Marathon, and carried the torch in the International Special Olympics where she has won medals in dozens of its events.

Tupac Shakur died on Friday, September 13, 1996 from gunshot wounds he received on September 7, 1996.

Bill Clinton gave a national apology to the victims of the Tuskegee Syphilis Experiment in 1997.

Wynton Marsalis was the first jazz musician to the win the Pulitzer Prize for Music for *Blood on the Fields* in 1997.

A Reflection

Marion Jones becomes the first woman in 50 years to win three events at the US Track & Field Nationals in 1997 and 1998.
Serena Williams won the U.S. Open Championship on September 10, 1999, the first African-American to win since Althea Gibson in 1958.
Muhammad Ali was crowned "Sportsman of the Century" by Sports Illustrated in 1999

Reflections on the Decade

Assessing the after-effects of the whirlwind decade that ended in 1999 is comparable to the morning after Mardi Gras or a big celebration, there were some great moments, but what had we accomplished and where do we go from here. There was quite a bit of distance ahead to get to the appointed destination and African-Americans were traveling without a map or GPS. As we prepared to move into the new millennium it seemed that we were still at the low end of the totem pole with very serious issues that continued to have profound effects on our growth and progress as a people, however, examination of these problems and concerns showed that most were preventable or at least manageable with some discipline.

The catalyst for change during the 1990s was a much improved economy that energized the economic circumstances of the black community and generated new momentum in the progress towards equality in America. The unemployment rate among blacks had plummeted to seven percent by the end of the decade, and the financial base of black businesses was much stronger. Huge numbers of blacks had chosen to enter the military as a career option, and in 1995, 40 percent of the United States military was black. Politically, blacks had advanced considerably during these years with a record number of forty-one African-Americans serving in Congress. A democratic president who was sympathetic to the plights of the poor and minorities was a welcome respite from the rigid conservative climate of previous decades.

Black women were moving ahead in educational attainment, but a disturbing trend among black men was becoming more apparent as their numbers graduating from high school and entering college faltered throughout the 1990s. "Black on black" crime and gang violence had not been contained and levels escalated with the consequence of close to one million black men locked up in jails and prisons across the nation. Issues that affected the stability of the black family, included low-income unskilled jobs, children being raised by women as single-parents, over-crowded segregated neighborhoods filled with negative influences, and homelessness.

1999

African-Americans have historically been a deeply religious and spiritual group, but we needed to become more cognizant of the responsibility of taking better care of our minds and bodies. There have been significant advances in the overall health of black people, but the health disparities that result from poverty, a lack of health insurance, and misinformation were costing many lives unnecessarily. Out of the top ten leading causes of death for black people, three of them, diabetes, AIDS, and homicide can either prevented or managed.

In many ways the 1990s were the calm after the storm and it seemed as if the conditions might be right for smooth sailing. Black people had moved in concert as waves against a shore, and similar to the contents of the ocean, some riding higher on the waves were propelled forward, while others on the bottom were pulled back out into the abyss. The divisions between the economic classes of black people separated the black community into several groups, fractions that couldn't operate as effectively as the whole unit. Although there are common issues of racism and discrimination, inadequate healthcare, and quality education for our children, there were problems that were unique to each group. Unable to identify with the problems of other groups we became agitated and uncooperative with one another and none of our problems were resolved. The middle class rejected the lifestyle of the poor and the poor rejected the mainstream existence which they perceived as just "acting white."

Our most gifted black people were moving singularly in search of their own achievements for self-satisfaction and that's not a bad thing. As individuals we all have the right to live our own lives, but as time progresses images have become more complex and distorted with positive role models fading into the background. The absence of high profile leaders to guide was a void filled by athletes and entertainers in these years. Young people followed the lead of ball players and rappers, and they became the heroes and success stories out of the "hood."

A Reflection

2009

jd2i.wordpress.com/263-2/barack-obama-michelle-obama-and-john-roberts-at-2009-inauguration/trackback

Praise Song for the Day
Say it plain: that many have died for this day
Sing the names of the dead who brought us here,
Who laid the train tracks, raised the bridges,
Picked the cotton and the lettuce,
built brick by brick the glittering edifices they
would then keep clean and work inside of.
Praise song for struggle, praise song for the day.
Praise song for every hand-lettered sign,
the figuring-it-out at kitchen tables.
---Elizabeth Alexander (inaugural poem)

The appearance of the decade ending in 2009 was an astounding vision to behold. The diametrically opposed forces operating in the black community reached to the farthest ends of the spectrum. On one end a black man had been elected president, the most powerful man in the world and in the United States is Barack Obama, an African American; bringing the long-term dream of African-Americans into fruition. On the other hand circumstances for many blacks in depressed black ghettos in desolate inner cities had reach a new low and the ticket to a better life stayed out of reach. The majority of African Americans were disadvantaged economically, in education attainment, in success in the workplace, and in home ownership.

The year of 2009 was a year full of contradictions for African-Americans. During this time it seemed that the multitude of possibilities that had been conceded and faded in our minds were reawakened and achievable. If a black man could be elected president, then there was still hope that black people could gain some momentum and make up some ground. Aside from the reality of the turmoil left from the terror attack on September 11, 2001, the loss of 8 million jobs in the decade, the stresses of two wars, corporate corruption and scandals on Wall Street, new rounds of homelessness, and above the top violence among young black males, blacks were still asking the question: when were things going to get better?

The years leading up to 2009 had been focused on color, but not black or white, brown or yellow, or the forgotten red, it was green, money green, and whether you were one of the haves or have-nots. Indignation at injustice was a thing of the past, as black people you had better be thankful for all you had because things could get much worse. Previously shut out by prejudice and bigotry, now shut out by corporate greed and recessions. Lay-offs and downsizing were widespread, and budget cuts in the public and private sectors were taken to a new extreme. The majority of blacks, along with other poor folk, were further mastering the art of living on next to nothing. The part-time work and gas prices of the 1990s were "the good ole days." Just when it seemed there was light at the end of the tunnel everything goes dark.

Demographics

According to U.S. Census data, blacks now make up 13.6 percent of the total population; with numbers around 42,020,743. African-Americans have dropped to the second largest minority population behind the Hispanics or Latinos. The life expectancy for Black Americans in 2009 is 73.5 years, with 31 percent of blacks under the 18 years and 8.2 percent over the age of 65 years.

The median age for blacks is 31 years. The sex ratio of African-Americans was consistently the lowest of all races again with 92 males per 100 females. The majority or

A Reflection

56 percent of the black population continues to live in the South, and with the inverse Great Migration pattern shifting, the numbers of blacks moving to the South was on the rise.

Further job losses in the Midwestern cities of Detroit, St. Louis, and Chicago after the period of de-industrialization have motivated African-Americans in urban cities to move where they could find opportunities for employment. The black populations of New York, Chicago, and Detroit declined during the 2000s for the first time on record, remarkably, Chicago dropped by over 180,000 residents. Conversely, Chicago's loss was Atlanta's gain as the city moved above Chicago as having the second largest black population in the country. During the 2000s, Atlanta had the largest net gain of blacks adding 518,784 residents for a total black population of 1.7 million black residents, equaling 35 percent of the Atlanta population.

Shifts in the demographics of the black population changed the ten states with the largest black populations to New York, Florida, Texas, Georgia, California, North Carolina, Illinois, Maryland, Virginia, and Michigan. The wake in the disaster after Hurricane Katrina displaced large numbers of the black population in Louisiana and the state fell from the top ten states with the highest African-American populations. Washington, D.C. or better known as "Chocolate City" was also losing some of its flavor as its black population dropped 11.1 percent while the white population grew 31.4 percent over the decade. Gary, Indiana has the distinction of having the largest proportion of blacks in its population numbering 83 percent.

The employment picture was drastically changed from the 1990s, by 2009, 17.8 percent of black males were unemployed with 64.6 percent in the labor force. The unemployment among black men was offset by black women with a lesser 11 percent rate of unemployment with 60.8 percent of black females in the workforce. The recession negatively impacted the incomes of African-American families decreasing the median household income from 35,575 in 2008 to 33,779 by the end of the decade, down to 65 percent of the median white household income. More blacks fell back into poverty during this decade raising the number to 24.7 percent.

Mood of the Black Community

"A lot of peoples holler about 'I don't like no blues,' but when you ain't got no money, and can't pay your house rent and can't buy you no food, you damn sure got the blues."

– Howlin' Wolf

2009

Why is every boom followed by a bust? Murphy's Law of "anything that can go wrong will go wrong" was proven true yet again. The exuberance of the 90s ended abruptly and black people were experiencing the uncertainty of the 2000s. Blacks along with most of the country had gone from wanting to move higher in pay and position to just being glad they had a job. It was a time of repossession. Employers took back our jobs, banks took back our houses, finance companies took back our cars, and credit card companies took back our available credit. For some, you couldn't miss what you never had, but for those of us who thought we had made it and had gotten our piece of the rock, discovered that it had to be given back.

Race consciousness was a sentiment of the past, and black people had become cynical about positive changes or things getting better. Efforts to assert ourselves as a race had diminished. Those who had achieved high levels of success celebrated themselves with awards and accolades while those without any hopes of being productive members of society denigrated themselves in their actions and appearance. Black males wanted to be thugs, wore sagging pants that exposed their behinds, covered their bodies in tattoos, and left their hair unkempt and called it gangsta. Black females wanted attention and acceptance, dressed overly provocative, tattooed their skin, and wore rainbows of synthetic weave in their hair and called it style. We were losing our heritage, our history, our identity, and our sense of pride. It seemed we had finally acquiesced and accepted our fate as second-class citizens.

We needed a leader, a savior, someone to save us from the unemployment, save us from our indebtedness, save us from ourselves, someone to make a way out of no way. Somebody or something had to bring us back from the brink. In the midst of this perfect storm, a black man was elected president. For many African-Americans we regained our identity and our sense of pride. We were full citizens of the United States of America. We had a leader, someone to save us, there would be better days. In the following months we realized Barack Obama was not the second coming we were praying for; he was a mortal man asking for our help instead of showering us with miracles, so we soon became disgruntled.

Political Climate

"I refuse to accept the view that mankind is so tragically bound to the starless midnight of racism and war that the bright daybreak of peace and brotherhood can never become a reality…I believe that unarmed truth and unconditional love will have the final word."
~Martin Luther King, Jr.

A Reflection

For African-Americans, the George W. Bush presidency was a series of cataclysmic train wrecks. The first would be the drama or trauma of the 2000 election. The allegations of a stolen election may have been imprecise; it was more likely that the election was purchased. It takes money to manipulate voting machines, to place police blockades in black neighborhoods, and to have three percent of African-Americans in Florida removed from voter rolls as ex-felons. These actions were a forecast of what the conditions would be under the Bush Administration. The political climate during the years of his presidency was oblivious to the struggles of minorities or the socioeconomically disadvantaged. At a Catholic charity fundraiser Bush joked, *"This is an impressive crowd, the haves and the have mores. Some people call you the elite, I call you my base."* Loyal to his base, Bush policies made them richer while the poor got poorer.

For Bush, civil rights were a non-issue even though the Civil Rights Commission reiterated that civil rights issues were a lingering concern for the nation. Discrimination was still pervasive throughout American society and continued to be a barrier to equal rights and opportunities for all Americans. Presidential leadership and support is crucial to the process of protecting and enforcing the rights awarded under the constitution to all citizens of the United States. A report on the civil rights record of George W. Bush during his first term in office found that he did not exhibit presidential leadership on pressing civil rights problems, that he did not have a civil rights agenda and furthering equal rights was not a priority for his administration. Instead of expanding freedoms and equality, numerous freedoms have been limited or eliminated in the interests of Homeland Security.

Bush encouraged diversity but was not a strong supporter of affirmative action, preferring "race neutral alternatives" that don't always achieve racial equality. His signature "No Child Left Behind" legislation did not address the unwavering 'separate but equal education system' or the unrelenting achievement gap between minority students and white students and between poor students and those with means. The injustice in the law was that schools who were unable to meet annual yearly progress, which were generally high minority and high poverty schools had their resources cut. Funding for rent assistance was shifted to home purchasing programs, ignoring the fact that the unemployed don't buy houses. There was not much empathy for African-Americans or the socioeconomically disadvantaged during these times.

The collateral damage due to the slow and inept political responses to Hurricane Katrina was second only to the initiation of two unnecessary wars. Briefed on August 29,

2005 about the magnitude of the disaster that was soon to strike with the breach of the levees, Bush told Louisiana state officials that "we are fully prepared." In spite of that, it took four days for him to sign a federal relief package or send troops to assist in rescue and clean-up efforts. The government response to New Orleans was called a "national disaster." Speculation has been that maybe if New Orleans had not been a majority black city or one of the poorest cities in the country that maybe there would have been a quicker response.

Most of the policies emanating from Bush and his Administration during this decade were geared toward corporations and the wealthier individuals of the country, from the tax cuts, to de-regulation of banking, from lowering the standards for toxic exposures to the public, and Wall Street bailouts. The poor were left to fend for themselves. Yet Bush said that the lowest moment of his presidency was when rapper Kanye West declared, "*Bush doesn't care about black people. He's a racist.*" Bush said that he can't think about that moment "without feeling disgust" and it was worse than the criticism he received for the Iraq war and his tax cuts for the rich.

Hurricane Katrina

A great tragedy in the lives of African-Americans during this decade was the aftermath of Hurricane Katrina. In this 21st century, many would like to believe that racism is a thing of the past, no longer relevant or pertinent to our everyday lives, but Hurricane Katrina blew back the curtains and revealed the depths of prejudice and discrimination in the United States and reminded us that some things may never change. On August 29, 2005 the gulf shores were bracing themselves for a category 5 hurricane, a storm so strong that forecasters had predicted the levees of New Orleans would be breeched. New Orleans Mayor Ray Nagin had declared a state of emergency in the city and ordered a mandatory evacuation.

In 2005, the population of New Orleans was 67 percent black and ranked as one of the poorest cities in the nation with more than one-third of its black residents living below the poverty line. Over 100,000 residents of New Orleans did not evacuate before the storm for several reasons, some say they weren't warned of the severity of the storm in time, others feared their homes would be robbed and stayed to protect their property, but the main reason was because of the lack of money. Most of the poor didn't have cash on hand or transportation to travel. Without money for gas, food and lodging, or any other incidentals where could you possibly go? Blacks who tried to walk across a

A Reflection

bridge to other parishes to find shelter were blocked by law enforcement.

The fact that the levees built to protect the city of New Orleans were not adequate for a storm above category 3 was well-know. It would have been too expensive for the government to build levees that would have withstood category five. After the storm hit, the levees were breeched and 80 percent of the city was flooded with nearly 10 feet of water. Black neighborhoods in low-lying area were completely destroyed, black businesses were destroyed, and thousands of lives were lost. Media coverage showed people stranded on the roofs of the homes, bodies floating in the water, and tens of thousands stranded at the overcrowded New Orleans Superdome and Convention Center.

The whole world was glued to the television watching the misery of the poor people in New Orleans and horrified at the lack of urgency in the rescue effort. Blacks who lived through the disaster believed that if they were white help would have come much sooner. President Bush waited four days before signing a relief package or sending troops. Five days passed as the crowds suffered in the August heat without food or water, without electricity, without toilets, without clean clothes, and being treated without dignity. Blame for the pitiful recovery effort was passed between the state, local, and federal government officials, but all were complicit. When the evacuation effort finally began, over 100,000 were shipped on buses to the Astrodome in Houston and other cities in the South. The relief effort was called a "national disgrace."

In the aftermath of Hurricane Katrina in New Orleans, more than 204,000 homes were damaged or ruined, and over 800,000 residents were displaced. The harsh truth is that a large amount of poor blacks who couldn't afford to leave the city until they were evacuated after the flood most likely will not have the financial resources to return. Many homeowners were issued FEMA trailers for temporary housing until they were able to rebuild, however much of the insurance on the flooded homes was inadequate to cover the repairs or rebuilding. Even in 2009, it still remains to be seen whether New Orleans will again be a majority black city or whether gentrification will turn the city into a majority white one.

Black Leadership

And so we shall have to do more than register and more than vote; we shall have to create leaders who embody virtues we can respect, who have moral and ethical principles we can applaud with enthusiasm. ~Martin Luther King, Jr., Where Do We Go from Here: Chaos or Community? 1967.

At the end of 2009 there were close to 10,500 African-American elected officials in the United States, 40 serving in the House of Representatives, and one serving in the Senate. Even with this new record number, the rate of increases in blacks serving in political offices has slowed considerably. Progress among black politicians in efforts to win higher offices has been minimal. There have only been three black senators, two governors, and eight lieutenant governors. The majority of black elected officials are housed in five states, Mississippi, Alabama, Georgia, Louisiana, and Illinois, and even though Mississippi has the largest number of blacks in the state legislature in the nation, their legislature is still controlled by Republicans, a common state of affairs seen in other Southern states.

Black political leader hopefuls have to walk a fine line in garnering support for their campaigns, and it has been problematic for some, purporting the issues of the black community, while trying to transcend race to appeal to white voters. New black politicians with high ambitions attempt to stay race-neutral to garner the funding and campaign contributions necessary to win elections in primarily white districts. Commitments to black issues are definitely unpopular on the campaign trail and can alienate potential non-black voters. Needless to say, even with political victories most black politicians are more symbolic leaders without enough political clout to effect positive changes for African-Americans.

In 2004, two African-Americans threw their hats in the ring for the Democratic Party nomination, Al Sharpton and Carol Mosely-Braun. Both candidates received less black votes than John Edward or John Kerry, and less support from the black community than Jesse Jackson did in his 1988 campaign, although they were able to bring a number of issues relating to minorities to the debate. Political polls show that blacks believe that black politicians have a tougher row to hoe than white politicians, feeling they receive harsher treatment from the media and are subject to more investigations and more severe penalties for improprieties. Two high-profile investigations of the decade were of Maxine Waters in California and Detroit Mayor Kwame Kilpatrick.

Although black voters are the core support for black politicians and are sometimes taken for granted by the Democratic Party, the Congressional Black Caucus' support was divided between Barack Obama, Hillary Clinton, and John Edwards. Those members who endorsed Clinton over Obama cited their long-standing relationships with the Clintons and her experience as the foundation for their support and insisted race was not a factor. The media questioned the hesitation on the part of some blacks in their support of Obama. The answer, "he's black, but not black enough." There was this notion that Barack Obama

A Reflection

had not lived the black American life or gone through the sordid black experiences, didn't come out of the black church, so maybe he couldn't be trusted. Yet as the primaries moved forward and Barack emerged as the winner, the doubters were convinced and he accepted the Democratic nomination for president.

According to a study conducted by the Pew Research Center, the 2008 election had the biggest African-American voter turnout in our history. Astonishingly, 65 percent of eligible black voters went to the polls to cast their vote. Sixty-eight percent of black women and 58 percent of young blacks between 18 to29 years of age cast votes in this groundbreaking election, with black youths playing a significant role in this political process. At the end of day, 95 percent of all black voters put their support behind Barack Obama and he won the election, becoming the first African-American president.

Extraordinary African-Americans
Barack Hussein Obama

Barack Obama is recognized as an extraordinary African-American not only because he was the first African-American to hold the office of the presidency of the United States, which in itself was dream for all black people in this country because of what it represents, but because of the example he set in the fulfillment of his goal. There are huge numbers of blacks who have had the desire to accomplish great things, but few who are willing to do the necessary due diligence to achieve these worthy aspirations. Barack Obama is an excellent example for black people to emulate in the efforts to realize our full potential. His journey has proved that we can make the changes that we want to see by rising above our failures, moving through our doubts, ignoring our limitations, reaching out to the community, and forging ahead in great expectation.

Barack Hussein Obama was born on August 4, 1961 in the state of Hawaii to parents, Stanley Ann Durham from Kansas and Barack Obama, Sr. from Kenya who met as college students at the University of Hawaii. Barack's parents divorced while he was very young and his mother remarried to Lolo Soetoro, an Indonesian college student studying in Hawaii. In 1967, all Indonesian students studying abroad were called home after a change in power. Barack and his family moved to Jakarta, Indonesia where he attended school for four years. Fearing for his safety and education, his mother sent him back to Honolulu in 1971 to live with his maternal grandparents, Madelyn and Stanley Armour Dunham.

Barack attended the esteemed private college preparatory school, Punahou School, on scholarship and graduated with honors in 1979. Not immune to the struggles of identity that affects most teens; Obama experimented with alcohol, marijuana, and cocaine to deal with the absence of his father and "push questions of who I was out of my mind." After high school, Barack worked his way through college with the benefit of scholarships and student loans, attended Occidental College in Los Angeles for two years before transferring to Columbia University in New York City. He graduated with a bachelor's degree in political science.

Obama worked for two years in New York before moving to Chicago in 1985 where he worked as the director of the Developing Communities Project, helping to set up job training programs, a college preparation tutoring program, and a tenant's rights program in the Altgeld Gardens community. He also worked as an instructor and consultant for a community organizing institute called the Gamaliel Foundation. Before entering Harvard Law School in 1988, Obama traveled to Europe and then Kenya where he spent five weeks becoming acquainted with his father's relatives and visiting the grave sites of his father and grandfather. During his years at Harvard, Obama was selected as an editor of the Harvard Law Review and became the first black president of the journal in his second year. In the summer of 1989, he met his future wife Michelle Robinson at Sidney & Austin where he worked as an associate.

After graduating from Harvard Law School in 1991, J.D. magna cum laude, Obama returned to Chicago joining the Davis, Miner, Barnhill & Galland law firm where he practiced as a civil rights attorney. From April to October of 1992, he directed a voter registration drive in Illinois called Project Vote which registered 150,000 unregistered black people in the state. On October 3, 1992, Barack and Michelle were married and moved to Kenwood. Obama also accepted a position at the University of Chicago Law School as Visiting Law and Government Fellow where he taught from 1992 to 1996 as a lecturer while writing his first book, and from 1996 to 2004 he taught constitutional law as a senior lecturer.

Obama ran for the Illinois State Senate in 1996 and won. He sponsored a law that created state earned income credit for low-income workers, promoted early childhood education, and supported payday loan and predatory lending regulations. In 2000, Obama made an unsuccessful bid for the U.S. House of Representatives, but was re-elected to his State Senate seat in 2002. In 2004, he successfully ran in the democratic primary for the U.S. Senate race and was invited to deliver the keynote speech in support of John Kerry at the Democratic National Convention. That now- legendary speech catapulted Barack Obama into national prominence.

A Reflection

In three televised debates with his opponent Alan Keyes, Obama clashed with different views on tax cuts, stem cell research, abortion, school vouchers and gun control. In the November election Obama claimed the largest electoral victory in Illinois history, with 70 percent of the vote, and became the third African-American elected to the United States Senate since reconstruction.

In 2007, Obama announced his candidacy for the 2008 Democratic presidential nomination with themes of hope and change, emphasizing the ending of the Iraq War, increasing energy independence, and providing universal healthcare. The field gradually narrowed down to Barack Obama and Hilary Clinton and after a hard fought campaign ended with Obama accepting the democratic nomination in June of 2008. Obama selected Joe Biden senator from Delaware as his vice presidential running mate. On November 4, 2008, Obama defeated John McCain with 365 electoral votes to his 173 and was inaugurated on January 20, 2009 becoming the first African-American president of the United States.

The Black Church

The black church is the supreme survivor in black communities throughout the country, in metropolitan cities as well as urban farm towns. Come what may the church has maintained its position as the fundamental institution for black America, but the relevance of the black church in the new millennium has been debated and what its focus should be in the new millennium has been questioned. The black church has always been the author of community activism in the past serving in the frontline in the battle for Civil Rights and the war against racial prejudice, but what is the present enemy of African-Americans and what is the strategic plan of attack. Robert Gaines (2010) says that the black church must be *"prepared to address not only the spiritual and psychological needs of its constituents, but also their socio-political needs."*

The black church has the greatest economic security of all black institutions with more than $6 billion collected annually, and the most consistent membership. Gaines (2010) proposed that the black church recast education as a contemporary civil rights issue as a means to further black educational achievement. Gaines recommends that churches "harness" their political power and use it to press for equitable and adequate opportunities in the schools for black children, and use their experience and resources to directly impact educational attainment for black students. Education is still the foundation for the social and economical uplift of African-Americans.

The black church of the new millennium, though comprised in eight major Protestant affiliations, has evolved into over 400 denominations with an estimated 45,000 congregations (Burch 2002). The absence of a charismatic leader like Martin Luther King Jr. with the capacity to unite these diverse denominations has been an impediment in the efforts to improve the plight of black people in America. Many lack the courage to admit that a lot of the problems within the black community are caused by a crisis of morality in the country and in the black community. Rev. Clarence James, author of *Lost Generation? Or Left Generation! Confronting the Youth Crisis in Black America* said, "*Black ministers must take the lead on moral issues.*"

Generally, prosperity preachers have abandoned the civil rights agenda, intent on following the models of Creflo Dollar, Eddie Long, and T.D. Jakes. They are proficient in stirring the emotions but aren't feeding the spirit; they don't require parishioners to give of themselves to help the whole community, the focus is on individualism. They tell us what we want to hear, that we can all be wealthy if we just have faith, and while we pray and wait, they command huge salaries, drive expensive cars, and live in luxury homes. Rev. Cain Hope Felder, professor at Howard University School of Divinity spoke to the issue in the Los Angeles Times, "*Too many preachers have become so enamored with fame, money, large congregations, and the art of preaching as entertainment that they have forgotten their calling.*"

African-American pastors and congregations alike got caught up in the excesses of the 1990s with expansions and new construction for church buildings. According to the U.S. Census, the money spent by churches on expansion and constructions tripled over the last decade and reached $8.6 billion in the early 2000s. The easy credit of the nineties allowed some churches to reach higher and spend more than they should have. The normal competition between churches in buildings, size of the sanctuary, add-ons, and new technologies escalated. Unfortunately the mortgage busts of the 2000s spared no one, not even the houses of God. The recession took its toll on church memberships and specifically on tithes in the collection plate. Black churches were going into foreclosure and filing bankruptcy unable to pay the debt of new construction.

During the 2008 presidential campaign, Rev. Jeremiah Wright, former pastor of Trinity United Church of Christ in Chicago of which Barack Obama was a member, was thrust into the national spotlight when excerpts of his sermons were disseminated through the media. Wrights remarks seemed inflammatory having been taken out of context. Accused of denouncing the United States when he said, "…not God Bless America. God

A Reflection

damn America," and "America's chickens are coming home to roost," Wright meant that American must be held accountable for the wrongs committed in order to be a just nation, and that funding terrorism in other countries will eventually come back to haunt you. Barack Obama described his experiences as a member of Trinity by saying:

> "Like other predominately black churches across the country, Trinity embodies the black community in its entirety – the doctor and the welfare mom, the model student and the former gang-banger. Like other churches, Trinity's services are full of raucous laughter and sometimes bawdy humor. They are full of dancing, clapping, screaming and shouting that may seem jarring to the untrained ear. The church contains in full the kindness and cruelty, the fierce intelligence and the shocking ignorance, the struggles and successes, the love and yes, the bitterness and bias that make up the black experience in America."

Black Press and Media

The negative impact of the Great Recession of the 2000s was definitely felt by the print media as advertising revenues declined nearly 20 percent by 2009, but the black press was still alive and well despite the dismal prognosis it was given some 40 years ago after the peak in the Civil Rights Movement. Most black newspapers stayed afloat with the monies from local advertising. There were reprieves for the black press in 2009, one welcome and the other unwelcome. They were the boosted sales from souvenir copies of the inauguration of President Barack Obama and the death of Michael Jackson. Additionally, fifty black newspaper publishers were invited to meet with President Obama, giving them unprecedented access to the White House.

In 2001, The Gales Directory of National Publication and Broadcast Media listed 247 black newspapers throughout the nation with a combined circulation of nearly 15 million, but halfway through the decade the number fell to about 200 black newspapers. About thirty of these newspapers had on-line internet sites. The internet changed the dynamics of the black press as they adapted to the new technology. Although it increased competition and reduced print readers, the internet does allow black newspapers to address the issue of daily news updates and provides local papers another venue to reach a national audience.

The Philadelphia Tribune is the oldest continually running black newspaper in the United States, serving the African-American community of Greater Philadelphia for over 123 years. *The Philadelphia Tribune* is published three times a week (Sunday, Tuesday, and Friday) and has the highest circulation of black newspapers with an average circulation of 270,000. In 2008, the *Tribune* was again named the "best black newspaper" at the NNPA Merit Awards, having won seven times in the last twelve years. The *New York Amsterdam News* and *The Baltimore Afro-American* were ranked second and third in circulation among the black press newspapers. The Los Angeles *Sentinel,* considered by many to be the best black newspaper in the country, is the largest subscriber-paid black-owned newspaper on the West coast with a circulation of 150,000.

Even in the new millennium the mainstream press and media don't have the capacity or the will to cover the news of the black community, so the black press is still a much needed commodity. However, the role of the black press has changed somewhat, particularly as a leader or major influence within the African-American community, not because their commitment has changed, but because of the changes in black culture and the media options available. The black press is faithful and stands ready and available for blacks to discuss social and political issues and provide a forum for new ideas to address the persistent problems for African-Americans but they need financial support and loyalty from the black community. A 2010 Pew Research Center Study reported that only 28 percent of African-American regularly read a black newspaper.

Black journalists who worked for the mainstream media were returning to the black press during this decade, some as a result of downsizing and consolidation, while others wanted to devote themselves to the coverage of African-American issues. The number of African-Americans working in mainstream newspaper jobs plummeted during the 2000s dropping 34 percent according to ASNE's 2010 survey.

Black-oriented magazines grew in popularity during the new millennium. The number of African-American magazines multiplied and expanded into a wide range of genres that included Hip-Hop, health and beauty, and hair care. Nevertheless, the shrinking economy led to larger declines in advertising revenue and drops in readership and national magazines felt the brunt of the economic hit. Some publications gained traction while others have faded quickly, but on average there were about 200 black magazines in circulation at any given time. *Ebony* and *Essence* have maintained their popularity and have the largest circulations in 2009 standing at 1.3 million and 1.1 million respectively, followed by *Jet* and *Black Enterprise.*

According to the Association of Black-Owned Broadcasters, there are 245 black-owned radio stations across the country. Radio One is the largest African-American

A Reflection

radio company in the United States with 53 radio stations covering 16 urban markets, and reaching 14.5 million listeners. Tom Joyner, the ultra-popular radio host of the nationally syndicated Tom Joyner Morning Show, is also an associate of Radio One. The 2000s took radio high-tech, webcasting or the streaming of radio now goes wherever the internet goes. In 2001, Tom Joyner, founder of REACH Media, launched the BlackAmericaWeb.com website as a "broad-based effort to become a timely and credible source for news and information covering all aspects of daily life, featuring a wide array of viewpoints and perspectives."

In 2004, Cathy Hughes of Radio One Inc., formed an alliance with Comcast Corporation to create the cable satellite network TV One L.L.C. The network was produced to provide alternative black-oriented programming for African-American adults. TV One is presently the largest black-owned cable television network in the nation. In 2009, the channel's audience has grown to an estimated 51 million subscribers.

Black Businesses and Professionals

A survey of African-Americans conducted by the National Urban League at the start of the new millennium showed that two-thirds of black people would like to start their own business. The high level of downsizing and layoffs from the Great Recession of the 2000s motivated large numbers of blacks to leave corporate American and start businesses of their own. According to Census data, blacks are more likely to start a new business than whites, but their ventures are less likely to succeed than those of whites.

The 2007 survey of business owners from the U.S. Census determined there were 1.9 million black-owned businesses in the United States, an increase of almost 61 percent over the last five years. In 2009, the buying power of black Americans was around $1 trillion dollars, sufficient enough to support twice the present figure of businesses. The top five states with the greatest number of black-owned businesses were New York with 204,093, Georgia: 183,876, Florida: 181,469, Texas: 154,255, and California with 137,875. Georgia had the fastest growth in black-owned businesses, with the number doubling between 2002 and 2007. In Detroit, 64 percent of the businesses are black-owned, the highest percentage in the country.

The total receipts from black-owned businesses were $137.4 billion, a 55 percent increase from the previous survey in 2002. African-American companies accounted for 7.1 percent of the nation's businesses and less than one percent of total employees. Most of the black businesses, 1.8 million or 94.4 percent, were enterprises without employees, where the owner was the only paid employee. These concerns generated $38 billion in revenues, a 69 percent increase from 2002; however, 87 percent of black-owned businesses had total sales less than $50,000. Only 5.6 percent of black-owned firms were employer businesses, but they accounted for 17.9 percent of the gross receipts earned by black businesses. Of these 106,770 employer firms, there were 920,198 employees, earning $98.9 billion in receipts with a $23.9 billion total payroll.

Black-owned businesses benefit the black community through the hiring of black workers, specifically the poor from inner cities. The largest percentages, 37.6 percent, of black-owned businesses were in healthcare, maintenance, personal, and laundry concerns with average gross receipts of $21,270. Thomas Boston (2006) found that the most successful black-owned businesses in Atlanta during the 1990s were located in the lowest income areas. He also clarified that black businesses employ blacks in higher skilled positions with higher pay than white-owned businesses. Boston also predicted that 8.6 percent of African-Americans will be employed by black-owned businesses in 2010.

A recent study revealed that the credit tightening of the 2000s caused 80 percent reductions in the lending to black-owned businesses in some parts of the United States. African-American businesses weren't able to access the necessary funding to run their operations and make payroll, or start new businesses. On June 15, 2009, empowered by President Obama, the Small Business Administration launched the "America's Recovery Capital" program. The ARC gave banks and credit unions 100 percent guarantees for loans of up to $35,000 made to small businesses. This should prove as a major boost to black-owned businesses that could borrow at no interest, make no payments in the first year, and have five years to repay the loan.

The economic crises in the banking, housing, and automotive markets negatively impacted black businesses during the decade. The top 100 black-owned businesses listed in *Black Enterprise* showed a 12.53 percent drop in revenues down to $17.9 billion and reductions in payroll to 67,937. Severe bleeding in the auto industry among the "big three" in Detroit caused the closure of about 900 dealerships. Financially, 2008 was so depressing that *Black Enterprise* decided not to name an Auto Dealer of the Year in 2009.

Beginning in January of 2009, an African-American couple living in Oak Park, Illinois, Maggie and John Anderson, decided to only make purchases with black-owned businesses for a year. This endeavor was called the "Empowerment Experiment" and was initiated to encourage more black consumers to support the black community by patronizing only black-owned establishments, reinvesting, recycling, and spending

A Reflection

their dollars to increase economic growth and job creation in underserved black neighborhoods. Twenty families joined in the yearlong effort and after four months Maggie Anderson remarked, *"We kind of enjoy the sacrifice because we get to make a point... but I am going without stuff and I am frustrated on a daily basis. It's like, my people have been here 400 years and we don't even have a Walgreens to show for it."*

Black Employment

The new millennium started on an upswing in the employment of African-Americans from the momentum of the economic expansion of the 1990s. The number of blacks in the labor force had reached a record high. The labor force participation for black men had surged to 74.2 percent. According to data released by the U.S. Bureau of Labor Statistics, the unemployment rate for blacks was 8 percent. Unfortunately, the economic rebound was temporary as another recession struck in the first quarter of 2001. The National Association of Manufacturers announced that another 2.6 million manufacturing jobs were lost nationwide from July 2000 to July 2003. This was more devastating for the black population who were disproportionately concentrated in manufacturing positions. The unemployment of blacks began climbing without pause reaching 11.8 percent in 2005, and as usual, twice the unemployment rate for whites.

African-Americans again walked hand in hand with adversity, a relationship that seemed unbreakable as the economic gains from the 1990s were reversed. The stability of the black community relied on strong job and wage growth and the jobless recovery didn't bode well for the future progress of African-Americans. In 2004, black males were again suffering the most, as half of the black men in their twenties were unemployed. According to the Department of Labor Statistics, the unemployment levels for blacks at the end of the recession were over 16 percent, and once again nearly double the 9.1 percent for the total population. Unemployment levels for blacks rise earlier than other races, faster than other races, and are more prolonged than any other races.

According to U.S. Census data, the median wages for black workers fell by $3 compared to $1 for all American workers. Additionally, the impact on weekly wages was different among gender; black men saw a decline of 3.4 percent in their weekly wages from 2000 to 2007 while black women saw a 2.6 percent increase. The median hourly wage for black men in 2007 was $13.47 and $12.23 for black women and the sentiment spreading throughout the black community among the employed was "just be glad you have a job." Hard times would only get worse as the Great Recession began in 2007 without blacks having experienced much relief in jobs or wages. The gap in the median annual income between African-Americans and whites was $22,000 in 2009, with blacks earning $.60 for every dollar whites earned.

Blacks were still disproportionately employed in industries that experience the brunt of the economic crisis, the automotive sector, manufacturing, and retail. Halfway through 2009, with the nation still in recession, the unemployment rate among African-Americans rose nine points during the year and stood at 16 percent. According to the Bureau of Labor Statistics in 2008, black women now exceeded black men in employment totaling more than 54 percent of blacks currently employed, but black women still earned less than employed black men. Black political and civil rights leaders frustrated over what they perceived as President Obama's lack of attention on the joblessness of African-Americans confronted the White House saying, "It's time to end the jobs crisis in the black community." President Obama responded saying:

> "But we're going to have a hole that we have to dig out of for a long time, and it has to do with structural impediments to opportunity that we are going to continue to try to knock down. But it's not going to happen in one year; it's going to take not just one term, but it's going to take years. The important point is that we're moving in the right direction."

The problem of persistent black unemployment has been blamed on the lack of training and education among African-Americans, but this has proven not to be the only explanation as unemployment for blacks is now an issue at every educational level. College educated and professional blacks are too suffering unemployment levels that are much higher than whites. At equal educational attainment there are still disparities in unemployment. The reality has not changed much over the decades and prejudices and discrimination are still factors in hiring and firing. The nation cannot afford to disregard institutionalized racism and must enforce anti-discrimination practices and revive affirmative action if there is to be reasonable measures of improvement in job creation and hiring to resolve the high rates of unemployment for black people in America.

Education

Considering the advancement of education for African-Americans in 2009, is the glass half empty or is it half full? Evaluating how far black people have traveled in education attainment is relative to the starting point of the journey and the pace of the progression.

A Reflection

One hundred years ago, 30 percent of the black population was illiterate, even fifty years ago the median grade for blacks was 9th grade with only 12 percent of black males and 15.5 percent of black females graduating from high school. Tremendous progress has been made, but has the pace of progression been enough? Presently, 80 percent of black children in the 4th, 8th, and 12th grades don't have the reading or math skills for their grade level. The majority of black students attend schools in high-poverty neighborhoods where student achievement is low. School districts across the nation offer high quality "magnet" schools as alternatives but funding is not always guaranteed.

Living in low-income urban areas doesn't supply an abundance of academic role models, and low expectations of success are the norm. Hopelessness and negativity breed more hopelessness and negativity. More black youths are rejecting the pursuit of academic excellence and viewing it as "acting white" fueling the vicious cycle of failure. Many young black students don't see education as a viable option for them or believe it's necessary for them to be successful or attain their goals; they have unrealistic aspirations without any foundation.

> "Forty years of research shows that the single most important prediction of academic achievement is the socioeconomic status of the family a child comes from, and the second most important predictor is the socioeconomic makeup of the school she attends." ~ Richard Kahlenberg, 2007.

Black students are graduating from high school in higher percentages, but they are still twice as likely to drop out as white students. Black females graduate from high school at a 10 percent higher rate than black males. In 2007, the NCES reported the graduation rate of African-Americans at 80 percent. The Common Core of Data (CCD), which excludes the General Educational Development (GED), reports the 2009 graduation rate for African-Americans as 63.5 percent with 449,261 graduates. Exclusion of GED awards from graduation rates gives a truer picture of the education attainment and academic circumstances for African-Americans.

One hundred years ago, black children filled one-room school houses anxious to learn to read, fifty years later, they were fighting to attend quality schools, today, so many black youths are choosing to dropout. The GED is disproportionately used by blacks and Hispanics in lieu of achieving a high school diploma, with more than 10 percent of GEDs being earned within the prison system. Students earning the GED distort the number of high school diplomas awarded when there is a distinct difference between the two credentials. Less than 50 percent of black males earn a high school diploma. Counting the number of GEDs earned by African-Americans along with high school graduates suggests that blacks are closing the gap on graduation rates, even though black males are twice as likely to have a GED instead of a high school diploma.

As in previous decades, more than half of black high school graduates are not prepared for college, algebra is typically the highest level of math completed, over 30 percent don't take science courses after general biology, and only around 11 percent opt to take an advanced course in the sciences. Less than 24 percent of all black high school students take an advanced English course. In 2008, 32.6 percent of 18- to 24-year-old blacks were pursuing higher education. The U.S. Department of Education data showed that 2,584,500 African-Americans were enrolled in degree granting educational institutions, comprising 13.5 percent of the total enrollments in higher education. About 14 percent of African-American students were enrolled in HBCUs.

According to the U.S. Department of Education, 142,420 blacks earned four-year degrees in 2006, the highest number in the nation's history, up 25 percent from 2000. Blacks increased their gains in earning bachelor and master's degrees during the 2000s, but there was a decline in number of professional and doctorate degrees earned. The persistent problem is the low college graduation rate for black students, only 40 percent earn their degrees within six years. The most common reason for black students dropping out of college is the lack of money. Financial aid is insufficient to pay for tuition and living expenses.

Black women were excelling academically, earning 94,341 of the degrees in 2006, almost double the number earned by black men, even though black men had increased their number of degrees earned over the last decade by 40 percent. Business management was still the most popular major among black students in this decade, 25.4 percent of the degrees awarded for this field were awarded to blacks. Blacks also earned over 23 percent of the degrees awarded in public administration, but they earned less that 8 percent of the degrees awarded in the science, technology, engineering, and mathematics fields (STEM). The top three fields that black students majored in 2009 were business management, social sciences, and the health sciences.

African-Americans earned 58,976 master's degrees in 2006, up 64 percent from the 2000 number, and close to 10 percent of the total master's degrees awarded. Alas, black women again surpass the black men, earning 42,017 master's degrees, 71 percent of those awarded to African-Americans. The most sought after master's degree was in education, and black's

A Reflection

earned 31 percent of those degrees. Business management was second, and blacks earned 30 percent of those master's degrees. Blacks earned about 7 percent of the degrees awarded in the professions of medicine, dentistry, and law. Nearly half of the 6,223 professional degrees earned by African-Americans were in law, and black women earned 63 percent of all the professional degrees earned by African-Americans. By the end of the decade, blacks earning doctorates were at an all time high.

The Issue of Crime

One hundred years ago, African-Americans were being terrorized and lynched by white supremacy groups to keep them from "getting out of their place." Fifty years ago blacks were fighting at the pinnacle of the Civil Rights Movement, suffering attacks and beatings from racist individuals, racist groups, and law enforcement. In 2009, we have become our own worst enemy, victimizing and terrorizing our own communities. Black people are the most likely to be victimized by violent crimes. Black men are the most likely to be the victims of crime, members of low-income households are more likely to be the victims of violent crime, teenagers are at the greatest risk for violent crime, and poor black neighborhoods or ghettos have the highest crime rates. Poverty and desperation walk hand in hand and lead so many to self-destruction.

The debate on whether African-Americans have a higher propensity to commit crimes or are simply overloaded with mitigating risk factors still rages on. Attempts to understand why black crime is so rampant in the black community requires an examination that goes deep beyond the surface. The reasons for higher crime rates among blacks point to a number of risk factors. A few risk factors are high school dropout, unemployment, single parent, and poor neighborhood. High dropout rates are seen among the majority of black males who commit crimes. Joblessness is an issue for black males, single-parent homes have been increasing over four decades, and black men place less importance on marriage. There is also a culture of crime that exists in poor black communities, where criminal behavior from black males is expected and accepted. High educational achievement, gainful employment, high levels of aspirations, two parent homes, and marriage are some of the deterrents to criminal behavior.

In 2009, the FBI Uniform Criminal Report data showed close to 70 percent of adult arrests were whites and 28 percent were blacks. In four categories of crime, blacks were arrested in higher numbers than whites, 49.3 percent of murders, 55.5 percent of robberies, 54.7 percent in suspicion, and 68.6 percent in gambling. Among juvenile arrests, 66 percent were white and 31 percent were black. Black juveniles were arrested in 51.6 percent of violent crimes, 58 percent of murders, and over 67 percent of robberies. Historically, blacks are convicted at higher rates than whites and receive higher sentences for similar crimes.

The numbers of African-American males in prison declined over the 2000s but remain at disproportionate levels. In 2009, according to the U.S. Bureau of Justice Statistics, African-Americans accounted for 39.4 percent of the total prison population with 905,800 blacks incarcerated in federal prisons and local jails, 841,000 men and 64,800 women. Almost 3 percent of the entire black population was in prison. Many of the states where black prisoners make up the majority are located in the South. The states with the largest black prison populations were Maryland with 77 percent, being followed by Louisiana with 76 percent, and Mississippi at 75 percent. Wisconsin had a mere 6 percent black population but 48 percent black prison population.

Although the murder rate has declined by 65 percent since the 1993 peak, homicides and gun violence are serious issues for the black community with 94 percent of black victims of homicide being killed by another black. Nearly half of the total murder victims in the U.S. were black, and homicide is still the leading cause of death for black males aged 15 to 24 years. Juvenile street gangs and drug dealing are the source of most of the violence. According to the National Youth Gang Survey Analysis, 35 percent of gang members are black.

Youth homicide rates, 1969 - 2007

http://www.hrsa.gov/healthit/images/mchb_youthmortality_pub.pd

The consensus among blacks is that the criminal justice system is biased against them. While black neighborhoods are the most policed, they are the most dangerous and

A Reflection

least protected areas. Black Americans are more likely to be arrested, prosecuted, and convicted. Blacks are also least likely to receive parole than whites, are more likely to get a death sentence, and are more likely to be executed.

Health Issues

According to the Centers for Disease Control and Prevention (CDC), nearly 14 percent of African-Americans of all ages are in fair or poor health. Research done by the Joint Center for Political and Economic Studies in 2009, found that blacks are much more likely to suffer higher rates of catastrophic illness and disease than whites, much less likely to obtain basic drugs, preventive screening, tests, and surgeries. Blacks are more likely to have slower recoveries, and die at an earlier age. Studies have shown that when blacks do receive treatment the care is more likely to be substandard to that of whites. Mortality rates for all Americans have declined, but the rates for blacks are still higher than those for whites. The health of black people is not what it should be, but we have come a long way, life expectancy for blacks one hundred years ago in 1909 was 33 years, the life expectancy for Africa-Americans today is 73.6 years, 70 years for black men and 76.8 for black women.

In 2007, 49 percent of blacks have employer-sponsored insurance and 23.8 percent have public health insurance. Over 19 percent of blacks under the age of 65 years don't have health insurance coverage which lessens their access to healthcare forcing them to use emergency rooms as substitutes for doctors or clinics for non-emergency health care. CDC health reports from 2009 show that the number of blacks with reduced access to medical care, prescription drugs, and dental care doubled over the last two decades. Hospitalization for blacks with diabetes, hypertension, and congestive heart failure has risen because of improper medical maintenance. A national study done in 2009, requested by the Connecticut NAACP, showed that African-Americans are hospitalized at much younger ages for chronic and acute conditions that are preventable with proper healthcare.

The leading causes of death for blacks, heart disease, cancer, and stroke, have not changed over the last decade and deaths from heart disease and stroke were twice that of whites. Thirty-nine percent of black men and 44 percent of black women have been diagnosed with high blood pressure. Black people are less likely to have a regular doctor, diet, or exercise. There are several risks factors that negatively impact the health of black people and several of those factors can be reduced or eliminated. In 2009, 25 percent of black men and 18 percent of black women currently smoked cigarettes.

Obesity has become a serious health issue for all Americans, particularly for the black community. In 2009, the Office of Minority Health reported that 80 percent of black women over 20 years of age were overweight and 51 percent were obese. Sixty percent of black men were overweight and 37 percent were obese. Black neighborhoods are overrun with fast-food restaurants and convenience stores with an abundance of fried foods and sugared drinks. Black people are also less likely to engage in physical activity. Black children too are more likely to be obese than other races. Obese children and adolescents have an increased risk for developing cardiovascular problems including high blood pressure, diabetes, and high cholesterol. School programs have revamped their lunches to educate children and their parents about healthier diets.

Campaigns to fight breast cancer have also gained momentum during the 2000s. Comparing CDC data over 50 years, from 1959 and 2009, shows that deaths from breast cancer for black women have risen from 27.9 percent to 31.4 percent while the numbers for white women have gone down significantly from 32 percent to 22 percent. Health professionals recommend routine mammograms for women after 50 years of age, however, one-third of black women who get breast cancer are younger than 50 years old.

Television campaigns during the 2000s were developed to bring more awareness to HIV and AIDS testing in attempts to reduce the spread of the disease specifically in the black community, HIV is a preventable disease. Although black Americans constitute only 13 percent of the total United States population, they account for 49 percent of the HIV and AIDS cases. Black males had seven times the HIV/AIDS rate of white males and black females had 22 times the HIV/AIDS rate of white females. The risks for HIV or AIDS infection were growing among the black population; the CDC estimates that 1 in 22 Black Americans will be diagnosed with AIDS virus in their lifetime, eight times the risks of whites and twice the risk for Hispanics. Poor communities have increased risk factors because of higher levels of substance abuse and incarceration.

A Reflection

Housing

There were several circumstances that impacted the housing and homeownership of African-Americans in the decade of the 2000s. Besides the Great Recession that cost millions their jobs and the ability to keep a roof over their heads, there was the gentrification of the inner cities, the demolition of distressed public housing projects, the relocation and housing of blacks displaced in the aftermath of Hurricane Katrina, the rising cost of housing and renting, and the huge numbers of blacks caught in the sub-prime lending fiasco with predatory loans that caused countless defaults and foreclosures across the nation.

The "urban renewal" and re-gentrification that began in the 70s and 80s, gained momentum in the 1990s, is now in full speed. This "white-flight" in reverse is changing the demographics of a number of metropolitan cities that have traditionally been black neighborhoods. Included in this "black removal" are predominately poor black ghettos that were located in close proximity to business districts downtown. Educated whites, many younger, were moving back to the inner cities in droves motivated by jobs, the cultural feel and entertainment, not to mention the shorter commutes in the midst of astronomical gas prices. As a result, home prices and monthly rents in urban cities have risen through the roof. Short supplies of affordable housing in the inner city forced low-income and fixed income residents to pack up and move further out on the fringes of the cities and into the suburbs. Unbelievably, the suburbs now have the largest population of poor people, having grown over 25 percent over the last decade.

The federal program, HOPE VI, planned to eliminate public housing projects nationwide because of its failure as a solution to the issue of affordable housing. Tenants in many of the housing projects objected to the plans and resisted relocating to what they saw as the same living conditions, only further out from the city. All of Chicago's public high-rises, considered to the worst in the country, including Cabrini-Green and Robert Taylor Homes, were to be demolished by 2009, uprooting over 40,000 people. The latest experiment in housing will be mixed-income neighborhoods, where the poor and well-to-do will live side-by-side. The New York Housing Authority was reluctant to tear down their public housing units opting to renovate, but in 2005 they relented and began to knock them down one-by one. The demise of housing projects in D.C. and gentrification has changed the demographics as the inner-city black population continues to shrink.

A controversial case of gentrification took place in New Orleans in the aftermath of Hurricane Katrina. Hundreds of thousands of poor blacks were evacuated out of New Orleans and put on buses to other cities in Louisiana, Texas, Oklahoma, and Arkansas. Countless others went to live with relatives in various states. The Lower Ninth Ward, devastated by the flood, with 14,000 residents, 98 percent of them black, was the last area to be re-opened. Although most residents in the Ward were poor, 59 percent owned homes that had been in their families for generations. Unfortunately, many of the blacks who left New Orleans don't have the resources to return or have anything left to come back to. HUD demolished 5300 public housing units along with scores of flood-damaged abandoned homes.

The rise in subprime lending for home purchases and refinancing exploded in the mid-1990s as a vehicle to help more low-income blacks become homeowners, but they were also very profitable for lenders. Blacks paid premiums on these loans, higher fees, higher interest rates, and greater penalties than on conventional mortgages. African-Americans and Hispanics were specifically targeted with predatory loans; more than half of the subprime loans were made to blacks from 2005-2007. Even middle-income blacks earning more than $100,000 a year were steered toward expensive subprime loans when they could qualify for conventional mortgages.

By 2009, blacks had the lowest rate of homeownership in the country. Predatory subprime lending and its higher interest rates were precursors to a barrage of foreclosures that disproportionately affected black homeowners. The "State of the Dream 2008:

A Reflection

FORECLOSED," a report by United for a Fair Economy said, *"the subprime lending debacle has caused the greatest loss of wealth to people of color in modern U.S. History...between $164 and $213 billion for loans taken during the past eight years."* Homelessness was back again.

Family Structure

In 2009, there were over 10 million African-American families in the United States. The decline in marriage among black people persevered. According to U.S. Census data, between 2000 and 2009, the number of currently married black Americans declined from 36 percent to 29.5 percent, and over 48 percent of black Americans had never been married. One hundred years ago, blacks valued the institution of marriage, over 73 percent of black females over the age of 15 were married. In 2009, married couples make up 44 percent of black families, but only 27 percent of these families are married couples with children, the lowest of all races. Close to 20 percent of black families were grandparents bringing up their grandchildren, double the average in the country.

In 1909, two-parent families were the norm, one hundred years later, nearly one-third of black families were single mothers with children under 18 years of age. According to the National Center for Health Statistics, about 72 percent of births to black women were out of wedlock. For most of these young black women their pregnancy is not a problem, and marriage is not a necessity. We're living in the age where "baby-mama" and baby-daddy" are the norm, and the traditional family is the exception.

Unfortunately children of single mothers are basically handicapped at birth, statistics show they are more likely to underperform in school, commit crimes leading to prison, abuse drugs, be economically disadvantaged, and continue the cycle by having their children without the benefit of marriage. Black families were intact and the norm fifty years ago. The answer is most likely in the moral breakdown in the country. Mary McLeod Bethune said that the uplift of the races begins at home, stating *"women are the moral role models in the home, community, and country."* Bethune saw black women as the moral authority; where the morals of black women go, so goes the black community.

A severe economic crisis dominated most of the 2000s after the Great Recession began in 2001. Rising unemployment coupled with declining incomes were straining families in 2009, particularly black families. The brief recovery during the 1990s had ended, and large numbers of black families were falling under the poverty threshold. Household incomes for black families fell by one percent each year during the 2000s. By 2009, the number of blacks living below the poverty line had risen close to 26 percent, the highest number since the U.S. Census began gathering the statistics. The poverty line for a family of four in 2009 was $22,050, and for a single parent and one child $15,030. The poverty rate for black children being raised in female single-parent homes was 74 percent.

The median income for African-American households was $32,584, with blacks making $.60 for every dollar whites made. By the end of the recession in 2009, the median net worth for black households was only $2170, compared to $97,860 net worth for white households. Economic disparities between blacks and whites have widened over the last twenty-five years, not even middle- or high-income blacks have been able to translate their earnings into greater wealth accumulation.

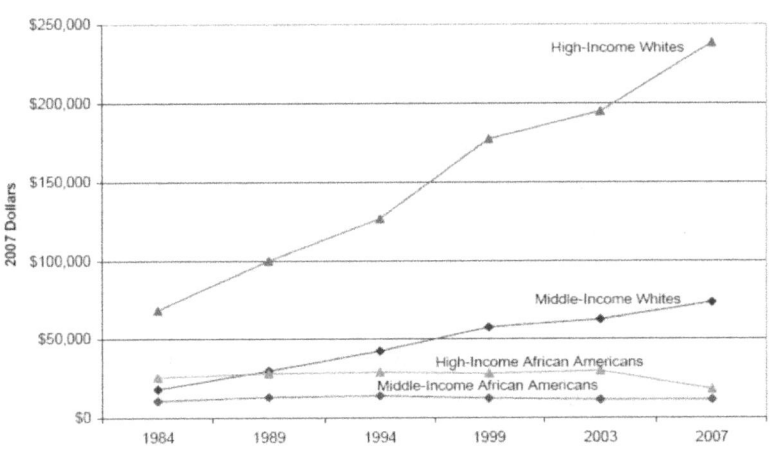

Figure 2: 1984-2007 Median Wealth Holdings by Income in 1984
(Not including home equity)

http://www.insightcced.org/uploads/CRWG?IASP-Racial-Wealth-Gap-Brief-May2010.pdf

The educational attainment level of the head of household and spouse influenced the income level for the black family. The less educated earned less and suffered greater income declines than those individuals with college degrees in the 2000s. Educational gains by black women were not being matched by the majority of black men, lowering the status of black men and further damaging the traditional black family. Black women, sympathetic to the plight of black men lowered the bar and then lowered it again in their expectations from black men. This lowers the potential for black men as human beings, as husbands, and fathers. Most of us don't require them to marry us before receiving all the benefits of marriage, a home, and children. Some of us keep them like children, feeding

A Reflection

and clothing them, stunting their emotional and mental growth. Larger numbers of black men must accept their role as heads of the family and do the work to elevate themselves educationally and economically.

Sports and Black Athletes

Black athletes in the 21st century have made tremendous progress over the last 100 hundred years. Reflecting back on 1909 when boxing was the only sport open to African-Americans to today where the sky is the only limit to black athletes shows two separate worlds. There are still some obstacles that hinder the participation of blacks in some sports, but the opportunity is there. In 2009, even though blacks comprised less than 13 percent of the total U.S. population, black athletes were well represented in professional sports. African-American athletes constituted 67 percent of the players in the NFL, 80 percent of the NBA, and about 9 percent of the baseball players in the MLB.

Black athletes have also come very far in college athletics; a NCAA report noted that 51 percent of collegiate athletes are black, 57 percent of the male basketball players, 39 percent of female basketball players, and 42 percent of football players. However, less than 5 percent of blacks play college baseball. Black students also account for 10 percent of the athletes participating in men's and women's outdoor and indoor track and women's cross-country. One discouraging trend is the decline in the number of black coaches at major college football programs, after reaching a mere five percent, the number of black coaches has dropped down to two percent. In the NFL there were now six black head coaches; Tony Dungy of the Indianapolis Colts, Dennis Green of the Arizona Cardinals, Marvin Lewis at Cincinnati, Herman Edwards of the New York Jets, Lovie Smith of the Chicago Bears, and Romeo Crennel of the Cleveland Browns.

A few wealthy black Americans were able to break the glass ceiling and become owners of professional sports teams. Deals were difficult to negotiate and many never made it to fruition. At the end of the decade, Michael Jordan had increased his ownership of the Charlotte Bobcats basketball team to 80 percent, Magic Johnson was part owner of his former team the Los Angeles Lakers, Shawn "Jay-Z" Carter was part owner of the New Jersey Nets, and Venus and Serena Williams were limited partners of the Miami Dolphins football team. Sheila Crump Johnson, former wife of Robert Johnson and co-founder of BET, was the first black woman to own or partner in three professional sports franchises, the WNBA Washington Mystics, the NBA Washington Wizards, and the NHL Washington Capitols.

Charles "The Black Cyclone" Follis, has the distinction of being the first African-American professional football player, playing from 1904 to 1906, prior to the complete segregation of professional sports, and it was fifty more years before blacks were reinstated in the NFL. One hundred years later from 1909, black players in the NFL are the norm rather than the exception. Yet, black athletes and coaches are held to a higher standard of performance than their peers, and being the last hired, black coaches are the first fired. The old adage that says blacks have to be twice as good to get in the game and stay there still holds true. Donovan McNabb, quarterback for the Philadelphia Eagles throughout the 2000s, played in the Pro Bowl six years, led the Eagles to four consecutive NFC East Division Championship, five NFC Championships Games, and the 2005 Super Bowl in 2005, but was still unappreciated and booed by the fans.

Michael Vick was the biggest story in the NFL during the 2000s. Drafted as the No. 1 draft in 2001 and signed to the Atlanta Falcons, Vick was an exceptional talent with amazing speed. In 2004, he was the first quarter back to pass for over 250 yards and rush for more than 100 yards in the same game and led the Falcons to their third division title. In 2005, Vick passed for 2,412 yards and 16 touchdowns, and was far ahead of all the NFL quarterbacks with 597 rushing yards and six touchdowns. Unstoppable, Vick became the only quarterback in NFL history to rush for over 1,000 yards during the regular season in 2006. Regrettably, Michael Vick was implicated in an illegal dog fighting ring in 2007; he pleaded guilty and served 21 months in prison. Even though Vick was technically a first-time offender, the NFL suspended Vick indefinitely without pay for breaching the NFL player conduct policy.

Professional basketball didn't exist one hundred years ago, although blacks played the sport in college, and it wasn't until the 1950s that a black player, Earl Lloyd of the Washington Capitols, actually played in an NBA game and integrated the very young basketball league. Fifty years later in 2001, there was a record-high of 14 black coaches in the NBA out of 29 teams. Michael Jordan, thought by many to be the top athlete of the 21st century retired for the third and final time in 2003. Jordan's retirement was a setback for the NBA, more than a franchise player; he was an ambassador for the game, and his absence impacted TV rating and stadium attendance. Nevertheless, the show did go on with feats of players that included Kobe Bryant, Shaquille O'Neal, Kevin Garnett, Dwight Howard, Dwayne Wade, and Lebron James.

The WNBA was the first women's professional sports team to last for ten straight seasons. Sheryl Swoopes, known for her great defensive play and having won three MVP

A Reflection

Award, three Olympic gold medals, four WNBA titles, was named WNBA Player of the Decade. Honorable mention also goes to Lisa Leslie who retired in 2009, winner of three MVP Awards, two WNBA Championships, and four consecutive Olympic gold medals. In 2008, Candace Parker was named AP Female Athlete of the Year Award after her second NCAA Women's basketball championship playing for Tennessee, and was drafted by the WNBA. Parker became the first player to win Rookie of the Year, MVP, and an Olympic gold medal in the same year.

African-American participation in the sport of baseball is coming full circle. In the early 1900s, blacks had been eliminated from profession of baseball by Jim Crow laws, and in 1909, Rube Foster at the end of an exemplary playing career, conceived the idea of a black baseball league. Fifty years later, the last game in the Negro American League had been played and major league baseball had been integrated. The proportion of blacks playing professional baseball was around 11 percent, similar to the number of blacks in the overall population. By 2009, the number of black players in the Major Leagues had declined to a 25-year low of nine percent. In 2005, the Houston Astros had no African-Americans on its roster, and in 2007, C.C. Sabathia and Dontrell Willis are the only two black pitchers on a big-league starting rotation.

One major event in profession baseball during the 2000s, but not without its controversy, was Barry Bonds' chase to break the all-time career homerun record. Playing for the San Francisco Giants, Bonds surpassed Henry "Hank" Aaron's National League homerun record of 733 homeruns on September 23, 2006. On August 7, 2007, Bonds broke Hank Aarons' all-time career homerun record with his 756th homerun. Bonds became a free agent in 2007, but at the end of 2009 he had not been signed or officially retired with 762 home runs.

***

The perpetual popularity of the sport of boxing in the United States seemed to wilt in the 2000s. The glamour division, the heavyweights, lacked a fierce but charismatic contender to excite the fans. Tyson floundered in the 2000s unable to stage a comeback and retired in 2006, Holyfield hadn't given up the fight but his strongest opponent was his age. One hundred years ago in 1909 there was a desperate search to find the "Great White Hope" to take the heavyweight title away from the brash and defiant, yet unconquerable Jack Johnson. Fifty years ago in 1959, Floyd Patterson reigned as champion, but in 2009, without a strong and tough black heavyweight contender, the boxing crown has been regrettably relinquished.

In the lower weight divisions, Sugar Shane Mosely won, lost, and re-won the WBC welterweight title, Roy Jones, Jr. continued his grudge matches against Bernard Hopkins and Antonio Tarver, but it was Floyd Mayweather who stood in the spotlight during the 2000s. Currently the welterweight champion, Floyd was the product of a professional boxing family, a father and two uncles. Mayweather was already a three time winner of the Golden Gloves before winning seven world titles in five divisions and the lineal championship in three different weight classes. The winner of numerous boxing accolades, Floyd Mayweather remains undefeated with a record of 42 wins, 26 by knockout, and is rated as the best pound for pound boxer in the world.

International competition has consistently served as a platform for African-American athletes to showcase their talent in sports. Although Jamaican athletes were giving African-American track and field competitors a run for their money, Maurice Green was the fastest man in the world at the start of the decade. In 2002, Vonetta Flowers was the first black athlete to win gold medal in the Winter Olympics competing in the bobsled. Joanna Hayes won the 100m hurdles and Lisa Leslie led the women's basketball team to another gold medal in 2004. One hundred years ago John Baxter won the first gold medal by a black person in the 1908 Olympic Games in the 440-yard dash, and in 2008, LeShawn Merritt won the 400 m gold medal of the Olympic Games.

There is no question that Marion Jones was a phenomenal athlete. No doubt born to run, Jones was the fastest female in history, had won both the USA Championship and World Championships in the 100m sprint, and the Jesse Owens Trophy Award by the age of 22. Always in fast-forward, she set her sights on winning five gold medals at the 2000 Olympic Games in Sydney, Australia in the 100m, 200m, 400m relay, 1600m relay, and the long jump. Jones did win five Olympic medals, three gold and two bronze, a remarkable feat never achieved by a female athlete before. Sadly, Marion Jones was stripped of these medals after her 2007 admission of using performance enhancing drugs.

Tiger Woods continued to astound the world of golf throughout the decade, having won 95 tournaments. In 2001, winning his second Masters, Woods became the first to hold all four professional championships simultaneously, including the PGA Championship and the U.S. Open, where he achieved "the greatest performance in golf history" according to *Sports Illustrated*. Woods went on to win a total 71 PGA Tour events and became the youngest golfer to the win the golf Grand Slam. He rounded out the decade winning three Masters Tournaments, three PGA Championships, and three U.S. Open championships including the 2008 U.S. Open.

A Reflection

Venus and Serena Williams towered above the rest in professional tennis during the 2000s. Venus started off the decade winning her first Grand Slam at Wimbledon and then became only the second player to win gold medals in both the singles and the doubles at the 2000 Olympics. Teamed together, the sisters won the Australian Open doubles championship in 2001. Later, the Williams sisters went head-to-head in the 2001 U.S. Open, and Venus became the third woman to win both Wimbledon and the U.S. Open two years in a row. In 2009, Venus won her 10th Grand Slam title at the Australian Open and regained her No. 1 ranking, becoming the all-time prize money leader in women's sports.

Serena Williams along with Venus, won all four Grand Slam women's doubles titles. By 2002, Serena had caught her stride winning the Wimbledon, the French Open, and the U.S. Open, and was named Female Athlete of the Year by the AP. In 2003, she won her second Wimbledon and became the fifth woman to hold all Grand Slam singles titles simultaneously. In 2005, Serena quieted the whispers that she and Venus were fading when she won the Australian Open. She came back strong in 2007 after a lull in her play to win her third Australian Open, giving what TENNIS.com described as "one of the best performances of her career." Gaining momentum, Serena won the U.S. Open as well as an Olympic gold medal in 2008. In 2009, Serena regained her No. 1 ranking, winning her third Australian Open, defeating Venus at Wimbledon and teaming with her at the U.S. Open to win their third Grand Slam doubles of the decade.

Black Literature

By 2009, most African-American writers were considered mainstream and their works were continuing to grow in popularity. Starting out the decade in August of 2001, there were three books written by black authors in the top fifteen of The New York Times Best Sellers' list, Lalita Tademy's *Cane River* was No. 2, E. Lynn Harris', *Any Way the Wind Blows* was No.3, and Alice Randall's, *The Wind Done Gone* was No. 15. One hundred years ago, the two most well-know black authors were Charles Chesnutt, *The Colonel's Dream* (1905) and W.E.B. Du Bois, *The souls of Black Folk* (1903) and *John Brown: A Biography* (1909). Black authors of the day were limited to black newspapers or magazines for publishing their work, and even the major writers weren't able to earn a living from their writing.

Fifty years ago in 1959, the premiere black authors, James Baldwin, Richard Wright, and Ralph Ellison had the literary world spellbound with the depth and power of their writing. The quality of the writers of today can be debated; however, most writers draw from their personal experiences and the times of which they live. Many of the prominent black authors from the 80s and 90s were still committed to producing good works in the 2000s, like Toni Morrison, Gloria Naylor, and Terry McMillan. Walter Mosely was expanding his range into more science fiction and teen fiction, but it was the black romance genre that women couldn't get enough of. Some of the books by the new generation of black writers were cookie-cutter novels in attempts in replicate the financial success of writers like Terry McMillan.

Edward P. Jones' first novel, *The Known World*, was a standout because of his more classical style and the subject matter, blacks owning slaves in the antebellum South. Jones states that his writing style was influenced by Southern writers, both black and white. In *The Known World*, ten years in the making, Jones mixed the fictional story with historical facts of the time, with an attention to details; he even created census records for his imaginary town to bring a sense of authenticity and "believability" to his book. Edward P. Jones' novel won the National Book award and the National Book Critics Circle Award in 2003, and in 2004, won the Pulitzer Prize for Fiction and the International IMPAC Dublin Literary Award in 2005.

In contrast, there was the urban literature genre which has evolved into "gangsta lit" that was dominating African-American literature in the 2000s. Mainstream publishers didn't waste time jumping on the band wagon to capitalize on the booming sales of these urban books. This genre emphasizes the underside of black life with unrestrained violence and sex, where the thugs are armed killers and the women are ghetto-fabulous. It's all about the hustle and how to get paid, roll with it or get rolled over. Mainstream black writers question whether street lit should be classified as literature and criticize publishers for not promoting other genres. In 1909, most black writers were concerned with promoting a "positive and beautiful" image of black people, wanting to lift up the race, in 2009; some writers of hip-hop literature are preoccupied with negative images that demonstrate how low you can go.

Artists of the Decade

African-American artists in the 21st century were fortunate to be living in an era where their talent is respected and appreciated. Black art of every genre is represented in the finest museums and galleries all over the world. Black artists have achieved critical acclaim and the benefits of commercial success, an accomplishment not to be taken for granted. Henry Ossawa Tanner, the first African-American artist to receive international

A Reflection

commendations over 100 hundred years ago, wasn't as privileged. Tanner spoke about racism and having to travel to France for artistic acceptance, where his race wouldn't be a barrier to him achieving his dream saying, *"I believe the Negro blood counts, and counts to my advantage – though it has caused me at times a life of humiliation and sorrow."*

As seen in the literary world, new artists were emulating the styles of those successful artists to make the quick dollar. However, the new generation of artists included some individuals that display unique ideas and passion through their work. One of those artists is Kara Walker, known for her expansive black cut-paper silhouettes that portray the hidden side of historical racial and gender issues that were prevalent in antebellum American and still exist today. Walker has had exhibitions in museums across the country and internationally, in 2002 she was selected to represent the United States at the Sa Paulo Biennial in Brazil.

There are two impressive African-American artists who have stood the test of time in their craft, with the relevance of their work stretching across two centuries, John Biggers, painter, and Elizabeth Catlett, sculptor and painter. Both artists were dedicated to honest depictions of the lives of black people and were described by Elton Fax as, "rebellious artists who speak in voices strong, articulate and shattering to the national conscience." Catlett has been teaching and producing masterpieces for over 75 years and was the 2003 recipient of the Lifetime Achievement in Contemporary Sculpture Award by the International Sculpture Center. On October, 8, 2009, the Swann Galleries auction of African-American Fine Art set a record for art by Biggers when his painting, Shotguns, acrylic and oil in canvas (1987), sold for $216,000. Elizabeth Catlett's sculpture in red cedar, Homage to My Young Black Sisters (1968), sold for a record $288,000.

John T. Biggers Shotguns (1987) Art © John T. Biggers Estate/Licensed by VAGA, New York, NY

Steppin Out (2000), Art © Catlett Mora Family Trust/Licensed by VAGA, New York, NY

Entertainment

August Wilson, one of the greatest African-American playwrights in our history died on October 2, 2005 at the age of 60, but not before he completed his impressive series of ten plays. The series was called *The Pittsburgh Cycle*, with each play set in a different decade of the 20th century, depicting the mood, challenges, and aspects of that time. A native of Pittsburgh, all but one of the plays were centered around the neighborhood where Wilson grew up. A brilliant body of work that blessed Broadway Theaters for more than twenty years, earned him two Pulitzer Prizes, one Tony Award, and seven New York Drama Critics Circle Awards. The whole Century Cycle of plays was produced by Israel Hicks at the Denver Center for the Performing Arts from 1990 to 2009. The chronological order of the plays for the century begins in the 1900s with *Gem of the Ocean* (2003), 10s- *Joe Turner's Come and Gone* (1988), 20s- *Ma Rainey's Black Bottom* (1984), 30s- *The Piano Lesson* (1990), 40s- *Seven Guitars* (1995), 50s- *Fences* (1987), 60s- *Two Trains Running* (1991), 70s- *Jitney* (1982), 80s- *King Hedley II* (1999), and 90s- *Radio Golf* (2005).

The 2000s were a red-letter decade for African-Americans in the theater. In 2002, rising star Susan-Lori Parks became the first black woman to win the Pulitzer Prize for Drama for her

A Reflection

play "*Topdog/Underdog*." Parks' play was about the sibling rivalry between two very different brothers named Booth and Lincoln. The play initially starred Don Cheadle as Booth and Jeffrey Wright as Lincoln. In 2004, *A Raisin in the Sun* triumphantly returned to Broadway, in 2005, *The Color Purple* was heartwarmingly adapted to a musical that sold-out on Broadway and across the country, in 2005 Denzel Washington played the title role in *Julius Caesar*, and in 2008, Laurence Fishburne was *Thurgood*.

Two successful Broadway Productions were revived with all-black casts during this decade, *On Golden Pond* in 2005 starring James Earl Jones and Leslie Uggams and *Cat On A Hot Tin Roof* in 2008 starring Terrance Howard, Anika Noni Rose, Phylicia Rashad and James Earl Jones. August Wilson objected to the casting of black actors in roles that had been written and played by white casts saying, *"it's a celebration of white culture... where black ideas and attitudes are not valid."* However, there are common emotions and relationships within the human experience that can be portrayed by any race.

The success of the urban circuit play was also garnering more criticism as they were being compared to the "blaxploitation" movies of the 1970s for their limited representation of black characters and plots and playing to the emotions rather than the intelligence of black audiences. That being said, there was a strong market for these productions, Tyler Perry was able to build his entertainment empire from the proceeds of his urban plays. Forbes Magazine reported that Perry sold "more than than $100 million in tickets, $30 million in his shows and an estimated $20 million in merchandise" and "the 300 live shows he produces each year are attended by an average of 35,000 people a week."

African-American films in the new millennium entertained us but lacked the depth and range of movies from the 1990s. Hollywood had gotten the message that black movies were profitable, but there were differences in the images that they wanted to portray versus what black audiences want to see. Hollywood obviously still perceives blacks as one dimensional failing to see the diversity in movie tastes. First-rate actors were still stuck in comedies or used as comic relief in other genres. Thankfully, a number of black actors who had earned Hollywood clout were moving behind the camera to produce and direct.

Denzel Washington and Will Smith were among the biggest box office draws of the decade. Washington starred in *Remember the Titans* (2000), *Training Day* (2001) for which he won the Oscar for Best Actor, and *John Q* (2002) before trying his hand at directing with the compelling and moving *Antwone Fisher* in 2002. Washington polished off the decade with *American Gangster* and the *Great Debaters* in 2007. Besides having starring roles, Will Smith was the producer of a respectable list of mega-hits in the 2000s that included *The Pursuit of Happyness*, *I Am Legend*, *Hancock*, and the *Secret Life of Bees*, as well as acting in *Ali* for which he received an Academy Award nomination for Best Actor. Chris Rock was also a wearer of many hats, as director, producer, and co-writer of *Head of State* (2003), director and co-writer for *I Think I Love My Wife* (2007), and producer of the documentary *Good Hair* (2009).

Spike Lee, never backing down from an opportunity to make a point shocked us again with *Bamboozled* (2000), stunned us with *When the Levees Broke* (2006), but entertained us with *Miracle at St. Anna* (2008). John Singleton didn't stray too far from his niche with his productions of *Shaft*, *Baby Boy*, and *Hustle & Flow*. Encouraged by Singleton, O'Shea Jackson or better known as Ice Cube, joined the group of writers and producers with his sequel *Next Friday* (2000), *Barbershop* and *All About the Benjamins* in 2002, *Barbershop 2: Back in Business* (2004), *XXX: State of the Union*, *Are We There Yet?* and *Are We Done Yet?* in 2005.

There were a number of movies that gave a more realistic view of the black relationships and black families in this decade, beginning with *Love & Basketball* (2000), *Finding Forrester* (2000), *The Brothers* (2001), *Brown Sugar* (2002), *Drumline* (2002), *Akeelah and the Bee* (2006), and *This Christmas* (2007). Two movies of this decade were based on actual events in Africa, *Hotel Rwanda* (2004) and *The Last King of Scotland* (2006). Starring in *Hotel Rwanda*, Don Cheadle deservedly received rave reviews and an Academy Award nomination for his performance as Paul Rusesabagina, who rescued well over a thousand Tutsi during the Rwandan Genocide. Forest Whitaker, an actor of the highest quality, starred in *The Last King of Scotland*, finally getting his due as an actor when he won the Golden Globe, the Screen Actors Guild, and the Academy Award for Best Actor for his vivid portrayal of Ugandan dictator Idi Amin Dada, becoming only the fourth black actor to win the Academy Award honor.

Tyler Perry had discovered his audience while touring with his urban gospel stage plays in the 1990s. Perry started out the decade as a screenwriter, producer, and actor, adapting several of his successful stage plays into feature films. His first movie, *Diary of a Mad Black Woman* (2005) was done with a budget of $5 million and earned $50 million. Perry followed quickly with *Madea's Family Reunion* (2006), *Daddy's Little Girls* and *Why Did I Get Married?*, both released in 2007. Perry released two more movies in 2008, *Meet the Browns* and *The Family That Preys*. In 2009, he released three movies; *I Can Do Bad All By Myself*, *Madea Goes to Jail* and paired with Oprah Winfrey to produce *Precious*. Mo'nique won an Academy Award for Best Supporting Actress for her portrayal of Mary, the abusive mother in *Precious*.

A Reflection

The number of black actors and actresses working was growing, but parts were still limited. Samuel L. Jackson, a consummate actor and box office gold, was one of the few actors who worked consistently, appearing in more roles than any other actor, black or white. Jackson is listed in the 2009 edition of The Guinness World Records for having appeared in 68 films that earned $7.42 billion. Black actors like Wesley Snipes and Cuba Gooding, Jr. have managed to work steady in Hollywood, and rising stars like Terrance Howard and Morris Chestnut seem to be up for the challenge. Popular black female actresses that have carved out a place in Hollywood include Halle Berry, Queen Latifah, Sanaa Lathan, and Nia Long.

The list of black comedians that have followed in the footsteps of Richard Pryor and Eddie Murphy parlaying their comedy beginnings into box office gold is long and continues to grow; there is Chris Rock, Martin Lawrence, Chris Tucker, Bernie Mac, and Jamie Foxx. In 2000, Spike Lee directed *The Original Kings of Comedy*, which was a stand-up comedy movie that featured Steve Harvey, D.L. Hughley, Cedric the Entertainer, and Bernie Mac. Filmed in front of live audiences with a $3 million budget, the movie grossed over $38 million in theaters. Jamie Foxx also appeared in two of the biggest hit movies of the decade, starring in the movie *Ray* (2004) and *Dream Girls* (2006). Foxx gave an outstanding performance in the movie *Ray*, playing Ray Charles, for which he won numerous awards and accolades including the Golden Globe and the Academy Award for Best Actor, the third black man to win the honor.

The new millennium brought significant changes to television programming. The Great Recession created a competitive atmosphere as financial reins were tightened after the free-flowing 1990s. Black hit shows were being canceled without notice, decreasing the number of black television shows by more than 20 percent, and dropping to 43 shows by the end of the decade. The most popular black shows of the 2000s were *All of Us, Barbershop, Eve, Everybody Hates Chris, Girlfriends, Half & Half, Meet the Browns, My Wife and Kids, One on One, That's So Raven, The Bernie Mac Show, The Boondocks, The Game, The Hughleys, The Proud Family, The Tracy Morgan Show*, and Tyler Perry's *House of Payne*.

The 2000s were without a doubt the decade of the reality show. Networks resistant to paying for quality writers and actors couldn't resist the less expensive programming of celebrities or individuals willing to put their lives on display. African-Americans were often featured in a number of reality shows, but not always to their benefit. The hard fought battle to remove stereotypical images and have black people portrayed in a respectable and positive light had become a moot point as blacks were voluntarily shown exhibiting derogatory and dysfunctional behaviors. Beginning with *The Flavor of Love*, *Being Bobby Brown*, and *College Hill*, the number of reality shows flooded with blacks grew like weeds.

Cable networks were creating more original dramatic shows in the 2000s. HBO broadcasted a first rate mini-series that featured blacks in the 2000 premiere of *The Corner: A Year in the Life of an Inner-City Neighborhood* by David Simon and Ed Burns. The six-part show won the Primetime Emmy Award for Outstanding Miniseries in 2000. Also in 2000, Showtime premiered *Soul Food*, a series focused on the Joseph Sisters, adapted from the hit movie of the same name. The series aired for 74 episodes over four years making it one of the longest running dramatic series with a predominately black cast. BET bought the rights to air the series' reruns in 2004. HBO also developed and premiered *The Wire* in 2002 which focused on urban life in Baltimore; the critics loved it but the show never found its audience.

Listening to black music in the new millennium is definitely not the experience it used to be, and I'm praying that the best days are not behind us. The lack of creativity is evident in the poor quality of music composition and lyrics. Wynton Marsalis gave his commentary saying, *"It's a shame what our youth calls music."* Radio stations with black music formats that play classic R&B and "old school" or a mix of R&B, neo-soul, and pop dominate the black markets as large amounts of the new hip hop or gangsta rap with profanity and sexual language is unfit for radio airwaves. The business of bootlegging, the unauthorized copying and sale of music has boomed and has had an adverse effect on record sales for all artists. Top black recording artists are changing their sound in efforts to cross over into the young pop market to optimize record sales.

Seasoned R&B artists who have made millions for the music industry with hit after hit in earlier decades can't get record deals while newcomers without much talent or originality are used to pump out CDs and are never heard from again. The premise for signing recording contracts of the past was that you had to be able to sing and you needed to have your own unique style or sound. In this decade, it's pretty obvious that you need to sound like someone who's already recording and you physical appearance is more important than your sound. If you have a marketable look the technology of the recording studio can fix your voice.

The most successful black entertainers of the decade were solo artists who crossed over into pop music which included Beyonce, Usher, John Legend, and Alicia Keyes. Jaheim,

A Reflection

Fantasia, and Mary J. Blige kept it real for loyal fans with their mix of hip hop and soul. Rapper Kanye West, with four platinum albums and twelve Grammy Awards, stayed at the top of the game by mixing electronica, R&B, and rock to hip hop. Other rappers who rose to the top during the 2000s were Nelly, 50 Cent, and Ludacris. The talent base the of neo-soul artists was very solid with mesmerizing performers like Jill Scott, Eryka Badu, India Arie, Maxwell, Eric Benet, Anthony Hamilton, and Kem and their fan base has grown considerably over the decade.

Prince had struggled a bit in the 1990s but regained his footing in the 2000s after settling the dispute over the use of his name. Rolling Stone magazine declared Price as the highest earning musical entertainer in 2004, with an annual income of $56.5 million. Whitney Houston and Michael Jackson both struggled with personal issues during the 2000s, but each seemed to be back on track in their careers by 2009. Houston released her new album, *"I Look to You"* in August of 2009. Michael Jackson announced that he would be doing 10 concerts in London, then shows in Paris, New York City, and Mumbai. His "final curtain call" was titled *"This is It,"* after which he would be retiring. More than one million tickets sold in less than two hours. Sadly, we would never see what was to be the most extravagant and spectacular show of our lives. On June 25, 2009, Michael Jackson died of cardiac arrest related to an overdose of medications. After his death, Jackson became the best-selling artist of 2009 in the United States, selling over 8.2 million albums.

Memorable Moments

In 2001, Retired General Colin Powell was the first African-American appointed to be US Secretary of State.

Halle Berry won an Emmy Award for the lead role in *"Introducing Dorothy Dandridge"* in 2000.

In 2001, Halle Berry became the first African-American woman to win the Academy Award for Best Actress for her role in Monster's Ball.

Robert Johnson, owner of BET, became the first black billionaire in 2001.

In 2002, Queen Latifah was nominated for an Academy Award for her role in the movie Chicago.

Condoleezza Rice became the first black female US secretary of State in 2005.

Shani Davis was the first to win an individual gold medal at an Olympic Game in 2006 in the 1000m speed skating competition.

In 2006, Jennifer Hudson won the Academy Award for Best Supporting Actress for her role as 'Effie' in the movie "Dream Girls."

Oprah Winfrey was declared the world's richest female entertainer and was the world's first black female billionaire in 2007.

In 2008, Barack Obama was the first African-American man to be elected President of the United States.

Michael Jackson, the greatest entertainer of all time died on June 25, 2009 from an overdose of anesthetizing drugs.

On October 9, 2009, Barack Obama won the 2009 Nobel Peace Prize for "his extraordinary efforts to strengthen international diplomacy and cooperation between peoples."

Reflections on Decade

"Either America will destroy ignorance or ignorance will destroy the United States."
---- W.E.B. Du Bois

Focusing on the decade that ended in the 2009 was a bit bewildering because of the lack of a center or meeting point for black people. These were the years of resignation without a common agenda or unifying issue visible that could shock us out of our state of unconsciousness. Seemingly we had been people of action, strivers, but now we joined the nation of spectators, reconciled to the reality that this may be as good as it gets. Financially, hard times had only been on hiatus and returned again with even more vigor. The "talented tenth" that Du Bois spoke of, the saviors for the black society, those who would lead and guide, were just as preoccupied with efforts to hold on to whatever they had gained as the rest of black folks. The competitiveness or capitalism of which America espouses had made us all rivals and jealous of another's success. The black community, the cohesive group that banded together in times of desperation had become disconnected leaving us vulnerable in the never-ending struggle for equal opportunity.

Simmering racism and prejudice were now boiling with a vengeance, opening old wounds that had never completely healed. Intolerance is always strengthened by financial difficulties in a tough economy and things were pretty tough all over. A daily diet of anger and animosity was served in generous portions through every form of media. The rich were desperate to get richer without any regard to consequences of their greed. Politicians had abandoned their obligations to the people while lining their own pockets. Religion had become one of the biggest businesses surviving the economic downturn

A Reflection

while the moral fibers of human decency had become unraveled leaving spaces where our discretion and self-respect had slipped away.

The catalyst for the changes in the decade was the crippling recession that began in 2001, eliminating millions of the jobs that had been created in the 1990s. Without even having a chance to dig out of the proverbial hole or build a nest egg, many of the black working poor found themselves in the familiar grips of poverty once again. At the end of the decade, more than half of all black households had incomes below $35,000 per year, the lowest median income of any of the races. Young blacks who were trying to educate themselves and move forward struggled with the high costs of college, limited resources, and insufficient financial aid.

The future which lies with our youth looks uncertain with growing numbers of black males, defiant, fearless, and poor dropping out of high school without job prospects, rejecting the structure of mainstream America for the dangerous hustle of the thug life. Stevie Wonder's lyrics said, *"We would not care to wake up to the nightmare that's becoming real life,"* but how long can you fight the good fight? Being told that you are inferior generation after generation, even with strong feelings of pride and self-worth, some chinks are made in your coat of armor, openings where drops of doubt can seep in from time to time. Self-consciously things are done on the outside to compensate for these inner self-doubts, we comfort ourselves with unhealthy food, we dress flashier, we buy shiny cars, black men try to conquer as many women as they can, while others feel white women can increase their worth. Black women devalue themselves with casual sex and have babies to connect to men who won't commit. Some of us pretend we don't care, so we stop trying, we quit school, and we sag our pants. We begin to prey upon one another and tear each other down in our frustration.

The struggle of today comes from within, but the will to fight is gone. In Martin Luther King Jr.'s I Have a Dream speech he said *"One hundred years later the Negro lives on a lonely island of poverty in the midst of a vast ocean of material prosperity"* and even more than fifty years later not a lot has changed. The ticket to a better life is still out of reach for nearly half of us.

Reflection on 100 Years

"History despite its wrenching pain cannot be unlived,
but if faced with courage, need not be live again."

--Maya Angelou

2009

Observing the reflection of 100 years in the lives African-Americans against a backdrop of inequality and oppression we can see that this has been an incredible journey. Black people have broadened their horizons far from the confines of the South to every corner and edge of this country we call home. Unsatisfied with second-class citizenship blacks fought valiantly for the civil rights and privileges that Jim Crown had cruelly and unjustifiably denied. One hundred years ago black people were disenfranchised and unable to change their circumstances in this democracy without the right to vote. The inconceivable battle of the Civil Rights Movement was successful in restoring our constitutional right to vote, and in 2008, 65 percent of eligible blacks went to the polls and made history, electing America's first black president, Barack Obama.

African-Americans had been guided through these years of change by a number of effective and charismatic leaders, but in the new millennium there isn't a national leader representing black people. The talented tenth that W.E.B. Du Bois had said held the responsibility of leading is quiet; the cream having risen to the top has dispersed, not condensed in its usual stance for solidarity, but diluted without substance. They have assimilated, integrated, and disappeared. The black church having always been the center of support and the first line of defense for black people in every aspect of our lives has withdrawn to a role of principally spiritual leadership.

Early in this century African-Americans understood that the catalyst for the changes we wanted was education. Many years were spent in the quest for an equal and adequate education that would open doors and opportunities for earning a living and building some financial security for our families. Educational attainment for black people has progressed dramatically over one hundred years, moving from 30 percent illiteracy and only primary education to blacks seeking post-secondary training, earning bachelor's, master's, doctorates, business and law degrees, and medical degrees in ever increasing numbers.

Black people are unarguable hardworking having built a good portion of this nation as slaves. Employment or the means to earn a living was essential to survival in 1909 and is even more vital in 2009. Blacks have transitioned over this century from working the fields as farmers and sharecroppers to the factories after World War I and II, to teaching institutions working as instructors and office personnel, to hospitals, courtrooms, and government agencies. The entrepreneurial spirit has increased the number of black businesses to nearly one million.

The level of crime in the black community has always been an issue, but has grown over the century to a very serious problem that jeopardizes the future progress of black

A Reflection

people. Scores of black men needed to head families and lead people are sacrificing their lives on the streets or subsequently to incarceration. Analysis by the most educated minds of the world says that crime is a symptom of deeper issues that have altered the mindset of persons to antisocial behavior. Subjecting any race of people to hundreds of years of oppression, degradation, and exclusion, would probably yield similar results. Undoubtedly, the years of mistreatment have affected the thinking and consciousness of us all, the perpetrators and the victims.

African-Americans have largely advanced their physical health over this century, expanding their life expectancy from 33 years to more than 75 years. The improved housing and living conditions have contributed to the better physical health over the decades, but the stability of the family structure that is crucial to our well-being has been shaken. The black family was basically intact in 1909, but in 2009 the traditional black family is in the minority, with 60 percent of black children living in poor families. Morals and values have shifted over 100 years, but we know the difference between right and wrong and need to encourage commitment to marriage and the family unit to revitalize the black community.

Initially I had the belief that something had gone terribly wrong in the evolution of black people, that the rollercoaster of a train ride had crashed or jumped the track, but the problem in this journey was that not enough of us boarded the train. Half of us are still at the station, so the evolution process is at different stages. Black people run the spectrum as do people of all races, from the mega rich, the super-talented, those driven by ambition, to the hardworking faithful, to the ones who just won't do the right thing no matter the situation. There are many who make us proud, and a few who make us feel ashamed, but we are all survivors with a rich legacy that deserves to be celebrated.

Vision of the Future

The beauty among the disturbing and distressing problems that have confronted black people on this journey is that as long as there is life there is hope. It gets dark every night but the sun comes up in the morning, and with that new day there's a new beginning. The blessing of life is that we are constantly changing. We have the opportunity to start something new, to change our directions, to change our attitudes, and to change our outcome. The journey doesn't have to stop here; we have the potential to move further and be more successful. There is no appointed destination, so let's ride this train until the wheels fall off.

2009

Ain't No Stopping Us Now

There've been so many things that have held us down
But now it looks like things are finally comin' around, yeah
I know we've got a long long way to go, yeah
And where we'll end up
I don't know
But we won't let nothing hold us back
We gonna get ourselves together
We gonna polish up our act, yeah
And if you've ever been held down before
I know that you refuse to be held down any more, yeah
Don't you let nothing, nothing
Nothing stand in your way
---Jerry Cohen, Gene McFadden, John Whitehead

A Reflection

Bibliography

An Annual Report on American Journalism: African American. (n.d.). Retrieved from The State of The News Media: An Annual Report on American Journalism 2010: http://stateofthemedia.org/2010/ethnic-summary-essay/african-american/

School Desegregation: Louisiana and Mississippi. Report of NEA Task Force III. (1970). Washington, DC: National Education Association.

A Progress Report 1964-1974, A Decade of Struggle. (1975, January). *Ebony*, pp. 25-36.

White Publishers Open Their Coffers to Black Writers. (1998). *The Journal of Blacks in Higher Education, 19*, 53.

New Evidence Documents That Large Numbers of Black Students Are Unprepared For College. (2007, Autumn). *The Journal of Blacks in Higher Education*, 27.

United States of America Overview: African Americans. (2009). Retrieved from World Directory of Minorities and Indigenous People: http://www.minorityrights.org/?lid=2607&tmpl.

Education for African Americans. American Decades. (2011, January 10). Retrieved from Encyclopedia.com: http://www.encyclopedia.com

"The 1980s: Sports: Overview" *American Decades.* (2012, Feburary 13). Retrieved from Encyclopedia.com: http://www.encyclopedia.com

A. Philip Randolph Institute. (n.d.). Retrieved from Gentle Warrior: A. Philip Randolph (1889 - 1979) : http://www.apri.org/ht/d/sp/i/225/pid/225

Allen, W. (1978). The search for applicable theories of black family life. *The Journal of Marriage and the family, 40.1*, 117-129.

Alridge, D., & Daniels, M. (2001). Black Violence and Crime in the 21at Century: A Socio-Historical Structural Analysis. *Journal of Human Behavior in the Social Environment, 4*(2/3), 17, 27.

Ambert, A.-M. (1998). *The Web of Poverty: Psychosocial Perspectives.* Routledge.

Anderson, J. (1973). *Philip Randolph: a biographical portrait.* Harcourt Brace Jovanovich.

Anderson, J. D. (1988). *The Education of Blacks in the South, 1860-1935.* Chapel Hill: University of North Carolina.

Austin, A. (2008, August 1). Understanding the black jobs crisis. *The Daily Voice.*

Austin, A. (n.d.). *Understanding the Black Jobs Crisis.* Retrieved from Economic Policy Institute: http://www.epi.org/publications/webfeatures_viewpoints_black_job_crisis

Balkaran, S. (1999). Mass Media and Racism. *The Yale Political Quarterly, 21*(1).

Bass, A. (1979, October). In the game: race, identity, and sports in the twentieth century. *Black Enterprise*

Beito, D., & Beito, L. (2009). *Black Maverick: T.R.M. Howard's Fight for Civil Rights and Economic Power.. ISBN.* Urbana: University of Illinois Press.

Biblarz, T. J., & Raftery, A. E. (1993). The Effects of Family Disruption on Social Mobility. *American Sociological Review, 58.1*, 97.

Boston, T. (2006). *The Role of Black-Owned Businesses in Black Community Development." In Jobs and Economic Development in Minority Communities.* (P. Ong, & A. Loukaitou-Sideris, Eds.) Philadelphia: Temple University Press.

Boyd, R. L. (1997, Jan-Mar). Protected Markets and African-American Professionals in Northern Cities During the Great Migration. *17*(1), 91-101.

Braithwaite, R. L., Taylor, S. E., & Treadwell, H. M. (Eds.). (1992). *Health Issues in the Black Community.* San Francisco: Jossey-Bass.

Brooks, D. (n.d.). Black Theatre and Performance Studies: Seminal Critical Essays and Articles. In H. Dodson, & C. Palmer (Ed.), *Cultural Life (Schomburg Studies on the Black Experience).* Michigan State University Press .

Brooks, R. L. (Sring 2010). The Crisis of the Black Politician the Age of Obama. *Howard Law Journal, 53*(3), 699-748.

Capeci Jr, D. J. (1942). We Shall Not Be Moved. In *Race Relations in Wartime Detroit: The Sojourner Truth Housing Controversy.*

Capeci, D. J. (1985, July). Wartime Fair Employment Practice Committees: The Governor's Committee and the First FEPC in New York City,. *Afro-Americans in New York Life and History, 9*(2).

Carnoy, M. (1994-1995, Winter). Why Aren't More African Americans Going to College? *The Journal of Blacks in Higher Education,* 66-69.

Carson, C. (1994). African – American Leadership and Mass Mobilization. *The Black Scholar, 24.*

Chafe, W. H., Gavis, R., & Robert, K. (Eds.). (2001). *Remembering Jim Crow.* New York: The New Press.

Coenen, C. E. (2005). *From Sandlots to the Super Bowl: the National Football League, 1920-1967.* Knoxville: University of Tennessee Press.

Committee, A. F. (1970). *The Status of School Desegregation in the South, 1970.* Washington, DC: National Education Association.

Conrad, C., Whitehead, P. M., & Stewart, J. (2005). *African Americans in the U.S. Economy By Cecilia Conrad.* Rowman & Littlefield Publishers.

Cooper Jr., W. J., & Terrill, T. E. (1995). *The American South: A History.* McGraw-Hill Companies.

Costa, D. L., Helmchen, L. A., & Wilson, S. (2007). Race, infection and arteriosclerosis in the past. *PNAS, 104,* 13219-13224.

Cowan, T., PH.D, & Maguire, J. (1994). *Timelines of African American History, 500 Years of Black Achievement,* . New York: Berkley Publishing Group.

Crack: Inner City Decay in America. (n.d.). Retrieved from Drug-Forum: http://www.drugs-forum.com/forum/showthread.php?t=42412

Crime, R. a.-B. (n.d.). Retrieved from http://law.jrank.org/pages/12128/Race-Ethnicity-Black-Americans-crime.html

Cunningham, E. (n.d.). *Putting Itself Out of Business.* Retrieved from California Newsreel: http://newsreel.org/guides/blackpress/putting.htm

Daniels, D. H. (2002, Winter). Los Angeles Zoot: Race "Riot," the Pachuco, and Black Music Culture. *The Journal of African American History, 87*(1), 98-118.

Darity, W., & Myers, S. (1984). Does welfare dependency cause female headship? *Journal of Marriage and the Family, 46.4,* 765-779.

Denby, C. (1989). Detroit Riots 1943. In *Indignant Heart: A Black Worker's Journal.* Wayne State University Press.

Drowne, K. M., & Huber, P. (2004). *The 1920s.* Greenwood Publishing Group.

Ellis, J. (2005). *Educational Psychology: Developing Learners* (5th ed.). Addison Wesley Longman.

Evanz, K. (n.d.). *The Messenger: The Rise and Fall of Elijah Muhammad.* New York: Pantheon.

Farley, R., & Hermalin, A. I. (Feburary 1971). Family Stability: A Comparison of Trends Between Blacks and Whites. *36*(1), 1-17.

Fields, C. D. (1997, January 23). Ebonics 101: What have we learned? *Black Issues in Higher Education,* 19-21, 24-28.

Fox, V., & Volakakis, J. (1956, January). The Negro Offernder in Northern Industrial Area. *The Journal of Criminal Law. Criminology, and Police Science, 46*(5), 641-647.

Franklin, F. E. (1964). *The Negro Church in America.* New York: Schocken Books.

Frazier, F. E. (1932). *The Free Negro Family.* Nashville, TN: Fisk University Press.

Gaines II, R. W. (2010). Looking Back, Moving Forward: How the Civil Rights Era Church Can Guide the Modern Black Church in Improving Black Student Achievement. *The Journal of Negro Education, 79*(3), 366-379.

Gates Jr., H. L., & West, C. (1994). *The African-American Century, How Blacks Have Shaped our Country.* New York: Touchstone, Simon & Schuster.

Gilbertlove, J. (Summer 1997). African American and the American Labor Movement. *Prologue, 29.*

Goldfield, M. (1997). *The Color of Politics, Race and the Mainsprings of American Politics.* New York: The New Press.

Goldfield, M. (1997). *The Color of Politics: Race and the Mainsprings of American Politics.* New York:

Neew York Press.
Green, E. (1970, June). Race, Social Status, and Criminal Arrest. *American Sociological Review, 35*(3), 476-490.
Harris, F. C. (2001). Black Churches and Civic Traditions: Outreach, Activism, and the Politics of Public Funding of Faith-based Ministries. *The Pew Program on Religion and the News Media* .
Harris, O., Kirsch, G., & Nolte, C. (2000). *Encyclopedia of Ethnicity and Sports in the United States* . Greenwood.
Harris, R. A., & Tichenor, D. J. (2009). *History of the United States Political System.* ABC-CLIO.
Harry Truman and Civil Rights. (n.d.). Retrieved from History Learning Site: http://www.historylearningsite.co.uk/Harry_Truman_civil_rights.htm
Heckman, J. J., & LaFontaine, P. A. (2007, December). The American High School Graduation Rate: Trends and Levels. *Nation Bureau of Economic Research*.
Hefner, J. (1980, August). The Black Balance Sheet. *Ebony Magazine*, p. 38.
Hicks Jr., H. B. (1994, Summer). Challenge to the African American Church: Problems and Perspectivs for the Third Millennium. *The Journal of Religious Thought*, 81.
Hill, C. V. (2010). *Tap Dancing America: a cultural history.* Oxford University Press.
Hill, E., & Hatch, j. V. (2003). *A history of African American theatre.* Cambridge University Press.
Hill, K. H. (2007). *Religious Education in the African American Tradition: a Comprehensivel.* Chalice Press.
Hill, R. B. (2003). ""The Strengths of Black Families" Revisited." *The State of Black America*, 107-149.
Hine, D. (1989). *Black women in white.* Bloomington, IN: Indiana University Press.
Hirsch, A. (1983). Chapter 2: An Era of Hidden Violence. In *An Era of Hidden Violence , Making the Second Ghetto: Race and Housing in Chicago, 1940-1960*. Cambridge University Press .
Hirsch, A. R. (1983). *Making the Second Ghetto: Race and Housing in Chicago, 1940-1960.* Cambridge University Press .
Hoch, C., & Slayton, R. A. (1989). *New Homeless and Old: Community and the Skid Row Hotel.* Temple University Press.
Hooker, R. W. (1970). Displacement of Black Teachers in the Eleven Southern States. *Education Resources Information Center*.
Huggins, N. I. (1973). *Voices from the Harlem Renaissance.* Oxford University Press.
Hughes, C. A. (2006, Spring). Grand Council of the Best Minds and the Economic Crisis of the Negro in the 1930s. *The Griot, 25*(1), 29-42.
Humes, E. (2006). How the GI Bill Shunted Blacks Into Vocational Training. *The Journal of Blacks in Higher Education, 53*, 92-104.
Hunter, A. G. (2001). The Other Breadwinners: The mobilization of secondary wage earners in early twentieth-century black families. *History of the Family, 6.1*, 69.
Hutchinson, E. O. (n.d.). *Obama's Balancing Act with Black Politicians.* Retrieved from The Hutchinson Political Report: http://earlofarihutchinson.blogspot.com/2008/11/obamas-racial-balancing-act.html
Johnson, K. E. (2004, Spring). Police-Black Community Relations in Postwar Philadelphia: Race and Criminalization in Urban Social Spaces, 1945-1960. *The Journal of African American History*, pp. 118-134.
Jonathan, L. (2006-2007, Winter). A Church Divided: The Dilemma of the Black Preacher. *The African American Pulpit*, 28-31.
Jones, F. G. (2010, November 26). The Role of the Black Press during the "Great Migration." *Education Resources Infromation Center*.
Jones, R. L. (2001, Fall). Between the Pulpit and the Polls: Black Ministers' Impact on Black Political Decision-Making . *The Griot*, 8-22.
Jordan, W. G. (2000). *lack Newspapers and America's War for Ddemocracy, 1914-1920.* The University of North Carolina Press .
Kahlenberg, R. D. (2007, June). *Rescuing Brown vs. Board of Education: Profiles of twelve*

schooldistricts pursuing socioeconomic school integration. The Century Foundation.
Kane, J. J. (1948). The Study of Negro gangs in West Philadelphia. *The American Catholic Sociological Review, 9*(2), 74-83.
Kelley, R. D. (June 1993). We Are Not What We Seem: Rethinking Black Working-Class Opposition in the Jim Crow South. *the Journal of American History, 80.1*, 75-112.
Kemp, M. J. (n.d.). *The Segregated School System in Atlanta: An Agent of Social Control and Black Oppression*. Retrieved from http://mgagnon.myweb.uga.edu/students/3090/04SP3090-Kemp.htm
Kersten, A. E. (2000). *Race, Jobs, and the War: The FEPC in the Widwest, 1941-46*. University of Illinois Press.
King, W. (1989, August 31). "Black Theatre in Perspective: An Abridged Introduction to Plays for the Black Theatre. *Black Masks, 5*(6), 6.
Klarman, M. J. (2006). *From Jim Crow to Civil Rights: The Supreme Court and the Struggle for Racial Equality*. Oxford University Press.
Kornweibel Jr., T. (1994). The Most Dangerous of All Negro Journals: Federal Effeorts to Suppress the Chicago Defender During World War I. *American Journalism, 11*(2), 154-168.
Kornweibel, T. (1998). *Seeing Red: Federal campaigns against Black militancy, 1919-1925*. Indiana University Press.
Kotz, N. (2005). *Judgment Days: Lyndon Baines Johnson, Martin Luther King Jr., and the Laws That Changed America* (3rd ed.). Houghto Mifflin.
Lanctot, N. (2004). *Negro league baseball: the rise and ruin of a Black institution*. University of Pennsylvania Press.
Lenworth, G. (1980, December). The Crisis. Black Health: Yesterday, Today, and Tomorrow. *Crisis , 87*, 546-548.
Leondar-Wright, B. (2004, May/June). Black Job Loss Déjà vu. *Dollars & Sense: Magazine of Economic Justice*(253).
Leondar-Wright, B. (n.d.). Black Job Loss Déjà vu. *Dollare & Sense: The Magazine of Economic.*
Levine, M. L. (1996). *Social Issues in American History Series: African Americans and Civil Rights from 1619 to the Present*. Phoenix: The Oryx Press.
Levitt, S. D., & Murphy, K. M. (2006). *How Bad Was Crack Cocaine? The Economics of an Illicit Drug Market*. Retrieved from Capital Ideas: http://www.chicagobooth.edu/capideas/apr06/5.aspx
Lewis, E. (1990). Developments in Research on Black Families: A Decade Review. *Journal of Marriage & Family, 52.4*, 993-1014.
Logan, M. (1973). *Harry S. Truman*. William Morrow and Co.
Madhunbuti, H. R. (2005, November 3). In Memoriam--August Wilson: 1845-2005. *Diverse Issues in Higher Education, 22*(19), 19.
Marable, M. (1980, March-June). Black Nationalism in the 1970s: Through the Prism of Race and Class. *Socialist Review*, 57-108.
Marable, M. (1985). *Black American Politics: From the Washington Marches to Jesse Jackson*. Norfolk: Verso.
Marable, M. (1999). *How Capitalism Underdeveloped Black America*. South End Press.
Marable, M., & Mullings, L. (2000). *Let Nobody Turn Us Around: Voices of Resistance, Reform, and Renewal, An African american Anthology*. Lanham, Maryland: Rowman & Littlefield Publishers Inc.
Mason, H. E. (1932, July 16). Depression. *Norfolk Journal and Guide, XXXII*(29).
Massey, D. S., & Denton, A. N. (1993). *American apartheid: segregation and the making of the underclass*. Harvard University Press.
McBride, d. (1990). "The Black-White Mortality Differential In New York State, 1900 - 1950: A Socio-Historical Reconsideration. *Afro-Americans in New York Life and History, 14.2*, 71.
Middleton, J. A. (2001, May). A Role for the African American Church in Urban School Reform. *Urban Education*, 426-437.

A Reflection

Miller, P. B., Steffen, T. F., & Schäfer-Wünsche, E. (Eds.). (2001). *The Civil Rights Movement Revisited: Critical Perspectives on the Struggle for Racial Equality in the United States*. The Civil Rights Movement Revisited:: Transaction Publishers.

Morris, A. D. (1984). *The Origins of the Civil Rights Movement, Black Communities organizing for change*. New York: The Free Press.

Negro League History 101. (n.d.). Retrieved from Negro League Baseball.com: http://www.negroleaguebaseball.com/history101.html

Nelson, S. (Producer), & Nelson, S. (Director). (2000, 2001). *Soldiers Without Swords: The Black Press* [Motion Picture].

Newkirk, P. (n.d.). *The Not-So-Great Migration From the black press to the mainstream-and back again*. Retrieved from Colombia Journailism Review: http://www.cjr.org/feature/the_not-so-great_migration.php?page=all

Nichols, C. A. (1988). Black Families headed by single mothers: growing numbers and increasing poverty. *Social Work Abstracts, 33.4*, 306-312.

Nichols-Casebolt, A. M. (1998, July- August). Black Families Headed by Single Mothers: Growing Numbers and Increaisng Poverty. *Social Work*.

Oby, M. R. (2009). *Black Press Coverage of the Emmett Till Lynching as a Catalyst to the Civil Rights Movement*. Lambert Academic Publishing .

Osofsky, G. (1996). *Harlem: The Making of a Ghetto: Negro New York, 1890-1920* . Harper & Row.

Ousey, G. C. (2000). Deindustrialization, Female-headed Families, and Black and White Juvenile Homicide Rates. *Sociological Inquiry, 70.4*, 391-419.

Owens, R. (2000). Review of Soldiers Without Swords. *The Journal for MultiMedia History, 3*.

Patton, S. F. (1998). *African-American Art*. Oxford University Press.

Petigrew, T. (1996). Negroes in Cities: Residential Segregation and Neighborhood Change. *AM J. SOC*, 112-13.

Philpott, T. L. (1978). *The Slum and the Ghetto: Neighborhood Deterioration and Middle-Class Reform, Chicago, 1880–1930*. Oxford University Press.

Porter, G. L. (1966). *The Negro Pioneers in Beauty Culture*. New York: Vantage Press.

Price, D. O. (2010, November 26). Blacks in the Labor Force in the United States. *Educationel Resource Informational Center*.

Rainsberger, M. (n.d.). *Marching on Memphis*. Retrieved from The College of Liberal Arts at UT Austin: http://www.utexas.edu/cola/depts/history/features

Ransby, B. (2002). *Ella Baker and the Black Freedom Movement: A Radical Democratic Vision*. The University of North Carolina Press.

Reed, W. (2004, February 08). *Blacks In Football: A Powerful Force Past And Present* . Retrieved from black press international: http://www.blackpressinternational.com/html/archives/article_ema020804.htm

Responsibilities, N. E. (1970). *Beyond Desegregation: The Problem of Power, A Special Study in East Texas*. Washington D.C.: National Education Association.

Reuben, P. P. (n.d.). *Chapter 9: Harlem Renaissance*. Retrieved from PAL: Perspectives in American Literature - A Research and Reference Guide : http://www.csustan.edu/english/reuben/pal/chap9/9intro.html

Rhodes, J. (1998). *Mary Ann Shadd Cary: The Black Press and Protest in the Nineteenth Century*. Bloomington: Indiana University Press.

Riddle, W. A. (1995). The origins of black sharecropping. *Mississippi Quarterly, 49.1*, 53.

Ronald W. Walters, R. C. (1999). *African American leadership By Ronald W. Walters, Robert Charles Smith*. State University of New York Press.

Schneider, M. R. (2006). *African Americans in the Jazz Age: a decade of struggle and promise*. Rowman & Littlefield Publishers .

Scott, M. (1993, June). Can Black Radio Survive an Industry Shakeout. *Black Enterprise, 23*(11).

Seitles, M. (1998). The Perpetuation of Residential Racial Segregation in America: Historical

Discrimination, Modern Forms of Exclusion, and Inclusionary Remedies. *Journal of Land Use and Environmental Law, 14*, 89.

Sidlo, R. B., & Kleiner, B. H. (1992). Discrimination in Employment by Race. *Equal Opportunities International, 11.2*, 1.

Simmons, M. (2007, Spring). Trends in the African American Church. *The African American Pulpit*, 9-16.

Slater, R. B. (1994, March 31). The Growing Gender Gap in Black Higher Education. *The Journal of Blacks in Higher Education*, 52.

Handy, W. C. (Producer), & Murphy, D. (Director). (1929). *St. Louis Blues* [Motion Picture]. Paramount Pictures.

Smith, J. C. (1993). *Epic Lives: One Hundred Black Women Who Made a Difference.* Boston: Visible Ink Press.

Spivey, T. (2002, April-May). Mama Put The Chicken Down And Start Sangin'. *15*(3), 9.

Stanford, K. L. (2002). *Black political organizations in the post-civil rights era By Karin L. Stanford.* (O. Johnson, Ed.) Rutgers University Press.

States and Black Incarceration in America. (n.d.). Retrieved from http://www.gibbsmagazine.com/blacks_in_prisons.htm

Steinbery, L. (1996). *Beyond the Classroom.* Simon &Schuster.

Stovall, M. E. (Autumn 1990). The Chicago Defender in the Progressive Era. *Illinois Historical Journal, 83*(3), 159-172.

Strickland, A. E., & Weems, R. E. (200). *The African American Experience : An Historiographical and Bibliographical Guide.* Westport, CT: Greenwood Publishing Group.

Suggs, H. L. (Ed.). (1983). *the Black Press in the South, 1865-1979.* Westport, Conn.: Greenwood Press.

Suggs, H. L. (Ed.). (1996). *The Black Press in the Middle West, 1865-1985.* Wesport, Conn.: Greenwood Press.

Sugrue, T. (1998). The Meanest and Dirtiest Jobs. In *The Origins of the Urban Crisis: Race and Inequality in Postwar Detroit.* Princeton University Press.

Sugrue, T. J. (2008). *Sweet Land of Liberty: The Forgotten Struggle for Civil Rights in the North.* Random House.

Sugrue, T. J. (n.d.). *Driving While Black: The Car and Race Relations in Modern America.* Retrieved from Automobile in American Life and Society: www.autolife.umd.umich.edu/Race/R_Casestudy/R_Casestudy5.htm

Swain, R. D. (2008). . Standing on the Promises that Cannot Fail: Evaluating the Black Church's activism Among African-Americans in the Present Day Context. *The Journal of African American Studies, 12*, 401-413.

Taylor, K.-Y. (2003). Civil rights and civil wrongs: Racism in America today. *International Socialist Review*(32).

Taylor, R. L. (1995, March 19). The Harm Wrought by Racial Stereotype. *Hartford Courant*, D1.

Thernstrom, S., & Thernstrom, A. (1997). *America in Black and White: One Nation Indivisible.* Simon & Schuster.

Thomas, K. K. (2006, November). The Hill-Burton Act and civil rights: Expanding hospital care for black southerners, 1939-1960. *The Journal of Southern History, 72*(4).

Tolnay, S. E. (1997, 1997). The Great Migration and Changes in the Northern Black Family, 1940 to 1990. *Social Forces, 75.4*, 1213-1238.

Topping, S. (2004, Winter). SUPPORTING OUR FRIENDS AND DEFEATING OUR ENEMIES": MILITANCY AND NONPARTISANSHIP IN THE NAACP, 1936-1948. *The Journal of African American History, 89.1*, 17-35.

Trotter, J. W. (2004). African American, Impact of the Great Depression . In *Encyclopedia of the Great Depression .* Macmillan Reference USA .

Turner, R. B. (2003). *Islam and African Americans Experience* (2nd ed.). Bloomington, IN: Indiana University Press.

A Reflection

Walter, L. (n.d.). *Samael Fuller Successful Entrepreneur.* Retrieved from Millionaire Mindset: http://kingslife.ning.com/profiles/blogs/samuel-b-fuller-successful?xg_source=activity

Walworth, A. (1958). *Woodrow Wilson: American Prophet.* New York: Longmans.

Warren, D. T. (2007). A New Labor Movement? Race, Class, and the Missing Intersections between Black and Labor Politics. *The National Political Science Review, 11*, 43-63.

Waters, R. (2007). *American Political Systems and the Response of the Black Community.*

Watts, J. (1992). *"These Outside Directions." God, Harlem U.S.A.: The Father Divine Story.* Berkeley: University of California.

Whitaker, C. (1992, August). Before Jackie ... black athletes made history and drew fans despite oppressive color barriers - Blacks in Sports: The Jackie Robinson Revolution. *Ebony*.

Whitaker, R. (2009). *On the Laps of Gods: The Red Summer of 1919 and the Struggle for Justice* (Reprint ed.). Three Rivers Press.

White, J. (1996). *E.D. Nixon was the One: Edgar David Nixon, The MIA and the Montgomery Bus Boycott.* New York: New York University Press.

Wickham, D. (n.d.). *Bill Clinton and Black America.* Ballentine Publishing Group.

Wiese, A. (2004). *Places of Their Own:African American Suburbanization in the Twentieth Century.* Chicago: University of Chicago Press.

Williams, E. O. (2008). *Harlem Renaissance: A Handbook.* AuthorHouse.

Willis, D. P. (1988). *Health Policies and Black Americans.* Transaction Publishers.

Wilson, B. (1988, January). The Black Church And The Struggle For Community Empowerment In New York City. *Afro-Americans in New York Life and History, 12*(1), 51.

Wilson, J. Q. (1970, April 27). The Moynihan Memo Revisited: Notes from an Academic Friend. *New York Magazine*, pp. 42-44.

Wilson, W., Baker, R. S., & Leach, H. S. (1927). *The Public Papers of Woodrow Wilson* (Vol. II). (R. S. Baker, & W. E. Dodds, Eds.) New York, NY: Harper & Brothers.

Wintz, C. D., & Finkelman, P. (Eds.). (2004). *Encyclopedia of the Harlem Renaissance, A-J* (Vol. 1). New York: Taylor and Francis group.

Wintz, C. D., & Finkelman, P. (Eds.). (2005). *Encyclopedia of the Harlem Renaissance K-Y* (Vol. 2). New York: Taylor and Francis Group.

Witkop, B. (1980). "Percy Lavon Julian. 1899-1975." in Biographical Memoirs. *National Academy of Sciences, 52*, 223-266.

World Directory of Minorities. African Americans. (n.d.). Retrieved from Minority Rights Group International.: http://www.minorityrights.org/?lid=2607&tmpl.

Wright, E. O., & Dwyer, R. (n.d.). *Boston Review. A Political and Literary Forum.* Retrieved from The American Jobs Machine. Is the new economy creating good jobs?: http://bostonreview.net/BR25.6/wright.html

Yeakey, L. H. (1973, Autumn). A Student Without Peer: The Undergraduate Years of Paul Robeson. *The Journal of Negro Education, 42*(4), 489-903.

Young, E. (2006, September-October). Urban Lit Goes Legit. *Black Issues Book Review, 8*(5), 20-23.

Zoba, W. M. (1996, February 5). Seperate and Equal. *christianity Today*, 14-24.

www.ingramcontent.com/pod-product-compliance
Lightning Source LLC
Chambersburg PA
CBHW071224290426
44108CB00013B/1287